WOMAN'S
GUIDE TO
HUNTING

0187 6/30

LEARN TO HUNT
Pheasant • Turkey • Waterfowl • Deer

BERDETTE ELAINE ZASTROW

799, 208
ZAS

Published by

700 E. State Street • Iola, WI 54990-0001
Telephone: 715/445-2214

Please, call or write us for our free catalog of publications. To place an order or receive our
free catalog, call 800-258-0929. For editorial comment and further information, use our regular
business telephone at (715) 445-2214 or www.krause.com

Library of Congress Catalog Number: 00-101582
ISBN: 0-87341-864-6

Printed in the United States of America

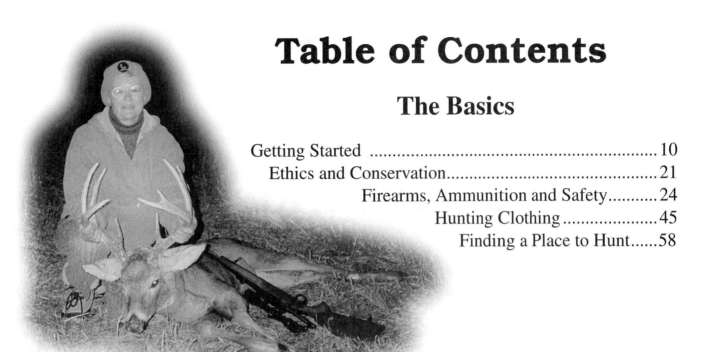

Table of Contents

The Basics

Let's Go Hunting

DEDICATION

To Sig:

My mentor, teacher, disciplinarian, neighbor, challenge-setter, ethics-reminder. Without him I'd never have written this book or been able to. Sig is, most of all, my friend, who now says, "I created a monster!"

To the South Dakota Conservation Officers:

The guys who dragged me over to the riverbank and taught me how to shoot. The guys who taught me how to hunt waterfowl and big game. The guys who gave me the confidence I needed, who, sometimes forcefully, made me get out and do things I was afraid to do, and who opened up a whole new world for me... so I could learn about ME.

To My Husband Bruce:

He has to be the best and most understanding man in the world.

INTRODUCTION

"Oh my Gawd, it's a woman!" I heard that countless times when I was first appointed to the South Dakota Game, Fish and Parks Commission back in 1986. I heard it whether I was a speaker at a meeting or at my place around the commission table, surrounded by seven men—the "experts," the "great white hunters." A name like mine, Berdette, can be used with either gender, so naturally everyone had been expecting a man. The "Oh my Gawd, it's a woman" phrase is now a joke, and actually it was quite funny to see the expressions on people's faces when they realized, in my presence, I was not a man.

I also heard that phrase out in the field. I was goose hunting one cold, frosty morning with friends and noticed some late-comers had crawled into a nearby goose pit. It was a wonderfully successful hunt, and I was lucky enough to be carrying a beautiful Canada goose as I left my pit. All bundled up in my camo overalls and two hats, I looked just like the rest of the hunters. As I approached the late-comers, I heard the now-famous "Oh my Gawd, it's a woman!"

"Well," I thought, "here we go again!" Twelve years ago I was an oddity in any hunting situation and I heard that phrase a lot. I was met with attitudes that ran the full length of the scale. However, I had fun educating people on the fact that yes, women CAN handle nontraditional roles.

I grew up loving the outdoors and fishing with my father. I thought I was an outdoor person; little did I know I had barely scratched the surface. My husband had hunted during high school but he no longer hunts. Marriage, raising two children and maintaining a radio broadcast career occupied my life. There was no time left to learn to hunt until later. I was 46 years old when I first learned to shoot a shotgun. I had been scared of guns before that. It was the game wardens (conservation officers) who took me under their wings and taught me hunting and shooting basics. Discovering the "real" outdoors was fantastic. Not only did I discover a whole new way of life, excitement and fulfillment, but the experience of being out in the field helped immensely at the commission table. The fun of hitting those first clay pigeons over the riverbank will always be a memory for me as that was "the beginning."

If you have grown up hunting, had a father, brother or friend as your mentor, that's wonderful. If you have not had that distinct advantage, don't despair! No matter what age or station in life, you can still learn, open new avenues, meet and conquer challenges, and accomplish goals you never before thought possible. And you can have fun doing it. If I can do it, you can, too.

When I started hunting I discovered I had to have knowledge of what to hunt and how to hunt it. I made mistakes; this book will tell what I learned and how you can avoid pitfalls. I want you to be so excited and knowledgeable you will start gathering your equipment and inviting friends to go hunting with you.

I'll tell you what you need and what you don't need. The information is offered in a simple and non-intimidating manner. Don't take yourself too seriously; have a good time and enjoy all the experiences—you are not in competition with anyone. There can be dumb things and funny things that happen; they do not necessarily ruin the hunt—they just add to the memories.

You know, it's more fun to talk about your latest hunting excursion than to compare laundry detergents! Hunting and enjoying the outdoors have made me a more interesting person, a more fun and relaxed person. I've gained much personal satisfaction in achieving new goals. You can become a more healthy person as you hunt. The fresh air and exercise will just make you feel good. We all know that when we feel good, our attitudes improve and our outlook on life improves. Hunting provides a special bond and shared fellowship. New acquaintances becoming a "family" and new memories will become very important to you for the rest of your life.

The husbands of several women interviewed for this book have very definite feelings about hunting with their spouses:

Phil Mitzel says, "There is just no other way to do it. My wife is very versatile, a great companion, good partner and there is no competition like I experience when hunting with the guys. I really enjoy the hunt—and it is truly a hunt — not just shooting. We both love the outdoors and it works well for us as we are both on the same time schedule—she is not left at home waiting for me."

Arnie Goldade likes hunting with Lori because, "It's very enjoyable. I like the companionship and being able to see her harvest her game. That is more important to me than what I harvest. I like showing her what I learned so she can do things the proper way. I let her take the best hunting spots and I take the second best."

Bill Antonides likes hunting with women, "because it is not so competitive. Most female beginners I helped knew very little about hunting; I taught them the way I hunt. There is less competition to shoot the most ducks or biggest deer. Since most beginners have not had outdoor opportunities, I like to see them really enjoying themselves as they learn. Men take a lot for granted in the outdoors because they have been hunting since they were children. Most women haven't been and they are awed by the sights and sounds of nature. When I witness this reaction to nature, it reawakens my appreciation."

I am concerned about the future of hunting and I believe we who hunt now must mentor others. It is extremely important to get children involved so the tradition can be continued; the way to do that is to get the "Moms" involved. My son-in-law's grandmother is 91 years old and has hunted most of her life. Granny Bowar's eyes sparkled, there was a satisfied smile on her beautiful face, and she was visibly moved when she told me her long-ago deer hunting stories. She grew up pheasant hunting, enrolled in a rifle course at college, and started deer hunting in 1945. Her husband hunted deer and Granny thought, "If you can't fight 'em, join 'em!" Granny and Grandpa Vic raised three children. Hunting was a big part of child-rearing. Safety was the number one rule, topping a long list of rules for everyone. They had 40 wonderful years with their host landowners in the western part of South Dakota; they all became family. Granny says, "It was a big deal when we all got out there—they dropped everything for us and we all had so much fun! We didn't have much money, we scraped so we could go because this hunting trip was the big treat for all of us! When our grandchildren were born, they were included—we always did everything together. Our grandchildren have grown up to be good hunters and I'm proud of that. Now I will be watching our great-grandchildren." THIS IS TRADITION! Passing on the desire to the next generation and paving the way for youth of the future to enjoy the wonders of the outdoors is the only way we can preserve this wonderful hunting tradition. Granny Bowar certainly did her part; I hope there is a little bit of her in all of us.

A Woman's Guide to Hunting is meant to inspire, educate and entertain you, giving simple down-to-earth help to those who are interested in hunting but don't know how to go about it or where to go for information and help. If you picked up this book to "just see what it's all about", I hope it sparks your interest and excitement and curiosity to open a new door in your life.

My red Jeep bears a special license plate that tells a story. After the conservation officers taught me how to shoot, to hunt waterfowl and big game, there was no turning back. I was having the time of my life. A whole new world opened up for me and I took advantage of it. I loved it. I grew. I became humble, proud, a more knowledgeable, interesting person and I had lots of fun. Fun that I always thought was just for "the guys." One day sitting around the table waiting for the Game, Fish and Parks Commission meeting to begin, the guys were talking hunting, very obviously ignoring me. Not to be left out, I said, "Hey guys, I hunt too!" They all turned and looked at me with rather sheepish looks on their faces and one said, "That would be a great license plate!" "I HUNT 2" was born!

SOURCES

•Beyond Fair Chase, by Jim Posewitz

•Hunting Whitetails Successfully by J. Wayne Fears, North American Hunting Club

•Ducks At A Distance, A Waterfowl Identification Guide, courtesy of Ducks Unlimited

•Guide to the American Wild Turkey, by Mary C. Kennamer, Ronnie E. Brenneman and James Earl Kennamer, courtesy of the National Wild Turkey Federation

•Wild Turkey Hunting, NRA Hunter Skills Series, courtesy of the National Rifle Association

•The Hunter's Guide, courtesy of the National Rifle Association

•Waterfowl Hunting, NRA Hunter Skills Series, courtesy of the National Rifle Association

•South Dakota Game, Fish and Parks 1999 Hunting Guide

•History and Management of South Dakota Deer, by Arthur H. Richardson and Lyle E. Petersen, courtesy of South Dakota Game, Fish and Parks Department

•Mule Deer, by Jim Van Norman and Tom Carpenter

•To Heck With Deer Hunting, by Jim Zumbo

•History, Ecology and Management of the Ring-Necked Pheasant in South Dakota, courtesy of South Dakota Game, Fish and Parks Department

•Wildlife Harvest, April 1999

PHOTO CREDITS

Cover Photo By Lila Antonides

Mitch Kezar Photographer
www.kezarphoto.com

Hunter's Specialties

Jim Zumbo

Ron Spomer

South Dakota Tourism

Steve Nelson

Daphne Kinzler

Kathy Butt

Foreword

A recent study indicates there are more women hunting today than ever before. That's not much of a surprise because the feminist movement over the past couple of decades has been accompanied by a huge influx of women into formerly male bastions.

Many women become interested in hunting because they want to accompany their husbands/significant others/brothers/fathers or other male acquaintances on their outdoor pursuits. Others prefer hunting with daughters, sisters or female companions. Some women learn to hunt on their own, with no mentors to offer advice and instruction. Whatever the case, hunting serves up some inherently different and sometimes difficult scenarios that can be bewildering and downright scary to the novice. Not only are the woods an intimidating place to prowl around in – but many aspects of hunting can be complicated. A newcomer to golf, bowling or tennis has only to learn how to deal with a sphere within a structured environment. The hunter, on the other hand, must begin the learning process by understanding the habits of the quarry, the land on which it lives and a myriad of other details, such as handling a firearm or bow, dealing with the elements of nature, woodsmanship, and processing game that is harvested.

A unique problem exists for female hunters. Because hunting has largely been a male activity, all the accessories and gear have been designed for men. Perhaps I should say, WAS designed for men. Nowadays, hunting clothing is being exclusively designed for women, as are firearms and other items. Without question, women are well-entrenched in hunting, and the sport is far better off because of it.

That still begs the question: How will women learn to hunt? Most of the information out there is still aimed at men. That's why this book is a valuable tool that should be in the library of every female hunter, be she a novice or a veteran. This book can be both an instructional tool and an aid in teaching others to hunt. Author Berdette Zastrow leaves no stone unturned as she delves into every aspect of hunting. An accomplished hunter herself, Berdette addresses hunting from the female point of view, including information on firearms, ammo, archery gear and clothing. She also describes the behavior patterns of and hunting strategies for most of America's common big game species.

Finally, here's a book that separates the fact from the fiction in a down-to-earth fashion, full of tips and techniques with an easy-to-read style. Berdette masterfully weaves anecdotes throughout, allowing the reader to learn vicariously through her experiences as well as from the solid information she provides. As one who has raised three daughters, all of whom hunt, I wish this book had been available when I began taking my youngsters hunting. The good news is — now it's here for you. Enjoy.

Jim Zumbo
Hunting Editor
Outdoor Life

THE BASICS

Chapter One
GETTING STARTED

I had gotten up well before dawn and made my way to our hunting site. We would be setting up in a pass between two sloughs. The day dawned cold. My hunting buddies were still getting settled when I arrived, but in a few minutes all was quiet. Before long a few ducks started to fly, and the numbers suddenly increased. Picking my shot carefully, I swung my shotgun, lining up on a nice drake mallard and the bird folded at the sound of the blast. Of course he fell into the water to my right. The wind was calm, so there was no breeze to wash him closer to me. We didn't have a dog to retrieve the bird or even a long stick with a nail on the end to pull the bird to shore. After puzzling on how I would retrieve my bird, an idea hit me.

"Yikes! Look at her!" shouted one of the other hunters. "Purple longjohns! Geez, that water must be cold! This is unbelievable! Here I thought we needed to have a DOG for a retriever!"

These were only a few of the comments as I tore off my hunting pants, took my boots and socks off and rolled up the longjohns. Yes, they were purple. I went wading into the slough to retrieve the second duck I'd ever shot.

Making a long story short, I had the desire to retrieve that duck; after all, it was my bird and I was pretty proud of being able to shoot it. It was a great day to be hunting waterfowl, there was more hunting to be done, and I didn't see any sense in wasting anymore time. I waded in and got my bird. The water was only about 8 inches deep. The mud washed off. I got the bird, dried off my legs and was ready to go again. The hunters with me (all male) couldn't believe it. As they watched me with wide eyes and open mouths, I heard the question "Is this what women do when they hunt?"

I've never lived down that event and remember it fondly as one of the unforgettable new experiences when I started hunting. I had the DESIRE to get that bird and I was darn well going to do it!

Both eyes open. The skills training at any Becoming an Outdoors Woman event puts you right in the action. You'll get a chance to try the things you want to learn and decide on your own if you want to continue. (Photo by Michael Pearce/NWTF)

DESIRE is the key word. If you desire to hunt, to experience all kinds of new actions, feelings and challenges, you can do it. If I hadn't had the desire to obtain my bird, I'd never have made a joke of myself that day. Desire can be the first challenge to hunting. Check your inner feelings, ask yourself some questions. Do I want to have more fun and diversity in my life? Do I want to meet new people? Do I want to learn about wildlife, their habits and habitat? Do I want to learn about the world through the eyes of wildlife? Do I want to learn about myself, accomplish goals and meet challenges I never before thought possible? Do I want to

become extremely proud of myself, more confident and a more interesting person? If you want any of these, or all of them and more, then you likely have the DESIRE. Remember the old saying, "If you always do what you've always done, you'll always have what you always had".

OK, so you have the desire. Now what? How do you get started? I was at a women's seminar at a National Wild Turkey Federation convention where a woman asked, "I wasn't raised hunting, I don't have a husband, my boyfriend doesn't hunt. I want to learn. How can I? Where do I start?" She had the desire, she just needed the knowledge.

My "Families in the Outdoors" seminars are designed to help jump start women into outdoor activities such as hunting. There is a lot of help out there, it's just a matter of telling women who they can talk to and where they can go to get the pointers they need. Once a phone call is made, the learning experience will snowball. One call, one person, one organization can lead to another and another. It's just knowing where to start.

The seminar includes discussion of WHO is in the outdoors, WHY they are there, HOW you can get there and WHERE to go. The "HOW you can get there" part is, by far, the most detailed. Part of the seminar includes a slide presentation and I conclude by demonstrating hunting/outdoor clothing and how women can dress to be warm, dry and comfortable, thus increasing enjoyment in the outdoors.

It's fun presenting these seminars because I enjoy encouraging women and telling them my story which is designed ultimately to help them get started. I have so much fun hunt-ing I want to share it and have as many women as possible involved. There is a lot to do out there and I don't want anyone to miss it. For the rest of this chapter I will pretend you are at my seminar seeking help, advice and information.

There is all kinds of expertise at your fingertips. Make a call to your game warden or conservation officer. They were the first ones to help me learn the basics and they helped me find other resources. They are a direct pipeline to your state's wildlife agency where you can find all kinds of programs. The officers can introduce you to the local sportsmen's club, to conservation organizations, and if the officer has the time, can maybe even give you and your friends personal shooting/hunting tips and advice. Contact them first, they are only a phone call away from expanding your horizons.

Even if you don't hunt now, but want to, join your local sportsmen's club and other conservation groups such as Ducks Unlimited, Pheasants Forever, National Wild Turkey Federation, Rocky Mountain Elk Foundation, etc. When you get there, introduce yourself and tell some of the other members you want to learn to hunt. You will find new friends whose interests are the same as yours. You'll learn about fun events that you will want to participate in and find new directions and opportunities. Business professionals call this process "networking." Hunters call it making friends.

Your sportsmen's club (yes, they are still named "sportsmen's clubs," I have not heard of one named "sportsmen's and women's club" — yet!), cooperating with your state's wildlife agency, likely sponsors a Hunter Education Course every year. Some have classes for women, usually taught by women.

Hands-on instruction is an important part of the Becoming and Outdoors Woman program. Here students in a waterfowl hunting class are constructing a hunting blind.

If you want to hunt ducks, you've got to place the decoys. The waterfowl hunting students at the Becoming an Outdoors Woman program get the chance to arrange their own decoys.

The author, foreground, and Kitty Beuchert show off a duck boat blind built at the Becoming an Outdoors Woman program. This is a great place for women to learn skills that will allow them to start hunting on their own.

Firearms safety is stressed in every hunting class at the Becoming an Outdoors Woman program. This is a great way to learn about guns and gun safety in a non-threatening environment.

Skip Meisenheimer, an archery instructor at the Becoming an Outdoors Woman program in South Dakota, provides some advice before people start shooting. When at all possible, classes at the BOW seminars are taught by women.

There is some classroom instruction followed by actual shooting on a trap range or similar place. I have participated in these classes and they are great! With women instructors, there is no intimidation, everyone is on the same level and there is never such a thing as a "dumb question." What a sight to see the beaming faces of the gals following their first shooting experience! Some of the women I've seen have started the course terrified of guns or indifferent because their husbands made them attend the course. Those gals were happy and proud of themselves at the course's completion and couldn't wait to start hunting. Not only do women learn to shoot, they are included in discussions of safety, ethics and wildlife management. This is a well-rounded course for the beginner and even if you don't hunt, what you learn about gun safety is worth the time you've invested.

BECOMING AN OUTDOORS WOMAN WORKSHOPS

Attendance at a "Becoming an Outdoors Woman" (BOW) workshop is a must for you. It is a wonderful three-day women's weekend where women have the choice of attending more than 30 different classes dealing with the outdoors. Hunting, fishing and other outdoor pursuits are taught. For the aspiring hunter, there are beginning shotgun, rifle marksmanship and waterfowl hunting classes. Other workshops include archery, big game hunting, game cleaning and cooking and more. It's a weekend of challenge, learning new skills or further developing already known skills. It is an introduction to outdoor opportunities for those who have never been involved in such sports. There are mostly female instructors and no competition.

The Becoming an Outdoors Woman program developed from a workshop conducted by Dr. Christine L. Thomas, Associate Professor of Resource Management, College of Natural Resources at the University of Wisconsin-Stevens Point. Dr. Thomas describes the workshop in some of the proceeding's prologue. *Breaking Down the Barriers to Participation of Women in Angling and Hunting* was a one-day workshop held on August 25, 1990 at the University of Wisconsin-Stevens Point. The objective of the workshop was to identify the barriers to participation, discuss strategies that have been used in addressing these barriers and to develop strategies that participants could use in their own situations.

In describing the event, Thomas wrote: "The workshop was up-beat and high energy. Participants were enthused about the topic and had many excellent ideas that could be used to help facilitate the participation of women in these sports.

"As media coverage intensified, just prior to the workshop, I began to receive letters and phone calls from women who wanted to learn how to hunt and fish and who thought that we might be teaching these activities at our workshop. Apparently, there is a need out there that could be addressed by clinics of that type."

Yes, there was and still is a need, and Christine Thomas addressed that need. She developed the Becoming an Outdoors Woman workshop program in 1991 in response to a growing number of women interested in outdoor activities. Since its inception, the BOW program has taught thousands of women throughout North America. Workshops are now conducted in 44 states and 9 Canadian provinces.

At the BOW workshops women have fun meeting new friends and networking with others so they will have companions with whom to hunt. Women of all ages are welcome. I taught waterfowl hunting for two years at the South Dakota workshop and had fun meeting a charming 70-year-old lady. She said she heard about it, thought the workshop would be fun and she was having a blast.

It was also fun for me to teach these women, watch their interest grow and now hunt with them in the field. The waterfowl class consisted of 90 minutes of classroom discussion including waterfowl identification, habitat, shotguns, clothing, regulations, decoy spreads, blinds, calls and shot shell sizes. The remaining 90 minutes consisted of hands-on activities. This part of the class was held outside at the edge of a slough. We had the women actually build a blind from scratch, using rushes they cut themselves. They wore waders, threw the decoys in the water, and helped position the duck boat and cover it with camouflage material. They also helped place goose decoys in a grassy area. It was wonderful to see the satisfied and excited faces at the end of the class. It may seem like three hours of instruction is a bit brief, but the goal is to provide a starting point and basic skills. All the participants had learned something new and were now on their way to being waterfowl hunters, and they had fun doing it!

During a BOW workshop, each participant chooses four of the 30 different classes offered at the time of registration. Every class is kept small, so learners receive individual attention. Each class is a three hour "hands-on" session. Every participant gets to try everything taught during that class. Equipment is provided so you don't have to purchase anything to attend.

The workshops are held over a weekend, with participants usually checking in on Friday and heading for home on Sunday. On the average, 100 women will pay around $150 to cover lodging, meals and instruction. State wildlife agencies are the primary local sponsors. Ask for your state BOW coordinator. Scholarships are sometimes available through your local sportsmen's club.

The program usually includes evening entertainment, so if you have a special talent let them know on your application. The first year in South Dakota we had an outdoor clothing fashion show, for which I volunteered to MC. I wanted to entertain the women and give them an evening they would never forget. I think the mission was accomplished! Rather than appearing on stage and just talking and describing clothing, I wanted to start with a bang. I dressed in my camo skirt and jacket, then proceeded to add almost every hunting article I owned, including my hunting shirt, pants, coveralls, big boots and topping it all off with my four-piece quad hunting bibs and jackets, hat, hood and big gloves. I sauntered out onto the stage "dancing" to stripper music and proceeded to throw off the hunting clothes amidst whistles, whoops and cat calls! They really wondered what I'd end up with! So after showing them what you need for hunting and then how you appear to others dressed in your "finest," things settled down and we got down to business with me in my camo skirt and jacket. I was thrilled with the cards and letters I received after that, and I was so pleased that I could contribute to the women learning AND having fun learning.

"Beyond BOW" is a new program designed to offer even more opportunity to women who want to learn more about the outdoors. Dr. Thomas says, "Our original workshops were so very popular, there was a 60 percent return rate. That severely cut down the opportunity for new attendees and limited a new audience. We saw a need to provide an opportunity for women between the workshop and the field so we developed the "Beyond BOW" workshops. The workshops are designed as a follow-up opportunity after completing an original workshop; however, a beginner is welcome and we do have many novices attending the "Beyond BOW" workshops in Wisconsin. Generally, the new workshops attract a mixture of beginners and "old hands." They have created more opportunities as there are now more workshops. For instance, in Wisconsin we had three beginning workshops and three "Beyond BOW" workshops. Texas has an advanced program called "Phase II"; that requires attendance at a Becoming an Outdoors Woman workshop so that you have taken a preliminary course in the activity in which you are interested. Phase II is a higher level and very popular."

Dr. Thomas is designing another twist on her programs to help bring more women into the outdoors and all it has to offer. "We are creating three pilot workshops, with the help of a federal aid grant, to offer outdoor education with a focus on minority women," she said. "The future of hunting is hanging in the balance and we must do all we can to insure that future."

The national Becoming an Outdoors Woman Web site is: www.uwsp.edu/bow. Punch up your desired state from there.

You may also call toll free: 1-877-BOWOMAN for information on any workshop.

We women are extremely fortunate to have an outdoor educational experience such as the Becoming an Outdoors Woman workshops at our fingertips. There are many international sponsors of the program. Those groups include sportsmen and women from around the world who feel our hunting heritage must be preserved for future generations and this is their method of showing their support. You and I are members of these organizations; let us take advantage of what is offered so we can do our part to preserve the hunting heritage. Whether it is a first-time experience at a workshop or if you are looking forward to attending a "Beyond BOW" workshop, take advantage of it — you will be glad you did!

NATIONAL WILD TURKEY FEDERATION: WOMEN IN THE OUTDOORS

The National Wild Turkey Federation's Women in the Outdoors project is an ambitious new program designed to provide outdoor learning opportunities that are hands-on and exciting for women ages 14 and over. The NWTF's goals are to teach the importance of responsible wildlife management, natural resource management, increased participation in outdoor opportunities, and help preserve the hunting tradition.

They train women as outdoor educators and provide a network for men and women within their local NWTF chapter system. They offer one-day events that are affordable for busy and budget-conscious women. The NWTF holds more than 150 Women in the Outdoors events throughout the country per year.

> "We started the Women in the Outdoors program to provide more opportunities for women to become involved."
>
> *Trish Berry*

"We started the Women in the Outdoors program to provide more opportunities for women to become involved and learn new skills in a non-competitive environment, work for the preservation of the wild turkey, preserve hunting traditions, and help them just to learn about the outdoors," said Trish Berry, Women in the Outdoors national coordinator. "We wanted to fill a niche that was void. When we started this program, the NWTF female membership was only 1 percent of our total. The NWTF had JAKES, the youth program, but nothing for women. When we started Women in the Outdoors, our female membership totaled 1,000. After one year, we grew to 10,000 women members."

In the program, women can become involved in various ways; they can be involved with local chapters and work with the banquet program, they can become a shooter, they can become a hunter, or they can help with the youth programs.

"With more than 200,000 members in the NWTF, we have a terrific mentoring system and that gives us our exclusivity," said Berry. "NWTF members are there for the women in a follow-up situation and they can just keep on going. We are truly excited about the continued growth of the Women in the Outdoors program. This new outreach program definitely complements the NWTF's efforts to involve entire families in the conservation effort."

Women in the Outdoors Regional Coordinator, Karyl Utke, said the group saw a need to train women as outdoor educators for other women.

"We want something there for the women so we can involve the whole family in the National Wild Turkey Federation because we are about God, family, country and conservation," said Utke. "By involving women in the Women in the Outdoors program and training them as educators, we are bringing the whole family together. Most times it is the women who decide on what the recreational activity is going to be; that's why this is so important. We are looking for any woman who wants to learn; we would really like to see single parent families attend these workshops."

Hands-on, in-the-field activities include archery, boating, camping, canoeing, deer hunting, flyfishing, map and compass, rifle marksmanship, shotgunning, turkey hunting and more. Erlene Mandrell is the national spokesperson for the Women in the Outdoors program and has hosted women-only hunts.

These events are hosted across the country. Contact your local NWTF chapter for details on the nearest event or how to help host an event. You may also call NWTF headquarters at 803-637-3106 and ask for assistance in locating your regional coordinator.

The National Wild Turkey Federation publishes a magazine, *Women in the Outdoors*. It is available only to NWTF members (so join!) and has "how-to" features, articles that entertain and inform women. It includes departments dedicated to the outdoors and conservation along with special features, recipes, gear for women and special-interest stories. Companies are now offering goods and services tailored just for women, and

Women in the Outdoors magazine highlights many of those. To receive the magazine, join the NWTF and request it. Call 1-800-THE-NWTF.

NATIONAL RIFLE ASSOCIATION OF AMERICA

The Women's Issues division of the National Rifle Association of America has a number of programs and projects to help the woman hunter get started. In late 1997, Women's Issues published the *Women's Shooting Event Handbook* and implemented a grassroots program to introduce more women to the shooting sports. In the first 18 months, more than 50 shooting programs were conducted exclusively for women.

"When the first one was over, the women wanted to know when the next one was. They wanted to know if they could set up a group totally just for women," said Melinda Bridges, Manager of NRA Women's Issues. "They wanted to know if they could set up once-a-month activities for women-only shooting. Now our NRA field representatives have gotten gun clubs interested in conducting the shoots for themselves. We received a call from a woman in New Jersey whose goal was to have 100 women in her shoot; 135 came. She is planning another shoot and she will be starting a women's club. The women that came are interested in actually organizing it."

Bridges continues, "We conducted all of this research at the beginning and

It's all about fun. Here country music star and outdoor activities ambassador Erlene Mandrell looks on as KarlaAnne Ballew takes a shot with a bow during the Women in the Outdoors event sponsored by the National Wild Turkey Federation. (Photo by Camille Roberge-Myers/NWTF)

one thing that we found why women did not go to a gun club to shoot is because nobody invited them! We were really surprised by that and, really, that's how this got started. We also talked to them, asking, 'OK, if you went to a gun club, what would it take for you to come and shoot?' They didn't want the event to be competitive. They wanted to be taught either by women or have women-friendly instructors. They wanted to have child-care provided if that was possible. They wanted to have instruction. They wanted the environment to be non-intimidating. Then they wanted to have a nice meal afterward so they could network and meet other women. But the real critical thing that we found when we started this was the follow-up. Once we realized all we had to do was provide the opportunity, it was going to take off on its own. That's exactly what it's done. One of the goals the first year was to conduct one hunt. We exceeded our goal. We had two half-day bird hunts and combined them with sporting clays. It was then four hunts and now 10 hunts per year. Knowing we cannot do this all on our own, we are working to develop partnerships. We want to work with the state wildlife agencies, the NRA state associations, local conservation groups as well as getting support from our office as to what they need in terms of supplies, support, PR, etc. We're really looking at this more to be on a grassroots level. Women's Issues will be working with programs such as the "Beyond BOW" to conduct hunts with instruction and opportunity as well as an actual hunt so women can actually go out and utilize the skills they learned."

Bridges said it makes absolutely no sense for everybody to have their own separate program if "we're all trying to do the same thing."

"So why not just bring it all together and those who are interested in partnering with us, we welcome them with open arms," she said. "If anyone is interested in attending one of the functions or getting one of these started on their own, we would be more than happy to help them get started. The whole goal really is to provide more hunting and shooting opportunities for women. For information, call us at 800-861-1166 or 703-267-1413."

The NRA Hunter Clinic Program is designed to help hunters develop practical hunting skills such as marksmanship, safety, responsibility and up-to-date knowledge of the hunting sports. NRA's *The Hunter's Guide* is an excellent reference for the beginner.

The Women's Issues department has a publication named *Women's Product Resource List*. It lists companies and small businesses that market shooting, hunting and outdoor apparel, and products just for women. Companies, businesses and vendors are listed by name, address, telephone and e-mail. They also have published *Women Hunters Network*. It is a state-by-state listing of outdoorswomen seeking to share their time in the field with other women. Join the NRA and you will receive information on these publications.

When asked how the NRA can help women start shooting and hunting Bridges said, "We have a program now that's been established to provide more hunting and shooting opportunities for women. We compile a list and a schedule of those hunts and shoots that are available for women across the country. If there is nothing available for the women in a particular area, we encourage them to get one started on their own. They can contact their local gun club or their state DNR (wildlife agency). We can provide a lot of support in regard to how to get them started and where they need to go.

We also have a *Women's Hunters Network*. It's a state-by-state listing of women who are interested in just hunting with other women whether it be in their own state or another locale. We can forward women a copy of that and let them get in touch with the women in their area to possibly share some experiences. The best vehicle we have right now is the quarterly newsletter called *The Ludington Letter*. It provides a schedule of all of our hunts and shoots as well as a description of the ones that have happened so they can see what we are doing and how to get involved."

For information on how to get involved or obtain copies of the publications, call 800-861-1166 or write to NRA, Women's Issues, 11250 Waples Mill Road, Fairfax, VA 22030.

WOMEN'S SHOOTING SPORTS FOUNDATION

The Women's Shooting Sports Foundation was founded in 1993 to introduce women and their families to the fun and excitement of the shooting sports and the great outdoors. Through many successful programs, thousands of women have picked up a gun or bow for the first time, were taught the safe way to use it, and had a great time learning a new sport. With participation in the shooting sports comes a responsibility to learn proper gun safety and ethics as well as an appreciation for our great natural resources and wildlife. These are all principles that the Women's Shooting Sports Foundation embraces with the intention of teaching women and their families the importance of preserving our shooting sports heritage.

The Women's Shooting Sports Foundation offers a number of programs and services in which you can become involved. WSSF chapters are an important part of the support system for women. These chapters help continue WSSF national programs on a local level, raise money to further the goals of the WSSF and provide networking, mentors and a social system for female shooters. Annie Oakley is quoted on their brochure: *If women and girls would learn to shoot, they would add to their happiness by falling in love with one of the finest outdoor sports.*

For more information, contact the Women's Shooting Sports Foundation at 1-800-820-9773, write 4620 Edison Avenue, Suite C, Colorado Springs, CO 80915 or e-mail at wssf@worldnet.att.net. Visit the Website at www.wssf.org. The WSSF has published a terrific catalog named *The List* that includes items "that every woman who shoots needs to have." Find accessories, firearms, clothing, footwear, equipment and more.

ORGANIZATIONS FOR OUTDOOR WOMEN

Many states have outdoor women's organizations. Outdoorwomen of South Dakota was organized following our second BOW workshop. Several of us women decided we needed an organization of interested women to network with others, be able to use the newly learned skills and learn still new ones. Contact your state wildlife agency for direction in your state. Always ask if they have a Web page, then check for outdoor women's organizations.

OUTDOOR TELEVISION SHOWS

There are many good outdoor TV shows from which you can learn a lot. Three good ones are the National Wild Turkey Foundation's *Turkey Call Television* and *Buckmasters*, both on TNN, and Indian Archery Video's *Hunting Across America* on The Outdoor Channel. They are so very professionally produced you can't help but become excited about hunting while watching them.

You should beware of some hunting television shows. Some of them I've seen always show the biggest game, the best, the easiest and fastest way to get a big trophy animal by disregarding ethics and personal challenges. They want you to see that every shot brings down the biggest and most beautiful game and it's usually men that are featured. Don't be intimidated by any of that! I enjoyed a career in the media and know there is a lot of smoke and mirrors!

I'll give you a funny example of how my uncle and I "produced" a whopper of a "live" waterfowl hunting radio show. At the time, I hosted an hour-long outdoor show on an FM station close to our lake cabin and hunting area. In fact, the station was at Eden, South Dakota, and our cabin and hunting blinds were "east of Eden." Really!

Well, I decided we would broadcast "live and direct" from the goose blind. Having my trusty tape recorder with me, it worked wonderfully. The duck and goose calls were perfect, a little wind made for realism. What was really perfect were the two geese that "just happened" to fly in front of us, not during a commercial you see, but during the "actual broadcast." And, what great sound effects when we took our shots! What a show! It was terrific! The listeners, some of them anyway, actually thought that show was live and the geese cooperated that well! In visiting with some listeners later, they just KNEW we shot those geese live on the air! Every once in a while I dig out that tape and Uncle Don and I just giggle! So this is what I mean when I say don't take some of those hunting shows very seriously. They are produced to entertain and impress you and encourage you to buy the advertised products.

VIDEO TAPES AND MAGAZINES

Check out your video rental store or library. I recommend contacting Indian Archery Video at 1-800-814-4117, write 115 David Drive, Madison, MS 39110 or visit www.huntingacrossamerica.com and request a catalog. They specialize in turkey and deer, but have videos on all species available. They even have *Turkey Tales*, a video of four of the South's most avid women turkey hunters!

You can learn a lot from reading outdoor magazine stories. Reading about a hunt is so different than watching a hunt on television. While reading the hunting story you can feel what the author feels, see through the author's eyes and become emotionally involved in the hunt. Outdoor magazines are starting to print more women's stories and hunting pictures. Let's give them enough material! Don't forget your local outdoor writer. He or she is an encyclopedia of outdoor information and can direct you to many sources of information.

EXPERT ADVICE

It is fun and interesting to talk to other women who shoot and hunt. You can always learn something in addition to making new friends. There are plenty of experiences out there to share with others, and women like to talk hunting just as much as men do. I had a wonderful time talking to the following women about hunting and what advice they would give to a beginner.

Kate Mewhinney, Communications Specialist with the National Rifle Association of America said:

The best thing is to go with somebody who knows what they are doing and who is going to be a good guide for you. The most important thing is for your first experience to be a positive one because you want to be encouraged. My Dad, who started me hunting when I was little, was very reassuring, very supportive.

I was on a feral pig hunt that the NRA sponsored in Texas. I didn't get anything but it was just really a great experience. It was just amazing to sit in the blind for so long, like three or four hours, just by myself. You have so much time to think and to see what's going on outside. You see the sunrise and see all the wildlife that comes in. It was just kind of a spiritual experience for me. It was really, really neat. I was worried. Could I shoot an animal? I knew I could shoot a bird, but didn't know if I could shoot a large animal. I'll tell you what, when I saw those pigs after sitting for three or four hours, I was ready! I was so excited and so was the guide. It's such a neat experience to be able to share that with somebody else. I love it now! It's really fun and I can't wait for the next one.

"The guides on our feral pig hunt were very supportive, very positive, and they also knew their stuff. They knew what they were doing. That helped my comfort level because I had not had a whole lot of experience. It helped me relax and feel safe," Kate said. "One of the guides told me, 'You know, this is what it's all about. It's such a kick for us to see how excited you are. It's the coolest thing for us to be a part of your first hunt.' The guides were really excited for us. When women would come in with their pigs, all the other women were so supportive. The guys just couldn't believe that. They couldn't believe there was no competition and no one-up-manship. Two of the guides had weddings to attend the last night; they missed the weddings because they wanted to see who came in with pigs. It was just a really special experience."

Melinda Bridges, Manager of NRA Women's Issues, has this advice for a woman who is starting her shooting/hunting activities:

I have found it is very critical that you work with somebody who has experience in that discipline, whether it be shotgun or whatever. When I went on my first upland bird hunt, I went with three very experienced bird hunters. They all supported me, shared with me and told me what I needed to do, helped me, praised me. I felt so comfortable in that environment. One thing we really stress is the safety. We never conduct any event, shooting or hunting without the safety instruction in the beginning. That person you go with that first time is very critical because you must have a positive experience. Some gun clubs do not invite women, or if they do, it is an intimidating atmosphere. How do we overcome that? Education, and a lot of it! I don't think many men realize that women are going to be the next generation to keep hunting alive. And why? Because women have the ear of the children and they have the ear of their spouse or significant other, and if women become involved in it, they are going to share their education and experience with them. Once that happens, it's on the road to victory.

Melinda shared some outfitters' and guides' opinions about women hunters following one of the NRA Women's Issues hunts:

They were extremely surprised about having women at the hunt as guests. They had a perception that the women hunters were going to be very demanding, that there were certain things the women had to have and how things had to be done. There were several things that were stereotypical towards women. The outfitters and guides said they would be more than happy to have the women come back. They also said that in many ways they preferred having us over their own gender because we were serious about what we wanted, the safety issue was important, we were polite, courteous and congenial. The whole mission was for us to get to know each other and support each other in the whole aspect of hunting.

Why does Melinda hunt? Because, "I enjoy it. It provides me with a tremendous opportunity to not only learn about what I'm doing, but I've learned so much about the outdoors and conservation, and I have developed an incredible respect for firearms and wildlife. It's provided me with a tremendous amount of education and joy combined," she said.

Susan Campbell Reneau, outdoor communicator from Missoula, Montana says:

I hunt because I love to be in the out-of-doors, and I go out and I have a purpose. I just love hunting; it is great! The only thing I got was an antelope which was good; that's a pretty big deal for me. I wanted to be out with my family and I wanted to have a chance to find out what it was that they loved and understand it better. One of the most important things to have is a pair of comfortable shoes and to have socks that properly take care of your feet because if your feet get blisters, you are in a whole bunch of trouble. It's important to dress properly for the weather; my husband had me over-dressed and I was miserable. Also pay attention to when your monthly cycle comes because it can be a real problem if you are hunting with all men. It can be very miserable if you don't plan. If your period comes and you are in the middle of nowhere and there are no grocery stores, you are REALLY going to be miserable.

Outdoor communicator Barb Henderson of Las Vegas, Nevada has this advice:

Number one is being very knowledgeable about what you are doing. Know your species and its habitat. Make sure you have a professional instructor, either male or female. I recommend attendance at a hunter safety course and repeat it in five years. My husband tried to teach me to shoot; I tried too hard to please him and not myself. He tried to be macho and I wouldn't listen. My instructor would say the same thing and I listened. Togetherness is important; a lifetime of hunting together can be fun. And get the right equipment, not your husband's old stuff." Barb stresses confidence is so important; start shooting trap and then sporting clays. She also states that women CAN learn from other women and they learn well when there is no competition.

Red Head Pro Hunting Team member (the only woman on the team), Brenda Valentine, outdoor promoter, outstanding bowhunter and BOW instructor, tells why she hunts.

"Hunting was a tradition in my family. In the part of the country where I come from (Tennessee), it was well respected; it was a means of entertainment and food in a very rural setting. Hunting was the main meat supply for our families. It was also the main entertainment. We kept hounds and we coon hunted and we did it all. Why do I hunt now? When they passed out personalities, some of us were hunters, others were gatherers, and the rest were just wimps that just didn't want to do anything. I suppose I ended up with more of the hunting genes. I think there are tons of women out there that have this in them but it's never been brought forth. They've never had the opportunity to realize that they actually are hunters. I think we are throwbacks in certain ways to the animal kingdom; in all aspects of the animal kingdom, you see the female that is more of a predator, more of a provider, and she hunts. Look at all the cat species; most of the time it is the female that is out there hunting and feeding the young. I don't see where we are much removed from that.

"I think a lot of women manifest their hunting urges in shopping. I teach at a ton of Becoming an Outdoors Woman workshops and women's schools all over the country. If I find a woman who is a continuous shopper, she's not trying to buy anything particularly, she just likes to shop. She's looking all the time; she wants to see what's out there; she's just roaming and shopping at yard sales, malls or whatever. You can take that same woman and introduce her to hunting and she goes nuts over it because it's the same thing. You (the hunter) are looking, you are pitting your skills at an animal where the shoppers are pitting their shopping skills to find that bargain. That is their reward, to find that bargain. A woman hunter gets that same satisfaction because she is pitting her predatory skills against an animal."

When speaking about women working their way through some of the problems of hunting, Brenda had this to say:

I think what we women lack in the hunting skills according to what men have, we more than make up for in other ways. We were taught patience. Servitude and patience were just part of your upbringing. You don't get in a hurry whether you're walking, stalk hunting, whether you're sitting on stand, whatever you're doing. You are just patient. If I get tired of sitting on stand, and I feel I just need to get out, I think, why? I'd just have to mop the kitchen floor! As long as I'm sitting here, I'm doing something. I'm hunting and it's excusable. If I get down and go into the house, that's when I have to be amounting to something and doing something.

I have hunted an animal, I have dressed this animal, I have cooked this meat. That is one of the most satisfying things you can do. I used to equate it with my garden. I'd pick my tomatoes, then I'd can them. It was so good in the winter to just open up a jar of tomatoes that I had grown and canned. I just thought they tasted better than any other tomatoes. It's the very same thing with your game; there is just pride when you can put a meal on the table and say, "I killed this animal, I dressed it and I cooked it." You just feel so self sufficient. It's a great feeling.

Brenda gives this very important piece of advice: Whoever you choose to help you, wherever you go, DO NOT BE AFRAID TO ASK QUESTIONS! There is no question that is 'too dumb' or 'too far out'. That's how we learn!

Kathy Butt, freelance writer/photographer had this to say:

I enjoy hunting. I've been married for about 25 years now, we are taxidermists by trade, so I've always been exposed to the outdoors. I just enjoy being out there; it's the challenge. I love getting close to the animals and I love out-witting them. I just enjoy the whole thing. I'm a

DO NOT BE AFRAID TO ASK QUESTIONS!

very "outdoorsy" person and I'd much rather be outdoors than indoors.

Margaret McDonald, Director of Marketing and Advertising for Gander Mountain outdoor stores advises beginners:

Hunt with someone you trust. In the beginning there may be some situations which arise that you are not adequately prepared to handle. You want someone there who you can really trust. In the beginning it can be scary, and sometimes you don't really know what to expect. You want someone who understands what it is like to be hunting for the first time and you want to share the experience. When you do become an experienced hunter, then it is time to think about asking someone else to get involved, to invite them along and introduce them to hunting.

Bertie Eastman is the designer for Eastmans' Hunting Journal, a magazine she and her husband founded. Bertie said she always loved nature, loved being in the outdoors with her husband. She has enjoyed the animals and appreciates how fascinating they are. She had never thought about hunting and she was scared to death of guns because they "can be so dangerous." She started hunting a few years ago and says:

It's the being out there, the challenge of having the animals close, being with Mike (her husband) and sharing his world. It's not the killing that is important, it's all that comes before and after. I didn't grow up in a hunting family, and for the first 23 years of our marriage I never hunted with Mike. Although I carefully dusted his elk and deer mounts, stacked the trophy photos, and listened to hunting stories, I never understood that part of him. His excitement was a total mystery to me. To be honest, the time and money he spent on hunting often made me mad at times. You can imagine my reaction when he informed me we were going to start a hunting magazine. After the second issue, I worried he had used up all his hunting stories and the ideas would soon come to an end. Not so. I just didn't understand the world of hunting.

Everything changed the day he asked me if I'd like to apply for an antelope license. I said yes, just to get a rise out of him. I did apply, and did draw a tag! After spending time at the rifle range, I felt I was ready when the season rolled around. When we started hunting, I asked myself, 'What am I doing? I'm not sure I can do this.' Mike told me, 'You don't have to if you don't want to.' With those words the pressure was off and I knew I was free to choose. I chose to go hunting.

Things did not go well, however, and it wasn't long before we figured out I could not be rushed. He could set up and shoot in a matter of seconds, where it took me at least a minute. It was frustrating for him. A few days later, I did take a 14-inch antelope with three shots. Mike was extremely proud of me and wondered why I wasn't as excited as he was. The truth was I had just struggled over a huge hurdle that even I couldn't explain until much later. My love of hunting would grow as I became a better hunter.

Bertie advises lots of hands-on instruction and "out-in-the-field" shooting to get ready to hunt. "You can do a lot of shooting at the range, but the shooting in the field is different. Prairie dog hunting was great and really helped my shooting," she said.

The following are some helpful hints Bertie and Mike have learned over the years.

Hints for Men:

•Make sure her first hunting experience is short and she is able to see a lot of game. A seven-day backpack into the wilderness is not her idea of fun.

•Hunt the same area for several years. It will be like a walk down memory lane.

•Make sure she has a gun that fits her properly. Consider a muzzle-break. It will help her keep the sight picture and prevent a sore shoulder. Let her become very comfortable with her gun before she goes hunting. Do a lot of explaining, but never take the gun from her to do it yourself.

•Practice at the rifle range is only the beginning. Consider spending several weekends out in the wild shooting. Make it fun. In our country we have an over abundance of prairie dogs which really help me with the reality of a live target.

•A woman is a nurse by nature and wounding an animal is like tearing at her heart. This is probably her biggest obstacle when it comes to hunting. Helping her perfect her shooting skills will make all the difference in the world.

•Be patient. Her best shooting position will probably be different than yours. After all, her body is put together differently.

•Sneaking through the willows, sagebrush, mud and cactus is not something a woman often does. At first, she may not react immediately when you tell her to sit down. She may want to glance around to choose a spot that looks more comfortable.

•Dressing with layers is best. Good walking boots are a must. DON'T get impatient. She's already nervous with so many new things to remember. It may be several seasons before the motions of hunting become second nature.

•Teaching her to hunt may give you a very enthusiastic hunting partner. The best part is she will be much more understanding when it comes to your love for hunting. Who knows, she may even encourage you to go more often!

Hints for Women:

•Learning to hunt can do wonders for your marriage. Your husband will really appreciate the time you take to share an important part of his life.

•Remember, you are totally on his turf and there is a lot to learn. When he says don't move, freeze. Even a slight hand movement can be seen by an animal's powerful vision. I've messed up more than one good stalk by peeking around Mike's shoulder just to see what he's looking at.

•Take time to enjoy watching him. He loves what he's doing.

•Hunting is an extension of who a man is. This drive to win is the same drive he uses when he wants to succeed at his job. Men will always keep score whether it is a football game, successful children, size of antlers, money or love. This is just a fact.

•You will quickly develop your own hunting skills and may even become a better hunter than your husband. For now, just listen to what he has to teach you. Relax and enjoy the adventure. You won't regret it.

Gail Swanston, former archery shop owner and now BOW instructor in South Dakota, says:

I started out hunting to make it a family activity, something we could do as a family. It's relaxing for me; it's a break from the phone and the hectic schedule of life in general. You can go out in the wild and enjoy nature and God's beauty in everything, not just the animals. That's what I like; it's peaceful. I also like the challenge that's presented. We eat and utilize everything we harvest and enjoy the entire cycle.

When asked why she hunts, Kay Richey, a freelance outdoor writer and game cooking specialist from Michigan explained it this way:

Hunting is being out-of-doors at a beautiful time of the year and being able to learn the habits and to see the communication between the animals that are out there. It's a very nice time to become aware of yourself. We have come to a point in time that it's very important for us women to start mentoring younger people. I try to take at least a half dozen kids out with me bowhunting every year. I have taken them rifle hunting when they are old enough and have their hunter safety class certificate. I feel women have more patience than a lot of men, and that we all should try to start mentoring.

Mary Clawson, a South Dakota Conservation Officer, BOW instructor and veteran hunter offers this advice:

Pick your hunting/instructing companions wisely. When you first start, go with someone who is concerned with the experience, NOT the result of the hunt. You are there for the entire experience, not the biggest and the best or quickest. You want to have a good time, enjoy the outdoors, and have fun learning the skills be to a good ethical hunter. You do not want to go with a person who cuts corners and does things unlawfully or incorrectly. That will not be a good experience. You do not have to harvest an animal to have a great time. It is the companions and the times shared that are important. Sometimes the unsuccessful hunt can be the most memorable.

Outdoor enthusiast and my hunting buddy, Lori Goldade says:

I hunt everything I can. I think I do that because I get to learn about everything I'm hunting. I love duck hunting because I have to know all the different kinds of ducks. I hunt everything because I can be out hunting for months. I start dove hunting in September and I can hunt other game through December. Hunting is a reason for me to get outside, it's a reason to learn more, and it gives me something to look forward to all the time.

Now you have some ideas on how to start hunting. Run to your telephone. Expertise, new friends and excitement are only a phone call or two away!

> # I hunt everything I can. I think I do that because I get to learn about everything I'm hunting.

Before you take off hunting, here are a couple of good tips:

• Get in shape before hunting season. It is important to be in condition to hunt. Get used to walking and carrying a gun. Practice with your arm muscles so carrying and shooting a gun is not such a shock to your muscles. Hunting activities can be exhausting if you are not used to it. A treadmill is wonderful to help you stay in shape in the winter. Jogging and walking are important, and if you have hills near you, walk or run up and down those to get in shape. In some areas the local hospital or medical facility will have a hunter "tune-up" program starting a few weeks before hunting season. Take advantage of that. Have your blood pressure and cholesterol checked. There's more information on being physically and medically fit for hunting in the Turkey Hunting chapter. If you experience any medical problems in the field, like chest pain, shortness of breath and dizziness, seek medical help immediately.

• Be aware of your environment. One situation that can be overlooked is this: There are animals out there other than whatever game you are hunting. Be aware of them and their actions. I speak from personal experience when I tell you to immediately dispatch an animal that acts in a peculiar manner, is wobbling while walking, is walking towards you, is foaming at the mouth or exhibiting any other signs of strange behavior. Fox, badger, coyotes and other animals can contract rabies, a serious disease, that can be infectious to humans. You will have a firearm or bow with you, so don't be afraid to use it in this situation.

• Walk, climb or crawl safely. Always have your firearm in a safe position. Watch where you are walking. If you are in a plowed field, for instance, watch for big dirt clods which can trip you. I know this from first-hand experience, too! I broke two fingers walking from a goose pit to the vehicle.

• Hypothermia (abnormally low body temperature) is extremely dangerous and can kill. Be very careful when waterfowl hunting from a boat. Always wear a life jacket. If you are walking on ice, know for sure how thick the ice is by taking a bar of some sort and testing it. Pay close attention to the safety section of your hunter education class.

My final tip will ensure that not only you, but your family will be happy when you return home from an exhausting day of hunting: Have some frozen meals and microwave meals available during hunting season. After being in the woods all day, the last thing you will want to do when you get home is cook.

CHAPTER TWO
ETHICS AND CONSERVATION

Jim Posewitz, author of *Beyond Fair Chase* and founder of Orion, The Hunters Institute, defines an ethical hunter this way: A person who knows and respects the animals hunted, follows the law, and behaves in a way that will satisfy what society expects of him or her as a hunter. A simplified version comes from a youngster's quote in the *Beyond Fair Chase* video: Ethics means the way we behave.

We all know the "gut feeling," the difference between right and wrong and how each feels to us. We know the good feelings and sometimes we have experienced bad feelings, depending upon how we handled a certain situation. We know when we do things right, we can feel it inside and it affects our attitude about a lot of other things in our lives. The feelings we experience while hunting are no different. In fact, hunting magnifies these feelings. We are dealing with wildlife, God's creatures, and their habitat. Wildlife draws us to their "living rooms." Wildlife puts on the show, gives us fodder for stories, creates great bonding moments, makes us look inside ourselves and provides valued memories. Because wildlife is so very unique and special and holds such a revered place in our hearts, we always want to have the good feelings knowing that we always acted with responsibility, respect and dignity.

There are anti-hunting segments in our world today. There are also non-hunters. We who are hunters are always on display and our actions are monitored by both groups and the ever-watchful eyes of the media. We must not give them any ammunition to use against us.

Let's look at why we hunt. If you asked five different people why, you'd probably receive five different answers. It's a very personal thing, something that emotionally involves every part of a person. It's a way of life. There is a personal fulfillment and thrill of being one-on-one with nature and its inhabitants. Hunting is full of challenges, fellowship, bonding, being in the great outdoors and really appreciating nature. When you are hunting, you become an integral, working part of nature. The challenge of doing this on your own, enjoying successes and feeling good about yourself and the way the chase and the hunt was conducted is what it is all about.

Who are today's hunters? Middle-aged males are the largest group. Female hunters are today's fastest growing segment of hunters. In the last few years, female numbers have increased. There are about 2 million of us in the United States today, that is 9 percent of all hunters, and that number has increased 8 percent in the last 10 years. That means eth-ics in the field are hopefully improving, thanks to the presence of women. I have heard men say at the beginning of a hunt, "OK guys, clean up your act, we have women here today". I have been told, by a male hunter, that women do make better hunters than men. They generally have a better standard of ethics and they are more patient. Women can accomplish many things. They can have fun changing attitudes, creating their own opportunities and making statements. Women can also bring class to the activities. Pink and purple longjohns certainly can add some color to the clotheslines at the camps.

Here are some guidelines to remember as you embark upon your hunting activities. You should always value what you harvest. A responsible hunter takes only what she can use, making sure that game is not wasted, avoiding unnecessary public displays of dead game, and treating animals with the respect they deserve. Clean and care for your game properly. A horrible display of irresponsibility is the hunter who throws a dead deer on top of his vehicle and parades around town. There are many people out there who would be offended at that, you and me included. The animal deserves more respect than that. Do not clean or dress your game in public view or leave the gut piles in inappropriate places such as road ditches or public areas. Clean your game in the field; the predators will appreciate that.

> **We who are hunters are always on display and our actions are monitored.**

Show that you are thankful for the privilege of hunting. Responsibility dictates that you pick up spent shells and other litter every time you hunt. Leaving an area better than the way you found it is just good manners and shows respect for public and private property.

Once, during a waterfowl season, I had received permission for the very first time from a particular landowner, one whom I was led to believe disliked hunters. I was thrilled, because his land held lots of ducks on various ponds and geese in his fields. We hunted his land early one morning, left and later returned to find both a discarded box and a big sack full of garbage just where we had been hunting. Of course, garbage was strewn all over the ditch. After standing and clicking our tongues about the "slob hunters" who did this, we picked it all up and took it home. No way was I going to have that landowner think it was me that made that mess. I'll never understand what possesses people to act in that manner as it ruins hunting for all of us. Sometimes we have to be watchdogs for others and clean up other people's messes to ensure that we all will have a future of hunting.

Responsible hunters do not HAVE to take a limit. You can have a great day simply by recognizing the challenge of the hunt, the pleasures of being out in nature, the companionship of good friends, and the simple rewards of just being responsible. Like a friend of mine says, "You do not have to kill something in order to enjoy hunting. If you bring home meat, that's a BONUS!"

There should be no competition in your hunting. Trying to shoot more and bigger game in order to earn bragging rights at the coffee shop is the wrong reason to hunt. Most often, such an attitude can lead to unethical and illegal behavior. If you want to compete, do it on the sporting clays or trap range, not on wildlife.

Using the correct firearm and ammunition for a clean, quick kill, makes for a most ethical hunt. It is extremely important. We'll talk more about this later.

You will encounter situations where you will have to decide, sometimes immediately, whether to shoot or not to shoot. You will have to ask yourself questions like, will it be a good, clean shot? Am I in a safe shooting zone? If I wound an animal and it runs to adjoining land, do I have or can I get permission to go after it? Do I have the correct license? Is it legal shooting time? The hunter safety classes will definitely be a help for you in this area. Every time I hunt, no matter what the game, I always identify my "shooting lanes" before a shot is fired. If there is someone else with me, we need to establish the safe shooting zones. If I am deer hunting, I remember that my bullet can travel "forever." I choose the directions and zones where I know I will have a safe shot.

Deciding whether to shoot or not can also depend on your feelings! If you are duck hunting and you see a big beautiful drake mallard coming in to you and you are admiring it, that's OK! Look at him, admire his beauty, his fluid movements adjusting his flight path after he has seen you. You do not have to shoot! You can enjoy just watching, too. I sometimes find it hard to shoot at big, beautiful Canada geese when they are flying towards me, setting their wings to land in the decoys at my feet. That is such an incredible sight, I just have to watch. While deer hunting with my friend, Lila, we had a young whitetail buck walk up to within 12 feet of us, stand there, blinking and staring at us. It would've been such an easy, fast shot. His antlers were not very big and he gave us such a thrill, I just told him to "Go back to mama!" I did not bag a deer at all that season, but still remember that hunt as so very special because of that little buck. Wildlife can entertain you, surprise you and fill you with such love for nature.

Knowing when to shoot and when not to comes with experience. You will have many self-educating and exhilarating experiences finding your way through all that is out there.

Yes, it is OK to cry. Bagging an animal, whether it is your first duck, pheasant or deer is a tremendous experience in your life. You have done something different, you have taken game, you have accomplished goals and met challenges. All these things come together when you lovingly stroke the beautiful pheasant feathers, place your fingertip in the curl of a drake mallard's tail, or place your hands on the smooth hair on your first deer. It's beautiful! It's wonderful! You actually did this! You are so proud of yourself! It's so emotional you burst into tears. It's OK! I still get "all choked up" when I feel my fallen deer. You can tell yourself that the harvest is part of wildlife management; the numbers must be thinned out; the landowners cannot tolerate too many deer on their farms and ranches. You can tell yourself all these things, which are true, but yet you can explain nothing. There is no way to explain your feelings at such a time. There are many feelings all wrapped up together and they're bumping into each other. Just enjoy the moment, feeling pleased with yourself, your accomplishment, and giving thanks for the animal's life. Knowing that you had prepared yourself and hunted ethically adds to the experience and THAT is when you have the really good feeling inside.

I recommend *Beyond Fair Chase* as required reading for anyone learning to hunt. Jim Posewitz says all the right things and makes us look inside ourselves. For the best dissection of ethics today, this book is a must. You'll be glad you read it. To order call 1-800-582-2665 or visit www.FalconBooks.com.

The more ethical we all are, the less reason there will be for anti-hunting and animal activists' existence. I have not personally been in contact with any of those people in the 12 years I've been hunting, but I have visited with hunters who have. It is not likely you will come in contact with them in the field, but just a word of caution in case you do. Our country is a democracy and we all have the right to disagree. They believe they are right, just as we believe we are right. Most states now have laws that protect hunters from being harassed while hunting. However, if you are approached, just keep quiet, don't overreact, just leave. The public and the

Hunters provide millions of dollars and even more volunteer hours to improve wildlife habitat. Groups like the Rocky Mountain Elk Foundation have volunteers even in states where there are no elk.

media are watching, do not give the antis any reason for publicity. If you can obtain names, descriptions of people and vehicles and license number, that can help. Contact your local conservation officer.

Noted outdoor writer, Jim Zumbo states, "As I see it, hunters have something to prove, not only to other hunters, but to the rest of the world. It's simply the notion that we're OK people, rather than second-class citizens who are constantly criticized by the press and non-hunters. For that reason alone, we need to be on our best behavior in the woods. Not only will we be better off for it, but we'll feel good about ourselves."

CONSERVATION

Each day, sportsmen and women contribute more than $3 million to wildlife conservation efforts. This amounts to more than $1.5 billion per year. Hunters contribute more than $14 billion to the U.S. economy each year, supporting more than 380,000 jobs. For every 50 hunters, enough economic activity is generated to create one job.

Through more than 10,000 private groups and organizations (such as Ducks Unlimited, Pheasants Forever, National Wild Turkey Federation, Rocky Mountain Elk Foundation, etc.) sportsmen and women contribute an additional $300 million each year to wildlife conservation activities.

In 1900, less than half a million white-tailed deer remained in the nation. Today, conservation programs have returned the whitetail population to more than 18 million.

Habitat destruction reduced Canada goose populations to a low of some 1.1 million in the late 1940s. Today, there are more than three times that number.

In 1907, only about 41,000 elk could be counted in the U.S. Today, populations in 10 western states total approximately 800,000.

In 1900, there were only 30,000 wild turkeys in the U.S. Today the population is 4.8 million.

Where does that $3 million a day for conservation come from? Here's where:

•License revenues provide more than half the income, on average, for state fish and wildlife agencies. The money supports wildlife management and restoration programs, habitat improvement and general conservation efforts.

•Excise taxes on sporting equipment (such as firearms, ammunition and fishing tackle) provide more than one-fifth the income for state fish and wildlife agencies. The funds are used to acquire, maintain and improve wildlife habitat and to make the nation's lands and waters more accessible and enjoyable to all its citizens.

•Other income sources include special taxes and receipts from the sale of duck stamps (required of all waterfowl hunters), income tax check-offs and interest collected on license fees. Duck stamp proceeds are used by the government to buy or lease wetland habitat for ducks, geese and hundreds of non-game birds and animals. This money comes from the states' overall budgets, supported by taxes paid by everyone including sportsmen and women.

All in all, hunters and anglers provide more than 75 percent of the annual income of the 50 state conservation agencies. Sportsmen and women are clearly the largest contributors to conservation, paying for programs that benefit all Americans and all wildlife.

Information on specific conservation organizations is found in each appropriate chapter in this book.

A free catalog of information on the shooting sports, hunting and conservation is available from the National Shooting Sports Foundation. To order one, write to: Literature Department, National Shooting Sports Foundation, 11 Mile Hill Road, Newtown, CT 06470.

CHAPTER THREE

FIREARMS, AMMUNITION AND SAFETY

SHOTGUNS

"I don't know if I really want to do this or not! It's heavy! Yes, I have my ear plugs in! What do you mean this is really gonna hurt my shoulder or my cheek? So will it throw me backwards? What if I don't like it? I'm afraid of it! OK, OK, yes, I'll shoot—no more excuses!"

That was me the first time I was to shoot a shotgun. I really was afraid of guns. But I had committed to learning to shoot and ultimately to hunt, so I had no choice but to follow through. The first shot wasn't as bad as I had been led to believe. I held the gun as instructed and I was wearing a heavy jacket, so it didn't hurt my shoulder.

"Wow! I actually did it! It wasn't so bad after all!" I said happily. Next came the clay pigeon shooting instructions. After I "kind of" knew what I was doing, I decided shooting was great and was going to be fun!

If you are contemplating learning to shoot and hunt, but are really afraid of guns, you are not alone. No one was more terrified of guns than me. Overcoming my fear of guns and learning to shoot were huge challenges to me, and I'm sure other women share these same feelings. The shotgun classes at the Becoming an Outdoors Woman workshops are perfect for you. In a non-intimidating manner you will be instructed on proper gun use with a great emphasis on safety for yourself and others. Just knowing the proper way to handle a shotgun, how it reacts to your actions and understanding the functions of the gun will go a long way to help you overcome a fear of firearms.

The word "respect" is defined in the American College Dictionary as: *to hold in esteem or honor.* You will arrive at the point where you will respect your shotgun or any firearm that belongs exclusively to you. There will be so many great times, good memories to share, good feelings to remember, all involving your firearm that yes, you will hold your firearm "in esteem and honor." Respect also means "deferential regard" for something. Mishandled guns can be dangerous, you must show the utmost respect for that firearm and be completely safe at all times.

I started with a light 20-gauge Belgian Browning shotgun, given to me by Sig, my first mentor. It was a perfect size and weight for a beginner. I still use it for my pheasant gun and I love it. When I decided I wanted to try waterfowl hunting, another mentor suggested a Remington 1187 12-gauge shotgun for more power. I just went to a sports shop, told the guy what I was supposed to get, and walked out with a new gun and camo coveralls. I thought I had the world by the tail and

was ready for some serious hunting. That 1187 gun served me very well for waterfowl hunting and I fell in love with that gun, too. I still use it for turkey hunting and it does a great job.

Something interesting happened as the years slid by — somehow that 1187 became heavier and more difficult to swing when out in the field. The advantages of a lighter gun started rolling around in my head and were intensified when I missed ducks because my gun was too heavy for a fast swing. As luck would have it, my decision coincided with the discovery by firearm manufacturing companies that women were interested in the shooting sports and in hunting. Light shotguns started to appear on the market. If you are a shopper, then shotgun shopping has to be the ultimate trip. I am not a shopper, but even I had a great time shopping in the gun store. There are more guns from which to choose today than ever before. You could literally spend hours looking over shotguns to pick out the one that fits and feels the best in your hands.

The most popular shotguns on the market today include Benelli, Beretta, Browning, Remington, Mossberg and Winchester.

Action styles include the break-action, which is typical for single-shots and double-barrels. To load, empty and reload this gun, you'll open the action by pressing on a lever somewhere near the rear of the gun. Each make and model is different, so get an experienced shooter to show you the ropes. The pump or slide-action gun operates by sliding the forearm to operate the action. Moving the forearm to the rear opens the action, removes the fired shell and prepares another shell for insertion into the chamber. Pushing the forearm forward pushes the shell into the chamber making the gun ready to fire. An auto-loader does this automatically, using some of the power from the firing of the shell to operate the action. These are just the bare-bones descriptions of the operations of these types of firearm. To really get a good feel for how and why these guns work, take a hunter education course or ask an experienced shooter to show you how they operate.

I recommend you start with an auto-loader rather than a pump shotgun. It will be lighter, easier to use and faster. A 20-gauge shotgun is a good size to start with, and has the power you need for smaller game. You can move on up to a 12-gauge which will enable you take bigger game, such as geese. Some hunters use 20-gauge shotguns on geese but you have to be a darn good shot to do it. It's best to start small and learn about the shotgun without fear of it's kick and report. Vic Carter, the owner of Kone's Korner, a gun shop in Castlewood, South Dakota, says, "Women need to feel good while they are shooting and not be scared of the gun — that will make her afraid to shoot. Starting with a 20-gauge auto-loading shotgun will help."

I have friends who use the 20-gauge for pheasants and waterfowl and harvest a lot of game with it. When they saw my trouble with missing ducks, I was talked into buying a 20-gauge Remington 870 pump shotgun just like theirs. Well, after learning on an auto-loader, I just cannot "get it together" to shoot a pump. Several times I failed to remember to "pump" after each shot and ended up missing even more birds than before. That's proof that no matter what gun you buy, you've got to practice, practice, practice so you know and understand the function of your firearm. You need to practice with your shotgun until its operation becomes second nature. There are other gauges available, but the 20-gauge and the 12-gauge are the most popular, offer the widest variety of loadings and you can get the shells just about anywhere. If you find a 12-gauge that weighs the same as a 20-gauge, I recommend buying the 12-gauge. You then will may be able to get by with one gun for everything you hunt with a shotgun.

After settling on the action style and gauge you desire, you can start the shopping process and begin looking for the perfect gun for you. Carter says, "Firearm companies are finally aware of women and are making lighter guns. Benelli makes a good one, the brand new Remington 1187 'light contour' will be good, and Beretta is now coming into its own in this market. If the gun needs to be custom fit, we can do that. A woman must have a gun that fits her."

That last one is an important point, get a gun from someone who knows guns, so that person can discuss with you things like stock dimensions and recoil pads and the like. There are plenty of questions to be asked and nothing is out of bounds when you are about to spend hundreds of dollars on a shotgun.

Melinda Bridges, Manager of Women's Issues for the National Rifle Association had her shotgun custom fit and gives this advice, "Yes, contrary to what some say, you can have the stock cut down on a shotgun. I had the stock cut down and added a special recoil pad to mine — it fits me perfectly. Find a very experienced gunsmith who knows what he is doing and has worked with women. He must know how to fit a gun to a woman."

Another option is having a stock custom made for your shotgun, but that may be cost prohibitive. There are thoroughly competent gunsmiths out there that can alter a stock to fit your measurements and do it for a reasonable price. Synthetic stocks can also be altered.

For years the "only way" to see if a gun fit your arm was to try this test: Place the gun butt in the crook of your elbow and if your index/trigger finger fits into the trigger guard, then the gun fits you.

You can still try the test, but add this one to it: Hold the gun up to shooting position and note the distance between your cheek and the base of your thumb. If the distance is 3

inches, you don't have to move your shoulder forward too much to make contact with the gun, and the gun doesn't get caught in your armpit as you raise it, then that is right length for you.

If you are left-handed, be sure to tell the gun dealer or gunsmith. The safety, if it is on the trigger guard, can be reversed making it more convenient for you. Or, you might want to look for a gun with a safety on the tang. Whatever questions you may have in selecting a gun, the dealer should know the solution and be able to help you. Don't be afraid to ask any question.

Scott McIntire of Sodak Sport & Bait in Aberdeen, South Dakota says, "The youth models can fit a woman shooter very well. It depends on the size of the woman. The basic things a woman needs is a lightweight gun and make sure it fits well. A woman should go to the gun store herself, try the gun herself and buy it herself. Lots of times the husband will buy his wife a gun, and he will buy what HE likes, with the idea being if she doesn't like it, then the gun will be his. The person who will use the gun should be the person who buys the gun. Changing the balance of a gun to better fit a woman's shoulder is important; look for that feature in any woman's model shotgun. I think the 24-inch barrel is the most popular for women hunters, but they need longer barrels for trap shooting. For women afraid of the recoil, Pachmayr® has a good recoil pad that can be added to the stock; it will absorb 40 percent more recoil than a standard rubber pad. You can do a lot to make the gun fit, but it can really add up; it is more economical to buy a woman's lightweight or youth model in the beginning."

When you walk into the gun shop, you may feel overwhelmed by all the firearms you see. Your eye may be drawn to the new camo patterns on some guns, to the beautiful shiny wood stocks on others or the slick black synthetic-stocked shotguns. There is a lot to look at, to admire and confuse you! Simply discuss your situation with the gun dealer, asking everything you want to know. In addition to the fit, try this exercise: choose a small point on a far wall, quickly hold up the gun into shooting position and find that point with the bead on the barrel. While still holding up the gun, move the gun away from that spot, then quickly return to it and see how fast you can find that spot with your bead. That will determine how fast you can draw on a bird. I found a 24-inch barrel was too short — I was moving the gun all over the place trying to find the spot. The 28-inch barrel was good, but later I found that barrel to be too long out in the field. The perfect barrel length for me and the most popular among all hunters is the 26-inch barrel. It worked great during my trial in the store and it works great in the field. Vic, at my local gun shop, also recommends a 26-inch barrel. Some gun dealers recommend youth models for women, others do not. Take it seriously if your instructor recommends a youth model to you; try it and see if it fits you properly. When starting out, stay with a basic shotgun.

> **No matter what gun you buy, you've got to practice, practice, practice so you know and understand the function of your firearm. You need to practice with your shotgun until its operation becomes second nature.**

Pick up the guns and hold them in both hands and compare weights. When I did that, I was very surprised to find that the 20-gauge Browning Gold Hunter with the 28-inch barrel weighed just as much as the Benelli and Beretta 12-gauge guns, both with a 26-inch barrel. The 20-gauge should have been lighter, but the extra two inches on the barrel added weight. I might as well have had a 12-gauge and have that extra power. You'll also want to have about half the weight of the shotgun between your hands. That will make for an easier and smoother swing. Too much weight at either end, which can be caused by a barrel that's too long or too short, will give you trouble swinging the gun smoothly. That can lead to missed shots.

I went shotgun shopping after realizing the Remington 1187 that I loved so much was just too big and heavy. I needed a lighter gun. I chose a Benelli 12-gauge with a 24-inch barrel. I found out the first day I used it that the barrel was too short for me; I had a terrible time finding the target. I was moving the barrel all over the place. The second day I took it out waterfowl hunting it started to malfunction. The shells would neither feed nor eject properly. I finally got a shell loaded, shot at a goose and felt my hand stinging. The trigger guard had blown off in my hand! My knees got weak and my friends' eyes were like saucers. Thank God no one was injured. My gun dealer, Vic, couldn't believe it when I returned the gun. He said he sells hundreds of Benelli shotguns and that had NEVER happened. I was recently told that the metal used for the trigger guard was defective and that the company had several guns returned for the same reason. The moral of the story is this: Even if you buy the number one most popular shotgun in the world, things can still go wrong. You've got to be alert to anything strange or odd that goes on with your firearms. And to notice those things you've got to be very familiar with your gun that means shooting it often.

After that happened, I just did not have the confidence in the Benelli anymore and wanted a different brand. Not that I'm knocking the Benelli, I know there are thousands out there in use and the vast majority work just fine. Anyway, I chose the 20-gauge Browning Gold Hunter. I liked that gun with two exceptions: It was heavier than I thought it was, and the 28-inch barrel was just too long for me to generate an effective fast swing for me. I was becoming frustrated because I just could not find the "right" shotgun. Several months later I found it. A wonderful Beretta 12-gauge, 26-inch barrel light weight model called the Pintail. The weight is perfect; it handles very nicely. The Mossy Oak Shadow Grass camo is perfect and there is no more recoil with it than with any other gun I have shot. However, I am still working out a problem. The gun didn't like goose loads when it was brand new. I have shot doves, ruffed grouse and ducks with no problem, but every once in a while, the heavier goose loads will not properly feed down into the chamber. I was told to keep it very clean and use Rem-Oil on all the parts. I have been following orders and it seems to be better; if not, that gun will go back to the dealer also. As you can see, you can have trouble with your guns, even when they are brand new. In some cases, it is NOT you, it is the GUN, no matter what any man tells you. The point of all this is that you may have to try several guns before you settle on the "perfect" one for you. If any of these problems should befall you, your gun dealer will become your best friend. And stock up on Rem-Oil.

The list of guns I have used includes the Remington 1187 12-gauge (that I loved but found to be too heavy), the old antique Belgian Browning 20-gauge that I still use, a Remington 870 pump 20-gauge that went back to the store because the shells would not eject correctly, a Benelli 12-gauge with a dangerous defect so it went back to the store, a Browning Gold Hunter 20-gauge that was still too heavy because the barrel was too long, and now my Beretta 12-gauge. I speak with some authority when I say this Beretta is terrific; I think I have finally found the perfect shotgun for me. But it took some shopping. So be ready. Once you get hooked on shooting and hunting, you can expect to be a regular customer at your local gun shop.

For a beginning shotgunner, Browning recommends the Gold Hunter, 20-gauge, semi-automatic with a 26-inch barrel (make SURE it has 26" barrel). Although the shotgun is not classified as a lightweight, Browning offers it as THE gun for women hunters. Having a gun that is somewhat heavier makes for less recoil; which is good not only for women, but for every inexperienced shooter. I really liked my Gold Hunter except for the 28-inch barrel, so I know this shotgun is a good choice.

Robin L. Sharpless, Senior Vice President of H & R 1871®, Inc. and New England Firearms®, says, "As the largest maker of single-barrel, single-shot shotguns in the world, we have many choices. My base recommendation is either a 20- or 28-gauge model in a size appropriate to the physical size of the intended shooter. We produce a wide range of models in each of these gauges and in both youth and adult configurations. The New England Firearms® basic Pardner® model can fit a unique bill as a first shot-

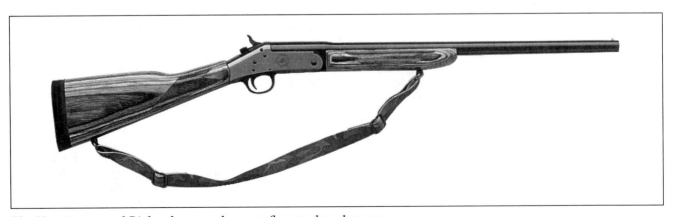

The Harrington and Richardson youth camouflage turkey shotgun.

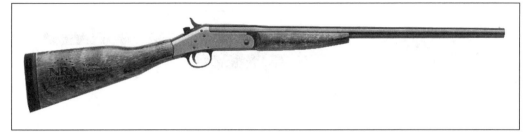

The New England Firearms youth model shotgun. This is a special NRA Foundation Youth Endowment Edition of the gun with engraving on the stock.

gun. It is simple, reliable and considered to be very safe. In fact, 38 states use this model in their hunter education programs, making these one of the most popular 'beginner's' shotguns in the world. Through a unique partnership with the National Rifle Association Foundation, New England Firearms® will produce three very special new youth shotguns, based on the current Pardner® Youth shotguns in 20-gauge, 28-gauge and .410. The safety is due to the use of a patented transfer-bar mechanism. Bird barrels to slug barrels all can be fitted to the same action. NEF has added a new youth version to its popular line of dedicated turkey guns and offers a new youth rifle chambered for the 22 long rifle. The new Harrington & Richardson® "NWTF Sponsored Edition Youth" shotgun is produced in 20-gauge with a 22-inch barrel with a modified choke for maximum versatility on turkeys and a variety of other game as well. It has a 3-inch chamber allowing it to handle the heaviest 20-gauge turkey loads with ease.

The shotguns offered by NEF and H&R are simple, light and inexpensive, making them perfect as a "first gun." But these are single-shot shotguns. They are not repeaters. You must open the action and insert a new shell after every shot. That may not seem like a big deal at first, but as you get deeper and deeper into hunting you might want that second shot or third shot, just in case you miss with the first one. Still, many people believe that having just one shot will make you a better hunter and a better shot. If you know you only have one crack at it, you tend to concentrate a bit more on making a good shot.

Another benefit of the single-shot is its price. Most of these little guns can be had for less than $100. Meaning you can get started for very little investment. But take Robin's advice from above, start with a smaller gauge gun. A 20-gauge will hit hard enough to bag pheasants, but remember, these guns are light. As you step up in power, the gun hits harder, but it hits you harder, too.

Benelli is promoting the Montefeltro, either the 12-gauge or 20-gauge as their women's shotgun. It is lightweight and has a shorter stock. My hunting buddy, Lori, has a 12-gauge Montefeltro and really likes it; she hunts upland game, turkeys and waterfowl. The 20-gauge comes in Realtree Xtra Brown Camo finish.

Ithaca has a "Women and Youth Model" 20-gauge that is promoted as a very good starter shotgun. It is available in turkey camo and waterfowl camo patterns. It has a shorter stock for youth and small-framed women. An advantage for youth is that as they grow, the shotgun can be returned to the factory and a regular stock can be placed on the gun.

Beretta recommends their AL390 with its adjustable stock in either 12- or 20-gauge for beginning women shooters. Also available is the AL390 Youth Model in 20-gauge. As I mentioned before, I have a lightweight Beretta 12-gauge Pintail with Shadow Grass camo and a 26-inch barrel. I am a tall person with fairly long arms and that gun fits me almost perfectly. I really like it.

Marty Fajen, President of Tristar Sporting Arms, Ltd, is promoting a special shotgun designed exclusively for women. Marty has worked in the gun stock business for 27 years so she knows women's shooting problems. She took all the stock measurements, had a pattern made and took it all to a factory in Italy. She is now selling double-barrel over and under shotguns by Emilio Rizzini Co. The shotguns feature a 13-1/2-inch length of pull (that's the length from the trigger to the buttstock) which women will like. The toe of the buttstock is flared out and faces away from the breast tissue, so it fits females well in the natural pocket of the shoulder.

"Ninety percent of the women who pick up this gun just smile," said Marty. "It is a fun shotgun to shoot— you can mount it more quickly for line of sight."

The shotguns are available in 12- and 20-gauge with different barrel lengths. The stocks are all wood and choke tubes are included. Starting price is under $1,000. If you want information, contact Marty at P.O. Box 7496, 1814-16 Linn, N. Kansas City, MO 64116 or call 816-421-1400.

A Benelli Montefeltro model shotgun designed for smaller shooters, especially women.

The Beretta AL390 shotgun is offered in full camouflage for those who want every advantage in the woods.

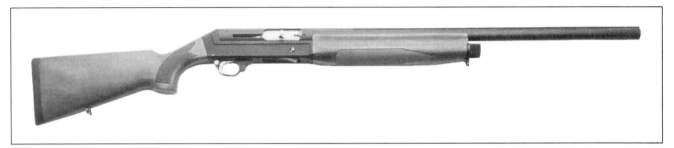

The Beretta Pintail model is a light weight shotgun with nice balance that's suitable for most women to carry in the field.

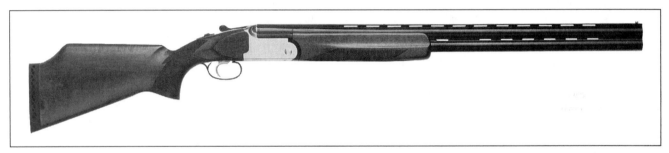

Tristar Sporting Arms, Ltd. offers a specially designed shotgun just for women. The TR-L is made to different specifications to accommodate differences between male and female shooters.

Ask for the TR-L model that was designed for the woman shooter.

As of this writing, Winchester does not have a shotgun designed specifically for women, but the Model 130 auto-loading shotgun does come in 20-gauge. This is a smooth-swinging and light gun that shoots very well. Winchester is expected to bring a women's model to market before too long.

When you are shotgun shopping, you will have a choice of stocks; that is a personal decision. The wood stocks are beautiful and probably still the most popular, adding much value to the shotgun. If you do purchase a wood stock, remember you will be hunting with this gun—it will not just be sitting in your gun cabinet looking beautiful. You will scratch it, gouge it, get it muddy, and certainly cover it with fingerprints and dust. Don't get something that you will be afraid to use in the field. The black synthetics are good and my friends love theirs. If you choose a gun with a camo pattern, be careful. Keep in mind just where you will be doing most of your hunting. When I purchased my Benelli, it had a Realtree camo pattern suited to turkey hunting. I did not notice all the white to light gray in the pattern until I had it out in a stubble field waterfowl hunting—it stuck out like a sore thumb! It would have been horrible in the rushes where I hunt waterfowl. There are other Realtree patterns that would be fine. I have a Mossy Oak

Swamp Grass pattern on my Beretta that is just absolutely perfect. While hunting in a cut wheat field with a new growth of grass mixed in with dry swaths of grain, I would have lost my gun if the barrel had not been black. That gun blends in perfectly in the rushes and any other place I hunt.

Camouflage is not always mandatory, but if you do purchase a gun with a black synthetic or wood stock, there are ways to camouflage it yourself. I wrap camo tape (the kind with no white in it) around my Remington 1187, barrel and all, for turkey hunting. It really disguises the gun well and you are confident there will be no glare from your barrel. I'll talk more about the importance of camouflage in the turkey and waterfowl hunting chapters. I kept the tape on it for waterfowl season, also--the geese do not see the glare or reflection of the gun and the tape does not hurt the finish on the gun. Besides, if you keep the gun taped all the time, who will see the finish?

My friends laughed at me, but I had the last laugh when I showed up with a "white gun" for waterfowl hunting in the snow. I covered the gun with a white opaque knee-hi nylon stocking! I placed the knee-hi on the gun, barrel included, held it tight and taped it with white medical tape. It worked great! Just use your imagination. Whatever conditions in which you will be hunting you can have fun trying new ideas!

When you buy a new shotgun it will be in a box. Have the gun dealer assemble it for you. Watch every step, then ask the dealer to take it part and allow you to try it, so you know the gun and understand how it works. Three different choke tubes will be in the box. The standard sizes are full choke (greatest constriction), modified (less constriction) and improved cylinder (least constriction). There are other tubes available, but for the beginner, stick with these three. A choke tube regulates the pattern size of your shot after it leaves the gun barrel. Shot pattern is usually described by the number of pellets that strike within a 30-inch circle at a given range. A full choke tube will provide the tightest shot pattern meaning it will put the most pellets in the circle at the longest range. As the amount of restriction is reduced, the pellets from the shotgun shell spread out wider as they fly. There is tons of information available on shotgun patterns and which tubes work best with which shot sizes and style of shot. We'll get a bit more specific later in the book.

There was a modified choke in my 1187 when I bought it and I never changed it. I used it for waterfowl and turkey and was successful with each. Later I was told an improved cylinder would be best for waterfowl, so I have that now in my Beretta and I am shooting better than I have for a long time. You will have to test your shotgun with different choke tubes and different size shot loads to find what is best for you. When using a 12-gauge, I recommend the improved cylinder choke with BBB or BB size shot for as the best waterfowl combination. Use Number 1 steel with the improved cylinder in your 20-gauge. The choke tubes screw in the end of your gun barrel and can easily be interchanged with the wrench that accompanies your gun.

Ask your gun dealer if it is possible to shoot your gun before you purchase it. When you have made your purchase, DEMAND that the gun dealer sit down with you and show

you EXACTLY how that gun functions. When you walk out of the store, you should know EVERYTHING there is to know about that gun and its operation.

When purchasing a shotgun, remember not to buy "too much gun." Start small. A gun with a lot of recoil and noise will instill bad shooting habits. Choose a light shotgun that you feel comfortable handling, can quickly and easily bring up to a target, and that you feel fits you well. Remember you are shopping for a very important item so try them all and carefully choose your favorite. It's like falling in love. You will know when you have found the right one!

Take good care of your gun. Each time you come in from hunting, clean the gun. There will be dirt, dust, weeds, and all manner of items that will be in the action and will need to be removed. MAKE SURE THE GUN IS UNLOADED BEFORE YOU START CLEANING! Use a small soft brush and good gun cleaning solvent (ask the owner of shop where you bought the gun) to clean the action. Dry carefully with a soft, clean cloth and lightly spray oil on the parts.

You can check the cleanliness of the barrel this way: MAKE SURE THE GUN IS UNLOADED FIRST, then shine a flashlight into the barrel. To clean the barrel, place a cloth patch soaked with solvent or Rem-Oil® on the end of a cleaning rod and pass it through the barrel. Follow this procedure with dry cloth patches until the patches come out clean. You can lubricate the barrel by pulling a lightly oiled patch through it. Do not use WD-40 to lubricate your guns, it will make your gun gum up in cold weather. Always use Rem-Oil® or a similar lubricant made specifically for firearms!

I take my shotgun to a gunsmith and have it thoroughly cleaned after every season. I do not trust myself to take it all apart, clean it and then try to get all those little pieces back together correctly. I had a so-called expert friend clean my gun once. After a hunting season of frustration caused by the gun repeatedly jamming I found out HE had put some rings in backwards after cleaning the gun. From then on, I have had a professional clean my gun and I know it will be done right. I suggest you do the same. Before you hunt, make sure your gun is clean and operating properly. If you take good care of your gun, it will work well and be with you for a long time.

An add-on you may want to try for your gun is the HI VIZ shotgun sight. It is a device that fits onto the end of your gun barrel to give you greater visualization of a correct lead. When holding up your gun to shoot you will see a bright green bead (it comes in four interchangeable colors for different light) that will improve your low-light shooting. Since you are more cognizant of the bead, you will have less tendency to stop or slow your swing on a target. I fastened the sight base on my barrel with hot glue. It came off and I lost it in a cornfield. I then used about three drops of super glue. That should hold it.

You will want a sling on your shotgun. Whether you are walking all day in the turkey woods or walking to your goose blind, you will want your arms free. When carried on a sling over your shoulder, you will not end the day with extremely tired arms from carrying your gun. If you are hunting doves, pheasants, grouse or waterfowl and feel the sling will interfere with your shots, just remove it and replace it as needed. Don't let a male hunter shame you into not placing a sling on your gun because it is not the "macho" thing to do. You want to be comfortable and have the right to do your own thing. My Beretta came with the sling loops already installed. If your shotgun does not have these, the gun dealer can install

Choke tubes are threaded steel inserts that change the constriction at the end of the barrel. The three basic choices include Improved Cylinder, Modified and Full choke. These tubes change the pattern density of the shot as it leaves the barrel.

The author tries out a shotgun at a shooting event sponsored by a writers' organization. Any time you get the chance to try several different kinds of guns at the same time, use the opportunity to see what you like and don't like. The experience is wonderful.

them easily for you. Make sure they are detachable; you may want to detach the sling while you are in your blind so you don't get it caught in something and miss a shot. (I know that one from experience)

You should also purchase a gun case to protect your investment. Most states have a gun case law, meaning your gun must be unloaded and in the case during transportation. Besides that, you want to protect while it is in a vehicle. When you have to throw the gun into the back of a pickup, you better make sure it is in the case or you could damage the gun. You have paid good money for this firearm so take good care of it. If you keep your gun in the case for storage while in your home, do not zip the case completely closed. Make sure it is open enough to get air so the humidity will not rust the gun. NEVER store your gun in your basement as it is too humid.

Before leaving the gun store, purchase a set of "ear muffs." These are hearing protectors. The kind that look like ear muffs and fit around your head offer the best protection. Wear them while you are patterning your gun and any time you practice. Buy several pairs of little ear plugs and keep them with your hunting/shooting gear or in your purse in case some day you forget your ear muffs. Hunters and others who have lost a degree of hearing will tell you how

extremely important ear protection is. Hearing loss is permanent, but completely preventable.

AMMUNITION

There are so many different kinds of ammunition you may be overwhelmed again when you look at the shelves in the gun store. Don't be. Let's keep it simple. First of all, there are two kinds of shot: lead and non-toxic. Lead poisoning became a serious problem in waterfowl flocks and is no longer allowed on federal lands and most states' public land. Waterfowl pick at gravel to help digest their food and they can easily die of lead poisoning when lead pellets are ingested. Wounded birds often fall prey to eagles and other raptors. If the wound was caused by lead shot, the raptors that consume the dead or injured bird can also die of lead poisoning. As a result, lead shot is now only used for upland and small game hunting and is banned altogether on some public lands. Be sure to check the regulations where you hunt.

Steel shot is the most popular non-toxic shot and the least expensive. Other non-toxic shot you will see are tungsten and bismuth. Do not concern yourself with anything other than steel for right now. As mentioned before, federal regulations require the use of non-toxic shot for all waterfowl hunting and for hunting upland game on federal Waterfowl Production Areas. Some states also require the use of non-toxic shot on public lands. You will hear all sorts of talk about steel shot, but know this: Steel is just as effective as lead. All you need to do is practice shooting with steel until you can hit the targets you are aiming at within the shot's effective range.

Some people initially complained, "I can't hit anything with steel shot." That's because it flies and patterns differently than lead. Everyone who grew up shooting exclusively lead just had to learn to shoot better, and they have. Since I started hunting, I have used steel shot for everything except upland game. I didn't have to learn how to shoot all over again. If you use steel shot for ALL of your hunting, things stay simpler and easier for you—you do not have to remember where and for what game you must use it.

Knowing you must use steel shot, you can then choose the length of your shell. Your shotgun will determine if you can use 2-3/4-inch or 3-inch shells. Shotguns are available that shoot 3-1/2-inch shells, but those are too big and heavy for a beginner and unnecessary at this point in your hunting career. The 3-inch shells have more power and hold more pellets. Those can be good things, but if the extra bang and kick cause you to flinch and miss your shots all the pellets in the world won't help.

Charts are available to show you which shells are recommended for each species of game. These can be found at sport shops, in magazines and in many states' hunting regulations. Please refer to the Waterfowl Hunting chapter for the CONSEP steel shot lethality table. FEDERAL Cartridge Company has published great charts showing a comparison of shot sizes, a pattern density table, pellet count for steel shot, etc. Call 1-800-322-2342 and ask for their catalog. Also ask for their Waterfowl Loads brochure for a good explanation of non-toxic waterfowl loads. Ask your gun dealer for charts, too. When you pattern your shotgun (see the "Turkey Hunting" chapter) you can use different combinations of shot sizes and chokes to find the very best pattern your shotgun will make.

If you have not attended a hunter safety class, contact your wildlife agency and ask for one of their manuals from which they teach. They are great books with a lot of good simple information for the beginner hunter. There are charts, graphs and tables included which can give you more information on shot sizes, how pellets pattern, and general shotgun/shell information.

SAFETY!! SAFETY!! SAFETY!!

ALWAYS REMEMBER TO BE SAFE! When you pick up a firearm, you are holding a lethal weapon in your hands. That lethal weapon has the capability of killing animals AND people, that includes your friends or relatives or anyone standing within range of the firearm. ALWAYS be cognizant of that fact! Another point: Choose hunting partners who possess a passion for safety as well as hunting. A best friend can be your worst enemy if he or she has even a momentary lapse in judgment. You can afford to be darn choosy about with whom you hunt. It is a fact that your hunting partner is more likely to harm you than other hunters.

Your gun can be dangerous; keep it safe by practicing your shooting skills, understanding your limitations and having a thorough knowledge of your gun's operation.

YOU are responsible for firearm safety. Here is a great list of safety tips found in the Browning shotgun owner's manual:

• There is no excuse for careless or abusive handling of any firearm. At all times handle any firearm with intense respect for its power and potential danger.

• Always keep the muzzle of any firearm pointed in a safe direction.

• Never rely totally on your shotgun's mechanical "safety" device. No guarantee can be made that the gun will not fire even if the safety is in the "on safe" position. A safety can sometimes fail; it can be jarred or inadvertently manipulated into an unsafe condition.

• Never test the mechanism of any firearm while it is loaded or pointed in an unsafe direction.

• Whenever you handle a firearm, or hand it to someone, make sure it is completely unloaded.

• Do not transport any loaded firearm.

• Hunting from elevated surfaces such as tree stands is dangerous. Make certain the stand is safe and stable. Make sure your firearm is unloaded when taken up and down from the stand. Remember a loaded firearm may discharge when dropped, even with the safety in the "on safe" position.

• Beware of barrel obstructions. Before checking, be certain the firearm is fully unloaded.

• Always completely unload all firearms when not in use.

• Use the proper ammunition. Be alert to the signs of ammunition malfunction. If you detect an off sound or light recoil when a cartridge is fired, do not load another cartridge into the chamber.

• Make sure of adequate ventilation in the area that you discharge a firearm. Wash hands thoroughly after exposure to ammunition or cleaning a firearm.

• Never insert a shell of the incorrect gauge in any shotgun. Examine every shell you put in your gun. Never put a 20-gauge shell in a 12-gauge gun. Use the correct length shells.

• Do not snap the firing pin on an empty chamber — the chamber may not be empty!

• Keep your fingers away from the trigger while unloading or loading, until you are ready to shoot.

• Be sure of your target and backstop.

• Always unload the chamber and magazine of any firearm before crossing a fence, climbing a tree, jumping a ditch or negotiating other obstacles.

• Wear eye and ear protection when shooting.

• Dropping a loaded gun can cause an accidental discharge.

• If any firearm fails to fire, keep the muzzle pointed in a safe direction.

• Be defensive and on guard against unsafe gun handling around you and others.

• Be certain your shotgun is unloaded before cleaning.

• Supervise and teach firearms safety to all members of your family — especially to children and nonshooters.

• Never drink alcoholic beverages or take any type of drugs before or during shooting.

• Perform periodic maintenance on your firearm.

• Do not, under any circumstances, alter the trigger, safety or parts of the firing mechanism of any firearm.

Another good point is when you unload your shotgun, keep that chamber open. If your action is open, the gun cannot fire.

According to Bill Shattuck, Hunter Safety Specialist for the South Dakota Department of Game, Fish and Parks, the rules for safely storing firearms in the home are few in number and easy to follow:

•Always unload sporting firearms carefully and completely before taking them into the home.

•Never load a sporting firearm in the home.

•Always make absolutely sure that firearms in your home are securely stored in a location inaccessible to children. Ammunition should be stored in a separate location, locked and also inaccessible to children.

•Always place firearms in their proper storage location immediately after returning from a hunting trip.

•Always re-check firearms carefully and completely to confirm that they are "still" unloaded when you remove them from storage.

•Always remember that it is your responsibility to make certain the firearms in your home are not casually accessible to anyone--especially curious young people.

If your child is receiving his/her first firearm, nothing is more exciting. It is proof the youngster is of age and ready to accept responsibility for the firearm. Parents will want to take some simple steps to ensure themselves that the firearm is used safely and responsibly. Shattuck suggests:

•Make sure your child reads and completely understands the manual supplied by the firearm's manufacturer.

•A responsible adult needs to be present anytime the gun is used.

•Enroll your child in a hunter safety course as soon as possible. Contact your nearest wildlife agency office for dates.

•Consider letting your child enroll in a 4-H Shooting Sports Program or a BB gun program sponsored by an area service organizations. These programs emphasize safety and responsibility as well as teaching marksmanship.

Bill Shattuck also says, the two most important points of safety are:

TREAT EVERY GUN AS IF IT WERE LOADED

KEEP THE MUZZLE POINTED IN A SAFE DIRECTION.

There would never be a firearm accident if these two rules were always followed.

Safety is of utmost importance to you, your hunting partners, your family and any child receiving a firearm for the first time. In summary, just remember always to keep that barrel pointed in a safe direction, be conscious of that fact when moving, and ALWAYS KEEP YOUR SAFETY ON UNTIL IMMEDIATELY BEFORE YOU SHOOT!! Never point your gun at anything you do not want to shoot, whether it's loaded or not. A terrible tragedy could occur because you "thought it was unloaded." You must treat your firearm with the utmost respect. If it is legal in your state to carry a firearm uncased in your vehicle, always unload completely before doing so. Even if it is pointed down and no one else is around — be safe — you don't need a hole in the floor or worse yet, in your foot or in someone else when you take that gun out of the vehicle. Better yet, put the gun in the case. There's really no need to carry it uncased anyway. When you treat your firearm with respect, you get that good feeling, knowing you ARE a safe hunter. You want to keep that feeling, therefore, SAFETY will always be uppermost in your mind. Don't be afraid of your gun, be SAFE with your gun.

SHOTGUN SHOOTING TIPS

The main difference between shotgun and rifle shooting is: with a shotgun you point and pull the trigger, with a rifle you aim and squeeze the trigger. When shooting a shotgun, do not aim at the target, point at it with the barrel. When holding your shotgun in shooting position, point your index finger of the hand on the forestock of the gun right at your target. Keep both eyes open when shooting with a shotgun. You must have confidence when target shooting or hunting; if you think you will not hit the target, then you won't. If you think you will, then you will hit it. Confidence is the most important part of shooting that you can be given by your instructor. While shooting, always concentrate on the target — never let your eyes drift back to the barrel. Never let anyone make you feel bad about missing. Your instructor is the one to analyze why you missed and correct it — you should just have fun shooting. Whenever a sportsmen's club has a shooting workshop in your area, attend it. Two personal hints: tie up long hair away from your face and make sure your shooting glasses cover your eyebrows so the rim doesn't obscure your vision.

Shooting a shotgun is different from shooting a rifle (which will be discussed later). A shotgun is not aimed so much as it is pointed, and most times you will need to get your shotgun moving and keep it moving slightly ahead of the target you intend to hit. This is called the "swing-through lead." Follow the flight path of the bird until the gun muzzle passes it, pull the trigger and continue the swing after shooting. DO NOT STOP THE GUN AND AIM! If you do that, you will miss shots. That is the most important part to remember! Here's a good way to learn and practice leading a target. With an UNLOADED shotgun, have a friend shine a flashlight on a wall and move it as a bird would fly; you come up behind that flashlight beam, overtake it, and say "shoot" when you think the time is right and keep on swinging that gun to follow through.

If the birds are flying straight at you or straight away, shoot straight at them. But remember, they could also be gaining or losing altitude at the same time. It takes practice and experience. Do not become discouraged if you cannot hit flying targets consistently at first; there are good hunters out there who miscalculate at times. Birds can be deceptively fast and timing is everything. Don't wait too long to shoot. But don't to shoot too quickly either. That's why you want a gun that's heavy enough to absorb some recoil, but not so heavy that it keeps you from getting the ahead of the bird quickly.

We learn through our mistakes. After you have hunted for a while, leading the birds will become instinctive and you'll figure out the timing as fire more shots. If whatever you are doing works, then keep doing the same thing the same way..

Also, pay close attention to the range. If you shoot when the birds are too close, the pellets from your pattern will not spread out to fill the 30-inch circle we talked about earlier. The farther the pellets are from the end of your gun barrel the more spread out they become, so at the moment they leave your barrel they are packed in close together, hence no pattern. At 30 yards, the pellets will have likely spread out to a nice even density. If you take long shots, like 60 yards for example, the pellets will be so spread out you may only cripple a bird. That is not ethical hunting. Accurate estimation of the range of your target is the key to making good clean kills.

Here the author scopes out a prairie dog town. Varmint hunting can be a great way to practice your shooting skills and learn about different guns.

Try to imagine a cone coming from the muzzle of your shotgun. Close to the barrel, the cone is narrow. Far away, the cone is wide. Thus the number of pellets per square inch drops the farther away from the barrel the pellets get. Ideally, you'd like to put several pellets into the body of the bird to bring it down quickly.

Shooting professional Tom Roster schedules seminars around the country. These information-packed seminars are valuable for every shotgunner and can teach anyone great things about shotguns and the range at which they are effective. Contact your wildlife agency to obtain the schedule of classes nearest you. It would certainly be worth your while to attend one of these seminars as you begin hunting— you will learn all the right things at the beginning!

RIFLES

The cockleburs were sticking me in the belly as I hugged the river bottom. With hearing protectors in place, and the 22/250 shouldered I listened as my mentor, Bill, told me how terrible the shock would be to my shoulder when I fired. We had milk jugs filled with water set up on the river bank, waiting for my perfect shot to empty them. I studied the crosshairs as Bill was still warning me how awful this would be. But I would still have to do it if I wanted to hunt deer. "Pow!" Water spurted out of the milk jug! What a shot for my first time! Bill refused to believe it, but my shoulder never hurt.

I know now he was using reverse psychology, and it worked. I shot until all the milk jugs were empty, and actually really surprised Bill with my shooting ability. I found out that day I loved rifle shooting and I still do. I shot my first deer with that 22/250 and now have my own 270 and two 22-caliber rifles. I have fun target shooting all year and really enjoy rifle hunting. Here is another opportunity for you.

When you start to look for a rifle, I'd suggest you contact your local gun or conservation or find a mentor. Ask if some one will let you fire several different rifles and assist you. Shoot several different calibers so you know how they feel and, if you can, try out several action types to see how they work. The caliber size will be determined by what game you are going to hunt. Knowing what game you want and knowing how different rifles perform, it is then time to go to the gun store and choose your personal rifle.

There are several good rifles for sale these days. Many are made by the same companies that make shotguns, but some companies focus only on rifles. Names like Remington, Browning, Winchester, Savage, Sako, Marlin, Ruger are common in the gun store.

As with shotguns, there are several action types to choose from. The action is the means by which the gun is loaded, made ready to fire and re-loaded. Typical rifle actions include the bolt action, auto-loaders and the lever action. There are also pump or slide-action rifles and a single-shot rifles.

The bolt-action rifle is operated with a handle at the rear of the receiver. This handle is pulled back to cock the firing mechanism and as it is pushed forward, a round is fed from the magazine into the chamber. After the rifle is fired and bolt pulled back, the empty shell is ejected. Auto-loaders use a similar system that is made to function by using some gas from the fired round to operate the action. Each time the trigger is pulled, a round is fired, the action cycles and new round is fed into the chamber. For the gun to fire again, the trigger must be released fully and pulled again. A lever-action, has an operating lever below the receiver. Rounds are fed from the magazine into the chamber by pulling the lever down and back up to the starting position. A slide-action works much like the slide or pump action shotguns described above. The same is true with single-shot rifles.

All of these actions provide pretty much the same function. I will leave it up to you and your mentor to figure out which one you like best.

The 22/250 with which I shot my first deer was a great gun, but I knew I wanted to hunt mule deer and elk some day, which meant I would need a bigger gun. I also wanted to have plenty of power and a good all-around rifle. After

The author loves her Remington rifle, chambered in 270 Winchester. It is comfortable, accurate and provides all the power she needs.

researching and pestering my mentor with all kinds of questions, I decided on a bolt-action Remington Model 700 chambered to shoot the 270 Winchester cartridge. It does kick, but I notice it only when target shooting. For some reason I never am conscious of it kicking when taking a shot at a deer. When I sight it in, I just make sure I have a heavy jacket on to cushion my shoulder. When you are expecting the kick and are ready for it, it's easier to take. It is a great gun, shoots and handles well and can be used for all game including elk. I have had people tell me to use a higher powered rifle for elk, but after researching the issue, I know the 270 will be fine. Shot placement (hitting the vital area) is the important factor. A bigger, more powerful bullet does no good if it's poorly placed.

My gun dealer, Vic Carter, says, "For a beginning female hunter who is going to hunt deer and antelope, I recommend a 243 caliber with a 100-grain bullet. That is just a nice middle caliber. If you hit a deer with that, you will get him. Unless you are a very experienced hunter, the smaller calibers like 222 or 223s are not heavy enough for a good clean kill. The next size caliber would be the 25-06 or the 270. I would be a little cautious with first-time hunters because the 270 is going to 'buck em' a little bit. A 243 is just about per-

fect. A 308 would also be good. It's the same case as the 243, it's just using a 30-caliber bullet. There you can get a 125- or 150-grain bullet. It will give you a little bit of a 'snap' (recoil) again, probably the same as a 270. The 308 is probably a little bit better than the 243 because you have a bigger bullet. I still think a 243 is the best for a female beginner. Staying with a lighter rifle in the beginning is the secret."

Scott McIntire says, "I recommend the 243 rifle for women hunting deer and antelope. It is in between the 270 and the 25-06, both of which are longer and heavier. A great new product is the 260 caliber which has 25 percent more knockdown power with minimum additional recoil. Both Browning and Remington are making these."

Of course there are heavier calibers, but for us women they are not necessary. I won a beautiful Browning A-Bolt Stalker rifle in the 300 Winchester Magnum caliber at a Rocky Mountain Elk Foundation banquet. That was several years ago and I have not yet shot it. That rifle is very heavy and with a scope mounted on it would almost be impossible for me to hold steady and shoot. Don't let anyone talk you into getting anything bigger than a 243 or a 270 and you will be fine.

A 100-grain bullet is the norm for a 243 and 130- to 150-grain bullet for a 270. I use ammunition by the Federal

The New England Firearms Handi-Rifle is offered in several calibers, including the 280 Remington for game as big as elk. The rifle is simple, durable and easy to master.

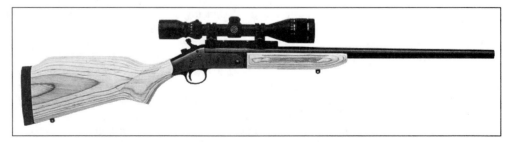

Here is the Harrington and Richardson Ultra Varmint Rifle in 243 Winchester. The caliber is fine for deer and also makes a good predator hunting round as well.

Cartridge company. Their trophy bonded 140-grain bullets are perfect for my needs; I don't need any heavier bullets than that for deer or antelope. Your gun dealer can help you with the proper ammunition. Again, find charts in the Hunter Education manual.

My friend Gail Swanston said, "I learned how to shoot by using a .410 shotgun out in the pasture on gophers. Then I worked up to rifles from there. We would go out to a friend's house and sight-in rifles and I shot until I was comfortable with that. From there I went out deer hunting. Through the bow hunter education course and the NRA rifle course I learned where to aim to hit the vitals. I definitely recommend that beginners take these courses. You will learn about your firearm and safety issues. For a beginner I recommend she go to the gun shop and get fitted, decided on what game she will hunt, decide on a rifle, then practice. When I shot my 270 for the first time and it kind of 'jumped me back' about a foot. I debated if I was ready to shoot it again. I did, and I use the 270 for my deer and elk hunting. It's just a matter of becoming familiar with how the gun operates. Then all you need to do is practice shooting, find your hunting spot, go out and enjoy yourself!"

Recoil can be a problem. If the "kick" from firing any gun is too great, it can cause you flinch when you shoot, thereby ruining your accuracy. That's why shooters should start with small-caliber guns to learn the basics of shooting, then move up as they feel more comfortable. One good way to reduce recoil, without adding lots of weight to your rifle is to have a muzzle brake installed. A muzzle brake vents some of the gas from the exploding gunpowder through a series of holes (called ports) to help reduce recoil. Vic Carter tells us, "A muzzle brake will reduce the recoil 30 to 40 percent, but it also increases the muzzle blast (shot noise) by about half again as much."

Put simply, that means you get less kick, but a louder "bang." The sound is louder because not all of the gas is going out the end of the barrel, some of it is coming out the ports. A 270 with a muzzle brake will have less recoil than a 243 (with no muzzle brake), but it's going to be a lot louder. You must definitely wear ear plugs. A muzzle brake will also keep the barrel from 'jumping' when you shoot. That allows you to see your target clearly as soon as you shoot. If you need a second shot, aiming will be a lot faster and easier.

Bertie Eastman, an avid hunter from Wyoming said, "I always used to shut my eyes when I squeezed the trigger, anticipating the shot and recoil. Since I had a muzzle brake installed on my rifle I do not shut my eyes because I don't anticipate the shot hurting. My shoulder is not sore anymore. I don't flinch and I can now see the animal in the scope and know that I hit it."

When you have chosen your rifle, the gun dealer will then recommend what type of scope you must have. He will know what you need. There are many types available and they carry various price tags. Don't automatically get the cheapest one, but you don't need the most expensive one either. Like everything else, ask questions and see if you can try a few rifles with muzzle brakes attached.

Most rifles are equipped with telescopic sights. Commonly called scopes, these sights provide magnification of the target and clear view of what you are shooting at. I like my Bushnell variable-power with thin crosshairs at the intersection point. Some scopes will have thick black lines throughout, even at the cross hair intersection (reticle). I want to be able to see as much as possible through the scope and that includes being able to see the vital spot at which I'm aiming. With those thick cross hairs it is difficult. The best scope for me is one whose lines are thicker at the edges and hair-thin where the lines intersect. With a variable-power scope, you can adjust the magnification of the scope. You can drop the power for close hunting or turn up the power for farther shots. The most common variable scopes are the a 3x to 9x models. They provide variable magnification making the target appear anywhere from three times as large as normal to nine times as large as normal. If you have a fixed-power scope, there is only one setting. Do not pinch your pennies when it comes to a scope; I would choose a plain basic rifle and spend more money on the scope. Besides Bushnell, Leupold, Burris and several other makers produce good scopes. Be sure to hold a new scope up and try it out to see if you like the view. Try several different types of reticles and styles of scopes. Purchase snap-on scope covers. They fit over the lenses and protect them from dirt, rain and snow. Some are clear so you can see through them to shoot if you have to make a fast shot.

Make sure you have a good quality sling on your rifle. Hunting done with a rifle usually involves a good deal of walking and a sling will make the miles more comfortable. When you add a scope and then maybe a bi-pod, that rifle will have some weight to it. You'll be happy to carry it on your shoulder. Make sure you have detachable swivels for your sling, because you may want to take the sling off if you are hunting in thick brush or crawling on a stalk.

> **Sight your rifle in 3 inches high at 100 yards. It will be right on at 50 yards to 250 yards and that is enough for deer and elk.**

Purchase a good rifle case for the protection of your firearm. You will want a much thicker and heavier case for your rifle than for a shotgun because you will have the scope to protect, also. If storing the rifle in the case, do not zip it all the way up. You will need to allow some air to circulate to keep the gun from rusting. And again, never store your rifle in a basement. It's just too damp down there.

When it comes to cleaning your rifle learn the basics of cleaning the bore and wiping down the outside. If you want to do more than that, take it to a gunsmith. Call your gun dealer, he can recommend a good one. Vic Carter says, "Rifles are touchy. Have a gunsmith clean it." If you do a lot of shooting, have it thoroughly cleaned after every hunting season.

Shooting Tips

Please refer to the "Deer Hunting" chapter for information on sighting-in rifles. Just remember you do not have to be perfect, but you have to be good. Do not get frustrated if you are not "dead-on" with every shot. That vital area in a deer or antelope is a large area, about the size of a paper plate, and if you can put your bullets into that space regularly, you will kill game. Jim Zumbo, a prominent outdoor writer, says, "It's easy. Just sight your rifle in 3 inches high at 100 yards. It will be right on at 50 yards to 250 yards and that is enough for deer and elk. RELAX AND BE EASY."

A good way to find out if you are holding the rifle steady is this: spot your target, aim, then shut your eyes. If you haven't moved from the target when you open your eyes, then you are holding it good and steady. Always hold that rifle TIGHTLY against your shoulder. You don't want to have a "white knuckle grip" with your hands but you do want to pull it in tightly into your shoulder. Be one with the gun.

PRACTICE, PRACTICE, PRACTICE! Use your off-season time to practice. Do not wait until one week before hunting season to drag out the rifle and start practicing; it should be an ongoing activity.

Small 22-caliber rifles are fun to shoot. Besides gopher or prairie dog hunting, you can shoot targets and plink at tin cans to your heart's content. This is excellent practice for your big hunting rifle. As with other rifles here are many brands of 22s and they come in all the various actions described above. I have a Marlin and love it. My advice is that you buy and use a 22. It will help with your marksmanship and you and your friends can stage all sorts of shooting contests. You'd be surprised how fun it can be.

Another tip to good shooting with a rifle is to find a steady rest. While a shotgun provides a large pattern to strike moving game, a rifle fires a single projectile at a precise point of aim. Moving the barrel a fraction of an inch can put the bullet several inches off target if the target is 100 yards away. So, always find a rifle rest. You can do that by assuming the most stable position that allows you to see your target and fire. That can be sitting and resting the rifle on your knee, flat on your belly and using your elbows, using a fence post, tree branch, rock, or anything solid to help you hold the rifle steady. Just make sure you have a rest so you can make a good clean shot and put the bullet where you want to. Place your hat, big gloves or coat (if you have time) underneath your rifle to absorb the shock and it won't bounce when you shoot.

Before firing, take a deep breath to steady yourself, let out half your breath, aim, then SQUEEZE the trigger.

Always use your ear protectors when sighting-in your rifle!

The only thing you need to add to your rifle may be a very light piece of yarn or tie a feather to monofilament fishing line and attach to the rifle barrel to tell wind direction when deer hunting. But that's not always needed.

Safety Tips

See the shotgun safety tips above. The same rules and more apply for rifles and rifle shooting. Always be cognizant of your rifle's safety switch; remember to click that safety back on after you take your shot. If you down a deer with one shot, PUT THAT SAFETY BACK ON! Most rifles hold four bullets, so after that one shot, you will have shells left in your rifle. If you have an auto-loader, you will have a live round in the chamber. Take the bullets out if you are finished hunting or get that safety back on if you are to continue hunting.

When you have loaded your rifle and are moving around or becoming situated in your hunting position, another safety tip is to pull the bolt up making it impossible for the gun to be fired. Even if the rifle is off safety, it will not fire until the bolt is pulled back down into position. When you are situated in your hunting position, don't forget to pull the bolt down; if you have forgotten to do that, you may miss a good shot at a deer!

Know your target and beyond. Rifle bullets travel more than a mile and can kill a human being at ranges as great as 1,200 yards. So know what is beyond your target. Do not take shots if the game is on the horizon and you can't see beyond it.

When you have your rifle ready to go, have practiced and are confident with your shooting, you are ready to rifle hunt. Enjoy!

The author shoulders a replica of a military musket during the annual festival at Fort Sisseton State Historical Park in South Dakota. Shooting a muzzle-loading gun is yet another way to get involved with outdoor activities.

PERCUSSION CAP MUZZLE-LOADERS

"You should get a muzzle-loader and shoot with that," my friend told me over and over.

"Why?" I asked, "I like my rifle, and my non-hunting husband complains that I have too many guns as it is."

"Yes, but you like to archery hunt and you also hunt with a rifle. So, it only makes sense that you should use a muzzle-loader. You like being close to the deer and most of the time you only use one shot anyway, so add another challenge and get a muzzle-loader!"

I had thought about this conversation for several years, never seriously thinking that I would ever try a muzzle-loader rifle. My method worked fine; I had never shot more than 80 yards at any deer I had taken in the last several years so why should I change? When I attended the Outdoor Writers Association of America annual conference at Sioux Falls, South Dakota in June of 1999 I was introduced to muzzle-loader shooting and was surprised at how it intrigued me and how much I enjoyed it. After spending the afternoon at the range shooting and watching others take their turns, listening to the "boom" and seeing the white cloud of smoke, and watching the cleaning and loading rituals, I was hooked. The only other time I had ever shot a muzzle-loader or black powder gun was during my tenure on the game commission. We had a meeting at the Ft. Sisseton (historical military fort) Festival and the commissioners participated in a friendly competition. It was fun to see the black powder enthusiasts dressed in their authentic period clothing and watch them load and fire the primitive guns. Since that was the first time I had ever held a black powder rifle, I was

Gayle Opp, an avid black powder shooting enthusiast, shows off her muzzle-loader and her buckskin dress.

apprehensive. When it was over I surprised myself with my good marksmanship, doing better than most of the male commissioners. Since that time, I've had a soft spot in my heart for muzzle-loaders but never thought I would actually ever hunt with one.

My good friends Dan and Gayle Opp are into traditional muzzle-loaders. They belong to a local muzzle-loader club and on various weekends participate in a black powder festival known as a "Rendevous," which is a re-enactment of a summer gathering of fur traders. (Fur traders and merchants would gather; the merchants would bring clothing and other items so the fur traders could restock for the next year). At the festivals, Dan and Gayle wear traditional period costumes, live in a tent, trade black powder items with other people, and participate in the fun of shooting competitions. Dan buys tanned hides from other traders and makes Gayle's beautiful deer skin dresses and does all the beadwork himself. By being so involved, they have developed a tremendous appreciation of our forefathers, the pioneers, and the way they lived.

Besides living the "black powder" way at festivals, Dan also uses his percussion cap rifle to hunt. He says, "I basically archery hunted with my regular rifle anyway, so I thought I might as well use my muzzle-loader to hunt deer. That allows me to hunt another season following the regular season, and it allows me to hunt two extra seasons in our neighboring national wildlife refuge. It's a fun and meaningful way to hunt."

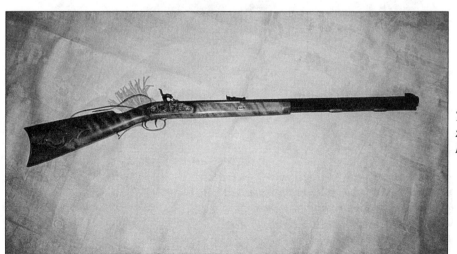

This is an example of a typical muzzle-loading rifle. This a 50-caliber Hawken model.

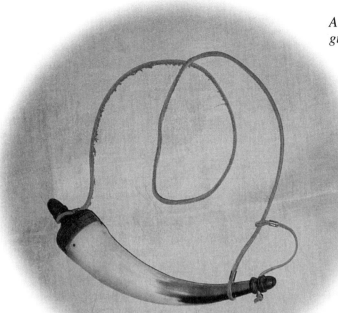

A powderhorn is just that, a hollow horn used to hold gunpowder.

A percussion or cap lock rifle is a muzzle-loader, meaning just that—all components are loaded into the muzzle. Dan's gun is a Richland Arms, styled after the Hawken rifle, from the 1820-1830 era. He demonstrates with it as he teaches muzzle-loading for hunter safety classes. The first thing he does is make sure the gun is not loaded by placing the ramrod down inside the barrel; if it goes all the way down, it is unloaded and safe. The ramrod is the small rod that is stored beneath the barrel and used to clean and load the gun. If the gun has been stored for a while, a dry patch (a small piece of soft cloth somewhat larger than a silver dollar) attached to the "cleaning jag" (ramrod cleaning attachment) should be run down the barrel to make sure it is clean and dry and there is no residue oil from the last cleaning.

Worrying about whether the caplock gun will fire or not is part of the challenge of muzzle-loader hunting. Make sure the rifle is well cleaned and dry or you will suffer through a misfire. This is critical: before loading the gun, make sure the ignition channel is clear by using a pipe cleaner and running it through the channel. Also before loading, two or three percussion caps should be shot to help dry the gun out from mold or oil. When loading the gun, keep it away from the face in case of accidental discharge.

Black powder is kept in a powder horn to keep it dry. The powder is poured into a powder measure, giving you the exact amount needed. Dan uses 70 grains of powder for target practice and 90-100 grains for hunting. The powder horn must be kept closed when not in use so the powder doesn't blow or fall out. The powder is then poured

into the barrel, and the barrel should be tapped near the back to settle the powder. A patch that is specially lubricated with oil or grease is then placed on top of the barrel and a lead ball (the bullet) is placed on top of the patch. In Dan's case, he used a 50-caliber ball. As with any firearm, ammunition must match the gun, so make sure you've got the right components to load your muzzle-loader. A "short-starter" is used to get the ball started down the barrel, then the ramrod is used to firmly place the lead ball on the powder. Care should be taken to not push so hard that the ball may become deformed. At this time, the gun is loaded.

There is no safety button as with a regular rifle, but until a percussion cap is put in place, the gun is safe to handle. The next step is to cock the hammer all the way back and place the percussion cap on the nipple. Dan's muzzle-loader has a double trigger; the back trigger "sets the trigger" and the gun is fired by pulling the front trigger. When the percussion cap is on, the hammer is pulled back and the trigger is set, the gun is ready to fire. For safety purposes, the muzzle-loader should be loaded only when you arrive at the hunting destination and be capped only when you are ready to shoot. Black powder burns differently than the smokeless powder used in modern cartridges. When the cap ignites the powder, there will be a loud roar and a cloud of white smoke. And there may be some sparks left glowing in the barrel after the shot. These must be extinguished before the powder is loaded for the next shot. Do not attempt to do this by blowing them out. Run a patch down the barrel. Then you are ready to re-load.

To make reloading in the field easier, many hunters use a quick-loading device. This is a small case containing pre-measured powder, a patch and a ball. Percussion caps must be carried and stored separately from

The possible bag or pouch is used to carry all the gear a black powder shooter needs. This fancy version is real buckskin covered with fur. The style of bag is up to the shooter.

black powder. Reloading can be accomplished in 30 to 45 seconds with a quick-load device. A "possible bag" is what period black powder shooters carry with them to tote around all the gear they need; it supposedly holds "everything possible."

Dan's hunting shots are all taken at 50 yards or less; 100 yards is considered maximum range. Short ranges should be the norm. Check your state's regulations regarding open sights, scopes, etc. Some states have will not allow scopes, others have various regulations concerning seasons and even locations where muzzle-loaders may be used.

Cleaning the muzzle-loader after shooting is extremely important. Black powder is highly corrosive and that can ruin a gun in a very short time. To clean a percussion cap rifle is simple. Use the barrel key and unlatch the barrel from the stock, then slip it off. Take the nipple out with the nipple wrench. Use hot soapy water (you can use laundry soap) to clean the barrel. Attach cleaning patches to the ram rod, work it back and forth

Barb Koch fires her muzzle-loader during a contest at the Sweetwater Rendezvous in northeastern South Dakota. Attending a rendezvous is a great way to see what muzzle-loading is all about.

and then flush the barrel out. Change water a couple of times. Rinse with hot water by pouring it through the barrel (the hot water helps to dry it). Run dry patches through it until it is clean and dry. Use a light lubricant on a patch and run it through if the gun will be stored; if it will be used soon it is not necessary to oil the barrel. Wipe off the barrel, replace it on the stock and secure with the barrel key. Replace the ramrod. The gun should be stored barrel down so oil doesn't run on the stock.

Since the powder used with a muzzle-loader is loose in the barrel and the percussion cap is on the outside of the muzzle-loader, care must be taken during rainy days. A balloon placed over the end of the barrel will keep the barrel dry and you can shoot through the balloon without any problem.

If you want to unload the gun without firing it, you can use a ball-puller or a carbon dioxide cartridge. When the CO2 cartridge is placed on the nipple it pushes the powder and the ball from the barrel.

Flintlock muzzle-loaders date back to the 1700s and are still made today. Flintlock guns have no percussion cap. They have a piece of flint to create the spark to ignite the main charge. Flintlocks are much more suseptible to moisture than are the percussion cap rifles.

If you are interested in learning to hunt this black powder method, I recommend you attend a hunter safety black powder/muzzle-loader session first. Muzzle-loaders are a completely different firearm and to be safe, you must know everything there is to know about them. Contact your local muzzle-loader club or sportsmen's club and ask for a mentor. Have the mentor with you until you are sure you can safely operate the firearm yourself. You must have complete knowledge about the gun's operation before you ever load it or shoot it.

The kind or type of muzzle-loader and the caliber you purchase will depend on what game you want to hunt. As with other firearms, choose a muzzle-loader that fits and feels comfortable to you. Your mentor can also help you with these decisions.

Barb Koch, an avid hunter from northeastern South Dakota, shoots a percussion cap muzzle-loader and enjoys hunting with it. She says, "It's another type of hunting challenge using a different weapon. I think my muzzle-loader, being a primitive model, even makes it more of a challenge. I like the "old fashioned" way of shooting and the challenge of having only one shot and to be accurate and consistent. I like the sound of the muzzle-loaders, it brings back that entire time period to me."

Laurie Root, President of OutdoorWomen of South Dakota, was only 13 years old when she received her first gun—a 45-caliber percussion muzzle-loader. "It made me a hunter instead of a shooter. That one shot has to count; I only take shots that are in my comfort zone. A female beginner should contact her nearest muzzle-loader club and visit with people who shoot muzzle-loaders. The most important points to learn are how to load it and how to clean it. The cleaning part is the unpleasant part; it's messy and the solvent smells, but it has to be done or you will ruin the barrel. Safety is important; always make sure the ball is seated on the powder properly. You should make a mark on the ram rod so you instantly know. If you have a misfire, always make sure the ball hasn't moved forward. Always check for a barrel obstruction. When I recently traveled in Germany, the people couldn't believe that I shoot a primitive muzzle-loader. I had fun convincing them," Laurie says.

This 50-caliber black powder gun by Knight Rifles in Iowa is a completely modern version of a muzzle-loader.

IN-LINE MUZZLE-LOADERS

In the mid-1980s some Missouri farmers, who loved hunting with muzzle-loaders, approached Tony Knight, their local gunsmith, and asked for help. They wanted to have the opportunity to hunt elk in another state, and they needed a muzzle-loader that was safer, more accurate, and more reliable than what they had. Tony went to work and designed the Knight In-Line Muzzleloader Rifle with all the needed features plus faster ignition, less recoil and the double-safety system.

An "in-line" muzzle-loader is just that, everything is in line within the rifle; there is a straight line of fire. None of the attachments, hammers, nipples, etc. are off to the side of the firearm; it is all included within the rifle.

I have a Knight DISC (Disc Ignition System Concept) .50 caliber 26-inch Magnum with Mossy Oak Break-Up® camouflage on the stock. It is a wonderful muzzle-loader and I'm glad I had the opportunity to learn with this model. Knight Rifles are the only muzzle-loaders in the world that feature the patented DISC technology. When Michele Bartimus, Marketing Manager for Knight Rifles, first introduced me to this muzzle-loader, she said, "This DISC system is great! It is so simple and easy for us women to use. A shotgun primer, instead of a typical percussion

The modern possible bag complete with bullet starter, Pyrodex pellets, ignition disc and modern bullet patches.

cap, fits into a little orange plastic DISC that drops right into the barrel so we don't have to fidget with tiny percussion caps when our fingers are cold. Women love this muzzle-loader!" The DISC rifle was designed for the hunter who appreciates the features of a modern in-line bolt-action muzzle-loader.

Before I ever had my hands on a muzzle-loader, I thought that type of shooting and hunting was done by a specific group of people and that I would never join them. It was kind of like my first idea of mule deer hunting. I thought that it was only for the "big boys". Was I ever wrong! Meeting Michele and seeing her enthusiasm for muzzle-loaders really impressed me. Her enthusiasm was contagious. Before I had talked to her, I had been somewhat afraid of the gun because I was told it had to be kept extremely clean after using or the barrel would corrode and the gun would be ruined. To me, the thought of my ruining this beautiful gun was scary.

I found the people at Knight Rifles extremely helpful. A detailed owner's manual and video tape accompanies each rifle. Personal help is only a phone call away. Your mentor will also be able to help you and so will the members of your local muzzle-loading club. My fears were unfounded. Do not be afraid of the muzzle-loader; do not let it intimidate you. It is a different type of weapon and you simply have to learn everything there is to know about it, as you did with shotguns and other rifles.

Learning how a muzzle-loader works is a great education on firearms and ammunition. When the gun is being loaded, you are actually making a cartridge. You can also vary the charge. For example, if there is too much recoil, then use less powder so it is lighter. Loading one component at a time makes you stop and think about what you are really doing and makes you appreciate the muzzle-loader. I have never had this realization when chambering another brass round into my regular rifle.

The double safety system of the Knight Rifle is another of it's advantages. In addition to the regular primary safety on the trigger mechanism, there is a secondary safety mechanism. When engaged, it prevents the hammer from striking the ignition source. It is a very confident feeling to be hunting with such a system. This is another reason why women will like this muzzle-loader.

When you are ready to actually load and shoot the in-line, follow this procedure: Take out the ramrod and run it down the barrel to make sure there is no obstruction (if the barrel is clear the top of the ramrod will be flush with the top of the barrel). Screw the cleaning jag into the end of the ramrod. Place a dry patch on the barrel muzzle and using small strokes, push the ramrod down the barrel until it stops and leave it. Place a disc containing a shotshell primer in its appropriate place in the barrel, and pull the bolt down. Holding the gun muzzle down, turn the safeties off and pull the trigger. This action will clean out any excess oil from cleaning, fouling, etc. When you pull the ramrod out of the rifle, there should be a blackened surface or a burned hole in the middle of the patch. The process can be repeated. The rifle is now ready to be loaded.

Now things get really good. Advances in muzzle-loading technology have created a new powder system that may even-

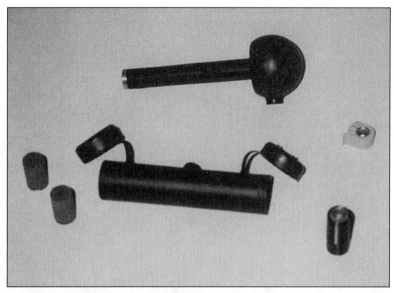

A speed-loading kit for a modern muzzle-loading rifle. At the top is the bullet starter. The compressed Pyrodex Powder pellets are at left and the bullet and ignition disc are at the right.

tually replace the use of loose powder. The Hodgdon Company is marketing its black powder substitute, Pyrodex, in a pellet form. These are pre-formed, pre-measured and easy to use. Drop them down the barrel, dark side down. I use two pellets of 50 grains each so I have a 100-grain charge (three pellets can be used for more power). Tony Knight calls the pellets the "greatest advancement in muzzle-loading propellants."

I use Swift premium 265-grain bullets with sabots. A relatively new idea to muzzle-loading, sabots are the plastic sleeves that house the bullets. Place the bullet on the muzzle and start it down the barrel with a bullet starter (short starter). Using the concave end of the ramrod, carefully drive the bullet down firmly onto the powder pellets. Do not pound or bounce on the bullet with the ramrod; if done so, the bullet could be deformed resulting in loss of accuracy. Remove the ramrod from the barrel.

When you are in your stand or ready to hunt, drop in a pre-primed DISC, remove the secondary safety (leaving the primary safety on) and you are ready! It's easy, it's fun and you have just made your own cartridge. A container holding pellets in one end and bullets in the other is called a "speed loader"; take some with you when you hunt, along with some extra DISCs just in case you may need a second shot. If, for some reason, you need a second shot in a hurry, simply reload and drop in the DISC. If you have time before reloading, first swab the barrel with a damp (use saliva) patch and the ramrod with the cleaning jag attached.

Tony Knight says, "Knowing you only have one shot makes you really concentrate on what shot you must make. You can reload, but it's best not to even think of that and make the first shot count. You will have a more ethical hunt. It's more fun because it's more of a challenge."

When finished hunting, return both safeties to the "on" position and simply push up the bolt and remove the DISC. The gun cannot fire. If you have not shot your muzzle-loader, it does not have to be cleaned at the end of the day. Because moisture is an enemy of muzzle-loaders, be aware of condensation. If you are finished hunting for the day but will go out again the next day, do not take the muzzle-loader into a warm

A close-up look at the Swift Premium muzzle-loader bullets. The plastic jacket or "sabot" around the bullet creates the seal and engages the rifling as the bullet travels down the barrel. Most modern muzzle-loaders use bullets like these.

The author tries out a Knight Disc Rifle at the shooting range. Having the chance to shoot several different rifles is a great way to learn what you like or don't like about the guns. Trying going to a local gun club and meeting with the members; someone there may become your mentor.

place such as your home. Leave it outside in your locked car or garage or someplace where it is cool so there is no condensation. If there is no option but to bring it in the house, pull the breech plug and take the powder pellets out. To be sure the gun will fire the next day clean the breech port by bending a pin and cleaning any tiny particles that may be in the channel. Ask your mentor to help you or refer to your owner's manual.

Check your state's regulations concerning scopes and sights. In South Dakota, scopes are only legal during the regular rifle season; I must use fiber optic sights or open sights during the muzzle-loading season.

Practice is very important. Spend time at the shooting range becoming acquainted with your muzzle-loader. You will have fun shooting, hearing the boom and seeing the smoke. Have plenty of patches, bullets and powder pellets. After each shot, moisten a patch with a little saliva, place on the cleaning jag and run it down the barrel with the ramrod. Remember to clean the gun when you return home at the end of the day.

When using two 50-grain pellets and the 265-grain Swift bullets, sight-in the rifle so it is "right on" (in the bull's-eye) at 50 yards. Shoot at 100 yards so you know where the bullet hits at that range. You will also see what your maximum range is. Whether you are using a scope, iron sights or fiber optic sights, you will need to sight in the muzzle-loader.

If you have shot your muzzle-loader, then it must be cleaned at the end of the day. Corrosion can occur quickly, and to maintain the quality of your muzzle-loader and it's accuracy, cleaning is imperative. You will need solvent, oil, breech plug grease, bore brushes and other items for the entire procedure. Refer to your owner's manual, watch the video and ask your mentor to help you clean the gun. Watch your mentor as the gun is cleaned, then have your mentor watch you and supervise as you clean it for the first time. The more you clean it the easier it will become.

"The Knight Rifles are easy to use, women can adapt to them easily, and they are simple to load. The hunt will be more enjoyable for women using this muzzle-loader because the game will be closer, and with the double safety system, this muzzle-loader is safer than any other gun. Women are more patient, calm and make better shots than their male counterparts. This style of hunting offers more opportunity with more seasons and not much hunting pressure," says founder Tony Knight.

Kathy Butt, freelance outdoor writer and photographer from Tennessee, says, "I like to shoot an in-line muzzle-loader. It's a lot faster ignition which means there is less time from when that first spark goes off until it reaches the bullet. It's much more dependable in foul weather, too. The main thing is to get fitted

A good solid shooting position is just as important with a muzzle-loader as it is with any other rifle. Here the author looks through the scope of her rifle before a deer hunt in Iowa.

Getting the job done. The author poses with Tony Knight, founder of Knight Rifles, and a beautiful buck taken on Knight's Iowa farm.

with a stock that fits your physical build. You can lighten the load up, too and not shoot a large amount of powder like guys like to do. Even if you do that, you must spend time at the shooting range. Also find someone who knows how to use a muzzle-loader and can go through the routine with you. Attend the Becoming an Outdoors Woman workshop and take the muzzle-loader class. Don't be afraid of the gun. When a woman knows the routine, she can go out hunting all alone. She doesn't need anyone else with her. I turkey hunt a lot with a muzzle-loading shotgun and I enjoy that aspect of it, too. Using a muzzle-loader is a one-shot challenge; it's a lot like archery hunting. I prefer the game to be at 50 yards. Hunting with a muzzle-loader provides another season; it's another way to hunt. I really enjoy being close to the game."

There are many states or portions of states that forbid rifle use during deer seasons. Only slug shotguns and muzzle-loaders can be used. While witnessing "party hunting" with shotguns I was very glad I was hunting only with hunters using muzzle-loaders. I know that person has to be an ethical hunter and I know there will not be a barrage of bullets or slugs flying in all directions.

We hunters can sometimes be our own worst enemy. There are "purists" who have not accepted the in-line muzzle-loader as a true muzzle-loader and this opinion also circulates in the political arena. There have been and will continue to be discussions around game commission tables across the country concerning which is the "true" muzzle-loader, the percussion cap or the in-line gun . Officials in Colorado decided to allow the DISC rifle and other in-line muzzle-loaders to be used in the 1999 hunting season after banning all in-lines for the 1998 season. We will have to get our act together and speak with one voice lest the anti-hunters claim victory and destroy our great American tradition of hunting.

The Bureau of Alcohol, Tobacco and Firearms had originally classified the DISC muzzle-loader as a "firearm" because of its shotgun primer ignition system. The BATF recently RECLASSIFIED the DISC rifle as an "antique firearm". The DISC rifle is a muzzle-loader by definition of the amended 1968 gun control act. Consumers now will not have to fill out the federal 4473 form and can purchase the DISC rifle from their retailer or catalog of choice. Some states have their own classification by state law; check the regulations in the state in which you will hunt to make sure you have applied correctly.

There certainly is room for all methods of hunting. Muzzle-loading allows us to seize the opportunity of new thresholds, whether we shoot a percussion cap rifle or an in-line rifle. It is a personal preference. There are some who very much enjoy the "mountain man/woman" experience of hunting with a primitive weapon and they should not be denied that. Neither should the opportunity to hunt with a safer, more reliable and more accurate weapon of the same type be denied. The main point is, when hunting with a muzzle-loading rifle, there are more days that can be spent out in the field. There is more opportunity available for everyone, using both types of muzzle-loaders. Let's not limit ourselves because of differing opinions. You select the type of muzzle-loader YOU want. As with anything, it is up to you.

Turkey hunting with muzzle-loading shotguns may appear next on my list. I am looking forward to experiencing that! A real neat lady, Verona Inabinette, is a professional turkey hunting guide and wildlife videographer (Indian Archery Video). She has the distinction of being the first woman to get a Grand Slam (refer to the Turkey Hunting chapter) all in one season with a 12-gauge muzzle-loading shotgun! (Verona also makes the best dang pecan pies you've ever tasted!)

The National Muzzleloading Rifle Association is our nation's oldest and largest organization dedicated to the sport of muzzle-loading. For more information contact them at PO Box 67, Maxine Moss Drive, Friendship, IN 47021 or call 812-667-5131.

CHAPTER FOUR
HUNTING CLOTHING

"You're dressed like THAT?? THAT'S ALL YOU'VE GOT??"

This was the greeting I received when I showed up at the hunting field the very first time I hunted waterfowl. My hunting outfit consisted of blue jeans with longjohns underneath, regular cotton socks, western boots, an old brown winter jacket that had given up the ghost a long time before, plain old cap and my driving gloves. I thought I was set. The guys couldn't help themselves; they tried not to laugh but their concern for my warmth showed through. That concern was justified. As I found out, you get hot and sweaty setting out decoys and scurrying around getting a pit ready. Then, you freeze while you lay on the frozen ground and wait for birds. Luckily it was early in the season and the warmth from the sun helped out a bit, when it finally rose. My freezing toes, however, are a memory forever emblazoned in my mind.

The morning was beautiful — still, warm and sunny. Flocks of green-wing teal dove in and out of the pond and each time a couple birds fell for the other hunters. The third flock was magic for me; I raised up, pointed the borrowed shotgun, fired and watched in awe as my first duck hit the ground. After that, the ducks disappeared so we waited and waited for geese to pay us a visit. When we were about ready to give up, we heard a lone "honk" from way back behind the hill. Our expert caller got busy and I will never forget the beautiful sight of that goose coming to his call, zeroing right in on the floater decoys. We now also had a goose to take home.

That first hunting experience changed my life. I knew instantly that I loved this and I wanted more. I also knew that I had to find the appropriate clothing or I would never make it. The guys all told me what to get, and it was very helpful. As my hunting trips increased and the weather became colder I knew I had to devise some of my own methods just to survive. The men could only help a woman so much. There was a lot I would have to research and try on my own. Being a woman in the field is so different than being "just another male hunting buddy." Your hunting buddies won't think of many things to tell you. Guys would tell me something, but then I would have to modify it and adapt it in my female way of thinking. This was the first lesson I learned. The guys are not to blame. They just have no idea of what it's like to be a woman!

Winter white camouflage can really make you blend in when there is snow on the ground. Just make sure you are wearing the required amount of orange in accordance with local regulations. Gail Swanston bagged this nice buck with the help of a trusty "snow" suit. It kept her warm and hidden.

I looked forward to buying hunting clothes, but when I tried them on I was severely disappointed. I felt that I looked like an old sack. But then, who would see me in the woods? There were no women's clothing available at all and whenever I asked a store clerk or manager, I only received shocked looks. I had to purchase all men's clothing and live with the discomfort of some of it. I wanted to hunt and really didn't care what I looked like; I was not out there to impress anyone. It was just the fit that was sometimes uncomfortable and the bulkiness of jackets sometimes could be unsafe.

In recent years, we have seen women's hunting clothing designers come and go. There would be excitement at a new women's product, then the product would soon disappear. The marketing system had to be improved. The clothing stores were not carrying the items because of lack of demand (women hunters are a minority) and when women did demand them, the items were not there. Hopefully, we are on the upswing in female items in both stores and catalogs. However, we must show these manufacturers and merchants that we women are serious and do want their products, We have to show support for them if we hope to keep what we have and have more developed for us.

Some would-be woman hunters have turned away from the sport because their spouse or friend took them out to a cold duck blind without the appropriate clothing. The women froze, were miserable and swore they would never do that again. Hunting is supposed to be fun, not an endurance test. With the hunting gear and clothing available today, a woman can be comfortable and enjoy her time outdoors. You need your own set of hunting clothing. Hand-me-downs are fine to begin with. You can hunt in them, and then you will know exactly what you need and want. There is quite a price range in clothing today. You do not need to have the top-of-the-line items and pay only for the name or label. You can go to your closest discount store for items and if they fit you, that's fine. Otherwise, there are catalogs available and they have a short shipping time. You just have to know WHAT to purchase, HOW to wear or use it, and ADAPT it to your situation.

OUTER CLOTHING

Just as with guns in a gun store, when you walk into an outdoor clothing store, or open up an outdoor catalog, there are so many items there of all types, material and patterns that it can be very confusing. A good rule to remember is "Keep It Simple." But we also must talk about how it looks. So we'll talk about camouflage patterns first. First of all, decide what game you will be hunting most. Let's assume for the moment you will be hunting waterfowl. That means you will be hunting in cold and sometimes

The author's Daughter, Andrea, blends in very well thanks to her Realtree Hardwoods camouflage. When you go looking for camouflage clothing, think seriously about the area where you will be hunting. The goal, of course, is to blend in.

wet conditions, so you will want something waterproof, windproof and warm. Determine what your surroundings will be; trees, fields, rushes, etc. While looking at the camo patterns, decide which one would fit the best where you hunt the most. Match your environment. If you will be hunting in plowed fields, wear dark coveralls; if you will be in rushes, wear camo that will blend in with them and not be conspicuous. If you will be in a snowy field, wear white camo or you can very easily cover your regular camo clothing with a sheet or white camo cover-up. (You can even use a mattress pad which is good because it is thicker, more substantial and you can even haul game out with it.) Just remember you want to adapt to your environment. With camouflage you learn from experience and experimentation.

Waterfowl hunting can take you to different types of habitats, from cattail rushes to stubble fields and flooded timber. The all-around best waterfowl camo I have seen is Advantage Wetlands Camo. Earthy brown, marsh-tone yellow, limbs and leaves all combine to make the perfect waterfowl camo. Advantage Wetlands Camo is also the official camo pattern of Ducks Unlimited. Before you purchase any waterfowl camo, you must check this out-- it's great!

The camo patterns available today are really exciting. You can "get lost" in a woods pattern or "blend in" with the rushes. The first camo I ever bought was the original green Realtree® for turkey hunting and I still wear it today. They have since designed great new patterns and allow you to mix and match. For example, during spring turkey hunting I wear the Realtree X-tra Grey pants so I blend in with the ground, but wear Realtree green on top to blend in with the foliage. All of the Realtree patterns will work for you in most situations. Their newest creation is the Hardwoods pattern; I think perhaps that is the best pattern I have ever seen for hunting in the woods. A lot of research goes into a design to create a 3-D illusion with shadows, limbs and leaves and many different shades of colors. I was once told a camo creator brought in dirt, stones and sticks and demanded that those items be incorporated into a new pattern. Whatever works and hides you is what you need.

Mossy Oak® Break-up™ pattern is very versatile and will be good when you hunt in the woods. Shadow Grass™ is a waterfowl pattern and is also quite good. I have that on my Beretta Pintail shotgun and love it Mossy Oak® has a new QT (Quiet Technology) Series of hunting items that allows you to be unseen and unheard. These QT items are made of a new micro fleece fabric that is waterproof, breathable, fade resistant and resistant to snags and pulls.

Sniper™ camo is a good pattern. It incorporates bark, limbs, leaves, background and 3-D effects. I have a Sniper™ jacket that is very versatile, quiet and comfortable. Skyline™ also has a couple of good patterns.

Just check them out and decide which pattern will be the best and most versatile for you and your hunting environment. Don't let someone in the store talk you into something you do not want; don't let anyone sell you a camo pattern you cannot effectively use because it's "on sale." Do some research and thinking (and maybe trying out old clothing) before you go into the store or order from a catalog. If the people you talk to do not handle women's clothing, politely tell them they should.

Again, the location of your hunt will dictate your need for camouflage. This Advantage Wetlands pattern works great in the rushes. The author almost disappears.

Then if they do, be sure and patronize them.

Because hunting is something you do outside, you'll want to be warm and dry while you do it. Look for the Thinsulate and GORE-TEX tags on any clothing items you buy. These products will help keep you warm and dry. Thinsulate "warmth without bulk" insulation is the warmest thin insulation on the market. It provides nearly 1-1/2 times the warmth of down, retains its insulating ability even in damp conditions, even after repeated washings and dries easily. GORE-TEX is a waterproof cloth found in boots and other items. These materials cost more, but they are worth it.

Clothing manufacturers are just discovering women hunters. Before now, if there was anything in the store for women, it was of inferior quality, fiber and insulation. The same story went for boots and longjohns. None of it was as good as what was offered for men. Women get colder faster than men and good, sturdy and warm clothing that fits was needed. Brenda Valentine, a RedHead Pro Hunting Team member, told the powers that be at Bass Pro Shops, "we need a good, heavy coat made with a high technology fiber, just like you offer for the men. We need to stay warm, we need to stay dry — even more so than men because we get colder." The result was Micro-Suede.™ It does not attract burrs and almost feels like velvet. This year women can get a parka made with it and this is a beginning; there still is a long way to go. Micro-Suede™ is soft, quiet, durable, and breathable material that wicks away moisture to keep you dry and comfortable. It's more durable and pill-resistant than fleece and it resists abrasions so common in hunting environments.

There's one problem every hunter faces: the call of nature. A few years ago, one of the first coveralls for women, designed by a woman, featured a back flap for easy access when a woman needed to relieve herself. (The company is now out of business.) It looked like the "real deal" but Brenda Valentine found a problem. "I tried turkey hunting

The Mossy Oak QT series not only helps you blend in, it is very quiet, too. Remember to try things on and make sure the clothes fit you. You might have to do a lot of looking.

I can pull the bibs down without getting totally naked; I still have my top on, and that overlapping layer keeps all the heat inside. If I'm stalking or rabbit hunting where I will be moving all day, coveralls pull on my shoulders and make me tired. Bibs don't do that; bibs are the most versatile hunting item for women."

Women, there are actually two FULL pages of female hunting clothes in the Bass Pro Shops RedHead Hunting Specialists catalog. Finally, WE can have hunting clothing that fits US!

Silent-Hide™ is a lightweight and durable fabric designed for noise-free movement, especially for deer hunters. Women's bibs, shirts, field pants and all-season jackets are available in Mossy Oak™ Break-Up™ or Advantage™ camo patterns.

Micro-SUEDE™ items for women include shirts, pants, and parkas, all in Realtree™ Hardwoods™ camo pattern. Red-Head™ women's insulated coveralls and bibs are available with 200 grams of Thinsulate™ Ultra Insulation. Coveralls are either Realtree™ X-tra™ Brown, or Advantage™ pattern. Bibs are either Advantage™ or Mossy Oak™ Break-Up™ camo pattern.

Run to your phone and call for your free catalog at 1-888-REDHEAD! Log on to the Web site at www.basspro.com.

RedHead also features fabric that inhibits scent and stops wind; let's hope they incorporate these fabrics into women's clothing soon.

Cabela's, the "World's Foremost Outfitter", has camo outer clothing available for women. They have a Northern Flight Wading Jacket, insulated parka and bib overalls. These are only available in Skyline Fall Flight camo pattern. The bibs are loaded with zippers--full-length side zippers and various zippered pockets. Camo uninsulated denim jeans and chamois shirts are available in women's sizes in Realtree® X-tra Brown™ camo pattern. Cabela's offers women upland game clothing featuring a blaze orange vest and brown nylon-faced hunting pants. Top-of-the-line rain wear for women is featured; it should be great stuff as it carries an exorbitant price tag. (As a beginner hunter, you do not need expensive rain gear.) Cabela's top-of-the-line GORE-TEX® MT050 Whitetail Extreme clothing is available in women's parka and bibs in Mossy Oak® Break-up™ only; they are insulated with Life Loft™ and available with Scent-Lok™ lining to eliminate game-spooking scent. They also carry a big price tag of $520. For a free Cabela's catalog call 1-800-237-4444 or visit the Web site at www.cabelas.com.

On the Wing, Inc. offers clothes made exclusively for outdoor women. In the brochure you will find an upland bird vest, brush pants, shooting shirt, T-shirt, cap and recoil pad to fit into the vest and shirt recoil pad pockets to provide more comfortable shooting. The items look like good quality, but they

with the ones with the backdrop. I was sittin' on the ground and scootin' around so much gettin' in position that the Velcro pulled off and there was my butt on the ground," she said.

Valentine also had trouble using the coveralls with the crotch opening (zippered from waist in front to waist in back for access), "I'm sure they would be great and handy and you wouldn't have to get totally undressed to go to the bathroom, but then you have to have all the undergarments that will work with that particular system. I never got into that. My favorite hunting outfit is insulated bibs and hooded sweatshirt under the bibs. This will keep my neck warm. For bowhunting it's great because it compresses the extra fabric in front, and it's warm. Then if I have to go to the bathroom, are spendy. Call On the Wing, Inc. at 1-877-THE-WING or visit the Web site www.onthewing.com.

There is a nice selection of women's outdoor clothing in "The Outdoor Woman™" catalog. Here is where you will find the zippered-crotch insulated coveralls and bibs and coveralls with "Nature's Door" built in the seat. They also feature the specially designed "pull-apart" briefs that have to be worn underneath the crotch-zippered garments. Upland hunting clothing, women's hunting boots, shooting vests and other outdoor items are available--all for women! Write "The Outdoor Woman" at P.O. Box 7603, Boise, Idaho 83707 or call 1-888-565-0907 for a catalog now!

If you are looking for women's hunting shirts, pants, dresses or a skirt and vest combo made in camo patterns (they are fun to wear!) "Babe in the Woods" is your place to contact! They also feature infant and toddler's camo clothing, plus youth sizes. Owner Shawn Young is gorgeous in all of her "dress-up" camo creations. When daughter Cheyenne was little, she was too cute in her tiny camo dresses and hats, sitting in her stroller that was made from the same camo pattern! Order a camo dress from Babe in the Woods; you will have fun and be the hit of the meeting or party! Write them at P.O. Box 1484, or call 334-393-6186.

I took two of my favorite skirts, a jacket, and plenty of camo material to a seamstress and had two camo outfits made. They are really fun to wear and you take a little of your lifestyle and the outdoors with you wherever you go!

Wool and fleece fabric hunting clothing are preferred by many hunters. Wool is probably the world's best insulator and is worn by many big game hunters. There are several companies making wool camo patterns, but I haven't found any exclusively for women. You can sometimes get military surplus, but

if you can't try it on, you don't know how well it will work for you. It may be a risk to purchase it mail-order, but that risk is sometimes worth it. Both wool and fleece are quiet, also. The modern fabrics and high-tech gear seems to be more popular, but there's a lot of good things to be said about wool and fleece does provide plenty of insulation. Here's a tip for fleece-wearing bowhunters: carry your fleece jacket in a plastic bag as you walk into the woods. When you are in your stand or at your hunting area, then take it out of the bag and put it on; this method keeps burrs and seeds from sticking on the fleece.

Providing comic relief with serious camo, the new Shaggie® 3-D cover system is hilarious, but really works. It's based on a system used by military snipers when they really need to hide. The Shaggie is made of 50 percent jute burlap and 50 percent cotton blends for quietness and depth of field. Hundreds of 10-inch long strips and leaf-shaped pieces are individually sewn to strong industrial netting. You slide this apparition over your street clothes and "viola!" you are no longer a person! You instantly turn into a bush with no definite form and your leaves flutter in the wind. Supposedly you can approach wary animals in the open much more effectively than with other camo that sharply outlines the human form. I think this would be fun to try! There are also 3-D camo suits, made of leaf-cut material that is sewn to a mesh backing. Again, you will "flutter in the breeze." Who said camo couldn't be fun??

For those of you who hunt during mosquito or tick season, there is an innovative outfit from Bug-Out™ Outdoorwear, Inc. Bug-Out offers you the ultimate in insect protection. The system uses a light-weight, see-through "no-see-um" mesh. Not only does the material guard against biting, stinging and crawling insects, it is proven to even guard against the nymph stage of the deer tick, the most aggressive biter! The jacket with attached hood creates a total enclosure that protects you but still allows for visibility and comfort. The Bug-Out™ System is available in Olive Drab or Mossy Oak™ Break-Up™ and weighs less than 7 ounces for the jacket, pants and mitts. With the complete system, you will be covered from head to toe. For information call 515-437-1936 or visit the Web site www.execpc.com/bugout.

Redhead Silent Hide BDU Bibs combine Mossy Oaks's Break-up pattern with material that allows silent movement, and it comes in women's sizes.

Who says camo is just for the field? This is a power suit if there ever was one.

The Shaggie, 3-D system takes camouflage to the extreme. This type of garment, developed by military snipers, completely obliterates the human outline.

Ready for anything. Waterfowling weather can be nasty. A complete outfit with bibs, jacket, windbreaker and hat will keep you warm and dry. Bring on the geese.

Gaiters are often overlooked, but a good pair will keep mud, snow or debris out of your boots and help when you are stomping through brush.

For extra protection while hunting in snow or wet conditions you may want to try gaiters. They are waterproof pant leg covers that slip over your boot and reach almost to your knee. When you are hunting in snow your pant legs will get soaked every time you hunt and there will not be enough time to dry them out between hunts. Gaiters will keep those pant legs dry. They are available in several camo patterns.

I have two basic hunting outfits and they work for every situation for me. I have a pair of very dark camo coveralls. They are great for plowed fields, lying in the mud if necessary, etc. The reverse side is white camo which I use in snowy conditions. My other set of camo is a three-piece bibs, jacket and outer windbreaker-type jacket with a hood. All of these are in a cattail/rushes pattern. The bib legs have long zippers which makes it easier to dress. When you purchase your parka or coveralls, be sure it has a hood as you will appreciate that when it is really cold. Because I do a lot of layering, I am comfortable in any situation with these two outer items. Basically, you will be fine with one universal outfit to fit in everywhere; you can also mix and match. If you cannot find a pair of reversible coveralls or bibs, etc. that switch from regular camo to snow camo, don't feel you must buy a pair of white camo coveralls also. You can buy a low-cost white plastic/paper type white coverup to wear over your regular coveralls, or wear a sheet poncho. You will also see blaze orange camo coveralls for big game hunting. Do not buy those! Conservation officers have told me a plain blaze orange jacket, sweatshirt or vest—solid blaze orange—is easier to see in the woods and therefore much safer! Just because the store is full of camo clothes and they all look exciting does not mean you have to "have it all" or "spend it all".

I've talked a lot about camo clothing and patterns, but all the same information holds true when you are required to wear blaze orange hunting clothing in the field. In South Dakota, where I live and do most of my hunting, the requirements for orange hunting clothing are less stringent than those of some other states. Some areas require that you wear a minimum number of square inches, others require that 50 percent of the upper half of your body be covered with an orange outer garment. You need to check those regulations,

The most important point concerning clothing is that you want to be warm, comfortable and fit in with your surroundings.

UNDERWEAR

Be comfortable. Make sure no undergarment is binding in any way or you will be uncomfortable and bothered during the hunt and that could even affect your shooting accuracy.

If you will be leaning against trees during the hunt, you may want to wear a sports bra or a bra that fastens in the front. You don't want to grind the back hooks of a conventional bra into your back. Don't wear a new bra. It might be tight or scratchy and hurt you at the end of the day. Don't wear an old worn-out one either, for the sake of comfort. I speak from personal experience! When I was elk hunting in 85-degree weather and climbing and crawling up and down very steep ridges with my backpack and rifle, something started to poke me under my arm. I was frustrated at the time

and let it go without checking to see what it was. The longer I went the worse it became; then it hurt under both arms. I finally got mad enough and stopped and checked; with all my movement, the underwires in my bra had broken through the material and were stabbing me! So, what was I to do? If I took the bra off and fell down (I was hunting alone), THAT wouldn't feel good. But there was no way I could leave it on. So, the only thing to do was take the bra off, pull out the wires and put the bra back on. You know Murphy's Law? I could see it coming: I would be standing there with my bra in my hand, hear a noise, look up and THAT is the time an elk would walk over the ridge. You can imagine the aftermath of that! Well, as fast as possible I got those wires out and the bra back on. I thought surely that episode would bring in an elk if anything would, but that didn't even help. I was also glad no other hunter peeked down over the ridge. I could imagine that story in the local watering hole! The moral of the story: check your underwear and make sure it is all OK before you put it on!

Layering is the secret of staying warm and comfortable. For that first layer, you will need some type of longjohns. I first started with a purple pair of cotton insulated regular longjohns. Of course no one knew they were purple until the day we downed a couple of ducks and had no dog to retrieve them from a pond. As the men stood around scratching their heads wondering how we would get those ducks, I just rolled my eyes, took my boots and socks off, rolled up my pant legs and proceeded to wade into the shallow water to get the ducks. When they finally noticed what I was doing, the cat calls began. They had spied my purple underwear! I was known as the "purple retriever" for quite a while!

Those little cotton longjohns just did not do the trick. They were not warm enough and did not wick away moisture. I tried pantyhose also; they are fine as a light liner under your hunting pants but don't count on them for good insulation. Years ago in some catalog I found a pair of wool blend, non-scratchy tights. They are wonderful! I have worn them for years; they offer tremendous insulation, wick away moisture and are very comfortable. They are an extra sock, too. I need a new pair but have not been able to find any; if you see a pair of these anywhere, buy them! Silk longjohns, and a top, are also good. Silk feels good on your skin, helps insulate and wicks away moisture. Any underwear set with M.T.S.® (Moisture Transport System) or any other moisture wicking system works well. I wear a polypropylene turtleneck as my top insulating, moisture-wicking underwear. Fabrics that wick away moisture are a must; when you are walking to a blind, setting out decoys or participating in whatever physical activity hunting requires, you will work up a sweat. If you are wearing cotton or something that does not wick away moisture, you will be damp, cold and miserable the rest of the day. Any of the above items can be found in outdoor catalogs. Get the correct size; if they are either too large or too small they will be uncomfortable. Major rule: Do not let your husband loan you his longjohns and do not let anyone sell you boys' longjohns! They do not fit! Get your own before you even start hunting!

LAYERING

Your next layers are personal preference and depend upon the weather. For very cold weather, on top I wear a wool blend lightweight turtleneck sweater. Turtlenecks are great. When it is really cold you can pull it up to your nose if you want and it makes another layer underneath your neck gaiter. I then wear a heavier wool sweater (chamois shirts are good, too) and top it off with an insulated hooded sweatshirt underneath my parka. I think the best sweatshirt is Walls Blizzard-Pruf® Vellux® fabric with polyurethane foam. They are warm, durable and very comfortable. For my bottoms, I will wear regular hunting pants or when it is very cold, I wear sweat pants under my bibs.

If you are turkey hunting, the weather will be warmer than when you are waterfowl or deer hunting in the north and you will not need so many layers. You also will not need your coveralls or bibs as they will be too heavy and too noisy; regular camo hunting pants and a jacket will suffice with whatever layers the weather dictates. You will be walking and sitting, so take that into account when you dress for turkey hunting.

For upland game hunting, you will need brush pants. These are camo or brown hunting pants with a nylon face on the legs. This helps you move through brush, grass and thickets easier. Any type of shirt, sweatshirt or sweater will be fine. You will need a blaze orange vest so remember that will be another layer. You will be constantly walking so you will not need a lot of insulation. The amount of clothing you wear will depend on the weather. Always take a jacket with you; it is better to have to remove clothing than to be freezing and not have anything else to wear.

Weather will also dictate how much layering you need when you are deer or antelope hunting. Bowhunting starts in very warm weather and maybe only a shirt and pants are needed. Deer hunting continues all the way through December and it can get mighty cold up north. That is when you need all of your layers! Antelope hunting is usually done during mild weather (except for freak snow storms) and hunting pants and shirt are fine. Brush pants are also good for antelope hunting as you will be lying on the ground at times and could be sliding over cactus!

When you are purchasing your top layer (your hunting pants and shirt), remember the same rule as for your outer clothing: fit in with your hunting environment. Shirts and pants will be found in many different camo patterns; choose the one that will be the most universal for you and your hunting situations. You'll also want to find good-fitting and durable clothing that will stand up to the rigors of the hunt.

When washing your hunting pants and shirts, use cold water only and a very mild detergent. Hot water and strong soaps can fade camo very quickly. There are products on the market that are known as "camo restorers" (for faded camo) and "UV (ultraviolet) eliminators" (takes away the shine animals can see). There are also products available to "descent" your hunting clothing as you wash them. I have not used any of these products personally, but I have been told more negatives than positives about them.

Rain gear can add another layer to your hunting outfit. You must have rain gear and be prepared for all weather situations. The temperature and type of rain gear you select will determine how many layers to wear. There is extremely good (soft and quiet) and very expensive rain gear available, but all you really need is something to keep you dry. Any durable camo-pattern rain jacket and pants found in a discount store will be fine. Do not get a solid color. Camo-pattern is best. My jacket is lined so I can forget about a layer or two. It has "air holes" in several areas for good ventilation. It was low cost and does the job.

HUNTING SOCKS

"Socks make all the difference in the world! Wear these! Wear those! Wear wool! Wear cotton! Socks do this, socks do that!"

"Yeah right." That's what I thought every time I heard these things. But I have found out that socks DO make all the difference in the world. They can help keep your feet dry and warm and can cushion boots that may not fit just right.

I wore heavy wool and wool-blend socks in my hunting boots for a long time. I thought they were fine until I started trying new upland hunting boots and I found out that socks are critical. Because I have a narrow foot and heel, I have trouble finding boots that fit well. I have suffered with terrible blisters and consequently found out that my regular socks were not helping one bit. I bought a different pair of boots and had the same problem. That is when I started my own boot/socks research project.

I had heard of Rocky® hunting socks but had never tried them. I contacted Rocky® Shoes & Boots, Inc. and got the lowdown on hunting/boot socks. The bottom line is I have found some dynamite socks! I was told "cotton is rotten"; it absorbs more sweat, causes more friction and feet get wet from the inside out. Wool is great; it is not itchy anymore, it wicks away moisture, feet stay dry and they can be worn in warm or cool weather. A wool blended with moisture-wicking properties makes the best sock.

Socks make all the difference in the world!

The best socks I have found are the Rocky® Dry Knit™ Bear Claw. They are specially engineered to be worn with ROCKY® boots, but work fine with everything. They contain Duraspun® Acrylic, Thermastat™ wool, nylon and elastic. Plush Duraspun® terry cushions the foot and wicks moisture away. Wool and nylon on the outside absorbs moisture. There is a flat knit area at the foot joint that reduces bulk. An elastic arch zone for extra support really feels good. Thermastat™ in the top, heel and toe add to warmth and wicking. These socks really have all the bells and whistles. They are expensive, but worth it. With all the trouble I have had, these socks get kissed. (Before the hunt!)

Rocky® makes another good sock named WildCat. These socks are made of Duraspun® Acrylic, nylon and elastic. They have all the moisture-wicking properties and terry throughout the sock to cushion the foot and protect against abrasion and blisters. The WildCat has been treated with an odor fighting anti-bacterial wash to ensure freshness. Although not quite the caliber of the Bear Claw, this sock is also very good and less expensive.

Merino wool is the softest, nicest, smoothest and best wool there is. So, are merino wool socks wonderful? You bet! I have a pair of Cabela's Outlast® medium-weight merino wool socks and I love them. Outlast® Thermal Regulating Fibers are specially designed to absorb body heat, and distribute it evenly throughout the sock. When your body heat drops, the heat that was stored is released back to your feet, allowing you to stay warm. These are magic socks and so very comfortable. When I wear my little rubber boots, my feet sweat and everything is wet and cold. My feet stayed completely dry with these socks, and the merino wool is so soft, I felt like I was hunting in bedroom slippers! I also had ROCKY's® DuPont THERMASTAT™ liner socks on underneath. That makes a terrific combination!

Liner socks with polypropylene are available in most places. My friends always wear them; they really like the moisture-wicking properties. They also help in preventing blisters. The polypropylene will not absorb water, so there is always a dry layer between your feet and the insulating properties of your outer sock.

For a free Cabela's catalog, call 1-800-237-4444 or visit www.cabelas.com. For Rocky® socks, contact D & R Sports Center, PO Box 139, 620 Fairchild Street, Nanticoke, PA 18634, call 570-735-1752 or visit the Web site http://www.dnr-sports.com. You might want to ask for a catalog as then you can read all the sock descriptions. They have some great heavy made-for-winter socks available. I can't even imagine how terrific the Bear Claw with merino wool would be!

HUNTING BOOTS

Don't let this happen to you: I was excitedly walking up the road to try out my new hunting boots. They felt good when I left the cabin and I thought I had finally found what I wanted. I had not gone very far when my heels really started to hurt. They were slipping and rubbing. I just thought, well, it will get better, but by the time I had only gone 1/4 of a mile, I had to stop. This was not a good day for this to happen. Those boots hurt me so badly I had to take them off; I

It took a long time for the author to find boots that fit and were comfortable. She finally settled on Rocky's Stalker boots. You will want to make sure you have good-fitting boots. If you will be doing lots of walking you might want lighter boots. Heavy-duty boots might be needed for really tough terrain.

noticed I already had blisters the size of quarters on both feet. The road was nice and greasy as it had rained an inch the night before, so I had no choice but to take my socks off too, and walk back. It was not fun to face the giggles of the resident construction crew as I meandered back barefoot, carrying my boots and socks and my feet covered in mud! The blisters were so bad I could not wear shoes for 2 weeks. Obviously, I would have to find another solution. This started me on my hunting boot research.

When I first started hunting, I bought a pair of L. L. Bean rubber duck boots. They fit well, were comfortable and except for my feet sweating (I didn't have the correct socks) I loved them. They were ultimately my upland game hunting boots, also. The first few times I hunted turkey in the spring it was cold so I wore my Sorel pac boots with grips on the bottom, so basically I was set for hunting boots. As I branched out into more hunting I decided I needed a regular hunting boot, with no heavy lining and good bottom grips. This has been quite a journey. The first ones I got were men's Rocky's®, on sale at a local outdoor store. I thought they would be fine with "fat" socks. They weren't too bad the first time I wore them turkey hunting in the Black Hills on rough terrain, but the next time I wore them my feet seemed to slip around terribly and I ended up in "blister city." My feet are narrow with a narrow heel and that is where my problem lies. I am sure I am not the only woman in the U.S. that has narrow feet and wants to hunt, but I feel like it!

After I healed up, I purchased another pair of Rocky® boots that were supposedly "women's". They felt and fit better than the first men's pair I had and again figured with "fat" socks they would work. I found out later they were just cut-down men's boots and not really women's boots made on a woman's last. (The Rocky® representative informed me of that and explained why they still did not fit me. He, too, has narrow feet and has two pair of boots he cannot wear!) This I found out after healing up for a second time in two months!

I was frustrated, disappointed and determined to somehow make something work. This was getting ridiculous! I just had to do some serious thinking and research. I remembered that a long time ago I had to have a leather heel cup installed in this one certain pair of western boots so they would fit better in the heel. I looked and called all over and couldn't find any like it. I settled for a $16 pair of heel cups that my western store owner ordered for me. After I trimmed some of the sole off of the cup (they threw my feet forward and my toes became numb!) the boots fit better but were still too wide for me. So, for one entire week I researched and "field tested" different combinations of items in my boots. Do not purchase those "heel strips" that supposedly stick to the heel area of the boot. They don't work. This is what I finally had to do to be able to comfortably wear these boots for any length of time and not get blisters: I have gel soles in each boot, I have two Dr. Scholl™ insoles in my right boot (my right foot is a tiny bit smaller than my left), I place the rubber heel cups on my heels underneath my socks, I wear good Rocky® socks, and I pull the boot strings extremely tight where my foot bends so my feet still don't slide forward. This is unbelievable! How wonderful it would be to be able to just slide your foot into a boot, lace it up and go and all is well. My friends all have wide feet and can comfortably wear ANYTHING! All the above mentioned items can be found in your local discount store, even heel cups. And, adding insult to injury, they are only $4.79 there!

The big problem is that boot makers do not make boots in narrow widths. They tell me there is not enough demand and that they are doing well to have a woman's boot at all. I researched Cabela's catalog and found two pair that sounded like they might work. One was made in Germany and was built with a narrow heel. The heel felt great but the backs of the boots were slanted and I felt like I was wearing downhill ski boots. I couldn't even stand up straight as they hurt the back of my leg. The other pair was Italian-made and came in a narrow width. I was sure excited to get those. But, they sent the wrong size so I had to go through an exchange. When I received my size, I was lacing up the boot strings and a rivet fell right out! I certainly did not want a low-quality boot, plus they still didn't fit. At this point, I screamed, "TO HECK WITH BOOTS! I might as well forget it and design a pair of camo high heels to wear in the woods!"

So, it was back to the phone to the Rocky® guy (we are good friends now!). He told me about the new woman's boot they have, that it is made on a woman's last so it is a "true woman's boot". Well, decision time. Did I want to invest in a THIRD pair of Rocky® boots? I had tried other makes of boots, but they were all too wide. I'd gone through so much already, I guessed it didn't make any difference. What I wouldn't give for a well-fitting and comfortable upland game boot that I wouldn't have to "doctor up." I did order another pair of Rocky's—this time women's boots—made on a woman's last! The Stalker® boots are great! Still a tiny bit too wide (I can fix that with a plain thin sole from the discount store), they fit like a dream compared to anything else I have ever had on my foot! They are waterproofed with GORE-TEX®, have 600 grams of Thinsulate™ insulation and a Direct Inject polyurethane sole. They are lightweight, comfortable, will be durable and look good. I heartily recommend them! If you cannot find them at your sports store, call Rocky® Shoes & Boots, Inc. at 1-800-848-9452.

I told you this sad story with a happy ending so if you have problems, you know you are not alone, that you should just keep on researching until you find a solution you can tolerate. If you are one of those lucky women who can wear anything in a boot with no problem, you have no idea how lucky you are. If your feet are comfortable, you feel good all over. If your feet hurt, you feel miserable all over and your hunt can be ruined. If you do have problems, tell the boot maker--that is the only way they will know!

My good hunting buddy Lori, wears Browning's Lady Nomad boots and is extremely satisfied with them. I tried the Lady Ridge Top. They seemed like very nice boots but, again, they do not come in narrow width. ECCO boots were recommended to me. My pheasant hunting friend swears by them and would never consider a different kind.

Look for boots in the RedHead catalog. They have two pages of boots, from upland game boots to waterproof rubber boots to winter boots. Refer to the address above.

When looking for a good upland hunting boot (regular hunting boot for wear in mild weather) look for durability, waterproofing, good bottom grips and height. Of course a good fit is important. You do not need a lot of lining in your regular hunting boot as you will be wearing them usually in milder weather. Take your boot socks along when trying them out in a store as you want to know EXACTLY how they fit. And, don't get "caught" in a sale. Know what you are buying! There are companies that custom-make boots to fit your feet (I may have to resort to that!). They are very expensive, but if they fit well, it would be worth it. Check at your local outdoor store and they can direct you from there.

An extremely well-made boot for big game hunting is made by Schnee's. They are tough, durable, reliable, great quality boots with good bottom grips. They do not come in narrow, so I have to follow my "Zastrow System" when wearing these. I have hunted the rough terrain of the Black Hills with them and they are great. Call Schnee's at 1-800-922-1562 or visit them at http://www.schnees.com.

When you get your boots pay attention to the "boot care" information. You have spent good money on those boots and you want to take good care of them. Before you wear them, spray silicon on them 2 or 3 times, letting them dry a few hours in-between. Never use paste or wax as that will plug up the leather pores. If your boots contain nylon uppers, spray a coating of stain repellent (Scotchgard™) before wearing. After hunting, clean off all dirt and residue. Use a quality leather cleaner and conditioner to keep your boots well preserved.

Rubber boots are good for waterfowl hunting. You can wear a couple of pairs of good warm socks and your feet will still stay warm and dry. You won't need waders or hip boots all the time, calf-high rubber boots can do the job. Some people even recommend that you wear rubber boots while bow hunting for deer. They say it keeps you from contaminating the area with scent.

For winter hunting I prefer Sorel pac boots, the kind with the rubber foot and leather upper and the thick felt inner boot. They are not too heavy, fit well and keep my feet warm. You can get different degrees of warmth in a boot, also. I have a pair of Sorel Dominators that are good to a temperature of minus 100 degrees. Living in South Dakota I have personally field tested them at minus 65 degrees and they work. They are big, clumsy and heavy and you don't want to walk very far in them. But they are good for stand hunting deer when it is cold and they are wonderful ice fishing boots. Check your Cabela's catalog for all types of winter boots and their descriptions; there are some good ones in women's sizes. My friend Gail Swanston has Columbia Bugabootoo boots in a women's size; she tested them well when she hunted elk in them and said they had good bottom grips, the heel fit well and they were very comfortable.

If your feet are blister-prone, here are some tips for you. Some women wear panty hose or knee-high nylons on their feet before adding socks. Or they wear liner socks to prevent blisters. This may or may not work for you as it really depends on the fit of the boot and what type of hunting socks you wear. The best prevention I found is, and this will sound crazy but it works, a combination of large self-adhesive bandages and duct tape! Scrape or pull the fabric off the Band-aid first; if you don't, the fabric will later bunch up and then

> **Rubber boots are good for waterfowl hunting. You can wear a couple of pairs of good warm socks and your feet will still stay warm and dry.**

hurt your heel. Place the Band-aid over your blister-prone area and wrap duct tape around your foot to keep it in place. Another idea that sometimes works is placing duct tape inside your boot from the heel to the top, then put duct tape on your sock--the duct tape will rub together, therefore preventing blisters. Moleskin, found in your pharmacy department, can be placed directly on your heel for blister prevention. It can be cut to any size to fit perfectly. There is a new Band-Aid product on the market called "Blister Relief"; they are little cushions to apply directly to the skin for blister prevention. There are different sizes for different areas of the feet, they conform to your foot to stay in place and can be worn for several days, even in the shower. Be sure to get the large size for your heels.

What do you do when you acquire bad blisters but have several more hunting days to go? Nothing is more painful than your boot rubbing over fresh blisters; that can prevent you from finishing your hunt. Here is my "Zastrow Blister System": Always have moleskin with you so you are prepared. When you get a blister, cut a piece of the moleskin larger than the blister and peel off the backing paper. Turn the paper around and place the shiny side on top of the blister, cover with the moleskin and tape it all up with duct tape around your foot. Moleskin has a good adhesive on it and combined with the duct tape, all will certainly stay in place. Use Avon Skin-So-Soft to remove tape residue when you are finished hunting. So moleskin and duct tape are two more items to add to your "getting ready" list! Believe me this works! I hunted for four days up and down hills with this combination and it saved the hunt for me. When you get home or finish hunting, take care of the blisters in this manner for fast healing (plan on not wearing shoes for a couple of days or wear open backed thongs): being extremely careful, cut away all the top dead skin on top of the blister (this is not fun!) so the air can get to it and heal it fast. To prevent infection keep the area extremely clean and spray with an anti-bacterial first aid spray. If the area becomes dry and cracks, use Mycitracin Plus™ ointment to help in healing.

HATS, GLOVES AND HAND-WARMERS

If you can keep your head, hands and feet warm, you will be toasty and comfortable while hunting. Most body heat is lost through our heads, so keeping the head covered is important. After you have

chosen your camo pattern in coveralls or bibs, choose a hunting hat in the same pattern. Of course you can mix and match, but we have to be stylish with SOMETHING in the field! My warmest hat is the one that matches my waterfowl bib/parka outfit. It is double lined and has a wool band around it that can be pulled down to cover my ears. A headband can also be worn under a cap for extra warmth. Make sure whatever hat you purchase has a bill so you will not have to deal with the glare of the sun, etc. In severe cold, I wear my headband, my heavy cap and top it off with a stocking cap on top. I have several stocking caps in camo, blaze orange for big game or upland game hunting, and white for winter waterfowl hunting. For big game or upland game hunting, always wear a blaze orange cap. I just makes you easier to see and that makes the hunt safer.

Caps with GORE-TEX® are good as they will keep your head dry in wet weather. I like my Browning Hydro-Fleece™ cap because it is soft, quiet and breathable and my head doesn't sweat. There are many kinds and styles of caps and hats. It's personal preference.

You will need face masks for two purposes: to keep warm and to camouflage your face. Look in the catalogs to see the different kinds and styles. I have a balaclava that can be worn four different ways. It is warm, but really tears your hair apart when you take it off over your head. Polar fleece face masks are warm and are good for concealment. If you wear glasses, be sure to try face masks on before you buy one; buy a mask that will fit around your glasses without obscuring your vision or steaming up your glasses. I had to cut and alter one of my masks so it would fit exactly.

Be sure you have whatever prescription glasses you need before you get to hunting season. If you go into the woods wearing sunglasses or shooting glasses remember it will get dark—bring your regular glasses with you. I have blue-blocker orange prescription shooting lenses in camo frames. The lenses block the blue in the light spectrum and highlight the green (makes greens darker) and also highlight movement. I did not have my bifocals put in these glasses as they distort images when you are lying on your back on the ground as for

When you want complete protection from the elements, a balaclava like this is hard to beat. As you can see the author even went so far as to have the frames of her glasses camouflaged. Too much? You make the call.

A neck gaiter can provide the warmth of a scarf without the length and bulk. Keep your neck and head warm and you will stay comfortable outside.

Chemical warmers can be just the thing to take the chill off of cold extremities. Read and follow the directions.

goose hunting over decoys. If you don't wear glasses, it is a good idea to wear shooting glasses for eye safety.

Neck gaiters (big neck bands) are on the market. They can be pulled up to keep your neck and face warm and even your mouth and nose. Caps that include a face mask are warm for your ears and neck and the knit hood can be rolled up and out of the way when not needed. An exciting product called a PolarWrap sounds promising. It is a neck gaiter that warms and humidifies the air before it enters your body and keeps your head, hands and feet

warmer as it prevents the blood from pooling in the center of our bodies when we get cold. (The less blood and circulation to the extremities, the colder they become.) The PolarWrap does not work if you wear glasses as they steam up immediately. If you do not wear glasses, it should work fine.

Face masks for turkey hunting will be in the spring catalogs or in your outdoor store in the spring. Please refer to the Turkey Hunting chapter for more information on turkey hunting masks.

The author's trusty muff. These come in several styles and work great for hunting from a stand or in a blind. Put a hand warmer inside and you might not even need gloves.

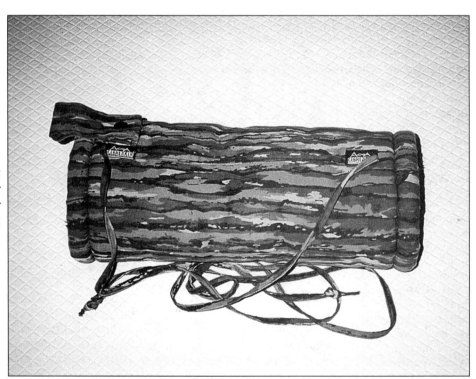

Keeping your hands warm will help your entire body to stay warm. There are many good, heavy hunting gloves available; the only problem is that they are bulky. Check out the styles of hunting/shooting gloves. Some will have a slit for the trigger finger for easy shooting. Waterproof and insulated gloves are a must.

Charcoal handwarmer packets can be purchased most anywhere. They are activated when the cellophane seal is broken. The reaction with oxygen causes them to warm, saving your hands and even feet on very cold days. They can be placed in your pockets for an instant hand warm-up. I have a pair of huge fleece mittens and place a handwarmer in each one during deer hunting; I wear my Equalizer (like Isotoner) gloves, place my hands in the mittens, and when I need to shoot, slip my fingers out of the slit in the mitten. My hands always stay warm! I have tried fastening the handwarmers under my toes--they stayed warm but it was an uncomfortable walk when I finished hunting. There are "footwarmers" with adhesive backing available. Hunting socks with special pockets for charcoal warmers are available. Large charcoal warming packets can be placed in your chest pockets to help you stay warm. Use your imagination and you can invent your own methods of using these handy items.

For maximum warmth, quiet and easy shooting, here is the "Zastrow Handwarming System." I have a muff; an insulated tube that my hands fit into during waterfowl and deer season. It can be tied around the waist so there is nothing to carry. I wear Equalizer gloves and place two handwarmer packets in the muff. I instantly have a nice warm haven for my freezing fingers! When birds are coming in I quickly pull my hands out, grab my gun and shoot. My gloves make for easy shooting and my hands are warm and flexible, not cold, numb and unmoving. It's great! Always take extra handwarmers with you--you never know when one might not work as long as it is supposed to.

Here is a private little Zastrowism for a certain group of female hunters: If you are having hot flashes, that's good!! Don't get estrogen therapy until after the waterfowl season and you will always be warm in the goose blind because you have your own heater!!

BACKPACKS AND FANNY PACKS

Where do we carry all of our "stuff"? Thank God for backpacks and fannypacks! Depending on what all you need to take with you to the field, you should be able to find the right size backpack or fanny pack. "Go light" and take only what you need. If you have big pockets in your hunting outfit, you won't even need to carry anything else. Backpacks are great for holding all of your general stuff for a whole day's hunting, but don't wear it hunting as it will be too heavy. I keep my shells, extra socks, gloves, etc. in the backpack and then take only the necessities (sunglasses, shells, tissues, etc.) in a small fanny pack to the field. My friend Lila wears a good sized fanny pack when we deer hunt. She has a compartment for everything and items are easy to locate. They are not rolling around all in a heap like in a backpack.

We women can have a problem finding the best place to carry our license since we don't carry wallets like the guys do. Place your license in a plastic baggie, fold and paper clip it and place it in a seldom used zipper pocket of your fanny pack. Don't place it in with your shells or something else that you often use — there would be more of a chance of it falling out and consequently losing it.

MPI Outdoors has great backpacks and fanny packs. Their rep explained to me the advantages of their new narrow backpack, just right for women. It is not bulky, does not stick out on the sides and is comfortable to wear. He also showed me the best way to wear a fanny pack — let it ride on your hips, not your waist. It is much easier to carry things using our hips than trying to control it mid-body. Contact MPI Outdoors at 85 Flagship Drive, Suite D, North Andover, MA 01845-6160. Call them at 1-800-343-5827 or visit their Web site at www.mpioutdoors.com. The MPI rep also had these tips for women: Carry a whistle with you. If you get separated from your group you won't panic; take wet naps with you for your hands, face, etc. because if you feel clean and good you will enjoy the hunt more and be able to stay out longer. You are in control of yourself and planning is the key. You will be proud of yourself as you can accomplish something few women have done!

BITS & PIECES

•Important tip: Keep all of your hunting clothing and equipment in one room so it is all in one place. It is not fun to be running around at 5:30 a.m. looking for "stuff" when your hunting buddies are waiting for you.

•When nature calls, do not be embarrassed! This, after all, is a normal bodily function! Discreetly find an appropriate place away from the group and do your thing. If this is a men's first hunt with women, they may be embarrassed, especially the younger guys, but they will get over it! Leave the outdoors as you found it; bring baggies in which to place the paper.

•Yes, you can wear make up! Just remember when you leave the house at o-dark-thirty, it does get light later! After watching a brilliant sunrise and the sun is shining, who wants to look like they just crawled out of bed? You can be a hunter, get down, earthy and dirty, but still look like a woman! Sure, my friends and I hunt with nails polished, too! Pushing shotgun shells into the shotgun can raise havoc with fingernails; keeping a nail hardener on at all times helps breakage.

•Jewelry: Yes, you can wear jewelry while hunting. Just don't wear big flashy inappropriate items and cover up anything that would reflect light. Leave your big rings at home as you do not want them to be caught in your gloves when you want to take a shot. Do not wear hoop earrings — they can get tangled in branches and brush.

Chapter Five

FINDING A PLACE TO HUNT

"The Point" was Sig's little piece of hunting heaven on a small northeastern South Dakota lake. Sig VandenAkker is a veteran hunter and fisherman, my mentor, friend and he used to be our neighbor at Pickerel Lake. He introduced me to The Point in 1989 and I've never been the same. At The Point the water is clear, the great expanse of sky is overwhelming, and the scenery is breathtaking. To the west are woods, hills, a dairy farm, more rolling hills, fields, and the prairie coteau in the background.

There is not a more beautiful sight than the dawn breaking over The Point and the world comes alive with the flapping of wings of all sizes. Whether a permanent home or a resting place on a migratory route, the lake is popular for all types of waterfowl. In the darkness on a good morning, you hear the deep-throated honk of giant Canada geese, chattering mallards visiting with one another, and the high-pitched flute tones of tundra swans.

Even driving into the area has its rewards. Deer, pheasants and partridge can usually be seen. The Point is a piece of land that Sig had leased for more than 20 years. He was extremely proud of it, as well as very appreciative of the owners. After photography and hunting trips there, I came to love the place just as much as he did.

To illustrate how times have changed, the landowner asked for only $1 for Sig to lease The Point for a hunting season! The Point was so well hidden, you really had to be an expert navigator to find it. When I asked how in the world he found such a place that was so far off the beaten path, he answered, "We were just driving around one day, followed some roads across some meadows and pastures, and there it was!" For anyone to "just find" a place like this was a pure miracle. Sig delighted in telling the story of how the farmer asked for only one dollar for the hunting rights. A true friendship and mutual respect existed for more than two

The Point at sunrise can be a magical place, even if when didn't offer exceptional waterfowl hunting. To find a place like this and secure permission to hunt there regularly will take some work, but it's worthwhile work that will build enduring friendships.

decades. The farmer was offered mega-bucks from big city hunters, but always turned them down in favor of Sig and his hunting buddies. How lucky I was to have learned to hunt in such a wonderful, beautiful piece of God's creation.

It was there that I shot my first waterfowl. It was there that I received my first lessons in making a blind and shooting over water. I listened to lectures on ethics, watched a great Chesapeake Bay retriever, videotaped ducks in flight and watched the largest flock of Canada geese I had ever seen. It was also there, at The Point, where I proved to myself that, yes, I am now a hunter. It was at The Point where I found my inner self and discovered how I felt about God's critters and hunting them.

One morning I surprised myself by arriving before dawn, entirely alone, throwing out decoys, settling in the blind and proceeding to bag waterfowl. What a terrific feeling I had at the end of the day, carrying my ducks back to the vehicle, knowing I did this all by myself, all alone, all day! It was wonderful to realize I had the intestinal fortitude to do all that. I had never thought I would ever be doing anything remotely resembling those activities. The Point was magical, drawing me like a magnet. I couldn't wait to get there and watch the ducks flaring in the pre-dawn light. I marveled at watching a most gorgeous sunrise and felt blessed watching the sun go down. There were many "blue bird" days — too nice for waterfowl to be active. Those days I made good use of the cameras and just watched and absorbed the feeling of the place. The days I went home empty handed were just as special to me; I was so thankful to have this heavenly spot. My uncle hunted there with me often; we really could define "bonding". We shared many memorable moments, the highlight probably being the morning we accidentally "crossed barrels" and brought down two 13-pound giant Canada geese at once!

Change is always a part of our lives. And change is what happened to The Point. After five years of above average rainfall in northeast South Dakota, accompanied by heavy snow in the winters, my wonderful Point is now under five feet of water. The Point ceases to exist. Ultimately, hunting excursions there have ceased to exist. Even though I cannot be there, The Point still affects me. There is the emotional tug on my heart whenever I think of it and remember everything that I used to do there. I'm lonesome for the "good old days", shed a tear or two and daydream about what is flying there now. I still am emotionally involved with The Point, and I know I will be for the rest of my life. I had no idea a human being could be affected so much by Mother Nature and her inhabitants. I now find myself doing what Sig did so long ago; driving around, looking for another very special hunting place.

I've told you about The Point just so you can know how much your hunting place can mean to you. You can find a place and experience all these things, too. You might have to work a little, take a little time, ask for some guidance, but these places are still out there, and so are the good landowners who will be happy to host you. You can become one with your hunting spot; it can shape you and change your life!

PRIVATE LAND

My husband and I farm near the James River in northeastern South Dakota. As I write this, the "river bottom" has been flooded for about five years now and the water attracts lots of waterfowl. It's great hunting, and I don't have to worry about getting permission. We have a lake cabin about 60 miles from our farm, in the glacial lakes area dotted with lakes, sloughs, beautiful hills and coulees. It's gorgeous country and waterfowl is abundant. I love to hunt there and

When meeting a landowner in an effort to secure permission to hunt on his land, planning on spending some time chatting. Remember, you are a stranger coming to meet someone and ask for something. That person will want to know a little bit about you.

with the disappearance of The Point, I now have to make the rounds of asking the farmers for hunting permission the same as any other hunter does. Being a landowner myself, I am aware of what it takes to make a good impression when meeting a farmer and obtaining his or her permission. I am aware that good conduct while hunting on his land, and thanking him for the generous opportunity given to me are even more important than whether or not I shoot my limit.

Before starting out on your mission to meet landowners to ask permission to hunt you must know where you are going and who owns what land. You will need a "Plat Book". That booklet is usually available at your county extension office or sometimes from a local bank. If they do not have one, they can tell you where to obtain one. The booklet is divided into townships included in your county. There are names of landowners and maps of which parcels of land they own. You will be able to tell exactly where the land is and how to get there. If you know whose land you want to hunt but the farmer isn't home or he is an absentee farmer (owns it, farms it, but doesn't live there) you will at least know his name and can call him later. This booklet will be yours to mark up, draw diagrams on and create a "huntable land" history for yourself forever.

Access to private land is becoming more difficult. With the downturn in the agriculture economy, landowners are looking for ways to supplement the farm income and hunting fees are becoming more common. Don't take that for granted! You do not know that a landowner will charge you until you talk to the landowner yourself. Do not assume anything. You can be pleasantly surprised at what you encounter.

I have been told several times that "so-and-so" doesn't like hunters, you cannot hunt on his land, don't even bother to ask, only to drive in the yard, visit with him and receive permission at no charge. I have also encountered the opposite type, but seldom; I realize it is the landowner's right to refuse me. I did recently have trouble receiving permission for an early Canada goose season in our lake cabin area. That was because the landowner's relatives were coming back for the special hunt. I was surprised at the various people who told me they were saving the field for their grandchildren, some of whom would be hunting for the first time. Even though I couldn't hunt there, I was very glad to hear that reason. Everyone who refused me at that time invited me back later during the regular season, and at no charge. If you are told there is a charge, you have to make the decision whether you want to pursue game on that particular land.

Here are some pointers on how to develop a good relationship with a landowner host. First impressions are important. That landowner can tell in a minute if you are the type of person he wants on his land. First of all, if you can help it, don't wait until the geese are sitting in his field or the first day of pheasant or deer season to ask permission. Being a landowner myself, I know how irritating it is to have car after car drive into the yard, or all at the same time, when there are geese in our field. Sometimes it cannot be avoided, but if you do your scouting and know that certain birds or deer are on a particular piece of land, make your contact as early as you can.

The only time of day not to go visit the farmer is high noon. Farmers work hard and want to peacefully eat their lunch. Drive SLOWLY into the yard. A farmer hates to see a vehicle come tearing into the yard and then perform a screeching stop. That's a big turn-off right there!

A smile is worth millions! Introduce yourself, tell a little bit about yourself. If the farmer is male, don't forget his wife, she may be the boss! And don't forget there are women who farm by themselves. I met one of my good hunting friends in that manner. You can ask first if the farmer allows

The author shares a cup of coffee with a landowner as they discuss the upcoming fall hunt.

hunting. You may have to listen to a lecture, stories, (farmers love to talk to visitors) or even view pictures before you get your answer, or at least the answer you want. Listen. Express an interest in their family life. They appreciate that. Finally you get to the question: "MAY I HUNT?"

When you secure permission, ask specifically and exactly what areas you can hunt. You must be careful about that. When you are out hunting and you are unsure about adjoining land and ownership of it, do not hunt it. Ask permission first; be certain you are where you are supposed to be. Whether knowingly or not, hunters who have ventured on others' land have found themselves in trouble with the landowners and that is what you certainly want to avoid. You should also ask the farmer if there will be any other hunters on his land. If there will be, find out where they will be and respect each other's areas. If you have the opportunity to visit with the other hunters, you may even find yourself some new hunting friends.

A polite touch is to ask the farmer to go hunting with you or ask if he would like whatever birds you may bag. If they do not hunt, those birds may be a real treat for that family. A follow-up with a favorite recipe is often really appreciated!

When the farmer tells you where to drive, what trails to take, what gates to open and close, LISTEN TO AND REMEMBER these instructions! Farmers do not want hunting vehicles making ruts and tracks all over their fields. If you open any gates, close them. The worst complaint I heard about hunters while I was on the game commission was the open gate issue. If you have never had to chase cattle around pastures and try to get them back into a place they do not want to go, believe me, you would understand why farmers hate to see gates that are supposed to be closed left open. The gates are there for a reason and they are closed for a reason. But some may also be open for a reason. If you find a gate that is open, don't automatically close it. You may be closing the cattle's only access to water or feed. If the farmer is gracious enough to allow you to enjoy his land, respect every one of his wishes and use common sense while you are there. Put yourself in a farmer's place; imagine all types of people in your yard. Of course, you would want your yard to look and be in the same condition it was before the people arrived there. It's the same way with landowners. Leave their property as you found it.

As for littering and garbage, do not leave so much as a gum wrapper on the property. If you find other hunters' garbage, be the good sport and pick it up. You do not want your host to think that you left it there. This gets back to ethics again and using common sense. Litter also includes shotgun shells. Pick them up. Clean game in appropriate places.

Ask the landowner how many people, maximum, he will allow you to bring with you. Even if he doesn't come right out and tell you, don't bring an entire 10-person hunting party with you. Landowners do not like hunters in "packs". If you have lots of friends you want to entertain, bring them one at a time. Tell the farmer your plans and stick to your word. Many hunting opportunities have been squelched because a hunter showed up with more hunters than allowed.

Finally you get to the question: May I hunt?

The hunter/landowner relationship is very simple and enjoyable; just treat landowners with respect. People are basically good and you get what you give. Kindness, courtesy and respect is returned. One day before waterfowl season opened, I had noticed giant Canada geese sitting in a pasture dugout at my neighbor's farm near our lake. I had never met the young couple, but knew this was the time. What a nice surprise to find a landowner who did not hunt but did everything he could to accommodate those who did. Not only did I receive permission to hunt at this his pasture dugout, the landowner jumped in my vehicle and said, "If you have time I'll show you a lot of other land I have that you are welcome to!" You just never know what is in store when you stop to meet a landowner. When we returned from our tour, he offered to move some hay bales into better position so I could use them as blinds! By this time I thought there would really be a charge for all this and I was afraid to ask him. When I finally did ask if he charged, his answer was, "Absolutely not! I used to enjoy hunting; I just don't have the time anymore. I now enjoy watching others having fun and want to give them as many opportunities as I can." Wow! What a surprise!

The landowner will appreciate the nice gesture of you returning to the house following the hunt and telling him what game you bagged. Farmers are curious and want to know the results of your hunt. It is little extra touches like this that help foster a good relationship with your landowner hosts.

If the landowner does not charge, then how can you show your gratitude? There are many ways. Gift certificates are available from local restaurants. Buy a couple of those and include them in a nice thank you letter. My landowner hosts for antelope hunting are terrific people. I sent them the thank you letter and gift certificates and the next time I was out there we had dinner together. I intended to buy dinner, but they beat me to the cashier with my own gift certificates! The certificates were intended for them exclusively, but these landowners are generous people and wanted to share!

You can offer to take the farmer's family to lunch when they come to town; set a date or they will never call you. I have given hams, turkeys, grocery store gift certificates and even sent small but nice Christmas gifts to the family. Remember, it's the thought that counts. A long time ago some hunters who were hunting on our land left a case of soda pop on our doorstep with a thank you note. That gesture was appreciated very much and gave us as landowners a "warm fuzzy" for hunters. If you bake and your hunting area is not too far away, take them some goodies. Just use your imagination.

When I was profusely thanking my host landowner for allowing me to hunt turkeys on his land, he sure surprised me! He would not take any money and said he would never charge hunters. "However," he continued, "I start repairing my fences around April first of each year and I sure would like some help with that!" I later took a friend to his place so she could photograph some turkeys. He told her the same story. As we left, we promised we would contact him the next spring. I applied for a turkey tag in his unit the next year but did not receive one. I called the landowner to tell him I would not be there and I asked how his fencing was coming

The lands of the American West can be wide-open, rugged and difficult to hunt. They can also pose a challenge when it comes to finding a place to hunt. For instance, without a farmhouse anywhere to be seen, who would you ask for permission to hunt on this land? That's why it pays to do some research.

along. He said they were just starting to work on them and everyone was welcome to help. He said hunters stop and marvel at his beautiful land; he asks them if they want a full tour, then "invites them to help fence and they can see it all!" If you have the time, it might pay to add a little elbow grease to insure that you can come hunt the next year.

Contact your hosts at times other than hunting season. Many times I have been told "the hunters never show up until the day before season opens. It sure would be nice if they would come out and offer to help with fencing or other jobs, or at least come and visit." Send landowners Christmas cards, birthday cards or remember their children at graduation times. Just pay some attention to them during the year. They will appreciate that and you will reap the rewards of making new friends.

To illustrate how this can happen involves dinosaurs! I hunted elk in western South Dakota and while visiting with my host landowner before the hunt he ordered me to follow him to the garage to "see something fantastic." It was Dinosaur bones. Yes, he had a dinosaur dig underway on his property, close to where I was hunting elk! He was very proud of that and wanted to show off the bones. He invited me to bring my family, especially the grandsons, out there the next summer. We all did make a trip out there and the first thing I did was to call my new friend for a dinosaur tour. He was delighted and we could tell it made his day to be entertaining us and showing us all the features on his land. We all had a great time and we appreciated the lemonade he served back at the house. The next time I saw the landowner was in the neighboring town where I was buying dinner for the folks upon whose land I hunted antelope. We all visited and enjoyed each other's company. Upon leaving, the "dinosaur landowner" asked if I hunted deer. When I told him yes, he said, "Well, I have deer, too, you know, some nice whitetails, so come on out and hunt those on my land, too, whenever you want to!" Another opportunity presented itself, all for just paying attention to the landowner, appreciating him and his permission. On the next trip out there I handed him a frozen giant Canadian goose, along with a favorite recipe. These guys appreciate game as most of them do not get the chance to hunt or fish. You should see their eyes light up when I take them some walleyes. They love it and I become a hero!

Always be prepared. Ask permission of the landowner early. The best time of course is before season opens. If you remember seeing birds in his field in previous years, get it all "sewed up" beforehand. Get it reserved for yourself. If he wants money for it he will tell you. Then it is the decision of how much it means to you to be able to hunt there.

Most landowners are good, nice respectable people who are willing to help you out. If it doesn't cost you money to hunt there, it just may cost you time. Visiting, to farmers, is important and means a great deal to them. If they invite you in the house or work shed for coffee or pop, you better go with them. They can become offended if you never take them up on their offer.

My friends invited me to snow goose hunt on a "new" landowner's land. We had a great hunt and were tired and ready to head for home. We had decoys to pick up and then make two trips with the landowner's four-wheel ATV (which he so graciously let us use as the field was too muddy to properly navigate with a pickup) from the field back to our

Sandy Hagny of the South Dakota Game, Fish and Parks Commission, center, chats with a landowner prior to a pheasant hunting outing. For reasons that are not exactly clear, women often have an easier time than men securing permission to hunt.

vehicle. It was dark and we all had things to do when we got home. Not so fast. The landowner insisted we come in for coffee. Gritting our teeth and sighing as we knew this would be another hour, we complied. Not only was there coffee, but homemade cookies, big dishes of cherry nut ice cream and a huge bowl of grapes! The farmer and his wife were delighted to serve us and visit. We did have a nice time; visiting and finding all the things we had in common was fun. Then came the unexpected payoff: The farmer said we could all hunt there come fall, could dig goose pits anywhere we wanted to, that he would even help us set up some semi-permanent blinds before the season. The older couple was all excited knowing that we would be hunting, and couldn't do enough to entice us there, probably JUST TO VISIT AFTER THE HUNTS! There was no monetary charge to hunt, just the investment of a little time for a terrific hunting place.

A few years ago my uncle and I used to hunt a particular area near a tiny lake east of our cabin at Pickerel Lake. The landowner was an elderly gentleman who personified the word "visit." He was fun to talk with and had many interesting hunting stories from years past. (Pay attention to those; you can always learn something while being entertained.) After waterfowl grew more abundant near our farm, I had not hunted on this farmer's place for a couple of seasons. I still stopped and visited with him, however, "just to be sure" when season rolled around that I would be ready if he had birds there. The last time I was there, he invited me in for coffee and proceeded to show me his gun collection. He had the entire closet torn apart and I heard every war story that matched each firearm. His grandson was usually around the farm brandishing a BB gun or riding his bike and blowing a duck call whenever I was there.

Before long, the grandson became a skilled waterfowl hunter and had permission from all the neighbor farmers to hunt their land. He had many decoys that he used to perfection and had become very successful at bringing home birds. At the end of this "grandson story", my farmer friend then

said to me, "Just tell me when you want to go with Jesse; he would love to have you along!" Talk about an opportunity there. So, just keep your eyes and ears open because you can be pleasantly surprised at unexpected times.

This reminds me of another story about a landowner whose farm was across the small lake from the fellow mentioned above. My uncle and I were told to check over there as the geese came off the lake within shotgun range and that could mean success for us on days the wind was out of the east. As my uncle and I walked to the door, a pickup truck loaded with goose decoys pulled into the yard. The young man behind the wheel called us to come over and talk to him. After visiting with him, he invited us to hunt the following morning with him in their pasture. What a deal! Of course we went, shot some geese, had a great time and were really surprised when Chris handed out our snack sandwiches. Still having two hours of hunting time left before the noon deadline, he invited us to his farm. From there we walked his pasture, looking for geese in the potholes. We didn't find any, but he had wanted us to have another opportunity to hunt. When we arrived back at his farm house he then invited us in and asked if we would like a "refreshment." Since shooting had closed for the day, we said "tomato beers" would be fine. Then it was a choice of which brand of beer, which kind of tomato juice and finally it was all served in frosted mugs. The only cost: looking at hunting pictures and listening to stories. The result: new friends, new places to hunt and an education on how one circumstance can lead to another. The world is full of great people!

I do not want to mislead you and make you think that all these good things will happen every single time you drive into a farmer's yard. As I mentioned before, most landowners are very nice, gracious people. There certainly are, however, the opposite kind. When you do run into a farmer or rancher who is less than hospitable or downright "owly and crabby" when he finds out you want to hunt, do not despair! It is not your fault! If you represented yourself well and he still acts this way, just remember YOU did nothing wrong. Maybe he was having a bad day, maybe all sorts of bad things happened on the farm that day, or maybe he just doesn't like hunters. Whatever his reason, that is the way he is and there is nothing you can do about it. If he expounds upon the circumstances and yells, you do not have to take it. Just politely thank him for his time and quickly leave. You will feel "bruised" and embarrassed and intimidated into thinking "the heck with it, I'll forget it". This is the perfect time to go on to the next one. Do not let one farmer of this type ruin your day or your hunting fever, just mark him off your list and continue on. There are times you will be told "NO" so expect it and deal with it diplomatically. The next farmer may present a surprise opportunity you can't resist.

PUBLIC LAND

Do you want a place to hunt without going through the "asking permission" part? Do you want a place that's entirely free to you and open to everyone? There are plenty of hunting opportunities on public land. There are generally state and federal lands available to hunters, but some areas, particularly in the east, have "County Forests" and even forest crop land owned by paper mills where hunting is allowed. The state land is primarily small tracks of wetlands, cropland and grassland. Federal lands consist of large tracks of land, such as the millions of acres of BLM (Bureau of Land Management) land in the western states and the national forests. County forests, like those in Wisconsin, for example, are usually fairly large tracts of managed forest land. Most county forests are found in sparsely populated counties where the timber sales from the land help fund the operations of the county government.

Public land means just that—it is land that is owned by usually either the state wildlife agency or the U.S. Department of the Interior (that means we taxpayers and license buyers have already paid for it) and is open and free for everyone to hunt. License fees and a special federal excise tax on hunting and fishing equipment sold (Pitman-Robertson Act) are just a couple of ways that agencies obtain funding for land they can purchase, set up management plans and then open to the public. With your license purchase YOU are contributing for the public use of these lands.

STATE LAND

State game refuges, game production areas and wetlands or grasslands purchased with license fees and/or land donated to the state as family memorials are usually included in the state's public hunting areas. Go to your local wildlife agency and ask for the most recent "Sportsman's Atlas" or public land directory. The cost is minimal for a wealth of information. On the atlas you can find state and federal lands of all types and their locations. When you have researched an area and drive there, be sure to note the signs stating it is public land. Be sure you know where the boundaries are and learn to recognize the signs.

South Dakota has a wonderful public access program known as "Walk-In Areas". The Walk-In Area Program was designed to allow hunters on private lands. The advantage for hunters here, where 85 percent of the land is privately owned, is a destination where they know they won't be denied access.

South Dakota's Game Production Areas are clearly marked. Most states offer similar lands that are open to public hunting.

In the past, most folks in South Dakota had an association with the land. Farms and ranches were smaller, so there were more farms. Agriculture then was more labor-intensive than today, and there were larger families to help with the chores. It seemed that everyone who didn't live on a farm had a cousin or brother who did; it was fairly easy to find a place to hunt. There was also once a law in South Dakota that allowed folks to hunt on any land that was not marked with "No Hunting" signs, as long as there were no woven wire fences, livestock or unharvested crops present. You could hunt just about anywhere you wanted.

Today, farms and ranches are becoming larger and there are fewer family farms. Families are smaller and most jobs are in towns and cities today. Many folks have no contact with anyone in the country. Hunting on private property now requires landowner permission. You can't just hunt anywhere anymore.

In the 1985 Farm Bill, the Conservation Reserve Program (CRP) was authorized, and by 1990 about 1.7 million acres of South Dakota cropland had been converted to grass cover for 10-year periods. The habitat created by CRP was followed by increases in many wildlife populations; pheasants for one. This was a rare and fantastic opportunity.

After careful study of the "Where do I find a place to hunt?" question, the Walk-In Area Program was developed.

Walk-In Areas provide hunters with hunting destinations that are certain, and they provide landowners with liability assurances and a fee for allowing unlimited public hunting. In South Dakota there are more than a half million acres enrolled in the Walk-In Area Program, and most of that land is CRP land. That land is public, open to you and me for hunting purposes, at no charge.

The WIA Program is updated every year and changes are made. Be sure to have the most recent map or public land handbook available so you know exactly where this land is located. Walk-In Area 2000 is an expansion of the South Dakota program. The program received a major boost from the state legislature, which established a $5 surcharge on most hunting licenses sold in the state. One-half of all funds generated through this surcharge, or about $600,000 annually, is earmarked for improved hunting access. All of us in South Dakota are proud of this program and very happy to be able to have the hunting access at no charge. It is a win-win situation as the landowner gets paid to let people hunt, the state shows cooperation with the landowner and the hunters can hunt at no charge. Look into this program in your state; if there is no such program, maybe YOU can be the catalyst to get it started by having your state agency contact the South Dakota Department of Game, Fish and Parks. If your

state does have such a program, obtain a Walk-In Area guide. If you do hunt one of these areas, just remember that it is still basically private land and treat the landowner's farm accordingly, with the respect we discussed earlier.

Your state agency will probably have a "Guide to Public Hunting" booklet. That will show you both state and federal public hunting areas. A list of the particular species found in each area will be listed, as well as explicit directions on how to find the public areas.

When the western lands were surveyed, and divided into townships (36 square miles) and sections (1 square mile), sections 16 and 36 of each township were set aside for school lands in some western states. These lands are administered by the state's Office of School and Public Lands. Although school lands are "public lands", they are not the same as federal lands managed by the federal land management agencies or the State Game Production Areas managed by the state. These trust lands are managed to produce income for the support of the state's schools, universities and other endowed institutions.

In South Dakota school lands are available for public hunting and fishing. These lands must be legally accessed. Anyone crossing private land to reach school land must have the permission of the private landowner. Off-road vehicle use is prohibited. All motor vehicles must remain on established roads and trails. No hunting is allowed in fields of unharvested grain, or on public road rights-of-way within 660 feet of livestock, occupied homes, churches or schoolhouses.

While permission is not required, users are encouraged to notify the rancher who has leased the land as a courtesy whenever possible. Notification can help avoid trespass and other problems. School lands are intermingled with, surrounded by, or fenced in with private land and are indistinguishable from private land. It is YOUR responsibility to know if you are on public land. If you are on private land without permission, you could be charged with trespassing. Never forget that fact. Call your state's wildlife agency for information on school lands.

FEDERAL LAND

Federal land consists of BLM (Bureau of Land Management), National Wildlife Refuges, WPA (Waterfowl Production Areas), U.S. Forest Service, National Grasslands and COE (Corps of Engineers) lands. They are all owned by the federal government; that means you and me. They are all open to the public for hunting.

BLM (Bureau of Land Management) started out as the "land nobody wanted" in our country's pioneer days. Today it represents a priceless legacy for the American people. The BLM is an agency of the U.S. Department of the Interior. The BLM administers the land. As taxpayers, you and I own it. There are millions of acres of BLM land in the west and quoting outdoor writer Jim Zumbo, "Imagine hunting in an area where you can walk for days, even weeks, without seeing a posted (no hunting) sign. Picture yourself spotting plenty of game and paying absolutely nothing for the experience." There are plenty of roads already established, but use them only for access. Your best hunting will be away from the roads so park your vehicle and walk. Do not depend on signage to identify your wherabouts. The cost of signage for the millions of BLM acres would be astronomical. Use your maps. Also be cognizant of the fact that these acres are grazed by cattle and private

Several states are now following South Dakota's lead in the creation of Walk-in Areas. These are privately owned lands leased for a nominal fee by the state and they are open to public hunting as long as the hunters do not use motor vehicles.

land can be intertwined with the BLM land. Just know where you are and where the boundaries are as you do not want to cause a problem if you would happen to stray onto private land without permission. The BLM has maps available for $4 showing federal, state and private land. To order the maps or check out the updated activities of each BLM office, you can call up the home page for each state on the Internet. For example, the Web site for Wyoming is www.wy.blm.gov, etc. Simply substitute the state abbreviation in the Web site address as required. If you don't have Internet access, call 202/452-5125 in Washington, D.C., and ask for the phone number of the state office you want.

The National Wildlife Refuge System is a national network of lands and waters specifically established for the conservation and management of fish, wildlife, and plant resources of the U.S. for the benefit of present and future generations. The first refuge developed was Pelican Island in Florida in 1903 by President Theodore Roosevelt. Now 100 years later there are 92 million acres in more than 500 refuges in every state in the union. The refuge system is the world's largest system of lands set aside specifically for the benefit of wildlife. Most refuges authorize some form of hunting, but not all of them do. You must check with your local unit of the refuge system for regulations. The national Web site is: www.fws.gov.

Waterfowl Production Areas are managed by the U.S. Fish and Wildlife Service. They are purchased with funds from the sale of federal Waterfowl Stamps. Instead of paying taxes on the land, the US Fish and Wildlife Service makes annual payments in lieu of taxes. Most WPAs include temporary or permanent wetlands and the associated uplands. These are important waterfowl nesting areas but provide habitat and public hunting for a variety of wildlife species. A list of WPAs is available in the free "Guide to Public Hunting Areas" booklet.

More wonderful hunting opportunities are available in our National Forests. These are public lands entrusted to the National Forest Service. They administer both the National Forests and the National Grasslands of which there are 191 million acres in 43 states. These lands are available to the public for a variety of activities including hunting, fishing, mining and logging. Their mission statement: "Caring for the land and serving the people". For information call your nearest forest service office in your state or visit the Web site www.fs.fed.us and click on the forest service national home page.

For those desiring information on wildlife agencies, BLM offices and National Forest Directories in nine western states, see the Appendix of Jim Zumbo's book, *How To Get An Easy Elk*. (Visit www.jimzumbo.com to order the book.) Addresses and phone numbers are supplied and will help you determine exactly where you want to go.

There is U.S. Army Corps of Engineers land available for public hunting. In the early years of our country, U.S.

National Wildlife Refuge lands are managed by the U.S. Fish and Wildlife Service. Hunting is allowed on many refuges, but only in specific areas and seasons may be slightly different than those set by the state. Check with the refuge manager before planning a hunt.

Army engineers blazed trails for westward migration and cleared waterways and harbors for commerce. The expertise gained in these early missions enabled the Corps to assume Congressionally authorized duties in the fields of flood control, hydropower production, shore protection and restoration, water supply, disaster assistance, fish and wildlife management, and recreation. Lakes impounded by Corps dams provide ideal opportunities for outdoor recreation. Corps recreation areas typically include campsites, picnic areas, swimming beaches, boat launching ramps, rest rooms and drinking water. Fishing is popular at most Corps lakes, and hunting is available on project lands at many locations.

No entrance charges are made to use Federal lands and waters at Corps projects, except in some areas operated by concessionaires or leased to other agencies. State and local agencies often lease land surrounding Corps lakes to provide additional recreation facilities. These agencies may charge fees for use of their facilities or services. These fees are set by the state or local agency and vary by location.

Complete rules and regulations are posted in conspicuous places at the parks. Become familiar with the rules governing use of Corps areas; violators may be subject to citations.

There is Corps land in every region of the country. Maps and brochures are available for all of them. Contact: U.S. Army Engineer District, Omaha, 215 N. 17th St., Omaha, NE 68102-4978. Phone: 402-221-4274.

There are certain advantages of hunting public land. There is no fee to worry about and you have unlimited access. You can hunt when and where you please — it is YOUR land. Public land will have more hunting pressure early in the season but then it usually tapers off, making it better for you later.

Although we are very appreciative of public land, there are disadvantages, too. You will not be visiting with a landowner one-on-one to tell you where to go or how to do it; there will be no "guide" to show you where to go. There will be competition from other hunters; in fact, the area may be overrun with hunters and dogs at certain times. You run the risk of someone else in your way, someone else bagging the game you had your eye on and safety becomes a concern. If you have no choice but to hunt heavily used public areas, don't feel too bad. Early in the season, learn to use hunting pressure to your advantage. The large influx of hunters from easily accessed points pushes game into small areas. Find these areas or strips of cover leading to them, and you will be successful.

My deer hunting friend talked me into applying for a deer tag within the National Wildlife Refuge near our farm. I had only hunted deer on my land and was used to solitude, quiet and stand-hunting at my convenience with no one else on the property. I was very skeptical about applying for a "public land" deer tag because of all the horror stories I had heard. I did apply however, hoping that the situation would be better than what I had expected. I was actually rather excited about going to the refuge — the first time in a new place can be educational and fun. What a shock I had when we arrived at the refuge. We had just removed ourselves from the vehicle and the first thing we saw was two other hunters, headed for

Maps can be some of your best sources of information. Get a good supply of maps for the region in which you plan to hunt. Plat books, which also list landowners names, are also great sources of information. Check with local government officials and state game departments to find the best source for maps.

the same place. As we were part way into the refuge, we saw two more hunters, then we heard shots. After hunting alone and seeing no other hunters, all these people suddenly appearing in my deer hunting area scared me. I know how far a rifle bullet can reach. I know the danger of hunting with others in the area and I certainly know when I am not happy with a situation. I was assured, however, that everyone would end up in "their own place" and no one would interfere with us. That did prove to be true, but I was nervous the entire time I was there. I just am not comfortable hunting on public land, especially with deer rifles surrounding me. But the truth of the matter is that if everyone follows the safety rules, you will be fine. But sadly some people do not. When hunting vast areas of BLM land out west, you could probably hunt for days or even weeks before seeing another individual. Here in the Midwest where tracks of land are smaller, there is a problem. Please do not take me and this message incorrectly. I am very glad there is public land as it allows an opportunity where none might exist. The state leased-land projects are terrific, allowing hunting for people who might otherwise never have an opportunity.

A friend just recently told me, "The hunting is better on private land, but the freedom isn't there." Your choice will be based on how you gauge the success of a hunt. If a hunt is successful in your eyes when you have the opportunity to be outdoors, enjoying what you are doing and want to share that with others, then, your day will be successful. You don't have to wait for other people and abide by their schedules — you go when and where you want and enjoy the day!

Private hunting preserves are common and can offer plenty of opportunity for you. Their specialty is upland game. You can find everything from a small "mom and pop" operation to a fancy, sophisticated first-class "hunting resort" and quite a few in between. Deciding where you want to hunt will depend on how much money you want to spend, how much time you want to spend and maybe how many different species you want to hunt. The hunting preserves' seasons run earlier and later than the regular state-regulated seasons so you do have more opportunity to hunt. On a hunting preserve you will find great wildlife cover and habitat, lots of birds, and learn about a different method of wildlife management. The game birds are artificially propagated, ensuring a good amount of them for you to shoot. In the past, hunting preserves were looked upon as a place for a "shooting event" rather than a hunting experience. The managers recognized that fact and today they want their clients to experience the

closest feeling to "open hunting" as they can. They can provide guides and dogs and really make your day an unforgettable one with all the shooting opportunities available. Decide if you want an experience like this; your budget will determine your choice. Contact your state wildlife agency for a list of hunting preserves in your area and the contact names and numbers.

If you want to plan a hunting trip and have a guided service with everything taken care, then you will want to contract with an outfitter. Contact your wildlife agency for a list of outfitters and their particular services. Be sure you check out the business before signing on with them; references are important as you want the trip to be a success, positive and as hassle-free as possible. When you want to check on an outfitter, obtain the name of a former client and give that person a call. Each state will have its own outfitter association.

Indian reservations can be a terrific place to hunt. Contact the Bureau of Indian Affairs, administered by the Department of the Interior, and receive information on the reservation lands in your state. You will have to obtain information from the specific reservation on which you want to hunt. Each tribe is governed by its own constitutional by-laws and has its own rules. You will very definitely need to know the boundaries of the reservation; maps may or may not be available. You will need to purchase a permit for any type of hunting on a reservation as state licenses usually are not valid. When you decide where you want to go, call that particular tribal office and ask for the hunting license office and they will direct you from there.

Be creative in what you want and what you are looking for in a hunting place.

You now have your choice of where to find a place to hunt — be it private land, public land, hunting preserve or Indian reservation. Be creative in what you want and what you are looking for in a hunting place. When you are attracted to a place, the game has cooperated with you and you want to return, then that particular place MEANS something to you. If you find yourself dreaming about other methods of hunting the area, other ways to find game, a different way to outwit the critters, and you can't wait to get back to "the place", then, you have found it. Not only have you found "it", you might have found a new and different part of yourself while you weren't looking. You might find more than just one of these special places; you might find several and they will all mean a lot to you. It's like falling in love — you "just know." Well, when you find a special hunting place that has captured a place in your heart and soul, you will "just know".

LET'S GO HUNTING

CHAPTER SIX
UPLAND GAME

My heart was beating quickly as I bounded out of bed, ran to the calendar and checked off another day. Only five more days and it would be here! My stomach lurched every time I thought about it. I was so nervous I couldn't eat. The dinner conversation always centered around it and the activities that went with it. Meals were planned, all the relatives were invited and that meant a lot of fun! What was going on? The opening day of the pheasant season was approaching, of course.

Growing up in South Dakota meant growing up with pheasants.

While driving to a pheasant hunting area with the anticipation of a fun hunt, I couldn't help but remember the effect pheasants had on my life during my childhood and teenage years. Opening day of pheasant season truly was a holiday. I was only the "gopher"— the guys shot them and my cousins and I would "go get 'em." There were so many birds they were falling everywhere. We kept count to see who could collect the most birds. Pheasants were thick in our shelterbelts (lines of trees planted as wind breaks) and walking or running through the thick brush and trees sometimes got to be a challenge. But no way would we complain! The days would be perfect — nice, warm, beautiful fall weather that had everyone in a good mood. Of course, after each walk, we would have to stop and check out the lunch coolers. Why is it that sandwiches, cookies, candy bars and pop always taste better out in the field?

One of my favorite uncles was in the U.S. Air Force and when he would come home for pheasant hunting it was a holiday. There was lots of hugging, laughter, good food and just an unbelievable amount of fun — all because it was the pheasant opener, the social event of the year. Later on, that same uncle moved to Wisconsin, was married and had a family. Then, hunting even became a bigger deal because he brought his in-laws with him. They were delighted to be hunting pheasants in South Dakota and we were delighted to have the company. They added to the fun.

In those days we had good-sized hunting parties, so there was lots of "gophering" for us kids. After the hunt, we would lay out all the birds, take pictures, look the birds over, compare them and their tail feathers. We would then choose the longest tail feathers and place them into an empty shotgun shell. Those were our precious souvenirs.

Pheasant-cleaning time was happily avoided by my cousins and me. We were, by that time, helping to prepare the evening dinner. My grandmother was a terrific cook and we always looked forward to the "pheasant company" meals with much anticipation. The first evening's dinner was delicious and served to whet our appetites for the next day's dinner which would be pheasant, of course. My grandmother and mother could make creamed pheasant to die for. I still remember the wonderful smell of pheasant cooking as we all came dragging in the house, hungry, dirty, tired, but oh, so happy and excited. I wonder now if they knew how much we really all appreciated their wonderful efforts. They had to do a lot of work, but we all loved it!

After a few days of hunting, it would be time for the visitors to return home. After all the excitement and fun, that day was always a disappointment. Then, we just talked about the next year, who would be coming, when they would come, what the pheasant population would be, etc. We always received some type of Christmas gift from them as a thank

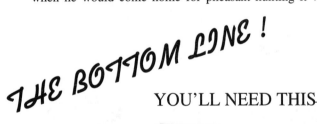

YOU'LL NEED THIS———

Pheasants are the most popular upland game bird with hunters in this country. Here the author shows off the results of a good day in the field.

you and a remembrance. Being busy with school, babysitting jobs, etc., we didn't think too much about pheasants until about one month before season opener. Then we would get into high gear, live at fever pitch and hardly sleep knowing that one of our favorite holidays, pheasant season opener, was just around the corner.

My father took me fishing, but never taught me, or even asked me, to shoot a gun. I grew out of the "gopher" stage, then became busy and involved with high school and college. After my husband and I were married, pheasant hunting was part of our lives, HIS life. Again, no one invited me to go along, no one offered to teach me to shoot or even talked to me about it. I didn't have the interest then to pursue it either. I wonder what those other 19 hunters who were with my husband would have thought if I had insisted on tagging along. In the 1960s, in South Dakota farm country, a woman's place was still in the home. My job was to help entertain the hunters' wives all afternoon while the men were all out hunting. Yikes! Today the thought of that is enough to put me into cardiac arrest!

That scenario continued for a few years. By then, we'd had our two children and I was occupied with them. My husband stopped hunting around that time, too. It was after the children were grown and gone and I was on the game commission that I discovered how much fun shooting a shotgun and pheasant hunting really were. It sure did beat "gophering." I thought I had had fun before (which I certainly did) but nothing compared to actually hunting! Carrying a gun, being one of the group, doing the "real thing" and then eating what I brought home was fantastic. I was hooked.

Every time I hunt pheasants I remember and relive the early memories. How astonished I would've been if someone back then had told me I'd actually be hunting them "when I grew up." I will cherish those memories forever. Opening day celebrations, laughter, fun, camaraderie and eating your game is what it's all about — and this certainly holds true for pheasant hunting.

GETTING TO KNOW YOU

Tony Leif, a pheasant biologist with the South Dakota Game, Fish and Parks Department, describes pheasants this

Pheasant hunting is traditionally a gathering of family and friends in places like South Dakota.

way: Pheasants are a chicken-type bird, in the same family, but are a little leaner and faster. They possess whatever is necessary to survive in the wild. The male is the larger of a pair, with beautiful colored feathers, a white ring around the neck and a blue/green iridescent head. There is red coloring surrounding the eye area. The male has spurs that can grow up to 3/4 of an inch long. They have long attractive tails, some of which can be 27 to 28 inches long. The female is smaller in size, is completely brown in color with a touch of red around the eyes.

While looking at a pheasant, you cannot help but marvel at the many gorgeous colors of feathers. From the dark blue-green head, accentuated by the white ring around the neck, the colors range from dark rust on the breast to gold, blue-green, black, tan and brown on the rest of the body. Pheasant feathers are a hot commodity; many people make jewelry, wreaths, flower arrangements and various other craft items using pheasant feathers. Ancient Chinese, Greek and Roman paintings and tapestries constitute evidence of the great antiquity and beauty of pheasant ancestry.

The first significantly successful introduction of pheasants from Asia came late in the 19th century. In 1882 Judge Owen N. Denny (then consul-general at Shanghai) bought four pairs of Chinese pheasants at a Chinese food market for 35 cents a pair and shipped them to America. These birds all died in Seattle, Washington, after a rough voyage. The next shipment of 50 to 70 birds arrived safely in Portland, Oregon, and were released on the old Denny homestead. By 1892 "Denny" pheasants had become so abundant in that part of Oregon that a season of 75 days was declared, and 50,000 birds were killed on the opening day.

After the spectacular success in Oregon became known, the country went wild about stocking pheasants. By 1907 pheasants of Asian and European ring-necked and black-necked stocks had been introduced and established in the wild in all but nine states. From the mixed ancestry, an American species emerged. The bulk of the good pheasant range in the United States lies in its northern half, with the largest block of continuous and superior range comprised of farmlands in the northern Great Plains. The preferred foods of pheasants are grains, weed seeds and some insects. It has been found that most grain eaten by pheasants is fallen grain that could not be used by the farmer.

"The best all-around pheasant habitat is undisturbed grassland with native grass plantings," says Tony Leif. "A grass and alfalfa mixture on our CRP (Conservation Reserve Program) land has been fantastic for the birds." The CRP has been called the most important conservation program in history — especially for the ring-necked pheasant. CRP is land that is rented from private landowners by the U.S. government for conservation purposes. Landowners are paid at least the going cash-rent rate for 10 to 15 years and are provided funding to establish permanent cover on the site. The objectives of the CRP program are to decrease erosion, improve water quality and increase and improve wildlife habitat. In South Dakota, the benefits of CRP for wildlife have been obvious. The pheasant numbers have been fairly stable and relatively high the last eight years. When you are out scouting land for pheasant hunting and you see large tracks of privately owned grassland that is CRP land, that is where you will want to go.

There are other types of good pheasant habitat providing what pheasants need — food and shelter. Farmland habitat includes small grain fields, corn, sunflowers and soybean fields surrounded by weedy field margins and fence rows. Woodland habitat is provided by farmsteads and field shelterbelts that include some evergreens. Wetlands such as small sloughs and cattail marshes are also good pheasant habitat. You will want to remember this when you are looking for a place to hunt pheasants.

The first significantly successful introduction of pheasants from Asia came late in the 19th century.

GETTING READY

Pheasant hunting is done in the fall, usually starting in October. At that time, the feel of autumn is in the crisp air, the sky is a most beautiful blue, the warm sun shines in golden streaks, and it is just great to be alive and outdoors. A good pheasant hunt is in order on days like these. This is the time to enjoy the fellowship of your hunting friends, watch a working dog do his job well, get plenty of good outdoor exercise, and if you bag a few birds, that's a bonus.

Contact your wildlife agency to make sure you have the correct license for pheasant hunting. An "upland game" or "small game" license is usually the name under which they are sold and they usually can be purchased over the counter. Some states also require conservation stamps, with the money going directly to improve pheasant habitat. Whoever you buy it from will be able to tell you exactly what you need. If you are not a resident of the state in which you wish to hunt, check the regulations early.

The next step is to decide where you want to go. Remember the pheasant habitat and where the birds "hang out." The number of hunters will determine where you go. If there is a large group you will want to check out the CRP fields. You will have plenty of opportunity there and there will be room for all of you to have a safe hunt. If you are going to hunt by yourself, or with one or two friends and no dog, then you should locate small cover (weed or grassy) patches, fence lines, seasonal wetlands (small sloughs), abandoned farmsteads or small tree claims. You will want small areas to cover. Refer to your "Sportsmen's Atlas" to find the public areas, or to your Walk-In Area guide if your state has that program. You should also consider contacting the wildlife agency in the state you plan to hunt to get maps and information about hunting sites.

The small areas are good usually only at the beginning of the season. When the weather turns cold and there is some snow around, the pheasants then migrate to heavier cover areas and cattail sloughs, etc. A farmer's small food plot can be a great place to hunt early in the season; cover will probably consist of corn, sorghum or sunflowers.

Farmers are the best sources of information when trying to find a good spot to hunt pheasants. They know where the birds are in their area. You should contact some farmers in the area where you plan to go hunting to get permission and to find out where the birds are. It pays to do some checking beforehand and not wait until the opening day. Refer to the chapter on finding a place to hunt for some general tips on getting access to good hunting areas.

If you and your friends are planning to hunt a large CRP tract or grassland area, be prepared for a tough walk. (Usually the best time to walk CRP fields is towards evening when the birds go back in there to rest.) That grass is a lot taller than you think and it is all wound up underneath and is just waiting to trip you! It is thick and hard to walk through. Be aware of that as you carry your shotgun through the field. And you can tell the guys not to walk so fast! Hunters do not have to RUN through CRP — take your time and enjoy it. And remember that if you are moving too quickly some pheasants may just stay put and let you walk on by. A slower hunt almost always ends up with more birds flushed.

You also have the option of hunting at a pheasant preserve. For a fee, you will have a good time and lots of shooting. Pheasant preserves, or game farms, can have a longer season than the regular state-regulated hunting season giving you more opportunity. Contact your wildlife agency to find the preserves in your area. The North American Gamebird Association publishes a directory of private-enterprise hunting resorts; order from www.harvest-1.com or send $3 to Wildlife Harvest, PO Box 96, Goose Lake, IA 52750.

Warne Ranches north of Pierre, South Dakota, can offer you outstanding bird hunting and are also very "women friendly." Pheasant hunting is done by hunting food plots of milo, sorghum and corn, adjacent to fields of waist-high grass. Patches of weeds and wild sunflower also provide excellent cover for pheasants, prairie chicken, sharptail grouse and Hungarian partridge. Cody Warne and his people will be your hosts and will transport you from Pierre. Accommodations will be in Pierre, only a few miles away so you can enjoy the nightlife also! Hunting groups can range in size from three to fifteen hunters for pheasants. They can also set you up with a combo hunt of upland game birds and waterfowl. They have wonderful land and I had a terrific hunt. Contact Warne Ranches at 29774 192 Street, Onida, SD 57564 or call 605-264-5325.

Hunting dogs play a large role in pheasant hunting. It is great to watch a good pointing dog (sniffs out the bird and then just "stands there" with his nose pointing at the bird, waiting for you to get there and shoot when the bird flies up). A hunting dog can be a wonderful companion, a great hunting asset for you, and most importantly, a terrific conservation tool. If you hunt in heavy cover with no dog, it could be impossible for you to find that downed bird. Or, if you would happen to cripple a bird, without a dog to retrieve it, you might never find it. Hunting in heavy cover is enhanced so very much by a hunting dog; depending on what could transpire, that dog could "save the day" and make the difference between a successful hunt and a long walk in the grass.

Pheasant hunting dogs come in all shapes and sizes. Some hunters prefer a Brittany Spaniel. According to those owners, the Brittany is bred to have the best pointing ability found in hunting dogs. They have the "best nose" for upland game and the ability to find the birds. I have hunted with Brittany Spaniels — some good and some bad. The good ones were a joy to hunt with. It was fun watching them point, enabling the hunter to get the shot. The bad ones were uncontrollable, running 200 yards out in front of the hunting line flushing birds too early and just generally ruining the hunt. However, that was not the dog's fault. It was the handler's/owner's fault. You can hunt the small areas without a dog, but for the large areas, you will not only want a dog, you will NEED one! Labrador retrievers (Labs) are most commonly bird flushers — not pointers. However, within the last 10 years, the pointing ability has been bred into them. It is great to watch them "get on point." After finding a bird, the dog actually freezes, pointing his nose at it and standing very still waiting for the command to "get him out of there." Other good pheasant hunting dogs include Springer Spaniels, German Shorthair Pointers, German Wirehair Pointers, English Pointers and Setters and just about any other dog that can be trained to find and retrieve the birds. Entire books have been written about each breed of dog and about successful dog training. Getting and training your own dog is a step in the direction of becoming an advanced hunter.

DRESS FOR UPLAND SUCCESS.

October hunting days can be warm and wonderful; they can also be

A good dog can sometimes mean the difference between a good day of hunting and getting skunked. Lori Goldade had the help of her yellow Lab to bring these birds to hand.

Pheasant hunting in the grasslands of South Dakota is often done with several people. Notice that everyone here is decked out in blaze orange. When the birds start flying, it's important to know exactly where everyone is. Orange clothing helps.

downright cold, blustery, wet and miserable. You must take the appropriate clothing and rain gear. Watching the weather is good, but you still don't really know what the weather has in store for you. You do not want to be caught with no warm clothing or rain gear and have to stop hunting. Be prepared for all kinds of temperatures and precipitation. Don't be dismayed if it snows when you are pheasant hunting — that makes it real easy to see their tracks and you can be more successful.

You do not need camo clothing for pheasant hunting. Of course, if you have it and that is your standard hunting gear, then wear it. A lot of hunters prefer the khaki-colored shirts and pants for upland game hunting. You should have some good quality brush pants (hunting pants with nylon or heavy canvas facing on the legs) as you will "put them through their paces" while upland bird hunting. Barbed wire, brambles and thorns can take their toll on your pants. The facing makes a world of difference while trudging through CRP and other tall weedy areas. The weeds, etc., that would normally catch on your pants just slide right off and that makes walking much easier.

As far as shirts are concerned, anything goes. Dress according to the weather. Layering is good; remember, you will be walking and working up a sweat so do not overdress. Wear your favorite hunting boots, jacket, cap, etc. REMEMBER THIS: BLAZE ORANGE SHOULD BE WORN FOR SAFETY'S SAKE! You can wear a T-shirt, sweatshirt, vest, cap, gloves, or jacket all of blaze, but a combination of a couple of items is the best way to go. Check with your state's regulations; some states mandate blaze orange be worn for upland game; other states just may suggest it. Whatever the regulations, be sure you have enough blaze orange on your person so you are very easily seen.

Lots of hunters prefer hunting vests. You usually shoot lots of shells while pheasant hunting and there are special pockets and elastic shell "holders" in those pockets. I prefer just to have all my shells in one big side pocket as then I can get them out faster and easier than if they were "stuck" in

elastic inside a pocket. Vests usually have a game carrier (big water-proof pocket) on the back of the vest for your birds. If, for some reason, you don't want to carry birds in your vest, you can purchase several different styles of game carriers; some have metal loops into which you place the birds' heads. Some are made with leather loops. Some styles hang off your belt and others sling over your shoulder. I do prefer hunting with a vest; and you can purchase them in various styles and colors.

I am very adamant about wearing blaze orange and I speak from personal experience. A large group of us were hunting a corn field in our river bottom. We had a huddle first and decided on who would be where and who would do what. I was one of the walkers and my nephew was to be one of the blockers. He was to stand on the river bank and shoot birds as they flew out of the corn (shooting up, of course, knowing we were in the corn). Many birds flew out of the corn and lots of shots were taken. As we neared the end of the field some more birds flew out and some guys were shooting. I did not shoot because I did not know just exactly where my nephew would be standing and I thought we were too close to the end of the field and the riverbank. I started to panic as I walked out of the corn and I could not see him. I saw the other blockers but I could not find him. I rapidly and nervously searched for him. It probably took only seconds but it seemed like an eternity until I saw him. He had on no blaze orange and I couldn't find him. The lesson was drilled in very effectively that day; everyone wears some blaze orange when pheasant hunting! While I was searching for him I had all kinds of bad scenarios flash in my head. Blaze orange must be worn so the shooters can easily identify the other hunters; blaze orange must be worn so YOU can be positive that everyone else can see YOU!

As for the rest of your clothing, use common sense and dress to be comfortable. You will be walking all of the time, so be sure you have the most comfortable boots with a lot of support. The first time I was invited on a large group hunt I did not have any hunting boots and wore my "work" western boots. They felt good and were comfortable for everything else, but they surely did not pass for hunting boots. I had hunting boots the next day! If you are hunting in the rain or a wet area, take that into account when you choose your boots. You may want to wear your "rubberized duck boots."

You must have your shotgun and shells chosen and ready for the hunt. Pheasant guns are a personal choice and there are many from which to choose. Refer to the "Firearms" chapter if you want some specifics about action styles and the like.

At one of the South Dakota Governor's Pheasant Hunts, a good friend of mine was on my team. He had just purchased a new "$1,000" gun and was bragging about it. My friend looked at my 20-gauge shotgun (I was carrying an antique Belgian Browning given to me by my mentor, Sig) with a condescending look and proceeded to extol the virtues of his new expensive gun. This went on and on. It didn't help that I had not been able to hit any birds in the first two walks. By the third walk I had it all together and really smacked a couple of birds. In fact, they were fantastic shots and I surprised myself. My friend was blocking at the end of the field and when I walked up to him he said, "By the way, forget what I said about you buying a new gun. I think yours will work just fine!"

I recommend a 20-gauge shotgun because they pack a lot of power, you can easily make a killing shot and they are light to carry. Remember, you will be walking all the time and you do not want to carry some big, heavy cannon around with you when a 20-gauge will suffice. Today there are many light-weight 12-gauge guns on the market and you may find one that is comparable in weight to a 20-gauge; if you like it, purchase it and then you will be set for every type of hunt.

Don't let anyone "embarrass" you into thinking only wimps shoot 20-gauge shotguns. I have talked with other women who have used them for decades for pheasants; I have spoken with many men who have used them forever and wouldn't think of carrying around a big 12-gauge to be "macho." Again, the main reasons for carrying a 20-gauge: they are light and they pack plenty of power. Also don't let anyone intimidate you into thinking you need a brand-new gun. There are plenty of good used guns out there, too. You just acquire what you need to get the job done and the heck with what anyone else thinks. You are not in the field to impress anyone; you are there to hunt, to have a great time in the outdoors and hopefully, bring home some birds for the table. And if you don't bring home birds, you will still be able to say you had a wonderful time in the field. Be yourself with your own type of equipment. You will be proud of yourself for just being out there!

Be sure to check the regulations concerning the type of shot you must use in your gun. You can use regular lead in most places on private land. Number 6 shot is the most commonly used shot size, but some hunters are fond of #5 and late-season hunters swear by #4 because it's heavier and will more effectively bring down birds that flush at longer ranges. Be prepared when you hunt public land as you must use non-toxic shot. Shooting with non-toxic shot (steel or bismuth shot) is different than shooting with lead. Here are some guidelines: for pheasants the best steel shot sizes are #2, #3 and #4. Number 4's (1 or 1 and one-eighth ounce) are very effective at the short ranges typical for much upland hunting. The #2's and #3's are better at longer ranges. Bismuth shots are much like lead, so use the same bismuth shot size as you would when shooting lead.

Steel shot patterns significantly tighter than lead, so most hunters have found that a modified or improved cylinder choke is the most effective for upland hunting with steel. Regulations state that steel, or other non-toxic shot, must be used on certain hunting areas because waterfowl pick at gravel and spent pellets to help digest their food and they can easily die of lead poisoning when lead pellets are ingested. Wounded birds often fall prey to eagles and other raptors. If the wound was caused by lead shot, the raptors who consume that bird can in turn die of lead poisoning. You might as well shoot with non-toxic shot everywhere you go; you will be protecting all birds everywhere and you won't have to remember where you need it and where you don't.

An important part of getting ready for your hunt is to secure a place to stay if you are traveling away from home. Motels fill up fast with a lot of people making reservations one year in advance. If you are planning to hunt in a "hot" pheasant zone, start making your reservations very early. Check with the local Chamber of Commerce as they sometimes will have lists of people who will rent rooms to hunters in private homes. The situation of staying in a private home can become the most fun part of the entire pheasant hunt! You will meet new friends that will mean a lot to you forever, so don't be disappointed if you find yourself in this situation.

THE HUNT

We have previously discussed the two methods to hunt: a big group, or hunting party, a small group or by yourself. Typically, when hunting in a large group, about half the hunters are walkers and the other half are blockers. The blockers take up positions at the end of a large field and the walkers "drive" the field working toward the blockers. Pheasants will sometimes run ahead of approaching hunters and stop when they get to the blockers. As the walkers approach, the birds get nervous and flush. Shooting at the end of the field, when the walkers and blockers meet can be fast and furious. Safety is very important. This type of hunting is what many people call a traditional pheasant hunt, and it was the only kind I was familiar with for a long time. When I was told to "go out and hunt by yourself. You'll like it," I couldn't believe it. I had never heard of anyone going out pheasant hunting alone. One day I wanted to go walk our corn field and no one else was available to go with me, so I decided to try this "pheasant hunting in solitude." Was I surprised — I loved it! You can go at your own pace, there is no one to keep up with, you can be extremely slow and quiet and really have good luck.

When you hunt alone work the small areas; go through the ditches, railroad tracks, small wetland areas and deserted farmsteads. Go slowly and quietly, not thrashing around; zig-zag through the area. If you have a dog with you let the dog work; believe in him, let him point, or if it is a flushing dog, follow him when he appears to be excited. When the bird flushes, you shoot. When you shoot, aim for the front half of

> *I recommend a 20-gauge shotgun because they pack a lot of power, you can easily make a killing shot and they are light to carry.*

the bird. Pheasants are not particularly fast, but many hunters shoot behind them. Lead the head, not the body, for a clean kill. Even though pheasants are not particularly fast, you will think they are in a situation like this: You are slowly walking along looking for birds and all of a sudden a rooster explodes out of the brush only a few feet in front of you. It takes a second for you to recover, (you've only jumped about 2 feet in the air) get your gun up, aim and shoot. By this time the bird can be too far away to connect for a clean kill and you've missed the shot. Eventually, you will learn to recover quickly, get that gun up and shoot immediately. But this "surprise explosion" is what keeps you on your toes. It can be a heart-pounding experience. You've got to be ready for birds which may fly in any direction. The surprise is part of the fun. I've heard many hunters say, "When I don't get excited at the flush of a pheasant, that's when I'll stop hunting."

This is important: When you do connect with a bird and he goes down, DO NOT TAKE YOUR EYES OFF THE SPOT WHERE HE LANDED! This is called "marking." This is especially important when you are hunting without a dog. Whether you are in a cornfield, wheat stubble or whatever, fallen birds can be very difficult to find. When you watch that bird go down, immediately walk to the "marked" spot, not taking your eyes off it. Even when you think you haven't taken your eyes off that spot, you may find the bird several feet away from where you thought it hit. You don't want to lose time by having to search for your bird, and most importantly, you do not want to lose any game. If you have lost track of the spot and cannot find the bird, place your hat on the spot where you think the bird hit and start walking in increasingly larger circles. Finding that downed bird is your responsibility. Diligently searching for every bird is part of being an ethical hunter.

Remember, in most places it is only roosters that you can shoot. Be sure you can identify a rooster from a hen. Sometimes it is very difficult to "ID" a hen due to the particular light. Many times I've had birds fly right up over my head, but because the sun was in my eyes, I could not ID the bird, so consequently I did not shoot. It is better to be careful than to be sorry. If you have no idea of what these birds will look like in flight then do some research before you carry a gun in the field. Watch videos, look at magazine pictures, or even walk a field without your gun before you actually go hunting so you know for sure how to ID those birds.

At all times, be cognizant of the fact that you are carrying a firearm and safety is the number one consideration. Leave that safety on as you walk in the field. You do not want to trip and have the gun accidentally fire. Obviously, you must be careful around other hunters. Hold the gun properly at all times, with the safety on. You will have time to click the safety off right before you shoot at a bird. Hold the barrel upright; never swing it around where it would be pointing at another person. Remember: always unload that shotgun before placing it in your vehicle! In most places you have to have your gun in a case in the vehicle. In the few places where you don't, remember: No shooting from the car window, or even allowing the barrel to protrude from the window. See your state regulations and just use common sense.

When hunting with a large group, there must be some organization. You will be hunting a relatively large area of land and a hunting plan must be identified. You will need to know how many hunters there are, what type of field you're to hunt, how many dogs will be with you and the correct amount of birds that can be shot. Most importantly, you will need to know where people will be. When you know where people will be you can be sure never to point a gun in that direction. Make sure everyone has on blaze orange. After it is decided who will be walking and who will be blocking or posting at the end of the field, then discuss the rule that no one shoots at a dangerous level. It is usually safe to shoot upwards at a 45-degree angle, but not always. Be safe. All shots must be aimed upwards, away from the blockers at the end. The blockers must also be told to shoot away from the walkers that are coming toward them. No one should shoot too low.

I suffered through a bad experience one time when the walkers did not remember shooting safety and shot low. I was blocking at the end of a huge CRP field, standing on a creek bank with others on either side of me. We heard shooting from the field and instantly heard the tree leaves rattling behind our heads. Knowing that someone was shooting low, we hit the ground in anticipation of more pellets headed our way. That was a terrifying moment and I never want to experience it again. The shooters received a good "talking to" and everyone learned from that. A lot of shooting accidents happen during upland game hunting, so just be careful and respect your firearm and other hunters.

If the area your hunting party is going to hunt is very large, then split it in sections and work one section at a time using walkers and blockers. Work each section like that. You may want to cover the same area two or three times. When I say the birds sit tight, I mean just that. Sometimes you almost have to step on them to get them to move. Here's another "nephew" story: There were about six of us hunting our alfalfa field near the farm. We were all in a row, keeping track of each other. I had a cold at the time and really needed to stop and blow my nose (I have since learned to "blow on the go") so I ordered "Halt!" When I was finished we all proceeded to discuss the situation, the birds, etc. We all stood in place, no one really moving. As we finally decided to push forward, no more than 5 inches away from my nephew's foot a rooster just exploded in a cloud of dust, wings loudly beating and his cackle echoing in our ears. We had taken a break, stood there all that time and that rooster had held tight just inches away from my nephew. You never know where they are (especially without a dog — we did not have one that day) or when they will surprise you. That is why it can be a good idea to cover your area a second time.

Be courteous to all the hunters with you. If you are walking down a corn strip, the shooting can be best off to the side as the birds fly out of the corn. Take turns with that position; do not think you must have the best position at all

> # Remember, in most places it is only roosters that you can shoot.

> # When hunting with a large group, there must be some organization.

times. You will want to keep your hunting buddies and being a "game hog" or "position hog" is the fastest way to lose those good friends. Make sure each hunter has a chance to shoot his/her fair share of birds. Hunters who are better shots than others should defer their shots to those who have not yet shot their limit.

Remember to be courteous to the landowner and respect the land. If you are walking through an unharvested corn field be sure to treat the corn carefully. Do not go barging through it and break it down. The same applies for other crop land you may hunt.

As you are walking down the corn rows or CRP, space yourselves out appropriately. Depending on how many hunters and how much land and the number of dogs along, have a good amount of space in between each hunter. Each person should have her own space and alley for shooting. If you do not have a dog with you, then you will want to be closer together. I'd recommend about 30 feet. If you have dogs, then close to 60 feet should work. If you have safety in mind, have done all the planning, and are walking through or blocking a pheasant field, you'll have some chances to shoot. You will also have a great time and will fall in love with the elusive beautiful ring-necked pheasant!

There are different methods of hunting pheasants, different areas, different fields and different habitat. You can have fun discovering them all and enjoy them all. Only when safety is in question may there be a situation that "isn't so fun."

While hunting at a pheasant preserve, we found the corn rows to be completely devoid of birds. The owner and dog handlers told us that the birds would be at the end of the corn strip, sitting tight in the 20-foot weed patch and would explode out of there as we approached. We walkers slowed down, anticipating this "rush" of birds and shooting. When we got to the end, between the walkers and the blockers, it sounded like a war zone and pheasants were dropping all over the place. It was interesting and exciting, but I found it very scary to have every hunter there shooting at the same birds all at the same time. I then found out what "pheasant hamburger" was! It was ground up before the bird fell out of the sky.

Here are some other options: Hunting can be good in the evening before roosting time in the rushes. Some of the best pheasant hunting can take place later in the season. The weather is cooler and the "hoopla" of opening weekend is over. Snow hunting can really be fun. The birds are more visible and it is fun to track them in the snow. If the birds haven't been hunted for a while, they will be less "spooky" and you will have better luck. You may have to work heavy cover areas quite hard to get the birds to flush, but that is where they will be in the winter. Dress accordingly so you are comfortable during snow hunting. Layering is best. Because of changing weather conditions during the winter season, it is a good idea to have a cell phone along with you for emergency purposes and be sure to put your vehicle keys in a safe place!

A good day. The author, front left, gathers with her hunting companions and a tired dog to show off the birds.

AFTER THE HUNT

If you are transporting birds to take home with you, check your state regulations and see just how you are to have them cleaned and if you must leave the head on, certain feathers on, etc. The regulations will be found in a pamphlet provided by the state. Read them carefully and abide by them. Refer to the Wild Turkey Hunting chapter for field dressing birds. If you hunt at a pheasant game farm or preserve the cleaning will be done for you.

If you are thinking of having the bird mounted, it can be done in many ways — flying, standing, enclosed in glass coffee tables, as a head or neck mount, etc. This bird might very well be the most beautiful you will ever acquire. To have a good looking mount as your goal, use these tips from Arnie Goldade, my friend and taxidermist: "Before you go hunting, put a paper bag and cotton balls into your hunting vest—plug the bird's mouth with the cotton balls so there is no blood on the feathers, wipe off any excess blood with a damp cotton ball, smooth all feathers down against the body, put the bird in paper bag until all body heat is gone (which could take several hours). If the bird is wet, dry it immediately and before putting it in a bag. After the body heat is gone, seal tightly in a plastic bag (tail feathers can stick out if necessary); fold a piece of cardboard long enough to protect tail feathers and wrap around the bird. NEVER gut the bird; keep the bird cool and freeze it as soon as possible."

You must treat the bird carefully while transporting him home from the field. Do not ring the neck or ruffle the feathers. Do not pile the birds up. What usually happens is that all the hunters throw their birds right into the back end of a pickup. If you are going to mount your bird, KEEP IT SEPARATE! Do not pile up the birds. Pheasants have a very high body temperature and they tend to start disintegrating immediately. Keep your bird where no one else can handle it. Also keep the blood off of the feathers.

Kevin Jorgenson, another taxidermist friend says, "The tail feathers are very important and you must keep them intact. The longer and straighter the tail feathers are, the more attractive the pheasant mount. The tail feathers cannot be restored, so treat them very carefully. If you cannot get the bird to the taxidermist immediately, you must freeze it. Wrap the head in paper towels and tuck it under a wing. Wrap him in a plastic bag and tie it tightly shut so no air can seep into the bag. Lay him flat in the freezer and keep him there until it's time for the trip to the taxidermist."

If you have forgotten to bring a paper bag, cotton balls, plastic bags or other gear with you, here is a tip: place the bird into a sock, head first. Make a small hole in the end for the beak (especially for waterfowl). When you get home, go through the other steps to freeze the bird; when you arrive at the taxidermists, he can just cut the sock off the bird. Throw an old pair of socks in your backpack and leave them there; you will always be prepared.

To clean and restore the luster to the feathers of your mount, dust with a feather duster first, then spray the duster with a little WD-40. That will bring back the brilliant colors and the sheen.

As previously mentioned, pheasant feathers are a hot commodity. If you do not want a bird mounted, you can still enjoy your trophy by crafting items using the beautiful feathers. Ask your taxidermist, ask your craft store people, or even talk to an artist for ideas. Pheasant-feather picture frames are becoming very popular. My favorite is a picture of a hunting dog holding a bird in his mouth and the entire picture is tastefully framed with pheasant feathers. You will likely have your camera with you and pheasant hunting pictures are a must. A nice trophy and reminder of the hunt is an enlarged good quality picture of yourself and the birds in the field, or a group picture of your hunting team, and frame it with pheasant feathers. Use your imagination; you can have fun creating your own personal ideas that will become a very special trophy.

Pheasant hunting can be one of the most fun hunts you will ever have. It is a very social type of hunt with lots of fellowship, and that means lots of new friends, stories, laughter, and new opportunities and many wonderful memories. A good way to prepare is to go to your local shooting range or gun club and go trap shooting. Besides sharpening your shooting skills and practicing up for the hunt, you may meet more new friends and that may mean new places in which to hunt. Take advantage of every opportunity that knocks on your door. If that door is open a crack, then crash your body through it and go for it. You want to experience all there is out there in the hunting world, so don't let it pass you by!

Pheasants can be found in a variety of cover types and the hunting can be both tough and exciting. The author bagged this nice bird by pounding through the dense cover behind her. (Photo by Ron Spomer)

You can meet new friends, have fun and do your part for pheasant habitat restoration by joining Pheasants Forever (PF). PF is a nonprofit conservation organization founded in 1982 in response to the decline of the ring-necked pheasant population. PF is dedicated to the protection and enhancement of pheasants and other wildlife populations in North America through habitat improvement, public awareness and education, and land management that benefits farmers and wildlife alike. Pheasants Forever is fortified by a unique system of county chapters that provides an incentive for sportsmen and women to raise money: 100 percent of the net funds raised by chapters remains at the chapter level for local habitat projects.

Mourning doves are popular and difficult targets. It takes a skilled shooter to bag a limit of doves.

A typical habitat restoration program includes elements of the following: nesting cover renovations, winter cover plantings of windbreaks and hedgerows, food plot establishments, wetland restorations and land acquisitions. In 13 years PF has spent more than $35 million on habitat projects alone, encompassing more than 1 million acres in North America. Pheasants Forever has 81,000 members.

In addition to various Pheasants Forever publications and other public awareness programs, the organization developed an innovative youth education program called Ringnecks. Complete with its own publication, *Ringnecks*, and an educational curriculum, the youth program is helping ensure the continuation of our nation's hunting and outdoor legacy.

In the South Dakota pheasant world, youth are taking over the spotlight. A couple of terrific ideas will go a long way to ensure our hunting heritage is continued. In an unprecedented move, South Dakota Pheasants Forever developed a tract of land exclusively for youth pheasant hunters. These 160 acres in central South Dakota will provide a safe place for youth pheasant hunting. Adults can only supervise youth and are not allowed to carry a gun. Hunting is open to licensed youth

between the ages of 12 and 16 years of age. Pheasants Forever members volunteer to supervise youngsters who want to hunt but don't have anyone to go with them. The local chapter cooperated with the South Dakota Game, Fish and Parks Department to achieve their goal. In a move to attract youngsters to pheasant hunting, the Game, Fish and Parks Commission approved a special youth pheasant hunt set for the weekend before the regular season opener. Check to see if your state sponsors projects like these. If they do not, maybe you can be the catalyst to get them started.

For information on Pheasants Forever, call 651-773-2000 or visit the Web site at www.pheasantsforever.org.

Close your eyes, dream of a beautiful, warm and sunny October day. You have your good friends with you, a good bird dog is ready to work, and you have just met a new landowner friend who has graciously let you hunt on his land. After a huddle where safety is the number one topic, you all start out with your plan. You tromp through the field, birds fly up, you take some shots. Some connect, some miss. You are having fun being in the outdoors, walking, shooting, watching your friends and the dog. As you bend down to pick up one of the birds you have bagged, you give thanks for this wonderful opportunity. You admire the beautiful ring-necked pheasant — one of the most gorgeous of God's creations. Tears well up in your eyes as you turn the bird over, inspecting every inch of him and give thanks again for such a beautiful creature. The hunt is over, the friends gather for socializing and sharing stories of "their shots." When you slide under your covers that night, you have a satisfied smile on your face and tell yourself, "I did it!"

Yes, you did. Another experience, another memory, another story, another completed opportunity.

MOURNING DOVES

"We're gonna do WHAT?" In the very dawn of my hunting career, my two game warden/mentors called and told me to get ready because it was time for me to learn how to hunt mourning doves. I really didn't know anything about doves or how you hunt them, other than picking up a few pointers here and there in hunting conversations. Well, after the fun I had that first time, I'm always ready to go after them now.

The guys picked me up towards evening and we drove only a short distance from the farm. I laughed as I watched the folding chairs and coolers being unloaded from the pickup, wondering just exactly what all would transpire. I was informed I would be shown how to hunt doves "Tennessee style." We drove up a fence line, unloaded the gear, then parked the pickup back near the road. The fence line, full of weeds and brush, divided two fields. We set up in a millet field (doves' favorite) a short distance from the fence line. There was a corn field on the other side. We had a perfect place as we would intercept the birds as they flew over our heads from one field to another.

It was the craziest sight I'd ever seen in a hunting field. Here was Lee Leuning, perched on his folding chair in the millet, cooler beside him, shooting doves right and left. He'd take a can of soda out of the cooler every once in a while but the cooler's purpose really was to hold all the birds and keep them cool. That cooler lid was being constantly flipped up and down. Lee was a great shot. After I settled down and realized he wasn't kidding, this really was his way of hunting doves, I decided I'd better take this more seriously. So, I positioned my chair a small distance from Lee and started shooting. I was no match for those guys! The doves fell right and left. With a limit of 15 doves each, the cooler filled in a hurry. I did connect with a few and was proud I had hit them!

Doves are small, fast, turn sharply, do "loop the loops" and anything else you can imagine while they are flying. They are hard to hit. Dove hunting is a humbling experience. You can be an expert on the trap range, but it's a whole different story when you are in the dove field.

With the cooler full and sunset coming on, it was time to go back home to the farm. Lee had promised he would prepare the doves and grill them for our dinner—that I would have to see! He cleaned and skinned the doves and rummaged through my kitchen finding all sorts of items in which to marinate them before cooking. Whatever he found was right — those doves were absolutely delicious! Of course, we had to try different dipping sauces, etc. The entire episode was great! Learning how to hunt them, learning how well a person has to shoot to get one, being thrilled when you can shoot a few, then dining exquisitely on them all added up to a tremendous time. I have been hooked on dove hunting since. Besides being fun, it is the best practice you can have at shooting. Dove season opens several weeks before waterfowl hunting and a full month or more before the upland seasons, so you will have many opportunities to "practice for the big stuff."

GETTING TO KNOW YOU

Mourning doves are small, sandy or buff-colored birds, with iridescent green and pink feathers. They have a long pointed tail bordered with white. They like to sit on telephone and power wires and fences; with their long tails they are easy to spot. Their habitat includes open fields (millet is their favorite food) and they will also frequent parks and lawns with many trees and shrubs. Doves are common in rural areas in all parts of the United States. In some states doves can be hunted and they are classified as "game birds." Some other states protect doves as "songbirds." BE SURE TO CHECK YOUR STATE REGULATIONS CONCERNING DOVE HUNTING!

The mourning dove is unforgettable because of its call. It is a low, mournful coo-ah, coo, coo, coo. I remember when I was a child on my parents' farm and first heard the mourning dove. I didn't know what it was at that time but I had fun imitating it and would have several calling back to me for what seemed like hours. I had fun doing that, but later found out how good they taste! There are always a lot of doves around both our farm and the lake cabin and I still enjoy calling back to them and listening to how long they will actually call back to me before getting bored.

GETTING READY

The first thing you need to do is check your state regulations concerning dove hunting. If it is allowed, then obtain all the necessary licenses, etc. If it is not allowed, check with other states' wildlife agencies and perhaps you can travel there to hunt. Be sure to check out the bag limit.

Before the dove hunting season starts, take the time to shoot clay targets. You can do it at the local trap range or you can buy an inexpensive thrower and a box of targets and practice with a friend. "Practice makes perfect."

Considering all types of hunting, dove hunting probably requires the least preparation time. Since doves are found anywhere and everywhere, obtaining permission should be fairly simple. Look for doves in millet fields, in corn fields, and by water holes. They also like cut alfalfa fields and that is good to hunt because if the farmer hasn't already moved his bales, you can use those to hide behind as the doves approach. Other than that, you don't really need any blinds. If you find a watering hole on a farmstead, set up between the water and any trees. Doves will probably be flying back and forth, especially near sunset. The birds always go for a drink before they roost for the evening.

As far as hunting clothes are concerned, you really don't need any. Since the season is during warm weather it's easy to dress for dove hunting. You don't have to have camo clothing, but certainly wear it if you've got it. You can wear jeans, a T-shirt and tennis shoes, or even wear shorts if you want to — the doves don't care! You will want a cap to cut the glare of the sun, and don't forget the mosquito repellent because early-season dove hunting is done in warm weather.

Because you must swing and shoot fast for doves, I prefer a light-weight shotgun. A light-weight gun makes shooting and swinging easier and you need all the help you can get when dove hunting. For just starting, I recommend a 20-gauge with #7 or #8 lead shotgun shells. If you are shooting a light 12-gauge shotgun, #7-1/2 works great with an improved cylinder choke. Remember to check non-toxic shot regulations when hunting on public land. If you are using steel shot, use #6 steel. Because the dove is such a small bird and you may be shooting at some distance, use the modified or improved cylinder choke in your gun, for either lead or steel. The birds are hard to hit and you'll want a wide pattern when you shoot.

Take plenty of ammunition with you. I take at least one box of shells. If you are just starting out, take two boxes of shells. The bag limit in South Dakota is 15 and you have to be a darn good shooter to get your limit. Most dove hunters shoot seven rounds (shells) for every bird in the bag. Dove hunting is very humbling — it will take lots of shots to fill that cooler. That's why it is such good practice for waterfowl hunting and pheasant hunting.

You will want something to sit on out in the field. Folding chairs are awkward and heavy. Lawn chairs are not conducive for shooting. I love my little folding hunting stool and recommend you purchase one of those. They have a shoulder strap and are very easy to carry and move around. Just don't place the legs in mud!

Take a cooler with you. You will be hunting in warm weather and will appreciate a soda pop or ice water. You will also want to put your birds in the cooler as you bag them.

DECOYS

Using decoys is a personal decision. I have hunted dove with them and without them and haven't really noticed any great difference. This is how we used the full body plastic decoys: We had six or eight of them and stapled them (heavy staples) to a small narrow board, placing the doves a few inches apart. Then fasten the board to an 8- or 10-foot pole of some kind (we used an old TV antenna pole). When you leave to go hunt, be sure to take some type of a pointed stake with you to punch the hole in the ground for the pole. This works especially well if you are beside trees; the doves will swoop in beside the decoy pole to check out their "friends." You can also set the pole in a fence line or wherever else you think it will attract the doves. Just setting the decoys on top of a bale of hay works, too. If it is windy, make a little hole in the hay and place the bottom 2-inch fastener into the hole. That will make doves anxious to check out their buddies on top of the bale. The doves then will come flying straight at you and that is a good shot. You can also place decoys on a fence wire or bare branches of a tree.

Silhouette decoys are also available. These are state-of-the-art decoys and the best ones I've seen are available from the Outlaw Company. They're a photograph screen-printed on heavy-duty vinyl and come with a clothespin attached to the backside so you can just clip them on wire fences, branches, etc. These decoys are very easy to carry and very simple to use. Just imagine, you can clip a dozen of these on a fence line between a millet field and another field or a water hole, and just sit there and shoot to your heart's content!

Late afternoon or early evening is the best time to hunt doves. They like the water holes at that time and also will be flying in and out of fields. The time schedule is great as you won't have to take any time off work to dove hunt! If you know where the roost trees are, be there just before sunset. The doves will flock in as the sun drops and you will have great shooting.

The dove season starts in South Dakota on September 1. Nine times out of 10, Murphy's Law appears on August 31. It can be very hot with lots of doves around everywhere until the night before dove season opener. For some strange reason the weather will suddenly cool off just that evening and the birds will begin their migration and disappear. Don't get impatient, though. Warm weather returns and so do the doves. Although it can be a very short season, I have hunted doves up here through the middle of September.

THE HUNT

You are all ready to have a "blast" in the field. Take your gear and get set up in your chosen area. After a few minutes, when things have settled down, the doves will start flying. You will be amazed at the acrobatic antics of these birds. As you shoot, you have to lead them by maybe a foot, maybe more. You will think you are right on and ready to score a direct hit, but whoops, the dove fooled you and went into a steep dive. When another one comes within shooting range you think you have that all figured out and antici-pate this bird diving, but nope, he decides on a 180-degree turn as he swoops upwards! While shooting, remember to swing through them with your shotgun — don't stop your swing and squeeze the trigger or you will be consistently shoot-ing behind them. (This is a rule to remember for all types of birds you are hunting.)

Remember to mark the spot where the dove has fallen when you shoot it. Doves are small and very difficult-to-find in any type of field. Again, it is your responsibility as a hunter to find all the game and you must mark the spot in order to do that.

If you are hunting with other people, always be aware of each shooting alley. Dove hunting can get exciting as the birds are flying all different directions. Don't forget to be safe! Set up those alleys beforehand and keep reminding each other of the safety factor. It is very easy to be swinging on a bird, caught up in the moment, and forget you are beyond your shooting alley. Be careful when picking up a fallen dove; the doves will still keep flying even though you are walking around. The other shooters must be aware of this and you must have the rule of no shooting when out picking up birds.

Get those birds into the cooler right away. It will be warm out and you want to keep them in the best condition possible until you return home.

Pick up your empty shells when you are finished hunting. The farmer doesn't want to get to his field and see a moun-tain of shotgun shells. Leave his field in the same condition you found it.

AFTER THE HUNT

Of course, you will want pictures. The doves are so small that they do not show up very well in pictures. Lay them out on the ground in a pattern or a straight line. They should all be lying the same direction, facing the same way for the best pic-ture. I hunted doves recently with my taxidermist friend, Kevin Jorgenson, and his young boys. They insisted on holding the birds for the pictures — they thought a "bunch" of them would look more impressive! After I heard Tim, the 11-year-old first-

Even the author's mother found that she liked dove hunting Ten-nessee-style. Often times you can hunt doves in shirt-sleeve weath-er while relaxing on a chair near prime dove habitat.

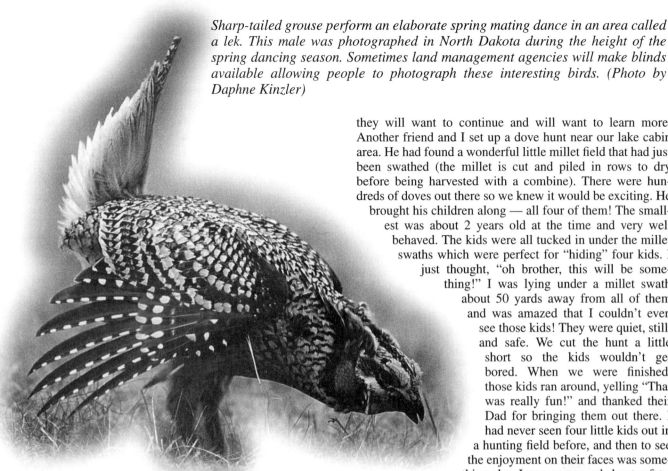

Sharp-tailed grouse perform an elaborate spring mating dance in an area called a lek. This male was photographed in North Dakota during the height of the spring dancing season. Sometimes land management agencies will make blinds available allowing people to photograph these interesting birds. (Photo by Daphne Kinzler)

they will want to continue and will want to learn more. Another friend and I set up a dove hunt near our lake cabin area. He had found a wonderful little millet field that had just been swathed (the millet is cut and piled in rows to dry before being harvested with a combine). There were hundreds of doves out there so we knew it would be exciting. He brought his children along — all four of them! The smallest was about 2 years old at the time and very well behaved. The kids were all tucked in under the millet swaths which were perfect for "hiding" four kids. I just thought, "oh brother, this will be something!" I was lying under a millet swath about 50 yards away from all of them and was amazed that I couldn't even see those kids! They were quiet, still, and safe. We cut the hunt a little short so the kids wouldn't get bored. When we were finished, those kids ran around, yelling "That was really fun!" and thanked their Dad for bringing them out there. I had never seen four little kids out in a hunting field before, and then to see the enjoyment on their faces was something else. I was concerned about safety, but they did what their Dad told them to do and they loved it.

Dove hunting can be fun for others — not necessarily hunters — to tag along with you. After I told my mother about my first "Tennessee-style" dove hunt, she thought it sounded like fun (she is not a hunter but grew up on a farm and in the outdoors). I invited her to come along and she accepted readily. For the fun of it, I dressed her all up in camo and we took off. It was a beautiful evening, the birds flew, I connected with a few and Mom had a ball! It certainly can be a "family affair." That was another unforgettable memory and a story to share forever. That is the only time my mother was ever out in the field with me and some special bonding took place.

Dove hunting is another opportunity for you. It's fun, it's exciting, you can improve your shooting, you can have fun with your family and friends, and you can devour these tasty birds that you bring home.

SHARP-TAILED GROUSE

"You better have your legs in shape and your best walking/hunting boots ready!" THAT was the truth! A couple of my friends wanted to introduce me to sharp-tailed grouse hunting in western South Dakota a few years ago and that statement started and finished the initial conversation. Truer words were never spoken! When the day was over, I felt like I had walked all around the world!

These birds inhabit the expansive grasslands of the west and yes, you certainly have to walk to hunt them. As we started out, with a very well-trained dog in tow (you do not necessarily need a dog to hunt grouse), I looked around me

timer, shot 10 doves out of only 20 shells, I didn't argue with them! Little 5-year-old Buck was the "gopher" and dove picker in the field; he wanted to hold his picked birds for the picture. I couldn't refuse his huge grin and the pride in his eyes! "JD" contributed to the hunt by being a dog handler at the other end of the field, and also bagging some doves. These kids have a terrific hunting future ahead!

When you arrive home, skin those doves ASAP or just filet the breasts (cut the breast meat away from the breast bone and peel the skin off). You can marinate them, put them on the grill with just butter, or bake them in the oven. However you fix them, doves are delicious. You will never find a more exotic hors d'oeuvre on a cracker, either!

Can you mount doves? Yes, you can. They are a pretty bird and if you want to keep them forever, that's fine. Two or three doves in flying position mounted on a piece of driftwood would be very attractive. They are yours; you earned them, believe me!

Dove hunting is a good way to get kids in the field and interested in hunting. The weather is warm, they can hunt after school, the action is non-stop and it is good shooting practice for youngsters. In addition to that, they can easily learn how to skin the birds and help prepare them for dinner.

The Arizona game commission approved a youth dove hunt several years ago. It was extremely successful and they received many thank-you letters. In one of those letters, a young girl stated that she was "so glad to have been able to hunt doves because it was more fun than going to Disneyland!" This is how we have to "hook" kids on hunting — make it so exciting in every aspect, make it so attractive that and all I could see was grassland, rolling, flattening, rolling again and then flowing into the horizon. When I received the answer to my question of "how far do we walk and where are we going?" it was just belly laughs! I just thought, "OK, I'll keep up with them!" I had been told sharp-tailed grouse hunting is a lot like pheasant hunting — only it takes place in a "bigger world." I remembered how pheasants flush, making your heart stop as they fly out in front of you, so I thought I was ready.

We walked the first half mile and found no birds. So we walked some more. No birds. By that time, the mind begins to wander and daydreaming can set in. That's when the first explosion occurred — a couple of sharp-tails flushed out just ahead of us! Was I ready? NO! Needless to say, my shots did not connect. I vowed I would pay more attention and be ready, but the country was so beautiful, it was a gorgeous day, and when all I could see was grassland in every direction, I had a good time just walking, really relaxing and enjoying just being there.

It was finally drilled into me to be ready at all times; no longer was I going to be daydreaming and miss shots. I turned into a hunting machine and worked my eyes back and forth, searching for the elusive grouse and expecting them at any second, my shotgun at the ready. It worked! I connected

Sharp-tailed grouse are birds of the grasslands. They prefer cover that is not quite as thick as that frequented by pheasants. The author shows a prime specimen taken in central South Dakota. When you hunt sharptails, get ready to walk.

with birds that day and was so proud that I had learned something new and proved to myself that I could do it!

Yes, we walked our legs off and I'm certainly glad I had on my most comfortable boots or I never would have made it through the day. But this was really a fun hunt! And there were birds to take home! Sharp-tailed grouse is wonderful on the dinner table. You will love it — especially if you bag your own for the first time!

GETTING TO KNOW YOU

The sharp-tailed grouse is named for the sharp tail feathers that stretch out beyond the rest of its short tail. They are pretty birds, mainly light brown with black and white speckles. They have a short tail which is white underneath (in flight this distinguishes the sharp-tail from the ruffed grouse) and weigh slightly less than 2 pounds. The male has a yellow comb over the eyes, but you can't usually see this as the bird flies.

Sharp-tails inhabit the northern plains states and range up into Canada. There are not very many east of the Mississippi River anymore. They are native to short- and mid-grass prairie lands. Depending on what region they are in, some like the open grassy areas and others prefer brushy areas. (They like the open grasslands in South Dakota and prefer brushy draws in Montana.) Winter is the only time they will be found in heavy cover.

The diet of the sharp-tailed grouse includes plant material and insects. Spring and summer they will devour mostly insects along with flowers, leaves, seeds and fruits. In the fall their diet consists mostly of native seeds like poison ivy berries (wear gloves when you clean these birds in case they have been eating these berries!), rose hips, cedar berries, cottonwood buds, etc. They also like grasshoppers and sunflower fields (when the flowers are ripe). Sharp-tailed grouse can also be found in alfalfa fields in the fall as the plants are green until frost.

Scott Glup, with the U.S. Fish and Wildlife Service at Sand Lake National Wildlife Refuge near my home, says, "The sharp-tailed grouse has a 'blind gut'— it's an extra little appendage in its intestine that harbors some bacteria that allows it to break down and utilize foods that other species, such as a pheasant, cannot utilize." (A pheasant would starve to death if he had a full crop of these 'other' foods.)

Sharp-tails are great flyers. As opposed to the pheasant that makes short flights, sharp-tails can fly for miles. Their roosting area can be farther away from their food source than can pheasants. Their mobility has allowed them to survive out on the plains. Following their spring dancing/breeding rituals, the young hatch out in June with an average of 13 to 15 eggs.

The sharp-tailed grouse is a fascinating creature and, similar to the prairie chicken, puts on quite a performance during the mating ritual in the early spring. To attract breeding hens to them, the males fly to an area known as a "lek" — their "stage" or dancing grounds before dawn. They proceed to dance around, stomp the ground rapidly while turning and flapping their wings while making a "cooing" sound. They will continue dancing for several hours if undisturbed. Dancing grounds are usually found on a knob or knoll, so the birds have good visibility. They use the same lek year after year. When the female is drawn near the lek, the dancing becomes more frantic! She picks the male of her choice and lets him breed her! (Yes, this is still grouse we're talking about!) After being bred, she looks for a nesting site, usually close to the lek. Following the beginning of nesting, the dancing ritual concludes.

What better entertainment and show could Mother Nature offer? This is a most fascinating display and you can be there and watch this production yourself. The U.S. Forest Service manages the National Grasslands and sometimes has blinds set up near leks, just for the purpose of observing this ritual. Contact them or your wildlife agency to find out where to go and what to do. Just imagine: You are sitting in a blind before dawn, you hear grouse flying in, then the dance begins in front of you with its own special music and erotic actions. Soon, the females approach, the dancing and sounds increase to a frenzy, and while the females are being bred, you are trying to keep your heart still. This show, my fellow nature lovers, is a MUST!

GETTING READY

For all the items you will need to hunt sharp-tailed grouse, please refer to "Getting Ready" in the pheasant section. The same clothing, guns, etc., also applies here. You will be doing a lot of walking, so be sure you wear your most comfortable boots — do not try to "break in" your boots during a hunt! You will not be walking and hunting in heavy cover so you do not need brush pants — regular hunting pants or jeans are fine. Remember the blaze orange items you will need to wear.

As far as equipment, and especially guns are concerned, Scott Glup recommends, "Go as light as you can. You will be walking a lot and you don't want anything heavy to carry. Use a light gun and a light load. Either a 12-gauge or 20-gauge is fine; I would prefer the 20-gauge shotgun as it is lighter. Use #4 steel or #6 lead shot. When hit and on the ground, sharp-tails don't run and hide the way pheasants do. Instead, they flop around and are easy to see. They are easy to bring down so you don't need a heavy shell (unless the shooting distance is longer during winter hunting)."

Refer to the chapter, "Finding a Place to Hunt." Since sharp-tails inhabit mostly grasslands and a lot of that type of land is public, it is easy to find a place to hunt; school and public lands are a great place to find sharp-tails. Besides the grasslands, sharp-tails like ripe sunflower fields and alfalfa fields in the fall (those will be private land so be sure to ask permission).

THE HUNT

The sharp-tailed grouse season starts in mid-September. They are still in small groups and sit tight during this time. In late November they can form flocks of 50 to 300 birds, making it a tough hunt. Earlier in the season you may flush the same group several times; late winter they will fly out of sight across the horizon. While you are walking the fields or grasslands there can be long lulls in-

A bird in the hand... that old saying was certainly coined by someone hunting ruffed grouse. The birds flush explosively from dense cover and can be a true test of shooting skill. It's no wonder they are called the king of game birds.

between bird flushes (causing daydreaming!), or there can be many flushes in a short period of time. Either way, you must be expecting them and be ready. It is not necessary to have a dog in order to hunt sharp-tails. Some hunters think it is better without a dog because it sharpens your senses — you are not completely dependent upon the dog to flush them — YOU need to pay attention.

Scott Glup says, "The best places to hunt will be the native grasslands. If you find one near an alfalfa field or sunflower field that's a good place. Typically what grouse will do in the morning is fly out to feed. They are usually roosting way back in the grass and fly a long ways to go feed. After they've finished feeding and are flying back, they generally don't fly way back where they are roosting, they fly to the edge of the grassland they are living in. So by mid-morning when they are starting back, a good place to hunt is those edges, next to the alfalfa fields, etc., but still in the grass part. They will loaf there all day and work back out to feed in the evening. So if you find big blocks of grassland, the best place to hunt sharp-tails is on the edge of those."

Scott adds, "Grouse don't like wind, so they stay out of it unless it's a very hot day and they can catch a breeze on the top of a knob. If it's a wet, drizzly, awful day, don't even bother to hunt grouse. They don't like to get wet or sit in wet cover so they sit right on top of the hills and it's hard to even get close to them — they can see you coming forever! If you are hunting in choppy hills, early in the

season when it's still rather hot and sunny, they will be on the northeast-facing slope of the hill because there is usually more cover there for shade and a little more moisture — that's a really good place to hunt. If you really want to see the grouse move, be out there at dawn and dusk when they are moving to feed. Another good place to hunt is near their lek — look for feathers."

The actual hunting of grouse consists of walking grasslands and/or fields and flushing birds. You will want to have practiced shooting so you have the best chance of connecting with birds. Remember to be safe when you are with other hunters; the surprising flushing can unnerve you and cause you to lose concentration. As with pheasant hunting, hunters line up horizontally and walk through the field. Know your shooting alleys.

When you are hunting on these large expanses of grasslands, you may hunt all day and not see another hunter. There is little pressure because of few grouse hunters so you can have a wonderful time thinking you are the only person in the entire world. This is another great opportunity for you. Not only can you have fun hunting and being surprised when they flush, you will bag a few and have some great eating. On top of that, you can see the "nature show of a lifetime" on their dancing grounds in the spring.

RUFFED GROUSE

"There he is!"

"Where?"

"There. Right there in that tree!"

"Where? I still don't see him!"

"Right there in the crotch of this tree! See his head sticking out?"

With our shotguns at the ready, My hunting partner and I move forward a bit. Lila finally yells, "I see him!" As the bird flushes it sounds like a small motor revving up as the bird takes off from the tree and soars into the thick brush 20 yards in front of us completely untouched by our shots. Kevin orders Echo, the yellow Lab, after the bird to make sure it was not hit, then turns around and yells at us, "Just SHOOT! You don't have time to DISCUSS IT!"

"Yes, I know we should have shot," I say, "but I was being polite and wanted to show Lila the bird so she would have a chance to shoot, too, and then when I had a chance, there were trees in the way!"

"You just have to shoot. You are using a light load with lots of pellets and some of those will get through the trees and hit that bird. If you have a shot, take it, quickly!"

And so it went, another on-the-spot lesson in ruffed grouse hunting in Wisconsin. Kevin Michalowski, my book editor at Krause Publications, had invited Lila Antonides, my deer hunting buddy, and I to a special ruffed grouse hunt in the northern Wisconsin woods. Never having hunted those birds before, we both jumped at the chance. Kevin's in-laws have a unique and quaint homestead nestled in a beautiful hardwood forest. It was used as our hunt headquarters. It came complete with colorful neighbors — specifically Ben, who graciously welcomed us, gave us hunting directions and even "helped" us hunt one afternoon. (I've never seen a man move through the woods like that. I literally could not keep up!)

"Just SHOOT! You don't have time to DISCUSS IT!"

After writing about the Wisconsin forests for *Outdoor Life* magazine, I was thrilled to be there, seeing first-hand why these people loved this land so very much, and I was anxious to see these "new" birds. The locals call ruffed grouse "partridge" — I never did find out why — it's just what Ben called them and whatever he said, went. Success during a ruffed-grouse hunt is often judged by the amount of "flushes" (birds scared up and flying out ahead of you) more than the amount of birds you bring home. Ben would always check with us to see how many flushes we had and if he didn't think that was enough, he sent us to another place in the forest.

Blazing with autumn color, the forest was breathtakingly beautiful. Living in a mostly flat agricultural area where the only areas of trees are shelter belts planted in long straight lines, river banks and coulees, this forest experience was extremely special. Aspen, known in eastern areas as "popple," abounded in the forest. There were spruce, white pine, hemlock, balsam (the best smelling stuff in the world!) and tamarack trees in the evergreen sections and lots of maple and oak on the hardwood ridges. The forest floor was carpeted with autumn's gold and red leaves, disguising the holes, deadfall, water, tangled vines, branches and all the other things that made Lila and I glad that we survived!

We discovered that being an Amazon woman would help in traversing this forest! It was a rough hunt at times. Living where it is flat, we don't have a lot of hills and forest in which to practice before a hunt of this type. It was difficult, to say the least, trying to make our way through all the obstacles, climbing over the dead trees, being slapped in the face by "wires" (tiny branches that would snap back and hit you) and still trying to keep track of each other so no one got lost. (We wore whistles just in case!) And, of course while fighting our way through this jungle, we were supposed to look under the pines and brush for ruffed grouse and listen for them to flush if we couldn't see them. Just trying to walk through this we made so much noise in the leaves, breaking deadfall branches, etc., that we even missed hearing a couple flushes! I don't think Kevin was pleased at that!

Lila, Kevin and I started easy by walking on an old railroad bed that snakes through the forest (that was used when the entire forest was clear cut generations ago). We saw our first bird there and kept remembering that fact as we fought our way through the woods to try and flush birds. We didn't have a lot of luck with flushing birds anywhere we went, so Ben decided he needed to lead us. He was raised in these woods and knew every inch of it by heart ("Trust me," he'd say!). I volunteered to be Ben's pupil first, not knowing that I would be begging for mercy at the end of the "walk." He wore no blaze orange and was very difficult to see in the forest but he assured me he would always be in view. Right! That lasted about two minutes in the thick cover that ruffed grouse love. I was just amazed at how he slithered through the woods, not even looking down, and just took off. I was struggling just to get my feet untangled and picking myself up after grabbing a small tree for support and have it snap in my hand! I was huffing and puffing at the end, but I made it and gladly turned Ben over to Lila. Later as she came dragging out of the woods, she did not have to say anything —

her eyes did the talking. We all flushed some birds, but some we never saw and only one or two of us ever got a shot. Even Ben thought we should've seen more birds than we did.

Ben had a good time hunting with us — mostly so he could laugh and poke fun at the way Lila and I fought our way through "his forest." "You guys step around like pixies on tip-toe and sweetly sing-song 'where arrrrrrrrre youuu-uuu'! Geez! That's no way to hunt in the forest! You just go with the flow," he would say.

Right Ben — and break our necks! I think we supplied his entertainment that weekend! He had to show us the forest "sights," the deer blind that has storm windows, heater and a radio, and the hunting cabin. We know he had fun and he was proud to dig up some tamarack trees from his farm and send them home with us.

Lila and I had driven about 900 miles, worked as hard as we ever had for any game, hunted hard for three days and only had one ruffed grouse in the cooler for the trip home. Disappointed that we didn't have more birds? Of course! So was the trip a bust? Absolutely not! The glistening white breast meat of that one little ruffed grouse is perhaps the most expensive piece of meat I've ever had, but that is not the point. The point is that we had a great time, hunted in beautiful country, met new friends, became reacquainted ourselves, planned future hunts, learned about a different way of life in our country and the people that inhabit it, learned about a different type of game bird, and concerning the tough forest conditions, we can say "been there and done that." A wonderful experience like that carries no price tag.

GETTING TO KNOW YOU

The ruffed grouse gets its name from the group of black feathers on both sides of the neck of the bird called "ruffs." These ruffs are more prominent on the males. Their body color is a basic brown with white underneath and the head is crested. They have a long fan-shaped tail that is barred and has a black band near the edge. The males weigh about one and one-half pounds, a little more than the female.

Ruffed grouse are mostly found in northwestern New England, the eastern and Great Lakes states and most of Canada. They inhabit aspen forests, enjoy mixed hardwood and conifers and sometimes may be found around cultivated fields. They also like cedar swamps and creek beds. Ruffed grouse especially like the aspen, or popple. They eat the popple shoots — our grouse even had a popple leaf in his crop. Clover and strawberry leaves are favorite meals along with many other seeds and berries. Popple buds sustain the grouse in the winter.

Like prairie chickens and sharp-tailed grouse, the ruffed grouse has a very definite spring mating ritual. The first time I heard the booming or drumming was during spring turkey hunting in the Black Hills of South Dakota and it scared me. It is hard to explain, but when we three women heard this sound, we first thought it was our hearts beating super fast — you can actually feel the beating in your chest! It is a low, rumbling, very rapid "boom boom" drumming sound. Once you have heard it, you will never forget it. Some people say it sounds like someone starting a roto-tiller. The ruffed grouse has a different twist on this from

his cousin the sharp-tailed grouse. He dances and drums on a log in the forest! Ruffed grouse like a large log which is 2 or 3 feet above the forest floor. When he finds one he likes within his territory, he stands on top and begins drumming (beating his wings). He starts out slowly and then works up to a rapid rate. This drumming sound can be heard up to one-half mile. The females then come into the area and the mating takes place.

Fall will find the family groups dispersed but regrouping can take place again in early winter.

Because of their ability to hide in the brush and then fly erratically when flushed, ruffed grouse are a popular game bird. They become very wary when there is a great amount of hunting pressure. Look for these birds in the mixed forests, especially places that are managed by clear-cutting. Ruffed grouse need several stages of tree growth to thrive and will often be found at the edges where a clear-cut patch meets a more mature forest. The birds spend a lot of time on the ground, but they will also spend plenty of time in the trees. Flushes can come from above you, below or behind you. The birds are tricky.

GETTING READY

The word "grouse" is synonymous with "walk!" That will be the first thing you learn! That means a good pair (or two in case you don't quite make it over the creek) of hunting boots is imperative! They should be comfortable, easy to walk and climb in, have good bottom grips, be waterproof and be oblivious to scarring. Comfortable boots are your most important item, next to your shotgun and shells. The other items are similar to what you need for pheasant and sharp-tailed grouse hunting, so please refer to those sections of this chapter.

A 20-gauge or 12-gauge shotgun will be fine with light loads like #7s and #8s.

After the "forest run" with Ben, I decided on the perfect outfit for ruffed grouse hunting: a football uniform, complete with helmet and face mask so you don't get hit by branches and scratched, shoulder pads so it doesn't hurt when you fall against a tree, knee pads for the same reason, and yes, even football cleats for a good hold on the forest floor! The gear might be on the heavy side, but that's what I told Ben I should've worn!

Brush pants are extremely important. They will help you slide through the brush easily, and you will end up with fewer seeds, thorns, etc., sticking to your legs. You will be walking, so do not overdress. Blaze orange is also extremely important. You will be hunting in very heavy brush and trees and it can be difficult to see your hunting partners even when they are wearing blaze orange. There is no excuse for not wearing orange; it can save your life. A hat is a must, but blaze orange sweaters, sweatshirts or vests are even better. If you fear becoming lost in the forest, seeing your partner's blaze orange through the trees is a comforting factor.

The shotgun information is also found in the pheasant and sharp-tailed grouse sections. A 20-gauge or 12-gauge shotgun will be fine with light loads like #7s and #8s. I recommend that you do not use a sling as it can interfere when you have to make a fast shot. If you will have a long walk to the hunting area, then use your sling but detach it when you reach the area.

A hunting dog is good for flushing birds and finding downed birds, if he is well trained. A bird dog that is not controlled and runs out too far ahead of the hunters is a detriment to the hunt. Echo made some good flushes for us, some we could not have made, and it was fun to watch her work, but the times we left her home we flushed birds ourselves. There is something to be said for the quietness of the pristine forest as you walk through it, minus dog commands and whistles. Using a dog is strictly a personal decision.

A compass is a necessary item for hunting in the forest. Do not forget it! "Overnights" in the forest can be cold, wet and scary!

The author, right, with her hunting partner Lila Antonides and their first grouse taken during a hunt in northern Wisconsin. Grouse can be found in the woods or along old logging roads and patches of clover.

Since you will be hunting ruffed grouse in forested areas, that usually is public land, whether it is federal, state or county. Please refer to the chapter "Finding a Place to Hunt." If you want to hunt on private forested land, be sure to obtain permission from the landowner.

When you have all of your hunting items assembled, have your hunting area chosen and are ready to go, play this scenario over in your mind: the birds will flush, and you will quickly draw on them, lead them and shoot where you think they will be. It's not easy to hit a grouse, so play this over in your mind; practice "shooting" those birds and pay attention to the correct method you must use which is swing and follow-through.

THE HUNT

The mystique of ruffed grouse hunting is the flushing of birds — that is the big deal here. If you happen to connect with birds, that is a bonus! If you have flushed 20 birds, whether you have hit them or not, while ruffed grouse hunting, that hunt is considered a success. These birds are extremely difficult to flush and that is where the challenge comes into play.

The birds have many favorite places to hide. They like the heavy brush cover of new growth on a clear-cut (new plants emerging on an area that used to be covered with trees); they like creek beds and cedar swamps. Look for them under the brushy cover, under pine trees and where tops of trees have blown down. They sometimes sit in trees and flush out from there, birds flying between the trees makes a shot very difficult. When they do flush, the noise is usually louder than a pheasant and will make your heart stop. They love to sit and hide in the popple because the hawks cannot swoop down and claim the grouse for dinner. The cover is heavy and thick and they just stay there until you push them out. If you are lucky, you may see them on a logging road, picking at clover, but their hiding ability makes these little birds tough to hunt — that is why they are so special.

When you are walking in the forest and hunting ruffed grouse, you must be ready to shoot at all times. You never know when the birds will flush and you will have to shoot immediately. Remember, "Shoot — don't discuss it!" Have your shooting alleys determined before starting to walk and always be cognizant of the other hunters. When those birds flush, your concentration is gone and you are immediately excited, but you must know your shooting area and where the other hunters are. I was concerned about shooting through the trees and not having a clear shot (impossible in an aspen forest) but was told to shoot anyway because "some of those BBs will hit that bird and none of the BBs will ricochet off the small trees — this is how you hunt here in the forest".

When you flush a bird, shoot and connect, MARK WHERE THAT BIRD FALLS! Do not take your eyes off that mark! The bird will be very hard to find in the forest, especially if you do not have a dog. All the hunters should mark where that bird fell so it can be found.

When you connect with a bird, congratulate yourself! They are tough to hunt and tough to shoot through the trees, but when you have done it, you can be proud that you have conquered another challenge and enjoyed the mystique of hunting ruffed grouse in the thick hardwood forest. Here is yet another opportunity for you to learn, have fun, enjoy nature while hunting, meet new friends, find out more about yourself and your capabilities, and give thanks for the beautiful world in which we live.

The Ruffed Grouse Society is a thriving national, nonprofit wildlife conservation advocate with the purpose to increase the numbers of ruffed grouse, American woodcock and other forest wildlife through state-of-the-art habitat management techniques and habitat improvement projects. Most of the income is received through the local banquet program. To join RGS, call 1-888-564-6747 or write 451 McCormick Road, Coraopolis, PA, 15108.

Ruffed grouse love thick cover. A good dog will help find downed birds even in the thickest brush.

Chapter Seven
WATERFOWL

"Be at the farm at 5 a.m.," I said,

"Oh no! That early?" he replied.

"The first thing you learn is to get up and get going," I said. "The birds won't wait for you!"

Well, Bill was there right on time. We loaded up the decoys and drove out to the field. What a morning! A tinge of pink identified the coming sunrise and a breeze was coming out of the northeast. We got the decoys set and Bill gathered corn stalks as I drove the vehicle back along the tree line, parked it and hurried back to the field. "This is going to be a great one," I thought, "I just know it!" After making sure the decoys were perfectly placed, we each chose our personal "pits" and completely covered up with the corn stalks. My goose call was at my fingertips, the gun was loaded, our spirits were high. Now it was up to the geese. I had a very positive feeling they would cooperate so waiting became difficult. "Settle down," I told myself, "we might be waiting for a long time."

This was very special, as it was the first time I had taken Bill Antonides out goose hunting. Bill had taught me how to shoot and taught me how to hunt deer. I then discovered goose hunting and that had become my passion. Bill had hunted geese only a couple of times with his friends so he really looked forward to having his "student" guide him goose hunting. As we set the decoys I instructed him on how to place them, where we should be set up, how I would call, where the geese would come in from, the height they should be when we could shoot, etc. I felt so important showing

HIM the ropes! As I lay waiting for the geese to appear I just enjoyed the circumstances of ME teaching HIM.

I started reflecting on some of the first times I hunted geese. My mentors were Sig VandenAkker, my lake neighbor, and Arlo Haase, a South Dakota Conservation Officer. With all the dumb things I did, it's a wonder they never gave up on me! I remember one day in particular at "The Point". Sig and I loaded up and arrived at the blinds with all our gear for a great day of hunting. I was nearly ready when I heard Sig say, "Hurry up! Shoot right now!" I looked up and saw about a dozen giant Canada geese flying right into us. "Come on! What are you waiting for?" Sig yelled. I screamed back to him, "I CAN'T! I DON'T HAVE ANY SHELLS IN MY GUN YET!"

"What have I told you? When you are this close to the blind, always have your gun loaded and ready," Sig growled as he went to pick up the nice goose he dropped out of that little flock. I sat there, stunned, mad at myself, disappointed, embarrassed and swearing to never let that happen again. You must ALWAYS be ready. Shortly before the "fly over" we had our gear placed inside the blinds, decoys placed on the water and I was basically ready. I just wasn't in the blind yet. I was doing some last minute "fooling around." I am very safety conscious and therefore did not load my gun and wouldn't have until I was in the blind and waiting for birds to appear. Waterfowl, however, fly on THEIR schedule, not ours, and I wasn't ready. It is OK to load the gun, carefully place it in a safe position while you are preparing to hunt, just in case. Then if the birds decide to take a look, you are ready. Well, I had dawdled and was unable to shoot and missed the only opportunity of the day.

This experience was only one of the many mistakes my mentor called attention to, all with the intention of making me a better waterfowl hunter. Sometimes, there were hard lessons to learn. When you have gone through all the paces

THE BOTTOM LINE !

YOU'LL NEED THIS————————————————

of buying your license, learning to shoot, obtaining the correct clothing and finding a place to hunt, its very disappointing to make a foolish mistake.

Because I was always the only woman in the hunting group and had taken no formal hunting classes, I experienced many pitfalls and learned from them. I want to prepare you and help you learn faster and with much less pain than I experienced. I have had great success hunting waterfowl and have had a tremendous amount of fun and excitement; I just want you to know my beginnings were humble and sometimes I had to learn the hard way. I want learning to be easier for YOU! I want you to know that mistakes will be made and that is how we learn. The ultimate confidence comes from learning lessons ourselves and we can be proud of that.

We have already covered information on how to start hunting, guns, ammunition and safety, hunting clothing and finding a place to hunt. You are now ready to dig into the meat of waterfowl hunting.

GETTING READY

Waterfowl Regulations

Before you start hunting, obtain one of your state's hunting regulations handbooks. This handbook will be your bible all through the hunting season. It covers regulations for all kinds of hunting and seasons. If after reading it you still have a question, call your local conservation officer. Don't ever go into the field not knowing what your limit is, what birds are legal, what are the legal shooting hours, etc. You must know the rules and remember they are always "black and white." You want to be an ethical hunter, a good hunter and an informed hunter. Read and digest the regulations handbook! Be sure to double-check shooting times in the handbook; it is in small print and can be difficult to determine when you can shoot!

Waterfowl Identification

You must know what you are going to hunt. It's very important that you are able to identify waterfowl properly. I was a pheasant hunter first and that was easy; I just had to be able to tell the difference between a rooster and a hen. Waterfowl hunting is a whole different ball game. I had to know the birds, their habits and habitat. I had to learn what they would do and when. When I started waterfowl hunting I was nervous about shooting the forbidden bird — the canvasback (it was not legal at that time). Many times my mentor would shout to me from his blind, "those are no-no's." I had to pay attention, know exactly what they looked like while they were flying as a group and what they looked like on the water. Canvasback populations have rebounded and the bird is now legal in some states but that doesn't mean you relax your identification skills. You still have to be able to identify hens from drakes; most regulations stipulate only one bird of one species per day. If you shoot a mallard hen and only one is allowed per day in your bag, you must carefully select your shots so you do not shoot another one. This is another reason why reading that hunting handbook is so important.

Ducks Unlimited publishes a great booklet, *Ducks at a Distance*. There are explanations of differences between puddle ducks (which inhabit fresh, shallow marshes) and diving ducks (which inhabit larger, deeper lakes and rivers). The illustrations are in color; they spotlight the birds in flight, body structure, flock pattern and wing samples. Two pages show the comparative sizes of waterfowl starting with the smallest ducks and following through to the trumpeter swan. There are more than just game birds in our sloughs, marshes and lake areas. The birds you are not allowed to shoot are called non-game birds and some of those are also pictured. A map of the flyways, the birds' typical migration routes, is found in the back of the booklet. I highly recommend this booklet; my booklet is a permanent resident of my backpack. Contact Ducks Unlimited at 1-800-45-DUCKS.

Experience increases your knowledge and abilities, and it can take a while. I still am very careful and question whether it's a drake or hen mallard swinging above me. Waterfowl shooting hours begin one half hour before sunrise. I think that is a half-hour too early; I have never been able to identify ducks at that time, as it is too dark. Be aware of this situation and shoot accordingly, not until you are positively sure it is a legal bird. I hunt a lot with a conservation officer and I am amazed at some of the shots he passes up because he

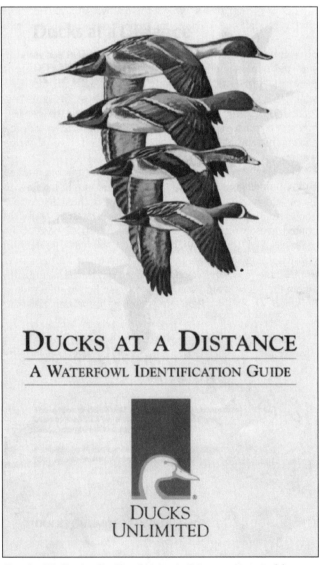

Ducks Unlimited's Ducks At A Distance pamphlet can help hunters of all skill levels identify ducks in flight. The booklet is reproduced in color and not only shows drakes and hens, but also the typical flock pattern of the birds you are likely to encounter in the marsh.

could not positively identify it. Don't become discouraged if you cannot "ID" the ducks your first or second time out hunting; ability comes with experience.

If you have a national wildlife refuge nearby go to the headquarters and ask to see the mounted waterfowl. You will be able to see the actual bird and more than likely someone can even give you a "short course" on waterfowl identification. If you have no refuge or wildlife office near you, call your state wildlife agency and ask where you can see some of these birds. A trip to your local taxidermist can also be informative. I suggest you rent some waterfowl videos either from your library or video store. They can be great teaching tools.

The more you learn about the animals you are hunting the more interesting it becomes. The booklets will help you with descriptions and identification. They will also help you to learn about how they are managed, both internationally (waterfowl flyways) and statewide, and about conservation of wetlands and habitat. Conservation officers and wildlife offices have the information you seek and should be very helpful in explaining this information to you. You can also contact a U.S. Fish and Wildlife Service office near you for management information.

A Hunting Place

The next thing to do is to find your place to hunt. How do you do that? Refer to the chapter, Finding a Place to Hunt, then apply waterfowl information. The evening before you want to hunt drive around fields and slough areas looking for birds. That is called scouting. A good rule to remember is "go where the birds are." It may sound obvious, but lots of people think decoys mean birds will come sailing right to you. Don't try to draw them into a field in which you've never seen them. If there are geese feeding in a field in the evening, chances are they will return the next morning. If you watch a wetland area or slough and see ducks flying, they probably will be there the next day also. Depending on what you want to hunt and where, be sure to ask permission of the landowner if it is private land. If it is public land be

A typical entry in the Ducks At A Distance pamphlet provides plenty of information about most ducks commonly hunted in North America.

sure it is open for hunting; there should be a sign posted indicating that.

When looking for fields that geese like, look for cornfields that have been harvested and disked, their favorite. Sometimes geese land in a soybean field and walk into the cornfield, if the cornfield is not disked. If the cornfield is not disked the stalks may hurt their wings so they walk in if they can. Just monitor the field, "mark" in your mind exactly where they are standing so you can remember in the morning. That is where you will place your decoys. Mallards feed in cornfields, too. A good thing to remember is that they will walk into the wind. So if you are lying between the cornrows, you can have mallards walk right up to you. That is fun!

If you find a wetland or slough area, watch and see where and how the ducks and geese are flying. "Mark" those directions in your mind and remember that the next morning. That will determine where you set your blind or set up in the rushes. Note the shoreline of the wetland and any good hiding places. Waterfowl always land facing the wind. Study different positions and choose what you think will be the best. A hunter can study, and put a lot of work into being in the perfect place, with the perfect blind and perfect cover and still the birds will not cooperate. Do not think that YOU messed up or did anything necessarily wrong. Birds will change their minds and do all sorts of things to confuse you and when they do, it is not your fault! I watched one flock of geese near our farm for five straight days and each day those birds did something different, like fly in or out at different times. All you can do is just play the game and have fun!

When the scouting is finished, you have permission and know how you are going to set up in the morning, your "night before" preparations are finished. You must be in the field before dawn to set up your decoys and prepare your "pit." That means getting to bed at a reasonable time the night before, setting the alarm allowing you plenty of time to get ready in the morning.

Starting the Waterfowl Day

If you are one to run for the coffeepot upon jumping out of bed you probably want to modify that behavior. Unless you have coveralls that are specifically made for women with a backdrop seat, etc., you will have to remove coveralls, or bibs or hunting pants in order to relieve yourself. It is an unwritten law that waterfowl know exactly when you are doing this and will choose that particular time to appear before you. Believe me, you do not want to be in that position! Limiting your fluid intake before going hunting will help in this respect. You can take a backpack with you and bring your coffee, tea, water or whatever, but be careful about

the amount you drink if you do not want to be continually disrobing in the field! This also brings me to another point on this subject. Leave the area exactly as you found it, and that means picking up waste tissues. Bring a baggie and discard the personal tissues in it. Never leave litter, including used tissues in the field.

Back to the preparations. If it is a very cold morning and you want to bring a hot beverage with you, I suggest a thermos of beef bullion. That will warm you up faster and keep you warm longer than caffeine. Granola bars fit well in backpacks, are securely wrapped and taste great for energy snacks. If you are planning an entire day out, then sandwiches, chips, fruit, and other snacks can be kept in a cooler in your vehicle. Just be sure to take some energy foods with you; you can become very miserable if you are hungry and thirsty and have nothing with you.

Be sure to listen to the weather forecast so you know what to expect for the entire time you are out. The temperature will dictate how many layers you wear, how many foot and hand warmers you take, what boots and gloves to wear. Please refer to the Clothing chapter for more details.

If you will be hunting near water, waders must be included in your "clothing list". I started out with a pair of hip boots. I do not recommend those! They are bulky. If you do not have them "belted up" the tops fall down, and they ultimately will not cover enough for you. You might drop some birds in water deeper than hip boots allow. Then what would you do? I found myself in that position. Buy waders. There are many kinds on the market today, from your basic rubber waders to fancy camo styled ones. I have the basic rubber kind, as they were the right price. They are somewhat bulky and heavy but they accomplish the job. Neoprene wad-

A bluebird day doesn't always mean you won't get some action. Here the author takes aim at an incoming duck from a makeshift blind in the rushes. Concealment and good calling will bring ducks close.

ers are more expensive but they are silent, lightweight and have additional insulation.

Don't forget the hand muff. You can use it for any type of hunting, but it works best for waterfowl hunting. Please refer to the Clothing chapter for a complete description of the muff.

Other needed items for your backpack include a selection of calls, a knife, binoculars, any medications you may need, and your camera. You may want to take a bird to the taxidermist, so bring along an old sock or nylon knee-hi stocking to slip the bird into so you will keep the feathers intact. (Slip the bird in head-first.)

SHOTGUN AND SHELLS

Next on the list is your shotgun and shells. Set them out the night before so you will not forget them. Feelings defy description if you would happen to be out in the field, all set up, the birds are coming in and realize you have forgotten your gun! Refer to the chapter on guns and ammunition for more specific information on the gun for you.

That Remington 11-87 treated me very well, bagging ducks, geese and turkeys. The last few years I began to have trouble swinging on ducks and I started missing a lot. The gun was just too heavy to pick up from a prone position, shoulder and follow through with ducks flying at supersonic speed. I started looking around for lightweight guns and settled on a Browning Gold Hunter 20-gauge. I was told in the beginning that a 12-gauge is the best for sure shots and heavy power and those 20-gauge shotguns were too light. Since I had gotten along so well with the 12-gauge I believed that. Not until I had taken a friend hunting and watched him connect with two great shots out of the same flock did I seriously start thinking about buying a 20-gauge. The heavier my 12-gauge became, the more I thought about a lighter gun. I liked the 20-gauge Browning; it fit me fine, felt comfortable, and had a long line of sight with the 28-inch barrel. I used it one season; I liked it but the 28-inch barrel was too long for me and the gun really wasn't all that much lighter weight than the old 11-87. Now I shoot a lightweight 12-gauge Beretta Pintail with a 26-inch barrel and it works much better for me. With the lighter gun models on the mar-

ket now it should not be difficult to find the shotgun that is really YOURS.

As for shotgun shells, again refer to the guns and ammunition chapter. For beginning goose hunting just remember a few pointers on what size shell to use. The area and method you will be hunting determine what size shells to use. If you are hunting over decoys you may shoot at birds that are just a yard or so above the decoys. Using a 12-gauge, I recommend #2 shot, steel of course. If you are pass shooting, I recommend a little more power for those longer shots. Choose BB or BBB shot size. They both have always worked extremely well for me. Don't let anyone talk you into F or T shot. Someone might try to tell you that you need it for "killing power." I do not like those size pellets as they can give a person a false sense of security. A person might think she can hit anything with the bigger pellets. But in reality, the bigger pellets just means there are fewer of them to hit the target. You'll actually wound more birds and that is a question of ethics. Stay with the recommended shells. As for duck hunting, I recommend #3 or #4 steel shot, in a 2-3/4-inch shell for a 12-gauge. For a 20-gauge use #1s in a 3-inch shell for all waterfowl. The advantage here is that you are always loaded for ducks and #1s are powerful enough for geese. Therefore, you do not have to be constantly changing shell sizes. That eliminates the problem of being caught loading your gun when the birds are overhead. Has that ever happened to me? You bet! Trust me, you wouldn't like it! I carry my shells in a small fanny pack and have it around my waist while walking out to the field. Then the shells are always close at hand.

Improved cylinder chokes are good for shooting large steel shot. Test fire your gun at a large paper target, it's called patterning, to show which of the various chokes and loads provide the most dense pattern of pellets. In your Becoming an Outdoors Woman waterfowl class, you will learn more about when to shoot, gauging distances, etc. For instance, never shoot at a Canada goose until you can definitely see the white patch on his head, etc.

Skybusting" is taking long distance shots at birds that are out of range. Skybusting is simply shooting and not hunting.

Lila Antonides prepares to tote a pole filled with Bigfoot decoys. Waterfowl hunting, whether done over fields or water, requires lots of gear. Plan to be carrying decoys, waders and other items just about any time you take to the field.

CONSEP 2000 STEEL SHOT LETHALITY TABLE©

Proven Steel Shot Loads For Waterfowl & Upland Game Birds[1]
Load Velocity: 1,225 - 1,450 FPS

ACTIVITY	Typical Shooting Range of Activity (Yards)	Most Effective Steel Shot Size(s) for Activity	Minimum Load Weight (Ounces)	Minimum Pellet Hits Needed on Lethal Areas for Clean Kills	Minimum Pattern Count Needed at Any Distance for Clean Kills (Number Of Pellets in 30" Circle)	Most Effective Choke(s) (Given in Lead Shot Designations)
Large Geese At Long Range[2] Giant, Western, Atlantic and Interior Canadas	50-65	BBB to T	1-1/4	1-2	50-55	Improved Modified
Large Geese Over Decoys[2]	40-50	BB to BBB	1-1/8	1-2	50-55	Modified
Medium/Small Geese Long Range[2] Snow, White-front, Lesser Canadas	50-65	BB to BBB	1-1/4	1-2	60-65	Improved Modified
Medium/Small Geese Over Decoys[2]	40-50	2 to BB	1-1/8	1-2	60-65	Modified
Large Ducks At Long Range Mallard, Black, Pintail, Goldeneye, Gadwall	45-65	2 to 1	1-1/8	1-2	85-90	Full
Large Ducks Over Decoys[3,4]	20-45	6 to 2	3/4 - 1	1-2	85-90	I.C. (20-35 Yds), Mod. (35-45 Yds)
Medium Ducks Over Decoys[3,4] Wigeon, Scaup, Shoveler	30-45	6 to 3	1	1-2	115-120	Improved Cylinder (20-35 Yards), Modified (35-45 Yards)
Small Ducks Over Decoys[3,4] Teal, Ruddy, Bufflehead	30-45	6 to 4	1	1-2	135-145	Modified (20-35 Yards), Full (35-45 Yards)
Ring-Necked Pheasants	20-50	3 to 2	1	2-3	90-95	I.C. (20-30 Yds), Mod. (30-50 Yds)
Turkeys (Head and Neck Shots)	20-40	4	1-1/4	3-4	210-230	Full or Extra Full
Swatter Load For Wounded Birds	20-35	7 to 5	1	1	175	Mod. or Full (7's or 6's), Full (5's)

This table summarizes analysis to date of the waterfowl and upland game bird lethality data base of the Cooperative North American Shotgunning Education Program (CONSEP). Responsible shotgun hunters not only engage in thorough pattern testing and ample target practice, but also restrict shooting to ranges less than 45 yards.
Note: To date, steel #BBB (.190") has exhibited the best all-around performance for taking geese; steel #3 (.140") the best all-around performance for taking ducks.

1 These findings are derived from testing 3" 20-gauge and 2³/₄", 3" and 3¹/₂" 12-gauge steel loads. As additional pellet sizes, load configurations, and gauges are tested and data bases completed, findings will be updated and may change.

2 Steel #F (.220") in all 12-gauge load configurations has exhibited the highest crippling rate on geese of all steel pellet sizes tested. Due to inadequate pattern density, steel #F has not proven lethal on geese beyond 55 yards.

3 Steel #4 (.130") has exhibited good all-around performance for taking small and medium-sized ducks, but has not proven lethal on large ducks beyond 45 yards.

4 Steel #6 (.110") has proven lethal out to 40 yards on all ducks tested. It has proven particularly effective out to 35 yards when used with chokes no tighter than modified.

This terminal ballistics information is provided courtesy of the members of CONSEP. CONSEP is a research and information service currently funded jointly by 25 U.S. state fish and wildlife agencies; the U.S. Fish and Wildlife Service; the Canadian Wildlife Service; the British Association for Shooting and Conservation (BASC); the Office National de la Chasse, France; the Victoria Department of Natural Resources and Environment, Australia; Winchester Division/Olin Corporation; and Remington Arms Company. Contributing members include Larry Gore's Katy Prairie and Eagle Lake Outfitters, and Briley Manufacturing Company.

© Copyright 1999 by Tom Roster.   Distributed by CONSEP.   Reprint rights granted only by written permission of copyright holder.

If shots are taken at more than 50 yards, the birds can suffer wounds that eventually prove to be fatal, but may not knock the bird from the sky upon impact. Do not "reach for the sky" while waterfowl hunting. Develop patience and knowledge of when birds are within range and when they are too far away and you will then have a good, ethical hunt.

DECOYS

Decoys are a must for most waterfowl hunting. You want to attract birds and the way to do that is to lure them to an area filled with their friends. As they fly over they can see other birds down in the field and think, " there must be something good down there, so let's go!" There are several types of decoys on the market now and companies are inventing new ones constantly. For our purposes we will talk about the basic decoys and how they work. The first goose decoys I ever had were huge (we use the term "magnum") body shells with detachable heads. I had a dozen, spread them out correctly and they worked well. The next decoys on the market were called "Big Foots". They are full-bodied plastic geese that stand on their own feet. I only have six of them. They are good decoys, however, and I have called in geese just using those six decoys.

If you have decoys like those described above, they will work for you. If you want something better, really state-of-the-art in goose decoys, run to your catalog or sports store and ask for Canada Magnum silhouettes from the Outlaw Company. They are terrific for a lot of reasons. They are a photograph screen printed on heavy-duty vinyl and they come with stakes to push into the ground. Since they are a photograph of a goose, they are the most natural looking decoys on the market today. The day after my uncle purchased his dozen we had to try them out. During the morning a goose landed amidst the decoys. I had seen the bird land but my uncle did not. He had a hard time finding the real goose; in fact he could not find it until it finally

The problem of viewing decoys from above has been solved with Outlaw's Hawkeye decoys that can be dropped into a standard spread to add realism.

moved his head! In addition to the regular silhouettes, new, "top down" or "hawk's eye view" silhouettes are now available. They resemble what a goose sees when he looks down. The silhouettes are very thin, about 1/16 of an inch thick, so at a certain angle flying geese may not see them. They should be placed "katty-wampus" to each other so the geese will see all of them from any angle. The new "top down" silhouettes eliminate that problem. Talk to your decoy dealer and tell him you want some of each. If your budget is tight, then gather your friends and pool your money. After hunting with all three types of decoys, it's like going from good (shells) to better (Big Foots) to best (silhouettes). I use the combination of all three types of decoys and it works well. If you have no decoys and are going to purchase some, then simply buy the silhouettes and you will be set.

Another great advantage of the silhouettes is their weight. They're light! I have carried a dozen out to the field with no problem. If the field is too wet and you cannot drive in and leave the decoys off, you must carry them in and that is impossible if you have big shells. You can only carry probably a maximum of five Big Foots, so being able to carry in several dozen silhouettes at once is great. The dealers sell carrying ponchos and side packs, also. Being a woman hunter, you want to have the lightest weight

It doesn't always take lots of decoys to bring in geese, but they have to be placed correctly. Here the author shows off a nice Canada goose that dropped in on a family group of just eight decoys.

The silhouette decoys produced by Outlaw look just like real birds.

equipment for all aspects of the hunt. In this case, light is best. The newest silhouettes manufactured are called Jenny Vane Canada's (from Outlaw). They are economically priced at $70 per dozen and weighs only 4 pounds per dozen! There are flying goose kites available, along with other "high tech" decoys, but don't worry about them yet. Learn with what I have told you, then proceed trying new ideas.

Snow goose silhouettes are available, too. Ask your dealer; he is your decoy resource. There are duck silhouettes for field hunting, but since most duck hunting is done over or beside water I'll recommend staying with floating decoys. You can always prop a few up on the ground if the situation calls for it. I can only think of one time in my hunting years where I duck hunted exclusively on land, so I will stay with the floaters. A couple dozen mallards, some blue bills and maybe some gadwall floating decoys will do a good job for you. You can buy decoys with weighted keels or the lighter-weight hollow keels that fill with water when the decoys are dropped in the pond. When you purchase your duck floaters make sure that heavy-duty nylon string comes with them or buy it separately. Attach the string to the appropriate place underneath the body. With the string approximately 6 feet long, attach a weight of some kind to the other end. You can use a piece of iron or steel, just so there is the weight to keep the decoy from floating away. There are snow goose and Canada goose floater decoys available; use them in the same manner.

Decoy arrangement is discussed later in this chapter.

BLINDS

When hunting waterfowl, concealment is most important. That is why you wear camouflage clothing. But clothing is not enough. We might think we are very cleverly hidden, but waterfowl's airborne inspections prove differently. Movement is actually more important to conceal than your body in some situations. Blinds are used to conceal movement and the "bumps" of hunters appearing where they normally are not. There are very many kinds and types of blinds. The best advice is to use your imagination and adapt to your environment. If hunting in a cornfield, then use the natural material — corn stalks. If

hunting in rushes, then make a blind of rushes, etc. Just use common sense and use materials that fit in with the area in which you are hunting.

I learned how to waterfowl hunt in an area covered with bull rushes. Labor Day weekend was always "blind-making time." It was important to make the blinds that early, about one month before season opening, so the waterfowl became used to seeing them and were not surprised by something new on opening day. The bases of the blind were boards

A pit and a layer of corn stalks makes a perfect blind.

The author's mentor, Sig VandenAkker, and his Chesa-peake Bay retriever Pat in a well-made waterfowl blind.

A good day of hunting at the blind on The Point.

This blind was made by simply piling grass and crawling inside. It offers total concealment. Be creative.

Sometimes you have to build a blind with anything thats available on the site. Here the author sits in a "thistle blind" in the center of a stubble field. It worked.

nailed together, and the sides were old pieces of plywood nailed up for walls. Be sure the height is about shoulder level when you are sitting down inside. Just a small piece of plywood is needed for a "door". Using your garden clippers, cut the rushes off near the bottom. When you have an armful, have a friend hold some up in front of the blind wall starting at the left side. Staple a heavy cord about midway down the wall while holding the rushes tightly against the wall. Continue holding up rushes and stapling all the way around the blind. You will want to repeat the procedure for reinforcement purposes. Finish up by stapling rushes on your little door. Move your bucket or chair inside the blind and decide if the rushes height is all right. If the rushes are too high and you cannot see anything you can trim them down some. There! You have your blind!

This same procedure can be used to make a temporary wall blind that can be moved. Just staple rushes on some plywood with the heavy cord. Using "products of nature" for constructing blinds is best. You don't have to spend any money, just use your imagination and make a fun day of it. Other "products of nature" include thistles, ditch grass or snow with which to cover up. I have gotten by with just lying or sitting in a thick bed of rushes, lying beside a rock pile or beside a big magnum goose shell. You can utilize dead trees by placing sticks or stakes around the tree trunk and draping burlap over them to break up your outline. Do this both in front and behind you.

Woven wire farm fence panels can be utilized as blinds. Have the landowner or another helper place the panel where you direct, secure it with three steel fence posts and using wire, attach camo or burlap material. That might only cost you a smile and a nice ham for the landowner's family. Some farmers dig pits in their fields for hunters. They can vary in depth and size. The best ones I have been in have been two-person blinds with

buckets to sit upon. Some goose pits are just round holes drilled into the ground and allow standing room only for one person. Snow fence can be used to hold camo or burlap material, too. I have even hunted from a blind made to look like a round hay bale. It held three people and the top flipped up for shooting. Just use your imagination!

There are many types of blinds available at your sports/hunting store or in catalogs. There is the corn stalk-pattern round bale which looks light and portable but is expensive. There is a super magnum goose you actually can sit inside of and a "stretcher" with a goose shell over one end under which you place your head. There are blinds that actually look like coffins; the top flips up for shooting. You will have fun exploring the blind department! If you were going to purchase one the best time would be after hunting season when they go on sale. I certainly would research the different types before I purchased one of these blinds. Some of them do not allow you the visibility you need; it would be a bad situation if you went to all the trouble of getting out to the field, buying the expensive blind then missed the birds because you couldn't see them!

Don't forget that MOVEMENT will scare birds. No matter what kind of blinds you use, you

Large round bails often provide great cover. Here Lila Antonides steps out to take a shot at a passing duck.

Learning to build a blind is something every participant in the Becoming an Outdoors Woman program learns. It takes practice, so learn before the season starts.

Attaching native vegetation to the blind at your duck boat will aid in concealing your presence from the ducks.

Good camouflage can be just as effective as a blind, especially in cut corn. Lila and Bill Antonides show off a nice snow goose that failed to see them until it was too late.

still have to remain still or the birds will spot you. You are in luck, though, as you are a woman and you will be patient! I've been told women make better hunters because they have more patience to sit still better and longer than men.

One word about little hunting stools or chairs: do not use a stool unless you are inside a blind. That's the only way you are low enough for concealment. They will not work in rushes because the ground is usually muddy and the stool legs will sink and you will tip over. I wonder how I know that!

Blinds can also be made to conceal boats. Wedging dowels in the boat framework and draping camo material around the edges is the simplest and easiest method. Your sports/hunting store and catalogs will also offer unique ways to camouflage a duck boat.

Just use your imagination. The long and short of it is that you need to have decoys to trick the birds into coming to you and you have to be hidden while the birds approach. Then all you have to do is shoot them.

WATERFOWL CALLS

You will want to talk to the geese and ducks, so you must obtain a call. Some of the most fun times I have had in the field have been while calling geese—I just needed the confidence to do it. I had no confidence in my goose calling when I was in a goose pit and listened to my hunting buddy's calling ability. I thought calling like that could only be done well by an expert and felt I certainly could never talk to the geese that well. But I got help in a round-about way at a Becoming an Outdoors Woman workshop. Women gaining confidence in themselves is a huge part of what Becoming an Outdoors Woman workshops are all about. While teaching the waterfowl classes at a BOW workshop I left the goose and duck calling abilities to my male partner. One of the gals in the class asked me if I called geese and ducks. When I told her the reasons why I didn't, she looked at me and said, "Well, you should! Why let the guys have all the fun? It can't be that hard!" How ridiculous I felt — having to tell her I'd never even tried it. I made up my mind right then I would get a call, practice and at least try. Part of my problem was that I thought a person had to have a $300 hand-made call in order for it to be good. How wrong that thinking was!

A week before waterfowl season opener I stopped at a local discount store and bought a goose call. I never got around to taking it out of the package until the night before the season opened, and when I did, WOW! What a surprise! It sounded great! I couldn't believe what I was hearing; the low and high pitches sounded just right! I could do it! The next question was, would the geese like it?

The waterfowl opener was miserable, ugly and wet — actually good for waterfowl hunting but we had to wait a long time before seeing any birds. When we spotted some geese I started calling. To my amazement, I turned one bunch, then another and another! It was incredible! I'll never forget the stunned look in my uncle's eyes as he watched this. Our marksmanship left something to be desired that day — we blamed it on the weather and being excited about the new call.

The Ducker, by Outlaw Marine is a handy duck boat that will help you get into areas you'd usually not be able to hunt otherwise.

The author's son-in-law, Mark, drew the short straw and had to pull the duck boat to the blind location on this hunt.

The next day dawned with a beautifully clear sky and bright sunlight. The geese had bunched up some and we saw some flocks in the distance. I turned a couple of bunches but they did not fly close enough for a shot. All at once I saw "specks" on the horizon and started calling. Three giant Canada geese were headed my way. They kept coming closer and closer and I knew I would have a great shot. It worked! Fourteen pounds of beautiful giant Canada goose was mine! My uncle was about a quarter of a mile away from me and I could still hear him yelling congratulations to me. That entire event gave me such confidence! See what I mean about being able to meet challenges and accomplishing goals you never before thought possible? Thanks to my waterfowl students I had taken another big step.

Don't think you will not be able to properly call waterfowl. All it takes is a call, a little practice and confidence. The call that I bought and still use today (I have more than one as I think they are so good) was a plastic Lohman goose call for under $10. There are many calls on the market for different types of waterfowl. I suggest a Lohman goose and duck call to start with. To further help you, buy an accompanying tape that demonstrates calls. You can then learn the feeding, welcoming, alarm and fly down calls and be able to practice them at all times. Don't be afraid to try them all out in the field — you'll surprise yourself at how good you can sound. Do practice outside, as the sounds are not the same in your living room. Along with your calls, purchase a lanyard from which to hang your calls around your neck so you don't lose them and they always stay within easy reach.

Good calls come ine all shapes and sizes. Find one that is easy to blow and learn to blow it well.

DRIVING TO THE HUNTING AREA

You now have your equipment loaded and you are ready to leave for your hunting area. You may have the question "what do I drive?" If you have a four-wheel drive vehicle at your disposal, that is perfect. You will have room for all of your gear and also

You should be proud of any bird you bag after you call it in, but your first goose is always something special. This 14-pound Canada fell to the author after she pulled it in with her calling.

the traction you may need when you get near your hunting area whether it's a field or a grassy trail. When I first started hunting I only had an old 1979 Cougar and I had to make do with that. I was able to get to most places but had to depend on other people when the going got rough. I was delighted when my husband presented me with my "goosemobile" — a 1979 Jeep Wagoneer! I love it and hope it lasts forever.

If you are able to drive into your area and drop off your equipment that's best. There will be many times when you may not be able to do that. You then drive as close as possible, drop off your gear, go park the vehicle, walk back and take your gear into the area. Where you park your vehicle is important. Parking can mean the difference between a good hunt and a disappointing one. Always be aware of where you leave your vehicle. Although it seems like a long way away, 1/4 to a 1/2-mile is a must. You do not want those birds to see the sun glare off your vehicle and then fly away. If there are trees that distance away, park beside them. If there are some trees in the ditch, park beside them. If you leave your vehicle on the road be sure to park far enough to the side to allow traffic to pass. Some hunters think you must cover your vehicle with camouflage material; that is a good idea but I personally have never done it. If you feel more comfortable doing that, by all means do it.

THE GOOSE HUNT

The following information applies to Canada goose hunting. If you can drive into the field where you are going to set up your decoys, that's great. Leave everything in a pile in one place, go park the vehicle and walk back. It's easier to see one big clump of gear than to find everything if you spread it out. If you have to carry decoys from your vehicle, make sure you have a decoy bag or some type of lightweight bag in which to carry them. When you return to the field, it's time to set out the decoys.

The most important thing to remember when setting up decoys is the wind direction. Geese come in to you by flying INTO the wind. There are two main patterns for setting up decoys: a fish hook pattern and a half moon pattern. See the illustrations. Whatever way you set them up, always place their heads primarily INTO the wind when the wind is blowing from one straight direction (some can be looking at other angles, but generally INTO the wind). I personally like the half moon presentation, leaving an alleyway in which they can land and "funnel" in to you. That way you do have some type of control of where they will land. When the wind is changing directions, then you can set the decoys in little family groups--maybe six to a group, depending on how many decoys you have. If my amount of decoys works for me it can work for you. More is probably better, but you do not need a lot more in order to hunt geese successfully.

You have your decoys set; now it is time for you to get set. Staying with the premise of hunting in a cornfield, use corn stalks and pieces to cover yourself. If there is little stalk material in the field, then collect it from another field the day before, store it in a big plastic bag and take it with you. Another idea, and I use this a lot, is to take the garden clippers and go hunt for some ditch grass (weeds in ditches). Cut some and place that in a plastic bag. When my decoys are set I like to find a depression between corn rows approximately 20 feet away from the decoys. Smooth it out some as you will be lying there and want to be as comfortable as possible. If the field is muddy or if I have to lie on snow I take a waterproof rubber hunting pad, plastic sheeting or black plastic trash bags with me and place in the bottom of the pit; that keeps me dry. As you get into position, pull the collected corn stalks over your entire body. Don't forget

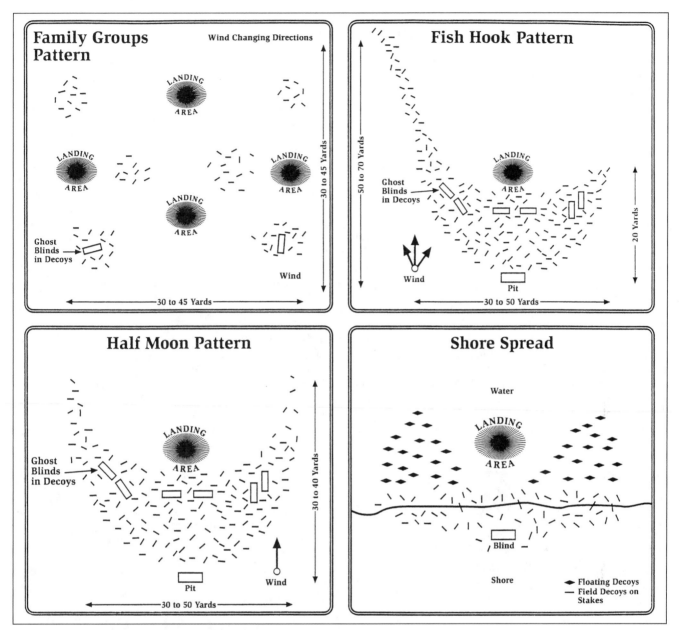

These illustrations show typical decoy spreads and where you should place your blind to be most effective. These are just guidelines. Experiment until you find what's perfect for you.

to place some around your head. I put my gun down on my body, pointing away from any other hunter and me. Cover the gun as much as possible with the corn stalks. To reduce the glare from my gun barrel I tape it with camouflage adhesive tape and I believe it really works. Another good idea is to wear a face mask. There are many types on the market but my favorite is the "half mask", just fitting under my glasses (glasses then will not steam up from breathing).

Hunting glasses are a good item to consider purchasing. They have camo frames with amber glass to cut down on the glare. I have mine made into my prescription, minus the bifocals. Believe me, you cannot lie in a pit and look through bifocals and expect to shoot geese, much less even see correctly. I did not believe the glare from glasses was as obvious as everyone told me until I witnessed it myself. On a sunny day I saw the reflection/glare of glasses on a hunter nearly 400 yards away! If you do not have or cannot afford hunting glasses, just make sure your camo cap or hood is pulled down as far as possible over your head and wear a face mask.

Pay attention to what direction you face when you lie down in your pit. Geese come in flying INTO the wind; geese land looking at the decoys' behinds. You get upwind of your decoy set, in front of the decoys and facing the decoys' faces so you can see the geese coming in toward you, facing you. Just remember you look into their faces. You must be able to see them coming toward you with the least amount of movement from you. If you are facing the wrong way, you will have to continually turn around in your pit and that movement can scare geese off from a long way away. You can choose to lie among the decoys, or off to the side somewhat or directly behind the decoy spread. Just lie there and watch until it is time to shoot. Do not move and keep your head down; when the geese are in range, shoot!

Practice your goose calls while you are lying there waiting for the geese to appear. When you hear some, start calling. Respond to their natural sounds. Don't be afraid to use the call. Bolster your confidence and just start right in talking to them. If they talk and call, you talk and call. Keep calling as they fly in over you. Don't suddenly quit, as they will wonder what's up. If you make a mistake, just try again, and have fun! The calls are not difficult to master. My 5-year-old grandsons both learned after a few minutes of coaching, so go for it!

So here you are all set and ready, you hear the geese, you see them and start calling. Lo and behold, they answer you! You are thrilled! You have done it! Keep on calling. As you do the flock swings in over your decoys. Using what you learned from your shooting classes, you know when to take the shot. If you miss and the geese fly away, you still had a breathtaking experience and should be proud of yourself. You should be proud of yourself just having the desire and knowledge to have set everything up and been in the field to SEE the geese! If you do connect and bag a goose, that's just a bonus!

Snow goose hunting involves huge flocks of geese. The general information is the same as for Canada goose hunting, except that you will need dozens of snow goose decoys and you will find that these light geese are harder to decoy than Canada geese. Hiding in a fence line and sneaking and stalking are common parts of snow goose hunting. I suggest you find an avid snow goose hunter and appoint that person as your snow goose mentor. That mentor can show you the difference in methods of hunting snow geese.

THE DUCK HUNT

Using all the suggestions, advice and principles we've already discussed, apply them to your duck hunt. After scouting for ducks and finding where you want to hunt, making a blind and deciding where to position yourself is the next step. With all the preparations completed, you arrive at your duck hunting area before dawn. One of the most beautiful sights you'll ever see is ducks flying over a wetland or slough at dawn. Their feathers glisten in the dawning light and they fly by as if to say "It's a beautiful morning and I want to share it with you." You certainly don't want to miss all this action, as it is the most spectacular of the entire day.

Be sure to take your waders. The first job upon arriving is "throwing out the decoys." Unwind the strings from the decoys and toss them out into the water. A pattern is also used for duck decoys. Arrange them in a horseshoe shape along the water's edge, probably wading out to knee-deep water. The horseshoe pattern allows the duck to come in and land with their "friends." If you have floating goose decoys you can also bring them. They will work together with duck decoys. Having set out the decoys, gather all your gear and hide it in your blind. Get your duck call out and have fun practicing. Ducks are very vocal and you will find imitating them to be fun. You will be an expert at the mallard highball call before you know it! I have had ducks also fly in to goose calls, so bring both kinds of calls with you.

The Becoming an Outdoors Woman program allows women to get hands-on experience placing decoys. Then they have to pick them up, too.

If your first hunt is this successful, you might be hooked on waterfowl hunting for the rest of your life. These are the first ducks the author ever shot. Not a bad day in the marsh.

Ducks provide nonstop action and are great entertainers. Depending on the kind of duck and how they fly and land, you will be able to watch them funnel in, swizzle in, wiffle, sail and dive bomb into the decoys. One time when my uncle and I were duck hunting we had extra entertainment. A hawk had been buzzing around the decoys and the blind trying to figure out what was happening. All of a sudden he decided he needed a closer look. BONK! He nailed one of the decoys thinking he would be getting lunch! What a stunning hilarious "double take" he did! I bet he never did that again. See, there is all kinds of entertainment out there!

Try to set up so you have the sun at your back. You need to identify the ducks correctly and be able to see perfectly to take the best shot. You cannot do either if the sun is glaring into your eyes.

So you are all set, ready and are calling. Mallards start whizzing by, coming in closer and closer for a look at the decoys. When the ducks come in, shoot as soon as they are within range — don't wait for more to come in — maybe there won't be any more! When they come in, drop

A good dog really helps when hunting waterfowl over water. Here, Sig VandenAkker's Chesapeake Bay retriever, Pat, brings in a duck.

your call; raise your gun and fire! If you have done everything right, a nice drake mallard will drop right into your decoys. Run right out there and pick him up, fondle his beautiful feathers and admire him. Bring him back to the blind and lay him where you can see him. Many times during the morning you will look at him and feel so proud of yourself, so confident and so glad that you decided to explore the waterfowl world. But what if everything was right and you just could not hit a bird? Be proud of yourself and all that you learned and accomplished just by being there. You were there, you watched the birds, you learned, you appreciated nature and you had fun. Again, if you bag a bird, that is a bonus!

HUNTING DOGS

What happens if you down a bird but he falls too far away and you cannot retrieve him? A retrieving dog is the best conservation tool you can have for waterfowl hunting. If you have a dog you do not have to worry about retrieving downed birds or wounded birds — the dog will retrieve them for you. If you ask 10 people their opinions on which breed of dog is the best waterfowl dog; you'll probably receive 10 different answers.

I have waterfowl hunted with only two breeds of dogs, a well-trained big Chesapeake retriever and young Labradors who had not yet been to school. The Chesapeake, Pat, was the retriever of dreams. He was fifth in a line trained by my mentor, Sig. It was wonderful to watch him retrieve so willingly, so expertly, bringing the birds back in perfect condition. Pat's last retrieve was bringing in my 17-pound swan, being beaten upon his head with the powerful swan's feet. It was a sad day when Pat went to "retriever's heaven." I saw what a properly trained dog could do and know what a great conservation tool a dog is. If you do not have a retriever there are certain shots you dare not take for fear of not retrieving your

downed birds. Before you shoot, decide just where and what shots you can safely take in order to retrieve the birds yourself. Since I do not have a dog, I take the next best thing with me: a pair of narrow (1-inch by 1-inch) boards nailed together making a length of about 12 feet, with a long nail pounded on the end. This board has helped me retrieve ducks many, many times. Some hunters take a fishing rod with a lure with multiple hooks along with them. Supposedly you can cast out and reel in the bird. Well, I have yet to see that work for me — maybe you are more coordinated than I am. Just don't have anyone watch you! The last time I tried this trick there was a sudden hard tug on the fishing line. I just thought, "No, it can't be! I don't want a fish when I'm trying so darn hard to snag this duck!" You guessed it, as I reeled in the line I felt a fish. A northern pike had taken the lure! I walked back to my cabin (about two blocks away in "unoccupied territory") left the fish there on the grass and went back to casting for my duck. I never could hook it and finally waded out and picked him up. When I got back to the cabin a while later all that was left of the northern was the head!

There was a coyote roaming around the area so I blamed it on him, or else the wild cat that lived up the hill got to it. So that was the story of my trying to "reel in" my duck! I'm glad no one was watching; I didn't plan on providing entertainment!

After telling you about Pat, the Chesapeake Bay retriever, I must tell you about Buddy, the young black Lab. He is a gorgeous dog, very well bred and someday I'm sure will be a wonderful retriever. His master Tori is one of my hunting buddies and local outdoor writer. I had said "yes" when asked if Buddy, on his first hunt, could come along with us. He promptly ran away. On the second trip he knocked me over twice, then bit me. So it was with some reservation that I consented to his presence a third time. We were out in my yard preparing to leave for the hunting area when Buddy really did it! I had my goose and duck calls on my lanyard around my neck, and yes, you guessed it, Buddy spied them. While running at me full bore he jumped up and grabbed the calls and pulled! I did not have my jacket on yet, only a couple of sweaters. I still don't know who was the lucky one, Buddy or me; it was a good thing he did not bite anything else that was on my chest! My friend then said Buddy would be going to school after the holidays. My only comment was, "do you think he will live that long?"

Nellie is a yellow Lab who belongs to my hunting buddy Lori. The dog is also young and rambunctious, but well on her way to being a wonderful waterfowl dog. She loves exploring our river bottom and minds fairly well. She truly earned her place in my hunting arena when she retrieved a duck for me that had floated to the middle of a slough. She hadn't been with us hunting there as we were conducting a very serious "swan stalk"; we had to drive back to the farm at sunset and take her back to the slough. Lori threw a couple of rocks in the water, Nellie tore right in and went right for the duck — all this in near darkness! Yes, Nellie can go with me anytime!

Lila Antonides, left, the author and Suzette Waszvick, pose with the fruits of a good day on the marsh. When everything comes together and the ducks drop in like rain, shooting can be good.

PHONES IN THE FIELD

Communications are necessary and access to a telephone is important while out hunting, but, so help me, if somebody's phone starts ringing while the geese are setting their wings to land in the decoys...! After a friend I took out goose hunting knocked down two nice Canadians, the first thing he did was call his wife! I had no idea he even had a phone with him. If that phone had rung at the wrong time, I don't think he would have ever seen it again. Now, whoever goes with me carrying a phone is checked and told to have the power off until we need to use it. A person can always call into the office or home for messages if needed. One of the reasons we all go hunting and spend time in the outdoors is to get away from the telephone. Take your phone, but use it wisely.

BEWARE OF BREAKFAST

One of the funniest things to happen while first hunting was being invited to breakfast. In fact, being invited to breakfast by some old prankster hunters. While picking up decoys from one of the first hunts I was ever on, the guys said "old so and so" is serving breakfast a mile over at the Smith corner and I was invited. I thought that was very nice and being hungry and thirsty made it all the more so. When all the decoys were back in the pickup, we took off for the Smith corner. I expected maybe a portable grill with pancakes, sausages, rolls, juice, coffee, tea, etc. My mouth was watering just thinking about it.

Well, there was no portable grill, no pancakes, no rolls, no nothing. Only a big red cooler sat down in the ditch beside an old guy's pickup. After the introductions I thought he'd finally get out sweet rolls and soda pop. He kept on talking and visiting and finally said, "Well, time for breakfast!" He opened the cooler and to my amazement all I saw was a good collection of whiskeys, ice cubes and a few cans of pop! Everyone else had been in on the joke and thought it was hilarious. If I hadn't been so hungry it would've been funny to me, too! As the old guy passed out "breakfast" to everyone, he told me I was the first woman hunter he had met and thought this called for a celebration. It was a nice gesture, but 10:00 AM was a bit early for a celebration. Moral to the story: Beware of old hunters serving breakfast by the roadside! and NEVER MIX ALCOHOL AND HUNTING!

BACK TO BILL

When I was supposed to be teaching Bill to hunt, I heard a voice.

"Hey... Hey!... What's the matter? Are you sleeping over there? Come on! The geese are flying!" Bill's shouting jarred me out of my daydreaming.

When I reflect on past waterfowl memories, I become very intense and emotional. I had truly been "out in left field" there for a while. As I rejoined the present I heard them!

"Hurry up and call for heaven's sake!" Bill was still shouting.

I grabbed my goose call and gave that flock everything I had. I was thrilled to see them turn and start looking over our way, and ecstatic when they were definitely on the pathway right into us. I talked and called to them, hoping they would continue on in, and not spy something we had overlooked in our preparations. They liked what they saw! They wanted to join some new friends on the ground. Closer and closer they came; I was almost breathless, my heart was in my throat and I know I was shaking. I held my breath as they made their last dignified swing over our heads, set their wings and floated down into the decoys. "Boom! Boom!" Bill's gun

was still smoking as I watched two beautiful giant Canada geese drop beside us. We did it! Everything worked perfectly! A classic goose hunt had just unfolded before my eyes. Words cannot express the feeling I had right then; I had just guided my deer hunting mentor to a most-successful first goose hunt. I was so proud to have been able to "show him the ropes" of giant Canada goose hunting. As we gave each other the "high fives" and congratulated ourselves, we both remembered only a few years previous when I knew absolutely nothing about waterfowl hunting. The point is: Never underestimate yourself.

You can start waterfowl hunting by jump-shooting (sneaking up on them) ducks or geese in ponds, jump-shooting in sloughs or marshes, pass shooting, and then work your way up to hunting over decoys. You will then be an expert and enjoy it more because YOU put more effort, knowledge and "brilliance" into bagging the birds and you will enjoy it more.

As for field dressing the birds, refer to the Turkey Hunting chapter. You can either pluck or fillet out the breast meat by cutting it off the breast bone. There may be local meat markets in your area that will process waterfowl for you. Obtain a good waterfowl cookbook for some wonderful eating! Refer to the Turkey Hunting and Upland Game chapters for taxidermy information, it's all about the same.

To become more involved in the waterfowl world, join Ducks Unlimited, Inc. The mission of DU is to fulfill the annual life cycle needs of North American waterfowl by protecting, enhancing, restoring and managing important wetlands and associated uplands. Nearly 750,000 DU members and over 50,000 volunteers helped to raise $118 million for wetlands and waterfowl conservation in 1999. There are over 3,400 local chapters working for waterfowl enhancement. DU is a national sponsor of the Becoming an Outdoor Woman workshop program. Youth are involved in the Greenwings program. For more information call 1-800-45-DUCKS or visit at www.ducks.org

CHAPTER EIGHT

DEER

WHITE-TAILED DEER

"No, I won't," I said.

"Yes, you will," he replied.

"No, I told you. I cannot do it," I said.

"Yes, you can and you will," he said firmly.

"I don't want to," I shot back.

"I will be there beside you to help you every step of the way. Remember the wildlife management principles — those deer are better off taken by hunters than starving to death in the winter or dying from a disease," he reasoned.

Thus began the conversation leading up to my first deer hunt. I knew he was right, but I just didn't think I could shoot a deer.

"Why?" he asked.

"All my life I heard the story of my father's only deer hunt," I said. "His words still echo in my ears. 'I shot that deer. But it was terrible looking into those big brown eyes and then pulling the trigger. I will never do it again.' And he didn't."

Naturally I thought that I never would either. After all, he was a man and if he couldn't do it, how could I?

My conservation officer/mentor/friend, Bill Antonides, and I were having this conversation at license application time. To appease him, I sent in my application and promised myself I wouldn't think about it until I either received the deer tag or I was unsuccessful in the drawing. Either way, I would worry about it later; I just needed to get him off my back about this. As luck would have it, I was successful and received a tag to hunt at Sand Lake National Wildlife Refuge

a few miles away from our farm. Yikes! Now what? Of course Bill had seen the list and knew my name was on it when he called me.

I had already become a fanatical wild turkey hunter, was learning to master waterfowl hunting and did some pheasant hunting. So why not try something new and completely different? I had trouble erasing my father's deer hunting story from my mind, but yet there was a streak of curiosity rising in me. I had quite the conversations with myself about deer hunting. If I loved other types of hunting, wouldn't I learn to love deer hunting just as much? Was I scared because this was now big game hunting? I was afraid of rifles. Could I conquer that? Was I using my dad's story as an excuse for my insecurity about this? After much thought and very patient and understanding instruction from Bill, my attitude was changing. He pushed me, but not too much. He made sure there was enough leeway for me to "duck out" if I honestly wanted to forget it. But, how could I ever live with myself if I said no to some new exciting opportunity? Besides, I had the tag and if I didn't use it, that meant I was unfairly keeping a deer tag from some other hunter.

The day came when I said, "Yes, I want to hunt deer. I want to give myself a chance. I want to see for myself what it is really like." In the days before the season opener, Bill made sure I had everything I needed, taught me about deer habitat and habits, brought out his friend's 22-250 rifle so I could become familiar with it, and started telling me exciting deer hunting stories. After making sure I applied for the tag and carefully instructing me about the rifle, the next best thing he did was NOT make me get up early in the morning and go into the refuge in the dark.

The first chance we had to hunt was a late afternoon "wait-by-a-water-pond" experience on a cool but nice day. After walking into the refuge and finding deer trails and

THE BOTTOM LINE !

YOU'LL NEED THIS ————

beds, we decided to set up beside a track-laden water hole and wait. I loved this already! It was nice, it was quiet, and it was the first time I had seen all the deer sign. I felt like I truly was in the deer's living room. I suddenly felt "close" to them — a feeling that bears no understanding or explanation. I was really going to do this — although if a deer appeared, I would have to pass the final test. The quietness and apprehension of not knowing if, how, or when a deer would make its appearance was addictive. No deer graced us with its presence at this first watering place, so we quietly and slowly walked until we found another one with even more deer tracks. We set up again and waited. Bill told me the most important time while deer hunting is the last 45 minutes to an hour before sunset.

I was facing one direction and Bill was facing the other as we discussed deer tactics. I looked up and there she was! A doe had miraculously appeared on the far side of the little pond. She was just standing there looking at me. I froze! Not wanting to move, speak or whisper, I placed my hand upon Bill's and pushed as hard as I could to get his attention. To this day he talks about the pain I caused and that his hand has never been the same. He whispered to move slowly and raise the gun, see her through

The author's hunting partner, Lila Antonides, and her first buck. If you decide you want to hunt deer, there is nothing stopping you. Just get out there and do it.

the scope, take the rifle off safety and then shoot. I took him literally and moved very slowly, like hardly at all. Bill gave me a loud whisper, "Move faster than THAT!" Somehow it all worked together. I raised the rifle, found her in the scope, whispered where I would aim and pulled the trigger. The rifle kicked and I'm sure I closed my eyes as I did not see what happened to her. Bill shouted, "Lady, you have just bagged your first deer!"

Shock, terror, relief, pride, sadness and joy were only a few of the emotions I struggled with as I stood beside her with my legs shaking. What a feeling! What an accomplishment! I could do it! She was beautiful and I viewed her as a harvested wild animal, one that would provide some wonderful meals and memories. My father's experience had been replaced in my mind by a good, ethical, and very enjoyable hunt with a happy ending and a tremendous sense of accomplishment and pride. I was now a deer hunter!

The next lesson of course was the field dressing — that was something to behold the first time! I have gone from thinking, "Golly, how does he know how to do that so well? I could never do that," to teaching my friend Lila (Bill's wife) how to field dress a deer of her own. Lila and I have successfully hunted deer, bagged them, cleaned them, skinned them and had them all ready to cut up while our husbands were watching TV!

Bill was a meat cutter while attending college, and he is extremely knowledgeable about the cuts of meat and how you obtain them correctly. Since he is the expert and enjoys saying who washes the meat, who cuts the trim, who does the wrapping and labeling, the entire process is done at Bill and Lila's house. It is a real "deer party" with friends stopping in and visiting during all the activity and a whole lot of fun. As I have said so many times, it is not just the bagging of the game that is important — it is all the fun before, during and after!

That first deer hunt has led to many, many wonderful hunts and memories. I will always be grateful to Bill for pushing me, but not too hard, to get started, and for the terrific calm and patient instruction. With the attitude I had in the beginning, any little mistake could've turned me off and away from deer hunting. I had a teacher who knew I had to be "pushed with kid gloves" or I would balk and that would be the end of it. This is why it is so very important that beginning women hunters have the right kind of instructor and instruction. I continually thank Bill for the strong encouragement as I had entered into an entire new world of hunting experiences.

Two years later, Bill "called in his marker." Lila wanted to learn to hunt deer. Bill did not have the extra time then and asked me to be the teacher/mentor. I'm so glad I jumped at the chance! Lila is now an expert deer hunter, a great shot, and a darn good hunting buddy. We hunt together most of the season and even have a "secret women's place" where no one else is allowed to hunt!

Lila and I hunt whitetails on our farm and our neighbor's farm. We both like to hunt the same way—slow stalks through trees, setting up on deer trails or just plain hiding in the woods and waiting. We have had great hunts, had plenty of meat to take home, and such a sense of pride knowing that we did all that by OURSELVES! I had fun teaching Lila, but she wasn't the only student. She has taught me plenty, also. I must say though, the first field dressing lesson really wasn't all that much fun. It was given in the snow and cold and dark, but we did it! We have a great sense of pride and accomplishment and always giggle when guys ask us if we really hunt alone with "no men. And you clean them, too?" You bet! Women can do anything they want to!

Lori Goldade is a special hunting friend with her own deer story to tell. She wanted to start hunting so she could spend more time with her son. The times she observed rifle deer hunting she was disappointed at the ethics she saw and decided to learn bowhunting instead. She attended Becoming an Outdoors Woman workshops and became a very proficient bowhunter of deer and bear.

One of Lori's first hunts was with another bowhunting woman friend. They made their way into a wildlife refuge area and split up. Finally deciding on the correct place to set up, she got into her ground blind. Lori tells it this way, "The doe started coming in, almost on the trail on which we walked. She was getting closer, I kept getting more excited and tried to hide behind this tree in front of me. She gave no indication that she knew I was there and stopped about 15 yards away. She was in a perfect position. I just said to myself 'I can do this!' It is a challenge, you know, just being

This is what you're looking for. The white-tailed deer is the most popular big game animal in the country. An entire industry has been built around deer hunting. Deer are wary, possess excellent senses and can be a challenging target for even the best hunters.

able to pull back on the bow without the deer seeing you! I pulled back and then came around the side of the tree and she was still standing there. Again, I repeated to myself 'I can do this!' I let the arrow go and, just like that, the arrow hit. I knew it was a good shot. It was so amazing that an arrow could do this — that I could do this! There was no noise — no blast from a gun. She ran over a hill and I waited 20 minutes and got my marking tape out and walked to the deer. I marked where I was at so my friend would know what was happening. I found the doe and had my 'admiration' time with her. I had her completely field dressed, ALL BY MYSELF, by the time my friend came over.

"The first time I cleaned a deer the landowner was driving around not too far from me. I didn't wave because I wanted to do this all by myself and not have anyone judging me or standing over me telling me what to do or push me out of the way saying 'let me do it for you.' The cleaning is an important part of the hunt. If I harvest an animal, then I'm field dressing it, too."

When I asked Lori how she knew what do, she explained, "I just saw the diagrams in a book (before hunting season) and knew what to do. I had never watched it being done before. I just did it."

Lori continued, "It was about dark when my friend showed up and she couldn't believe I got a deer. She thought we were just going out to hunt/have fun, not actually really get something and then have to work! We had to drag that deer out 1-1/2 miles (head first so we wouldn't ruin any hair). When we were walking back to the vehicle, dragging my deer, I was so proud! The feelings I had were hard to explain. I felt like I was one with my human predecessors. I had hunted. I had harvested. I had cleaned my animal and I was dragging it out of the hunting area. I did all of it! I really felt like an 'Amazon Woman'! What a feeling! I don't know what this brings out in other women, but it was cool!

"I saved everything I could from that doe. I had the head mounted, the hide tanned and the skull saved. The skull is hanging in the bedroom! We had jerky, steak and ground venison and enjoyed all the meat."

I told Lori that I had wanted to have my first deer, a doe, mounted but was told it "wasn't the thing to do." I was told only antlered deer ever were mounted, so I didn't do it. Lori's response was, "It's because most of the hunters are men and men wouldn't do it! Some men maybe would want to do it, but they didn't because it just wasn't the macho thing to do!"

Why did Lori want her doe mounted? "Because she was my trophy; I was as proud of that doe as anybody could be of a big-antlered deer.

GETTING TO KNOW YOU

Whenever you are in the woods or the forest and you suddenly see a flash of bright

Brenda Valentine, the only female member of the Red Head Pro Hunting Team, says she still gets excited when a big deer comes into range. You need skill, confidence and a little bit of luck to bag a deer like this. With a little practice, your turn for a trophy will come.

white waving back and forth and disappearing into the brush, you can bet that was a white-tailed deer — the most popular big game animal in the U.S. Their color varies throughout the seasons; they are dark gray in winter to almost a deep red in the summer. The color of the underside of their tail never changes. It is brilliant white. Hence, our forefathers named them "white-tailed deer." When whitetails are alarmed or feel threatened, their tails go up; it will look like they are waving a flag as they bound away through the woods. Imagine the surprise of early explorers as they first witnessed the actions of whitetail deer in this new country, all "waving the flags" in their hurry to get to cover. Whitetails are found throughout most of North America with the exception of the extreme western U.S.

In the latter part of the 1800s, the west was being settled. With habitat being destroyed and over-hunting occurring, the deer herds became sparse. Laws prohibiting market hunting and regulating sport hunting were enacted soon after the turn of the century and deer numbers have increased. Whitetail populations have increased rapidly

An adult white-tailed buck weighs anywhere from 100 to 300 pounds and does weigh between 85 and 130 pounds. They mate in the late fall; this period is known as the "rut". About one month following the peak of the rut, bucks will be after does again to breed the ones that were not bred the first time around. Bucks will also breed the 1-year- old fawns, usually in January, so there can really be three parts to the rut. The first rut is the most important. (My South Dakota deer hunter friends tell me the peak of that first rut is always November 11.) The buck's hormones are running on high and breeding a doe is his only purpose in life at this point in time. Bucks in the rut eat very little. You may have heard the statement "drive carefully as there may be deer on the road this time of year"; bucks will be chasing does and they don't care if they have to cross a highway or not. Bucks rub dried velvet off their antlers on small trees and saplings, (that is what is known as a deer "rub") and in the process overdevelop their neck muscles making their necks appear huge. They use small twigs to rub their scent gland which is near their eye. My friend Jeff Nodsle told me, "I have watched deer do this — you would swear they are trying to poke their eyes out!" They paw the ground and urinate there to mark their territory; that is called a "scrape". These are both good places to find a buck during hunting season, because bucks are announcing their territory to all other deer. They are trying to attract hot does and will also attack any other buck that comes into the area in search of does.

Fawns are born in the late spring and weigh between 4 and 8 pounds. A doe's first birth is only one fawn; twins and sometimes triplets are born to older does, but this depends on the availability of good food for the deer. The fawn's spots on his body help conceal him from predators, but the young deer's primary defense is that it emits almost no scent. That combined with camouflage and the ability to lie completely still allows the fawns to elude predators.

Throughout their first year, the fawns stay with their mother forming a family group. Deer make only three sounds: they snort, grunt and bleat. Does use short, mono-

An adult white-tailed buck weighs anywhere from 100 to 300 pounds and does weigh between 85 and 130 pounds.

tone bleats to summon their fawns. Nothing will jerk a buck's head around faster than a doe bleat during the rut.

Whitetail buck antlers are extremely special to hunters. Some hunters will go through "hell and high water" to acquire a trophy whitetail buck. The antlers grow up and forward with single, unbranched spikes or tines projecting up from the main beam. They are grown and shed each year. Genetics, quality and quantity of food determine the antler size. Velvet supplies nutrients to the fast-growing antler tissue. Once the antlers reach full size, the blood vessels in the velvet begin to die, become dry and start to peel. This is when the buck starts to "rub".

Whitetails stay mostly to themselves or in mother/fawn family groups throughout most of the year. Depending on the winter weather and the snow cover, deer can form herds and "yard-up." In January of 1999, my family hosted a whitetail herd of around 250 animals on our farm. The deer bedded down in a state game production area about one mile away, then walked, in single file, across the frozen river bottom, up the river bank and helped themselves to our hay and corn. We had about 100 inches of snow that year and the deer either came into the farmyards for food or starved to death. Our wildlife agency's "deer crew" brought out ear corn and dropped it off on the riverbank to "shortstop" the deer and keep them from coming and eating any more of our hay. This procedure was followed in several states that winter. Deer depredation can be a terrific problem for landowners, wildlife agencies and hunters. There is a delicate balance between landowners and the hunting public and the way deer depredation is handled can either make or break relationships. A good idea is for local sportsmen's clubs to participate in this deer feeding and build good will.

During that hard winter, the deer started across the river bottom every day at 4:30 p.m. Their timing was unbelievable. They formed a mile-long stretch in single file. I spent many wonderful hours observing the deer and their habits during that time. Sometimes I would dress in my white snow camo suit, take the video camera and lay underneath a sheet near a tree on their trail. It was hilarious when they would figure out I was there, but sometimes they went by and ignored me. If they smelled me they snorted, flashed their white flags and ran around in circles. It became a waiting game; they were determined to eat and would wait me out. During the days it was 25 degrees below zero, they didn't have too long to wait. One time when I had the video camera, I just happened to catch a fox running across the ice from about a quarter of a mile away. He was headed to the deer string and when he got there he bit the ankles until the deer stomped him enough times that he caught on and split. What a thrill to get that on tape in my own back yard. My mother couldn't wait to watch all this excitement. It was 30 degrees below zero the day she chose to observe. I dressed her warmly and we stood behind the big tree on top of the riverbank and watched the procession. She was thrilled. Not too many 78-year-old ladies would probably list that as a highlight of their winter!

The home range of a whitetail may vary from 40 to about 300 acres with total movement generally restricted to about one square mile.

Whitetails are browsers in the winter and feed on such trees as chokecherry, birch, maple, dogwood and aspen. They also consume some grasses and herbs when those plants are in season and nuts and fruits. In farming sections of our country, deer consume agricultural crops adjacent to woodlands and use the woods primarily as resting and escape cover. Whitetails are most often seen in the early morning or late afternoon when they move out on the edge of open areas to feed. Hunting pressure determines feeding hours. If the pressure is heavy, deer may only move out and feed during the night. During bright, moon-lit nights, they may feed all night long and stay bedded all day. The bottom line is, to successfully hunt deer, you must know them and their habits.

GETTING READY

Some states require that you apply for a deer hunting license. Other states allow you buy a license over the counter. Some of the over-the-counter states my have an application deadline for "bonus" tags available in areas were there are too many deer. Application time is usually in the summer. Check with your state's wildlife agency and find out when the deadline is and write it down on your calendar. The agency will tell you where you can find application brochures. The sooner you send in the application the better; if there is a mistake on it there will still be time for it be to returned to you for a correction and resubmitted before the deadline. Here in South Dakota, there are several choices on each application. We have to select our preferred hunting unit, which type of deer (whitetail or mule deer), and what type of tag. There are a large selection of tags available, from single doe (anterless) tags to combinations of two tags (antlerless and buck, any whitetail plus any antlerless whitetail, etc.) "Any deer" means it can be either a doe or a buck. The list may seem confusing, but it is not. Just read any application you have slowly and carefully and select your preference. If you have any questions, contact your local conservation officer or the agency office. Your local sportsmens club's members will also help you

The author making some noise with a pair of rattling antlers. It is not always required that you stay quiet while you are in the woods hunting deer. During the rut, the sound of two bucks battling for the right to breed a doe will usually draw some deer to your location.

with any questions you have from finding a place, applying for the tag, finding the right equipment, and deer hunting tactics in your area. Just remember every state will be a bit different when it comes to deer management.

In some states, if you do not draw a license, you can check out the "left over" list to see if there are any licenses available. If you change your tag preference (perhaps from buck to antlerless) and reapply you may receive a tag. Check your state's regulations.

Some states' wildlife agencies require you to send them incisor teeth from your harvested deer. If your state requires this you will probably receive a "tooth envelope" along with your license. The incisors are used for various biological information and helps to effectively manage the states' deer populations. It is an easy procedure; use your knife and just cut out one of the lower front teeth. Have your mentor or buddy do this if you do not want to. It is important to send in these teeth and it is a responsibility of a good hunter to do all that is required as you will be contributing information for the resource. Other states require that you take any deer you kill to a registration station where an official will record specific information about the deer. This is done to assist in deer management.

GETTING STARTED

So, you've got your license. Now what? You must research your chosen unit more carefully, use your maps to find public and private land. If you choose to hunt on private land, you must obtain permission. Please refer to the chapter "Finding a Place to Hunt". Be sure to read all your state's big game regulations and know them forwards and backwards!

You may have applied with a hunting buddy in mind, or been asked to accompany a seasoned hunter on your first deer hunt. If you have not done either and have jumped into this entirely alone, that can be scary. But it doesn't have to be! I recommend you call your conservation officer or sportsmen's club (they do have women members, too!) and find a mentor for your first few times out hunting. There will always be someone who will be honored to take you and "show you the ropes". You should still follow all the steps and study and scout for deer before the hunt. After doing this, your mentor or hunting buddy will make it all "come alive" for you, show you the real deer world, open up new experiences and opportunities for you to discover yourself in your new world.

Scouting for deer is important. You will want to know where the deer are, what times they appear, the directions they take on their trails, where the trails lead to and from, where the deer rubs, scrapes and beds are found and everything else you can about your hunting area. Scout your hunting area about a month before the season opens so you know the terrain exactly; the last scouting should be done closer to opening day as deer do change their habits (they do this to confuse us!). Do not scout a day or two before the season opens — you might spook the deer out of the area. If you are on public land, contact your conservation officer and ask where the best place to hunt deer would be. Take a map with you and mark where you have seen sign. If you are on private land, take a notebook with you and make your own map. Mark where you have seen tracks, trails, fresh scat, etc.

A good time to be in the deer woods is late winter, after season closes. The deer return to their regular habits and schedules and will not take much note of you. Watching them, observing their habits and their feeding times can be quite an education for you. Remember where the rubs and scrapes are as bucks usually return to them year after year. Take a notebook and write down specific details, making a map of rubs and scrapes, trails, etc. Keep this information and use it to your advantage the next hunting season.

Fresh scat are black, oblong and glistening small pebbles; older scat will be lighter and dry. Deer leave a lot of droppings during the day. Scat is a good sign, but if you see a lot do not mistakenly think there is an entire herd right there — it could only be a couple of deer.

Finding scrapes and setting up close to them is effective not only during the rut, but after the rut also. A scrape is an area of ground the buck uses to mark his territory. He paws and scrapes the ground, then urinates on the spot. If you find a scrape you will know deer have been in the area. "Doe-in-heat" scent can be utilized in conjunction with the scrapes. Here is how to use it, if you desire: place the scent on a rag, then connect the rag to a string and drag it into the woods behind you to cover up your human scent; place it where you want a buck to stop. When a deer smells the scent it will and stop to investigate. THAT is when you take your shot. By using scent you can control, somewhat, the actions of the deer. But this system is not sure-fire. If you will be sitting on the ground, DO NOT spray your boots with the scent (a buck could come in and attack you — really!). Sprinkle a few drops of the doe in heat scent in the scrape, then go to your blind or deer stand. Make sure you are at least 10 to 20 yards away from the scrape so you don't spook the deer.

Mark the feeding areas and note the trails leading to those areas on your maps. Trail intersections are good places to set up; as you draw out the trails on your map you will automatically see these places. Plan on setting up just off the side of the trails. Mark them and you will have your place to hunt your deer. If you find deer beds, mark the general area because deer seldom bed in the same spot each day. Always ask the landowner where and when he has seen deer; he lives there with them and knows their habits and

can direct you and save you time. Don't forget that deer can swim; check for tracks and trails leading into or out of streams and up the bank. Deer usually tend to cross water where it is shallow and slow-moving. A heavily used deer trail at a creek or river crossing can be a good place to hunt.

You want this to be a successful hunt — you have invested a lot of time and enthusiasm already, so do the best possible job of scouting so you are confident you have done everything possible to ensure a good hunt. Get into the woods before daylight and actually observe the deer; go there again in the evening and watch their habits at that time. Be as quiet as you can and be concealed. Make mental notes of what you see — where and when the deer are moving. You can write in your notebook later. If you do not see any deer, just note the sign you see to determine if they are still in the area. You know what to look for in the woods or fields; don't forget to look at the edges of water holes. If they are using that water hole, there will be tracks all around it. If there is cover such as trees, bushes, or a nearby field edge, you can plan on setting up right there. While you are scouting, ask yourself the questions: Where would be the best place to sit? What cover would there be for me? If there is no cover, what do I bring with me for concealment? How can I change the plan when the wind direction changes? Where would I park my vehicle for concealment and safety? Would this be an easy place from which to drag a deer? How much time does it take for me to walk in here from the vehicle so I know when to set the alarm clock?

There are some "tricks and gizzmos" to help you bring in deer. Rattling antlers, sticks or bags and deer calls can be used effectively. However, these items should NOT be used as a substitute for hunting skills. You should learn about them, but DO NOT be concerned about them until you have some experience deer hunting. Learn all the basics mentioned above.

When you feel you are ready, place "rattling sticks, a rattling bag or rattling antlers" on your list of items to take with you. Rattling for deer is clacking together a pair of deer antlers to imitate a fight between two bucks, the purpose being to attract bucks. The "home" buck will run in to see who is in his territory; younger bucks will slowly walk up to the racket expecting to see a fight in progress and therefore steal away any does that

Brenda Mitzel of Aberdeen, South Dakota, bagged this nice buck with a muzzleloader. Hunting with a black-powder rifle offers an even greater challenge because you get only one shot and range of a muzzleloader is limited when compared to that of a centerfire.

may be watching. Some experts say rattling will work only during the rut, but others say it will also work later. Rattling antlers can either be real antlers or you can buy synthetic ones. The brow tines (the first tine on the main beam) are sawed off and the rest of the tines can be sawed off one inch from the pointed end. You can smooth off the area where you will be holding them, then drill a hole through the antlers so you can attach a cord.

The author calls this buck "William" and he responded nicely to the sound of clicking antlers. His desire to be the dominant buck in the area was his undoing. Patience and a little practice, along with a well-placed shot could give you a buck like this.

Brenda Mitzel says, "if a buck hears rattling, it thinks another buck is in its territory and it will come to look. When the deer comes it will be very, very alert. They are hard to shoot if you have been rattling because they are not just 'moseying along' on the trail; they are looking for the other deer with their eyes wide open and they are mad! Most likely their ears will be all the way back — that happens when they are really mad. A lot of times the little guys also come in to check, thinking that they may get a chance at a doe. These little guys usually just run away when the big guy comes in. I use real antlers to rattle and I also have a rattling bag. When using real antlers, you clack and rattle them for about 2 minutes, wait a minute and a half, or 2 minutes, then rub them on the tree bark and paw the ground once or twice for a minute and a half. Wait another 2 minutes and repeat the sequence three to four times, then stop and wait and watch. It usually takes a good 20 minutes before you might see anything because they are really cautious. If you want the deer to get closer, just tickle the tines a little bit. This works well with a rifle or muzzleloader; they might not get close enough for a bow shot."

The first time I rattled antlers, it was just like magic. I listened to Brenda's instructions, completed the sequence, waited and watched. In 25 minutes this very nice whitetail came looking for excitement. He was only 75 yards in front of me, standing broadside. "William" was not only the nicest whitetail I had ever harvested, he proved to me that I had learned another hunting skill.

The rattling bag works very well because you can carry it in your pocket. It is a small bag about 7 inches long and the diameter of a baseball. It contains several wooden sticks, like 3/4-inch dowels. When you hold the bag in your hand and click the sticks together, it sounds just like the rattling deer antlers. If the deer are starting to come in but are hesitating some, just click the bag a little bit to make noise and that might be enough to get them to come closer. Movement can be held to a minimum with the rattling bag and that is a great advantage, however, I prefer the real antlers and the sound they produce.

A grunt call (grunt tube) is another important thing to take with you. Brenda says, "The best thing to do is to go out before you are actually going to hunt, just to play with the deer. You can watch tapes and educate yourself on grunt calls, but you really don't know what it sounds like until you are in the woods. When you hear the deer make these sounds, it is easier to imitate them and easier to learn. You will hear the grunt sound and really know how long or how quick it is. One day before season I spent two hours in a tree stand, just grunting. A buck came by and really got mad at me. He would grunt, then I would grunt. He would come in and look all over and just couldn't find where that sound was coming from. He would run outside of the tree claim, then I would grunt and he would just come barreling in to me again. This is how you learn. The best way to learn how to use the grunt call is to be in their world and listen to them. A lot of times they will be following a doe while they are grunting."

It doesn't look like a great deer call, but this bag filled with sticks can be just the ticket to bring in a buck. Just roll the bag around a bit between your hands and wait to see what happens.

The True Talker grunt tube by Hunters' Specialties is said to be as easy to use as "fogging a mirror." Grunt tubes like this can produce a variety of sounds, from a buck grunt to fawn bleat, that deer will come to investigate.

The first time I heard a buck grunt was unforgettable. The strange and unfamiliar sound came from behind me as I sat against a tree. I heard it a second time, then finally realized that a buck was behind me. His third grunt was even louder and to my right. I slowly turned my head and there he was, only 18 feet away, looking directly at me! I had to make a 90-degree turn to get a good shot and I knew he would leap right over the riverbank and disappear when I moved. He did exactly that, but what a fun experience to hear that grunting sound when he was right there!

A compass is necessary if you are in an unfamiliar area or may become confused about directions in the dark. This is especially true when you are hunting in the big Eastern forests. Hunting in the forests is quite different from the deer hunting done where I live in South Dakota. The differences are largely due to the woods. It's tough to see deer in the woods. They have lots of places to hide. You still need to scout, find trails and set up your hunting site much the same

way. But you have to remember that during most hunts in the forest, your longest shot might be less than 75 yards. Hunters in the deer woods also often use deer drives to bag their deer. A drive is nothing more than a couple hunters walking through a likely looking section of forest, hoping to spook deer out past standers waiting along deer trails at the other end of the drive. Many times, those hunters walking on the drive never actually see the deer they spook up. In most cases, the deer move out long before the hunters are within gun range, but the standers get the shots as the deer try to sneak away.

To ensure you don't get lost in the woods, become thoroughly educated on the use of maps and compasses. It's a good idea to take the Map and Compass class at a Becoming an Outdoors Woman workshop. The most important thing to remember is that the red needle always points north and you can get your bearing from that. Look at your compass before you walk into the woods to know which way you are headed. Then check from time to time to keep your bearings. Be sure to stand away from your vehicle so you obtain a true reading-- any metal will throw the compass off.

Take binoculars with you, especially in open country, and glass for deer. Carefully and slowly look through the trees, brush, cornfields. Deer are experts at hiding and they will make your mission of finding them as difficult as possible! Look for an antler tine, an ear sticking up, a rump or any other part of the deer that might give away an animal trying to hide. Because of the whitetail's notorious reputation for hanging tight and letting hunters walk by, it pays to spend more time looking than walking while you are in the woods.

Don't forget to add toilet paper, paper towels, tissues and Wet Ones or baby wipes and any other personal items, including any medications that you must take to your day pack or fanny pack while hunting or scouting. Either activity can become an all-day affair, especially if you find what you are looking for.

If you are scouting in mosquito season, take your mosquito repellent along. You do not want to be fanning and slapping mosquitoes and thereby causing quite a stir while you are watching a deer trail. You also do not want to be covered with bites!

Please refer to the Turkey Hunting chapter for information on "Where do I stay on the hunting trip?".

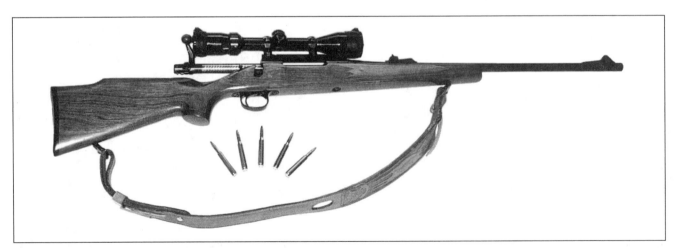

The author's rifle is a Remington Model 700 chambered for the 270 Winchester cartridge. It provides adequate power with moderate recoil and is very accurate.

DEER GUNS

Rifles are the most commonly used deer guns. Some areas require the use of shotguns with slugs and a few areas still allow buckshot to be used. Muzzleloaders can also be used. First of all, find out what firearm your state requires and plan accordingly. Contact your conservation officer or state agency.

I hunt deer with a Remington chambered for the 270 Winchester round. It has a Bushnell 3- to 9-power variable scope and I shoot Federal trophy-bonded 140-grain shells. I love my combination of rifle, scope and "silver bullets". It is lethal. The 270 packs a lot of power and does kick some. When you are sighting it in or practicing your shooting, be sure you have a heavy jacket or other clothing covering your shoulder for padding. You will be wearing heavy clothing when you are hunting so you won't have to worry about it then. Just don't injure yourself, or scare yourself by practicing with a big rifle in a thin shirt. Do not have your eye too close to the scope; you do not want to start out with a black swollen eye.

When you have made your rifle and scope choice, the gun dealer will have it bore-sighted for you. Bore-sighting is a preliminary sighting-in done by the gunsmith after the scope is mounted--you have to fine tune it yourself. You must fine tune it by sighting it in yourself so it is "right on." Ask your mentor or members of your local sportsmen's club for help here. They may take you out to their shooting range and give you the instruction you need. Most likely they will have a paper target that will be divided into 1-inch squares, with the bull's-eye area clearly designated. The standard by which rifles and shooting are judged is to shoot a cluster of three bullets into a group that measures 1 inch at 100 yards. Do not shoot any less than three. If you shoot only two, you could have a "wild" shot the first time and be right on the second time, or be way off and you would have no way of knowing for sure how you are consistently shooting. I know! I have made the mistake! I was frustrated and nearly in tears because I couldn't figure out what was wrong and how I could be shooting so badly. Remember this tip: shoot during the cool hours of the day, not in direct hot sunlight, and don't shoot more than six or nine shells at one session. The rifle barrel expands with heat and can really throw off your shooting. I know that personally, too — been there, done that. I was doing all this sighting in by myself and when everything started going downhill I didn't know what was going on. "Frustrated" does not even start to describe my emotions at that point. If I had had someone with me I would have been spared and learned faster. This is another reason I say find a mentor and have that person go through all the steps with you.

When sighting-in your rifle, you want it to be as steady as possible. Sandbags are perfect. Go to your nearest transportation department and have them assist you in obtaining sandbags and filling them. Two or three half-filled bags are better than one full one and a lot easier with which to work. They are heavy, so you won't want to tote them around any more than necessary. I left mine in my hunting vehicle and they were always there and ready when I decided to practice my shooting. If you don't have access to a shooting range, get permission to shoot at an area with a safe backstop. Then you can place the bags on the hood of your vehicle, use them on a shooting bench or even place them on the ground. If you have a local rifle range, become a regular shooter there.

The desired result of your sighting-in should be a cluster of three bullets all in a square inch, exactly three inches above the bull's-eye where you aimed your rifle. With the trajectory (path) of the bullet, you will be within the vital area of deer at ranges anywhere from 50 to 250 yards with most rifle bullets. This is the best and most reliable way to sight in your rifle. It is difficult to obtain this "perfect result", but work at it because you want to harvest that animal as quickly and cleanly as possible. If you cannot perfectly shoot the 3 bullets in that tiny space at 100 yards, make sure you get as close as possible. Remember the vital area on big game is large — much larger than one square inch. When hunting you will have a much larger target area. However, while hunting you won't have your sandbags, shooting bench and perfect wind conditions, so every inch you are off at the range is greatly magnified in the field.

I had deer hunted for a few years and had good shot placement each time I harvested an animal. When I received my elk tag I was told to use the above procedure to "make sure my rifle was perfectly sighted-in." In my first three attempts (different times, different days) I just could not get the three bullets on that paper the way they were supposed to be. I cannot tell you the frustration I felt! I called various people and always received the same answer: "yes, it's three-bullets in 1 inch, 3 inches high at 100 yards." I could not do it! My confidence level was in the cellar — where it had NEVER been before. I just couldn't figure out what happened to me. It got to me so badly that I entertained thoughts of ripping up the elk tag and giving up. (I didn't dare do that — here in South Dakota receiving an elk tag is almost a once-in-a-lifetime event!)

I finally called my game warden/mentor/friend Bill and whined a lot about all this. He couldn't understand what was happening to me either. He had witnessed my rifle shooting and knew I was rather proficient. He came out to the farm and down to the river bottom we went, paper targets and pop cans in hand. We measured off 100 yards and began what was to be the biggest confidence-lifter I've ever experienced. Bill used my rifle and aimed at the bull's-eye on the paper target; yup, there were three bullet holes in a cluster the size of a quarter, 3 inches high! The rifle was sighted-in perfectly. OK, so then what? Was it my eyes? Was it the "barrel heat" factor? Was I just too nervous about being absolutely perfect and my perfectionism took over? I still don't know. Bill handed me my rifle, replaced the paper target with pop cans and when he got back to the firing line, gave the signal for me to fire. Three bullets later I had taken out three pop cans at 100 yards! I repeated the performance with the same results. I could not believe it! We then placed dirt clods on a fallen tree trunk — same story — I disintegrated them! Bill then said it was time again for the paper target. Finally, this time, after all this trial and tribulation, tears, frustration and hopelessness, I HIT THE PAPER CORRECTLY! I can't even describe what that did for my confidence!

Now knowing I still had "what it takes", I put the rifle to rest for a couple of days while I prepared for the elk hunting trip. The evening before I left I went again to the "magic place" on the river bottom and nicely shot a few cans — just to make sure. I really still don't know what happened that caused all the trouble for me — I guess a combination of things. Heed my advice if this ever happens to you: DO NOT GIVE UP! Do some research and ask for help. Don't let the paper target intimidate you--find some pop cans and go to work! You must have that confidence level up there where it is supposed to be and you can do it!

Cardboard life-size deer targets are great for shooting practice. The vital area is drawn out and you will see exactly where you need to shoot for a killing shot. You will see your bullet hole and know how to adjust your sights or aim if you need to. Practice your shooting from sitting, standing, kneeling and prone (flat on your belly). You should be able to shoot well from all positions, but when you are in the field, always try to find the most stable position you can. Do what ever you can to support your rifle. Shoot from a standing position only as a last resort.

I love my 270 for hunting deer, but there are many other calibers that will work for you. My friend Lila really likes her 243 Winchester and the 100-grain Power Point shells; it is lighter in weight and does not kick quite as much as the 270 Winchester. It still has plenty of power to knock down a deer. I shot my mule deer with a borrowed rifle chambered in .308 Winchester and that was OK, too. Other rifles that can be used include the 223 Remington, 22-250, 6 mm (close to the 243), 30-06, 7 mm Magnum and dozens of others. The one rifle that has likely killed more deer than any other in this country is the 30-30 Winchester. It's a good rifle, maybe not the greatest caliber in the world, but it has been around since 1894 and hundreds of thousands of hunters (maybe even millions) have carried a 30-30 in the woods. Talk to your gun dealer about what size shells to use in whatever rifle you choose. Tell him what game you are hunting and where you are going; he will be able to recommend a good shell for you. An important point to remember is always be cognizant of the availability of shells for your particular rifle. If you will hunt with an "off beat" caliber, make sure you either have enough shells for the trip because you may not be able to buy them once you get off the beaten path.

Remember to purchase a hearing protector that you will use when you are sighting-in your rifle. Also purchase a sling for your rifle so it is easier to carry in the field. A sling that is wide over the shoulder area is best and most comfortable; it will not cut into your shoulder and hurt after carrying it for a while.

If you are sighting-in your rifle at an established shooting range, mark off the yardage so you know what targets at 50, 75, 100, 200, 300 really look like. Think about that a lot.

When you are out hunting you must take range into consideration before every shot. Remember when you sighted-in your rifle 3 inches high at 100 yards that enabled you to be "right on" anywhere from 50 to 250 yards. Shots of less than 50 yards or more than 250 require that you compensate your aim. Aim low for short shots, high for longer shots. If you are shooting at a target less than 50 yards away, aim a little lower. If you are shooting more than 250 yards, hold the rifle higher.

You also have to adjust for the wind velocity. If it is blowing from your right, hold the rifle a little to the right, etc., depending on your yardage. Remember this: if you are shooting uphill, hold the rifle higher than normal; if you are shooting downhill, hold the rifle lower than normal. Adjust for the angles.

A clean, killing, humane shot is what you want and unless you are completely confident that you will do that at long range, don't shoot. You should learn to be a good hunter so you will not have to take long shots — you will have the game closer. I am not saying it is wrong to take long shots; just be confident enough that you can do it correctly before you take that shot. Do not take any long, 250- to 300-yard shots at running game during your first time hunting. In most cases shots at running game are best avoided. It takes experience to know how much to "lead" the deer (how far out in front of the deer to aim so it will hit the vital spot — some experts say you should lead 20 feet at 300 yards when you are shooting at a running deer) to make a good shot. All but the closest shots at running deer greatly reduce the chances of hitting the vitals. It is most ethical to save your shots for standing game. A friend told me he whistles and yells at running deer to get them to stop so you can have a standing shot. You can learn all this at a later time. If you have questions about any of the above, get to your sportsmen's club and rifle range and ask for help.

Some states have regulations requiring only shotguns firing slugs may be used for deer hunting; high-powered rifles are not allowed. Because of the close proximity of farms and dense rural populations in southern Minnesota, for instance, only slug shooting is allowed because the distance a slug will travel is much less than that of a rifle bullet. My friend, Pinkie, has hunted with a shotgun in Minnesota for years. He says, "A slug shotgun is still your basic shotgun, usually outfitted with a "slug barrel" (a barrel with rifle sights). Slugs look like regular shotgun shells, only the top is not crimped

Combination gun. In areas where rifles are not allowed for deer hunting, a shotgun equipped with a barrel designed to fire slugs is an effective deer hunting tool. The key ingredient to a slug gun is rifle-style sights.

It is quite easy to see the difference between a shotgun slug and a regular shotshell.

in and you can see the top of the slug. It is one big piece of lead that, depending on the type you purchase, will mushroom as it hits and down an animal the same as a rifle bullet."

Do you have to purchase a new shotgun to shoot slugs? No. You can use a regular barrel or you can buy a slug barrel to "remodel" your waterfowl or pheasant shotgun into a slug gun. The barrels are usually 22 or 24 inches in length. Some are rifled (they have grooves such as those in a regular rifle to make the bullet more accurate). The biggest difference is, as mentioned above, a barrel for shooting slugs will have rifle sights, as opposed to the simple bead of a standard shotgun barrel. If you desire a scope, then you must purchase a slug barrel that is specifically designed to allow the mounting of a scope. If you don't want to buy a new barrel, you can purchase rifle sights that fit right onto the vented rib of your wingshooting gun. Ask your gunsmith.

My friend Pinkie sights his slug shotgun in at 50 yards and compensates for any other distance by holding the barrel higher or lower. Slugs are heavy and slow, so they drop fast after 50 yards. Most shots in slug country are short anyway. Rarely will you get a shot longer than 75 yards in areas where you are required to use shotgun slugs for deer hunting.

Most deer are killed with one shot; the slug is just as lethal as a rifle bullet. Pinkie says, "I have shot deer in brush, woods and cornfields, and I hunt the same as with a rifle.

Check your regulations and go see your gun dealer. You won't have the range of a rifle; learn what the slug range is and hunt accordingly. I usually shoot deer at around 50 yards and this system works fine for me."

The day we were out shooting targets with the slug shotgun was interesting. I found the gun to have quite a kick — a lot more than with waterfowl shells and a lot more than my .270 rifle. When you first shoot the gun, be sure you have a good heavy jacket to protect your shoulder. We hit targets at 50 yards and nearly 100 yards. The closer targets were easier to hit. We were shooting with open/iron sights (no scope) and I found it difficult to be accurate much beyond 70 yards. I was surprised at the large size of the hole left by the slug in a piece of wood and the hay bale. Hit in the correct place, a deer certainly would be yours.

If you have trouble calculating yardage while hunting, a rangefinder may be your answer. They will enable you to determine distances out to where the target is likely to appear. They can be found in your gun shop or any outdoor catalog.

CLOTHING

You need to be visible to other hunters and they need to be visible to you. Your state deer hunting regulations will tell you if and how much blaze orange clothing is required during the season. My state, South Dakota, requires only one

This single-shot slug gun by H&R 1871 is accurate, easy to use and tough as nails. It would make a great starter gun for a new hunter.

A selection of hunting blades from Buck Knives shows the wide variety on the market. You don't need a huge knife to field dress a deer, but you need a stout one. Pick one you are comfortable using. (Photo courtesy of Buck Knives)

orange garment be worn while hunting. In Wisconsin, a deer hunter must cover at least 50 percent of the upper half of her body with orange and hats, if worn, must be solid orange. You can obtain blaze orange hats, stocking caps, face masks, sweatshirts, jackets, pants, coveralls and gloves. In fact, most any type of hunting clothing will be found in the blaze orange color. Plastic and webbed vests that fit over the outer garments are available but not advised because the blaze usually isn't bright enough or there isn't enough of it for safety reasons. I wear a front zippered hooded sweatshirt over my coveralls and that more than suffices. I also have a blaze stocking cap. Here's a vanity tip for the field: Do not wear pink lipstick with your blaze orange jacket — the colors clash and look terrible!!

The weather will dictate what type of clothing and how many layers. If you are hunting from a stand or blind, be sure to have enough layers on to keep you warm when you are sitting still. If it is cold when you hunt, be sure to have warm boots. If you are walking you can wear lighter boots, but sitting in cold weather demands good warm winter hunting boots. Rubber-soled boots are good for deer hunting as they will carry little if any, human scent. If you will be hunting in hilly, rocky areas wear boots with good terrain-grabbing grips. Be sure to take some hand-warmer packets with you. When hunting in stand or blind, place them in a muff for

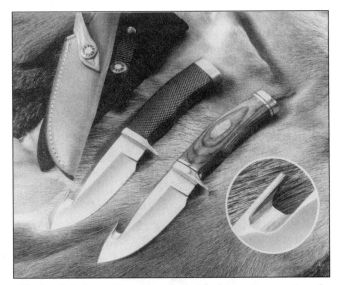

Gut hook knives, like these from Buck, make opening the deer's abdomen quick and easy. A gut hook will cut the skin and muscle of the abdomen but not penetrate to the intestines, an area you really don't want to cut.

your hands or inside your boots to keep your feet warm. Refer to Waterfowl Hunting chapter for tips here.

Weather will also dictate what type of gloves and how heavy they should be. Refer to the Waterfowl Hunting chapter. I use many of the same "keeping warm" ideas for deer hunting. My favorite method is to have hand warmers inside big mittens that have a slit on the palm for your fingers to emerge. I may wear a lighter glove on my left hand, inside the mitten. My right hand may remain bare inside the mitten so when I'm ready to take the shot I can just quietly, slowly and with no visible movement slide my fingers out and get my trigger finger in place and make the shot. It is important to not wear gloves that will bind or in any way hinder your ability to shoot. If you have a hand warmer inside that mitten, you shouldn't need the extra glove and should be limber enough to shoot well. If your hand is cold, wear a light glove inside the mitten. Try different methods until one works for you.

Purchase some type of a fanny pack or a backpack. You will need it for all the items you should take with you. Take your license and your deer tag with you. Some states require that your license and tag be displayed in the middle of your back while hunting. Special protective sleeves are sold for that purpose. If you are allowed to keep the license or tag in your pack, keeping it in plastic bag will protect it from dirt, rain and snow. Have a pen with you in case your state requires your signature on your tag when you bag your deer. A small scissors is also helpful to cut the little month and day wedges out of the tag. You can also carry some extra ammunition in the pack. A folding wallet with individual pockets for each shell works well, too. Take your binoculars, camera, water, snacks, mosquito spray (if it's warm) and a good, dependable flashlight, extra batteries and bulb (for deer tracking, cleaning or finding your way out of the woods in the dark). Take a rope or a deer drag strap for hauling the deer to the vehicle. A roll of blaze marking ribbon will help you mark your place if you have to track a deer, or even if you need to mark a trail from your vehicle. A good idea is to wrap reflective tape around clothespins and tie blaze ribbon from them; attach them to tree branches, etc. to mark your trail. You can then easily find your trail with a flashlight. A cell phone can be invaluable as another safety measure — just make sure it is turned off until after the hunt. You don't want to have a great shot ruined by a ringing telephone. If you want to use grunt calls or rattling antlers, put them in the backpack. A first-aid kit should also be included, along with some disinfectant or germ-killing salve in case you nick yourself while cleaning the deer. If you take your lunch with you, pack it in an air-tight bag so no odors escape and spook any deer.

Have a good, heavy hunting knife with you. I received a Buck knife as a gift the first year I deer hunted and that has proven to be one of the best gifts I've ever received. My knife has a 6-inch fixed blade (non-folding), is 10-1/2 inches overall and comes with a leather sheath. It is a Special Master Series (119MS) Buck knife. When the knife does need sharpening, use whatever method you desire, but be sure to sharpen it at a 10- to 20-degree angle. If you have questions about knife sharpening, talk to your mentor or get a good book on the subject.

> ## Purchase some type of a fanny pack or a backpack. You will need it for all the items you should take with you.

There are so many knives on the market now, don't be surprised if you end up owning several before you find "the perfect one." Buying knives just gives you another reason to shop.

Here is a great idea, compliments of my buddy Lila. The ground can get mighty cold in the north in November and December, especially if there is snow. Lila found the perfect thing for a gift: a warming seat you heat in the microwave! I place it in the microwave for 3 minutes just before leaving the house (we hunt only a short distance away). It folds up and fastens with Velcro and can be easily carried. By the time you get to your hunting place, it is nice and warm and makes a wonderful "nest bottom" to sit on! It stays warm for several hours; even if it does cool off, you will still have a very thick seat to protect your bottom from the cold ground.

Hunting white-tailed deer is a billion-dollar industry in the United States. You can spend as much or as little as you want. There are calls, decoys, deer stands, clothes, guns... you name it. For some people, it is a year-round pursuit. Others plan their annual vacation around the hunt. States like Pennsylvania, Michigan, Wisconsin, Texas and New York regularly see more than half a million hunters in the woods each year. If participation is any indication, the white-tailed deer can become an addiction.

THE HUNT

There are several ways to hunt deer: stand hunting, still hunting, spot and stalk hunting, and organized drives. Stand hunting consists of sitting in a tree stand or sitting on the ground and waiting for deer to come into range. Still hunting is very slowly walking through an area looking for deer. Spot and stalk hunting is finding a deer, then sneaking up to get the shot. An organized drive is a method of pushing deer to sitting hunters. Personal preference, deer habits, environment and your particular situation will determine how or which hunting method to use. No matter which way you decide to hunt, remember the phenomenal senses of smell, hearing and sight that deer possess. Never forget to be cognizant of wind direction. You want to be DOWNWIND from the deer at all times, if that is possible. When you are still hunting or stalking, always move into the wind.

Most whitetail hunting is done where there is fairly dense cover. To stand hunt, you should be in place before dawn and again during the last couple of hours of daylight. Deer usually feed and water at these times and bed during midday. (There are exceptions because they like to tease us, you know!) Refer to your scouting map and choose the best place to sit — usually beside the well-traveled deer trails. The place where the trails converge is the best place to sit. As you are looking for the "perfect spot" to set up, keep in mind the cover, what is in front of you and behind you, and your safe shooting alleys. If you find a good tree to sit beside and there is no bushy cover, gather some branches and make a little "blind" in front of you. You want your outline broken up but you want to be able to see and shoot well in just about any direction. Sit where you are comfortable, placing your backpack behind you and rifle in your lap. Make sure there are no branches, etc. on top of the rifle so you can bring it up slowly and quietly when needed.

When I sat on a bare hillside beside a fence with no cover whatsoever, looking down over the river bottom, I took some camouflage burlap with me, "wired" it up into the fence and gathered it around me and my backpack on the other side. Use your imagination and you can devise some ingenious methods of concealment. Burlap comes in different camo patterns and you can do a lot with it. There are camo folding blinds on the market that can be used for all types of hunting, including deer. If you do purchase one of these, try it out first before deer season so you know exactly what you are doing. You don't want to be fussing around trying to get the thing set up when the deer are starting to move. You also don't want to find out a window zipper does not work when you are ready to take a shot.

Hunting from a tree stand is not necessarily just for bowhunters. Rifle and muzzleloader hunters also make the climb. There are very definite advantages to be above the deer. We discussed the keen sense of smell that deer possess — the elevated hunting position keeps the human scent above the deer. You can have a great view of the surrounding cover from a tree stand and you can observe the deer and place your shot without spooking the animal. Some of the disadvantages of hunting from a tree stand are restriction of movement, no wind protection, and you have either a permanent stand to maintain or a portable one to carry around. In most cases you look for the same deer sign whether you are hunting from the ground or in a tree. You can refer to the

Bow Hunting Chapter for more information on tree stands, deer rubs and scrapes and where to set up.

I have never hunted from a tree stand and have enjoyed venison every year I have hunted. I like sitting on the ground, a few yards off a deer trail or convergence. I make sure there are shooting alleys around me. I gather branches and pile them up in front of me for some concealment. I sit with my back against the tree, on my warm "deer seat", rifle at the ready and hand warmers in my gloves. I just settle in to watch the sunrise or sunset and the wonderful wildlife. I hunt more in the evening hours and seem to be more successful at that time. Only twice have I shot deer during mid-day.

If there are two of you hunting together, sit at angles looking away from each other. That way both the sides are covered. Decide on a spot in the middle of the front alley; one hunter takes the right, the other takes the left. This is no time to get chatty. Keep your talking to a minimum and use signs or signals to alert each other to deer.

Stand hunting in a ground blind is my very favorite way to hunt deer. In fact, I daydream many times during the year about the wonderful deer hunting place — the "women's secret place". It is quiet; I'm the only one there unless Lila is with me. I have enjoyed so very much watching the fawns play, watching does run in and out of the trees and witnessing most beautiful sunsets. The neatest thing I have ever seen there was the evening my buck came sauntering up the path, his antlers silhouetted against the blaze red setting sun. He walked towards me without a clue I was there. He stopped to munch on a branch, started slowly moving again and at that time I just lightly clicked my tongue, he stopped and looked at me and that was it! He was only 15 yards in front of me. That he was so close was completely cool. The entire scenario is a wonderful memory.

The beauty of sitting on the ground or in a tree stand is that you can watch the deer and they have no idea you are there. It is calm, it is relaxed, it is ethical, and believe me, you will enjoy this much more than a more active drive or big push through heavy cover. You become so aware of the deer's habits and habitat; you can learn so very much by watching them. The secret is to wear the right combination of clothing so you are comfortable and can enjoy everything you see.

When I stand hunt, I stay in the same place in the evening and don't move. I know the habits and know that if there are deer in the area they will be coming across in front of me. Sometimes early morning hunting can be different and if nothing has shown up on the trail for an hour I might move to a different place on the trail. Morning and evening are best for stand hunting. If you are stand hunting a heavily hunted area and deer are moving around, you may want to stay all day. In that case, plan ahead and bring a sandwich or heftier snacks. Stand hunting takes patience; women have that patience and do very well. You will like stand hunting! You will not only learn about deer and deer hunting, you will learn about yourself.

Still hunting also takes patience and women are good at this method, too. Still hunting must be done very slowly. Here's how: take a few steps, then stop, look and listen for a couple of minutes. Taking a half hour to walk 300 yards is a good point to remember. Just walk very slowly. Plan your steps and when you stop, balance yourself so if you have to freeze instantly or take a shot you are balanced. You would not be able to shoot if you were standing on one foot. Try to

Doris Schocker with her Nebraska whitetail. Notice the kind of forest land in the background. White-tailed deer can adapt to a wide range of habitats. You will need to adjust your hunting style to suit the terrain.

avoid cracking sticks, walking on leaves or anything else that would make noise. Deer sometimes just materialize in front of you and other times they can sound like a truck coming through the brush. The point is that dry, crackling leaves make noise. If you must make noise, make noise like a deer — take a few steps, stop and look. A deer then hears "another deer". Use hand signals between hunters. When you do stop, get beside a tree or bushes. Hold your rifle vertically, the most natural way it would appear to deer. Never walk on top of a ridge; walk below the ridge line. When you are walking this slowly, it is difficult to stop for the few minutes and wait and watch. It seems like forever and feels like you are wasting time. Not so. Be patient. Slowly look around, remembering that a deer may already be looking at you. You must move very slowly and stop for minutes (some say up to 5 minutes at a time) so you do not spook a deer that may be in ahead of you. You do not want them to flush and run, you want them to just stand and hopefully you will get a good shot. If all you see are white "flags" (their tails) you are probably going too fast.

I think the best and most enjoyable time to still hunt is immediately following a snowfall of several inches. Everything is quieter, brighter, and the deer tracks seem to just jump out at you. Deer are more visible at this time, also. When you are still hunting in snow you will very much appreciate your environment. The air is clean and fresh and everything looks beautiful. You will thank God that you have the opportunity to be out there, appreciating all creation in this winter wonderland. Enjoy!

Deer are extremely hard to find when they are bedded down. Look for parts of a deer such as an ear, antler or face. They can so expertly hide that you may be walking right by them. On one still hunt through our tree claim Lila and I had that very experience. We were about half way through the trees when something exploded in front of us. The racket was more on my side of the trees; I froze and felt like my eyes were microscopes I was looking so hard for a deer. I never saw anything, but I knew for sure something had been there. I motioned to Lila that she should watch for a deer to come bounding out on her side of the trees. We walked, now more slowly than ever, almost getting a headache from looking so hard in the trees and watching the edge of the trees so intently. I saw nothing and assumed the deer ran out in front of Lila on the opposite side of the trees. When we arrived at the end of the tree claim, we both looked at each other quizzically and each expected the other to say the deer had run out on her side. But, no deer had run out anywhere! Absolutely no deer had left those trees. That told us one thing: we had walked right over him (probably a buck since they are best at hiding) or beside him! Unbelievable! I thought I had looked at everything so closely and scrutinized everything so well — and here I had walked right beside a deer and never saw it! Deer lie low and take their chances that the hunter will never see them. This is why you must walk very slowly, stop for a long time and peer into the woods ahead of you, around you and even behind you extremely carefully. This is how the bucks live to become true trophies — they are smart!

The spot and stalk method, or "stalking" works best when hunting mule deer. It can be done while hunting white-tailed deer, but the opportunities are limited.

The deer won't know you are there if you have played the wind correctly and are walking slowly enough. If you see one before he sees you, freeze. Then slowly get into shooting position. When you are in the woods you can scan a tree for a "Y" branch and fit your rifle into it for the shot (if it is close and you can move without drawing attention to yourself), or just hold your rifle against a tree for a rest. If the deer hasn't seen you and is walking toward you, do not move. Get ready for the shot; he may come within a few feet of you. If he walks away from you, stalk him ever so slowly and quietly, waiting for the animal to turn and give you a good shot at the heart/lung area. The adrenaline will be pumping in your body and you may think you won't be able to breathe because this can be such a hair-raising experience. Stop and take a couple of deep breaths to calm yourself. (Where else can you get these kinds of thrills?)

A couple of other things to remember are not to stop and lean against small trees — the tops will move and sway and give away your position; if you cross any water, do it quietly. Wear quiet clothing, not something like noisy nylon which will advertise your whereabouts. When you see a deer and he doesn't see you and he puts his head down to feed, that is the time you move into shooting position, when he cannot see you. If you can help it, do not ever walk directly on a deer trail. Walk parallel to it. If deer are spooked, they may return on the same trail and you do not want him to catch your scent. If you are walking through really thick cover, you may not have any choice but to walk on the deer trail. (Deer don't really like to walk through the thick brush either.) Still hunting takes a monumental amount of patience, but can be a most thrilling hunt!

The spot and stalk method, or "stalking" works best when hunting mule deer. It can be done while hunting white-tailed deer, but the opportunities are limited. I'll discuss it later in the chapter.

Another method of deer hunting is known as the drive. Basically, the drive is a method of pushing deer to hunters waiting at deer stands. If you are hunting very dense cover like thick brush in creek bottoms, CRP fields, river bottom rushes or even dry noisy forests, an organized drive may be the way to hunt. A drive hunt is organized in this manner: there may be 5 to 10 hunters who have scouted the terrain and know the deer runs; some hunters will be drivers and some will be standers at the end of the field or a chosen place where they think deer will run out and be very visible; as the deer are driven out of their hiding places and into the open, the sitters have their shots. The most important ingredient of the drive is to know where the deer will run and where the hunters will be. It is imperative that if you are a stander, you stay in the your spot. The drivers will be working the cover and working toward you. They need to know where you are so they can safely shoot, if they get a shot. You as a stander need to make sure that you positively identify everything moving in the woods before you shoot. If you see a deer, make sure there are no hunters anywhere near where you intend to shoot.

A drive can be noisy with hunters shouting and whistling (I've never seen this but heard about it!) and generally making as much noise as they can to drive out the deer. The general idea is that the deer are so spooked they are not cautious by the time they reach the sitters and the sitters will then have a better chance of taking a deer. I have never hunted in this manner. This method does not appear to me to be an enjoyable way to hunt. Smaller deer drives can be just as effective, in some cases even more so. The trick here is to post a shooter or shooters on known deer escape routes, then send a few drivers to slowly move through the area. The deer will hear the drivers coming and try to sneak out ahead of the drivers. Quiet drives don't often get the deer running like a noisy drive. Sometimes the shooters will get shots as trotting or even walking deer if the drive is conducted quietly.

Dogs are used to drive deer out of heavy cover in the southern U.S. There are usually lots of hunters on dog drives with the end result being fast running shots with a shotgun and buckshot. This type of hunting is illegal in most states.

Some deer drivers prefer to take their time on a drive, moving slowly and quietly. The deer can be seen in front of the hunters standing or walking, not spooked into a dead run. There are several conditions that call for a deer drive and the drive may be the most effective way to hunt in that particular situation. Bad weather can cause deer to stay bedded; snowstorms, extreme wind, heavy rains or extreme heat will limit the deer's activity. Hunting pressure may push deer to very remote hiding places, and a small drive through the area

Janette and Judi Zumbo pose with a nice little mule deer buck.

could yield results. If you have hunted an area and think the deer have been pushed out of there, try a small, quiet and slow drive to off-beat corners. You may be pleasantly surprised at what you will find.

No matter which driving method you use to flush deer, always remember BE SAFE. There are other hunters around you. There will be hunters sitting or standing in front of you, beside you, and maybe even behind you. Always be cognizant of them and their positions and never point the rifle in their direction. Hunters tend to get overly excited when deer flush and there is potential danger. Just remember to be safe.

Road hunting is NOT a good ethical way to hunt deer. When you check your state's deer hunting regulations you will probably find it is illegal. However, that does not stop unethical hunters from obtaining a deer in any manner they choose. Road hunting consists of driving around looking for deer, finding one, jumping out of the vehicle and shooting, or, worse yet, shooting from inside the vehicle.

Yes, there are people who do this! There are also shooters, (I do not call them hunters) who drive their pickups up and down the tree claim or shelterbelt edges waiting to see a deer, then shooting from the vehicle. These types of people have no concept of what hunting is all about and they are missing the point. Greed and laziness determines their priorities. This behavior is disgusting and when observed gives all hunters a bad name. In these days of strong anti-hunting sentiment and animal rights activism, hunters' behavior needs to be as good and ethical as possible. We need more WOMEN in the field to improve hunting ethics! Women DO improve ethics — I have watched this myself!

If you encounter any illegal activity while you are out hunting, call your state's wildlife agency's hunter hotline. In South Dakota we have the "TIPS" (Turn In Poachers) line available 24 hours a day. You may remain anonymous while doing your duty for wildlife, and rewards are offered for reports leading to arrests. Check your hunting regulations booklet for the phone number and use it if you have the chance.

LET'S GO HUNT DEER!

I want you, the beginning woman deer hunter, to have the most meaningful, ethical and best hunt possible for a first time experience. Here's the scenario: Late one November afternoon we go the "women's secret place." We have done our scouting, found rubs, scrapes and trails and have decided where to sit. We will lean against a couple of big trees, just off the deer trail. We noted good shooting alleys around the spot. We picked the place where we would like a deer to stop and sprinkled a couple of drops of deer scent there. We will set up by the tree, build a little blind in front of us using some small branches, sit down, get snuggled in and comfortable, agree on communication signs, and then watch and wait.

We are after your first deer. Since we are out for your first time we will keep it simple. You will have enough things to think about without any "extra" frills to concern you so we left the rattling antlers and grunt calls at home. After a few initial experiences, you will want these items and they will come in handy.

I will show you how I sit "turkey hunting style" and how well it works for me. I keep the rifle on my lap, at the ready, with no restrictions on top of it so I can pick it up and be ready in a hurry. I use my right knee as my rifle "rest" and it works out beautifully!

Shot Placement for Whitetails

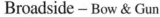

DEER & **FROM THE PUBLISHERS OF**
DEER HUNTING **MAGAZINE**

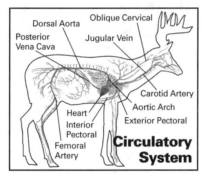

Broadside – Bow & Gun

➤ Gun-hunters can drop deer instantly with a broadside shot by putting a bullet through the shoulder blade. A well-constructed bullet will pass through the blade and hit the spine, destroying its major nerve bundles.

➤ The broadside shot is also good for bow-hunters, but it doesn't leave as much room for error as the quartering-away shot. Arrows that pass through the vital organs produce quick, clean kills. Aim for the heart, knowing that a high shot will still hit the lungs. Archers must avoid the shoulder blade.

Quartering Away – Bow & Gun

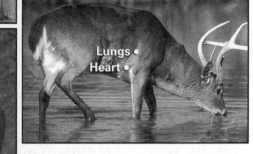

➤ For archers, the quartering-away shot offers the best chances for success. Even if the arrow hits a bit too far back, it can angle forward into the chest cavity for a quick kill. When taking this shot, the point of aim should be through the deer to the opposite shoulder.

➤ This is also a great shot for gun-hunters. As with the bow, the gun hunter's point of aim should be through the deer to the opposite shoulder.

Head-On – For Guns Only

➤ This shot presents gun-hunters with three vital targets. A shot in the chest will hit the heart or lungs. A bullet in the neck will usually break the neck or cause enough shock to drop the animal instantly. It could also destroy the esophagus and/or carotid artery or jugular vein.

➤ The head-on shot is not good for archers. Unless the arrow hits the chest dead-center, which presents a very small target, it can easily deflect off bone.

Deer Anatomy Facts

➤ Making quick, certain kills should be the main goal of every hunter, no matter if using a bow or gun.

➤ When shooting at deer with a bow and arrow, aim for the heart region. If the deer "jumps the string" by dropping sharply before bounding away, the arrow will still hit the lungs.

➤ The average white-tailed deer, weighing about 150 pounds, carries about 8 pints of blood in its circulatory system. Massive hemorrhage is necessary to bring a deer down quickly.

➤ A deer must lose at least 35 percent of its blood, or 2¾ pints in a 150-pound animal, before falling. The better the hit, the quicker blood loss occurs.

➤ Deer blood carries high levels of Vitamin K1 and K2 in early autumn. Vitamin K is an antihemorrhagic agent, which greatly aids blood clotting.

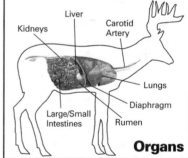

➤ Frightened whitetails produce high levels of B-endorphin, which supports rapid wound healing. Endorphins consist of morphine-like chemicals from the pituitary gland, allowing the animal to control pain.

➤ Hunters must study white-tailed deer anatomy to learn to put their bullet or arrow where it can quickly destroy the deer's circulatory and/or respiratory system.

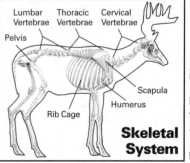

Illustrations by Wayne Trimm

The vital area of deer is your intended target. You should make every effort to put your bullet into the heart/lung area in order to make a quick kill. If you don't have a good shot at the vitals, don't shoot. If the deer is so far away that you are not confident you can hit the vital area, don't shoot. Hunting ethics starts with knowing your own abilities and those or your firearm.

It is a solid rest for the rifle and still allows me to move somewhat if I have to. As the afternoon light fades into dusk I have the rifle on my knee because a deer can appear out of nowhere anytime. Suddenly, one does. I watch as a deer comes in and when it is behind a tree or brush and can't see me, I make the final adjustment for the shot. That reminds me of something.

When hunting in this spot, in this particular position I do not need a rifle rest. One of my neighbors can't understand my method of sitting, holding the rifle, etc. and one day he insisted that I needed a rifle rest. He made one out of PVC (hard plastic) pipe; it worked great for him and one day he gave it to me to try. The pipes were connected a few inches from one end, forming an "X" with a small top and a large bottom. "The rifle fits perfectly; if you need to move it, just pick it up and turn it." The rest was tall, so I had to take my little hunting stool with me. (There have been so many goofy things that have happened while using that stool I sometimes wish it could talk and tell the stories itself!) So, this was a first--taking a stool into the woods and using this big rifle rest. Imagine me walking into the deer woods trying to be very quiet--but with the rifle on my shoulder, backpack hanging on my back, and the metal-legged stool clanging against the PVC pipe! I think every critter within a mile was alerted! Shaking my head and giggling to myself about how ridiculous this was, I arrived at my place and proceeded to set up. After arranging and rearranging the stool 50 times I thought I was OK. So, then it was time to set up the nifty PVC pipe rifle rest and try it out.

I finally got the height adjusted OK so I could see out of the scope, steadied the rest after it clinked on a couple little rocks until I got it right, and thought I was ready. So, there I sat and waited. After awhile I got to thinking about shooting from different angles and wondered how I would turn the PVC rest carefully and quietly with the rifle in it. I tried it but it was difficult. This "easiness" must be a "man thing"! I would carefully look around me and seeing no deer, I would practice moving this contraption and hoped that it wouldn't fall down, leaving me with no rest at all.

When I was reasonably confident I would be able to move it if I had to without it falling down, I breathed a little easier and sat still and waited. I was still worrying about it when all of a sudden I heard a noise off to my right. There stood a nice doe. If she would stand between the right trees, I would have a chance. It seemed like forever before she moved into the perfect spot. Then HER position was great, and MY position was terrible. I WOULD HAVE TO MOVE THE PVC REST! Geez, could I do it? Yes, I would. I took a deep breath, tried to pick up the rest with the rifle in it as I had practiced. All went well until my fingers slipped! CRASH! The darn thing fell down with a clatter as it hit a tree branch, bounced off and landed in the brush! I still remember the shocked look on the doe's face! I could almost hear her yell, "What the hell was that?" It was hilarious! Needless to say, that was the ONLY time I used the PVC pipe rifle rest and the damned stool!

For whitetail hunting, I do not use a rifle rest other than my reliable knee. If I am stalking or still hunting I use a fence post or tree trunk or branch to steady the rifle. My favorite rest is my knee. It is always with me and is nothing extra to carry!

After hearing my sorry rifle rest story, Jim Zumbo took pity on me and gave me a device that doubles as a walking stick and a rifle rest. It's a great idea! It is a strong but lightweight walking stick and with a twist of the hand becomes a rifle rest; it flips back into a folded-up position with another twist of the wrist.

Back to our hunt. We are set up, I have answered the last few questions you have asked. We have both commented on how quiet, beautiful and peaceful it is here in the deer woods. We are sitting about 75 yards back from the river and we watch deer moving along on the far river bank. Suddenly a fox appears and we wonder what his plan of action is. The time is passing and we have not yet seen a deer on our side of the river. Just when we are readjusting our bottoms, I catch movement way out on the deer trail. Yes, it is a doe and she is headed our way; I motion to you and point toward the trail with my eyes.

No matter if its a fawn, buck or doe, whenever I see a deer walking in my general direction, my heart starts beating, my breaths get shorter, all the senses pick up and go into "afterburner" phase. I look at you and see that all these things are happening to you, too. Your eyes are as big as saucers and I can almost see your heart beating! Since the doe is still down the trail and behind some trees at this point, I motion for you to get your gun ready.

We have discussed at length the vital target area on big game. You know that a heart/lung shot is the desired placement and that is where you will aim.

We have discussed at length the vital target area on big game. You know that a heart/lung shot is the desired placement and that is where you will aim. The shot should be at a spot straight up the front leg and then a little bit back behind it. You have correctly sighted in your rifle; you know the deer will be only maybe 15 to 20 yards in front of us and you are confident your rifle is "right on" and you can and will make a good clean shot.

The doe slowly comes closer and you are ready. You make your final adjustment as she stops with her head behind a tree. She does not see, hear or smell us! We have it made! As she steps out directly in front of us, I make a "click" with my tongue, she stops, looks at us, and you instinctively pull that trigger. It connected! We watch her jump and run into the cover on our left. In a matter of seconds, a "crash" comes from that general direction — she is down. You did good and remember to mark the spot where you last saw her. After making sure you put the safety back on your rifle, we walk over to where we she entered the cover, seeing a blood trail on the way. This one is easy. We walk 50 yards right to her. You on shaky legs and your adrenaline still pumping. Lady, you have just felled your first deer! YOU ARE A DEER HUNTER!

There is one ritual left: a traditional, sobering, glorious, proud and tearful application of a spot of deer blood drawn across your cheek by your mentor. This signifies you truly are a deer hunter, in every sense of the word. You appreciate the opportunity to harvest one of God's beautiful creatures and to give thanks for the deer's life and yours. This memory will stay with you forever.

There are many responsibilities you encounter as a deer hunter and tracking and finding a downed deer is one of the most important. When at all possible, deer hunters use a "blood trail" to lead them to the downed deer. When you make a successful shot, there will usually be blood on the ground or weeds in that area; you follow that blood trail and it will lead you to the deer. Sometimes there is a lot of blood and that makes tracking easy. Other times, there may be no blood, or very little blood, making tracking extremely difficult. There may be big splotches of blood or tiny almost pin-head-size drops on the ground, bushes, weeds or snow. Use toilet paper or your blaze ribbon to mark places on the trail, in case you lose the trail and have to "start over." If you lose the trail completely and can't find the deer, go back and pinpoint where the deer was when you made the shot and start over. Having a flashlight or two is imperative when you have to follow a blood trail at night.

> **The most important point to remember when field dressing your deer is to do it as soon as possible and get the carcass cleaned and cooled as soon as possible.**

There are times when there will be no blood to follow. That is why it is very important to mark EXACTLY where the deer was when you took the shot. When I rattled in "William: the big whitetail" and took the shot, I thought I had the spot marked well. There was no blood and we had an extremely difficult time finding him in the tall grass. We went back to where I was sitting and started over. We found him in just a few minutes, thanks to my hunting buddy.

Good shot placement in the vital area is extremely important. You want a good, clean, killing shot and hitting the deer in the lungs or heart will do that. If you hit the deer elsewhere, you may not have a killing shot. You may only wound it and then you will have a tough tracking job ahead of you. If you lose the blood trail while you are tracking and become frustrated, it may become easy to get tired and just quit looking. DO NOT GIVE UP! You owe it to that animal to find it, and you owe that to yourself as a hunter. Finding that animal is your responsibility and comes under the heading of "hunting ethics." Sometimes it really is impossible to find a wounded animal. If you have spent a lot of time and energy looking for that animal and you and maybe others who are helping you absolutely can not track it or find it, you may have to give up the search. This holds true not only for deer but for anything you hunt. You will know inside that you have done everything you could possibly do to find it. In the event you have had to forsake the search and feel very badly about it, remember that there are coyotes and fox out there that need to eat, too. That may be little consolation, but that's all there is.

When you have successfully followed the blood to your downed animal, approach it with caution from the rear so it can't see you if it is still alive. To make sure the deer is dead, gently touch the eye with the muzzle of your rifle. Always take your rifle with you in case you have to make another shot.

AFTER THE SHOT

The high five's, whoops, hollers and hugging are over and it is time for the photos. Place yourself behind your deer, hold the head up, shove the tongue back inside the mouth. Push your cap back on your head so your face will not be shadowed. Hold your rifle in one hand or lay it down beside the deer. You will not have to be told to smile! Have several pictures taken. You will love them all.

Some states require that you attach your deer tag immediately. Others allow you to haul the deer home before you attach the tag. Know the law and follow it. I suggest you field dress the deer where it lays. The residue will not be seen by others, scavengers will take care of it, and the deer will be lighter to drag to the vehicle. Your knife, latex gloves, deer strap or rope, etc. will be used at this time.

Please refer to the illustration: "What Do I Do Now? How to Field Dress Big Game".

The most important point to remember when field dressing your deer is to do it as soon as possible and get the carcass cleaned and cooled as soon as possible. Venison is free of chemicals and preservatives and is perhaps one of the most pure meats we can eat; that is why it is so important to treat the carcass and the meat carefully. When I hunt I field dress the deer immediately and wash out the carcass very well. I then make the 20-mile trip to Bill and Lila's house, our "deer processing center." We hang the deer and skin it while the carcass is still relatively warm. Skinning deer as soon as possible makes the job much easier. Be sure to cut away any bullet-damaged meat or that tainted by any bodily fluids. We either hang the deer overnight, for a day, or cut it up immediately. You do not have to let deer hang/age for a certain length of time to improve the quality of the meat. The typical hunter, butchering a deer in the garage doesn't have the right facilities to age meat anyway, so don't try it. We fry chislic (small chunks of deer meat sprinkled with spices, deep fried and then use the dip or sauce of your choice) as we are cutting up the meat and it is delicious! There have been times when we have gone hunting, shot deer, cleaned, cut, wrapped, labeled the meat and had it in the freezer all in a matter of hours. Tip: cut away all possible fat — that can give deer meat an unattractive odor and taste.

Remember, if you are new to deer hunting, it may be easier to simply drop the field dressed carcass off at a reputable meat processor immediately after the hunt. That will save a lot of work, but I think it takes away a little of the post-hunt camaraderie.

If you are hunting in a remote area and do not have access to water or any of the above-mentioned facilities, you will have to plan carcass care beforehand. Put some plastic milk jugs full of water into your truck so you can wash the carcass and clean rags or paper towels to wipe it out. To allow cooling, prop open the chest cavity with sticks. If you leave the deer hanging for a day or two, the easiest way is to loop a rope over a tree limb. There is a device called a gambrel that will allow the deer to hang by its back legs. You can also tie the rope onto the antlers or around the neck and hang it that way. There is no right or wrong — whatever is easiest for you to do. You will want to keep flies away so sprinkle some black pepper on the exposed edges of the deer meat or cut off the legs and use a mesh bag. Keep the carcass cool and clean on your way home from hunting. If you do not want to take the deer home with you, find a deer processor near your hunting area; the only problem there is picking up the meat when it is finished.

At cutting and freezing time, or when you take the deer to a processor, you will have to decide on what cuts of meat you want and how much processed meat you will want. The butterfly chops are terrific, and you will want some roasts. My family loves deer chili so we have a good share of meat ground, with 8-10% beef fat added for moisture. We also like deer sticks (like beef pepper sticks) and summer sausage. Talk to your mentor and processor for other ideas.

For those who are unsure of their fondness for deer meat, Jim Zumbo's *Amazing Venison Recipes* cookbook is a must! He is a master at cooking venison and shares terrific recipes. There is even a section on Proper Field Care, From Field to Freezer and Tips for Beginners. Order your copy from the Web site: www.jimzumbo.com or call 800-673-4868. I kid you not — this book should be on every deer hunter's shelf. You will truly be amazed at the wonderful big game recipes at your fingertips.

If you are planning on taking your deer to a taxidermist, be sure you have left enough of the cape (neck to shoulder skin) for a nice looking mount. Ask your mentor about this. Never make any cuts in the throat; never put a rope around the neck; never drag a deer over rocks or other sharp objects that may cut the hair; never allow a deer skin to be exposed to direct sunlight. Your taxidermist will skin out the head, cut off the antlers and place the skin in the freezer. A styrofoam-type form in whatever position you desire will then be ordered. The job is time-consuming, so do not be in a hurry — it will usually take several months for completion.

When you have your mount, place it on a wall away from heat and direct sunlight if possible. Those two elements can dry out a mount very quickly, causing the hair to become brittle and break off. Want to place your deer over the fireplace? Wrong! Unfortunately, that is the worst place because of the heat. To clean a dusty mount, carefully use your brush attachment on the vacuum cleaner or wipe it with a clean soft cloth, doing both in the direction of the hair grain. Use a Q-tip sprayed with a good quality glass cleaner to keep the eyes sparkling. It's best not to touch the mount after it is on the wall, but if you must, handle it only by the antlers or muzzle. "Melvin", my mule deer, (Have you noticed that I'm so fond of the big deer I've bagged, that I named them?) has been my "escort" to several Rocky Mountain Elk Foundation banquets; handling him by the antlers has definitely saved the hair from breakage. He's had fun at the banquets and still looks great!

FIELD DRESSING

Dress deer or antelope immediately to ensure rapid loss of body heat. Hang animal head up or lay it on a slope with rump lower than shoulders.

1 Cut through hide along center line of belly from brisket to vent. Deepen cut through belly muscles, using fingers to guide knife and avoid cutting intentines.

2 Cut deeply around anus. Remove it with intestines. Separate hind quarters by splitting pelvic bone with sharp, heavy knife, or hand ax.

3 Open chest cavity, front to back, through breast bone. Split muscle (diaphragm) separating chest from stomach cavity.

4 Sever gullet and windpipe as far forward as possible. Pull heart, liver, lungs, paunch and intestines out on the ground.

5 Prop body cavity open with sticks and cool quickly by hanging, head up, in a shady, airy place. Let it hang this way for about an hour before moving it to camp or car.

A basic guide to field dressing a deer can usually be obtained from your state's game department. These illustrations are used with the permission of the South Dakota Department of Game, Fish and Parks. Notice they are not in color or in graphic detail. Field dressing a deer is not the most pleasant thing in the world, but you must learn to do it correctly to protect the quality of your venison.

I was so very proud of the very first duck I shot and brought home all by myself that I saved the wing as a reminder. It was only a "spoonbill" duck (unimportant in some people's opinion) but the entire experience meant a tremendous amount to me. This was something I did on my own — at one time never believing I would ever do anything like it. An experienced hunter acquaintance stopped at the lake cabin one day, spied the duck wing and chuckled saying, "when you become experienced and have beautiful good ducks completely mounted, you will laugh at yourself for ever keeping a silly wing!" Well, I do have other "good ducks" mounted, but that duck wing is probably the most precious prize I have. It was a FIRST experience. I was all ALONE, and I'll never forget the exhilaration of the moment. You can become good friends with your taxidermist, but there are other ways to enjoy the critters forever, too!

I have various animals mounted and love every one of them. When I am asked "why?" I answer: Each and every one of them are my friends, they will no longer have to search for food, look for protection, will never again be cold and will live with someone who loves them! As I look at each mount, I relive the hunting experience all over again. I can hunt them over and over again as I go around the room. They are so very beautiful to look at. I marvel at the intricate feathers and their design, the aerodynamic design of their bodies, the nice horns or antlers, the brilliant colors they display and I give thanks to God for giving me the opportunity to have experienced nature. Yes, Billy the bufflehead, George the gadwall, Rachmaninoff the redhead, Sammy the swan, Melvin the muley, Arthur the antelope, Big Shot the blue/white hybrid snow goose and Cameron the Canada goose are all my friends. They keep us company at the lake cabin, and never cease to remind me how very fragile our resources can be and how we must each do what we can for their preservation.

Lila and I have hunted together now for several years. We always seem to have new encounters and experiences with each whitetail season, and no matter what time of year it is at the time, we always rehash our deer hunts and the great times we had. Stories and memories are a huge and enjoyable part of hunting. Lila says ethics and safety were the most important things she learned as a beginning hunter. She explains, "From my mentors I learned to respect the animal and only take a SURE shot. You must remember to look and see the pathway of your bullet and always look for other hunters. You must know when it is better NOT to shoot. I found out by personal experience that I do not want to fill my tag on opening day of the season! I love to be in the outdoors and love hunting and certainly want more than just one day to be in the deer woods! I appreciate the entire cycle of hunting — of finding the game, harvesting it, cleaning it and having our family dine on it. For years I watched my husband and friends go hunting and finally decided I wanted to go, too! I was also persuaded by my mentors and friends and

I'm glad I was! I enjoy being outdoors, the camaraderie and the constant situations of challenging myself. My most important tip to beginners is: Don't wear huge mittens because you can inadvertently bump the trigger! (Sounds like a story here!) Learn how to hunt, have fun and enjoy yourself!"

Whitetails Unlimited, Inc. is a national whitetail deer conservation organization. Its purpose is to raise funds in support of educational programs, habitat conservation and preservation of the hunting tradition for the direct benefit of the white-tailed deer and other wildlife. Founded in 1982, WTU has made great strides in the field of conservation. They have gained the reputation of being the nation's premier organization dedicating their resources to the betterment of the white-tailed deer and its environment. WTU's Adopt-A-Hunter program is another avenue for you to explore as a beginning hunter. WTU has a grassroots banquet program in which you can become involved. For more information write Whitetails Unlimited, P.O. Box 720, Sturgeon Bay, WI 54235 or call 1-800-274-5471.

Whitetail deer hunting is a wonderful and always exciting experience. You will not only learn a lot about deer, but you will learn a lot about yourself. Be ready to explore these new horizons!

And hey, if you skipped the archery chapter because you don't hunt with a bow, read it anyway. There is a lot of good information and tips for deer hunting.

MULE DEER

"Oh, you'll get a big one!" "Don't worry. You'll drag a trophy home!" These were the farewell statements from my friends. The crowning touch came from Wild Bill, our helper on the farm. As I waved good-bye to my husband, Wild Bill hollered, "If you don't get at least a five by five, don't even bother coming home!"

Sure, just what I needed, more pressure to bag a big mule deer. Never mind it would be the first buck I'd ever shot, forget that it was my very first trip out to "West River" country to hunt. Suddenly, I'd let my thought that mule deer hunting is "in the big boys' league" float right out of my mind.

South Dakota is divided by the Missouri River which runs through the middle of the state, from North Dakota to Nebraska. "East River" is mainly

Angie Zumbo shows off a nice mule deer. A steady shooting position helps make for clean kills.

agricultural and flat. It is great whitetail country. "West River" is endless miles of rolling prairie, contains the badlands, Black Hills, buttes, breaks and in the extreme northwest, rough hills. This is great mule deer country. Living in northeast South Dakota, I had listened with fascination to many stories of trophy mule deer bagged out west. I'd heard about the physical challenges involved, the deer camps, the camaraderie, the bragging and the taxidermy of trophies when the hunters returned home. I had always secretly thought I'd love to try a hunt like that, but shrugged it off as something beyond my hunting skills and ability, just something I'd love hearing about but would never do.

Finally, in a moment of reckless abandon, I agreed to apply for a mule deer two-tag license for extreme northwestern South Dakota. A friend of mind had begged me to do this for two years and I just thought, "OK, I'll never get drawn anyway. Then I'll have the perfect excuse not to go because the thought of actually doing this scares me to death."

Our mailman never knew how the shot of adrenaline hit me as I collected the mail one August day and found West River mule deer tags with my name on them! I was now committed; I had to go! I couldn't chicken out because everyone I worked with knew I had a lucky draw. I called my friend and conservation officer Brian Meiers to be my guide and arrangements were made. He was extremely excited and made the entire ordeal sound simple and easy. Sure it was easy for him! I had only been deer hunting for two years, had only bagged whitetail does, and had hunted no further than 7 miles from our farm. After two months of suggestions, advice, encouragement and sheer terror, I gritted my teeth and packed my hunting gear .

Driving through the West River prairie grasslands and listening to country music tapes worked together to calm me down. I told myself that I would enjoy just being in this new country and situation, appreciating the fact that I had the opportunity for a new experience, and if I got a deer or not was beside the point. I just did not want to make a fool of myself. At least I'd be able to say I drove 600 miles and had hunted.

Lost in my own dream world, I didn't pay any attention to the vehicle appearing on the horizon until I met the van. The hair stood up on the back of my neck, I got goose bumps and an immediate stomach ache! Perched on top of the van was the biggest buck I had ever seen! "Oh my gosh! They get that big?? This is what I'm expected to get?? I can't do this!" I shook the rest of the way and wondered how I could get out of actually going hunting.

I met Brian and some colorful locals and tried to choke down some dinner as I listened to "the plan." I didn't even think about sleeping, knowing that would be impossible. At a dark 6:30 a.m. I met Brian at his pickup with the order of muffins he demanded from the motel and we were off.

I felt like I was in a fantasy world as we left town. I wondered what would happen on this "day of infamy." As we came around a small knoll, the muffin I was trying to eat suddenly stopped in my throat. There was a huge monster mule deer buck entertaining his does. Everything flew in the pickup as Brian slammed on the brakes and screamed, "Wow! Where did he come from? I thought I'd seen all the bucks around here!"

I will never forget the beautiful sight of that buck looking at us, looking at his harem, back at us, and arrogantly walking away back down the breaks. I couldn't speak. I couldn't breathe. What a truly magnificent creature! Breaking the silence, Brian finally said, "Berdette, that was the biggest muley buck I've ever seen!" I knew that buck was very special. If that buck was all I had seen and I would have had to go home right then, the trip would have been worth it. It was just incredible to me. When we were 5 miles down the road and breathing had been restored to normal, I KNEW this was beyond me. After bagging only two white-tailed does in farm country, how in the world could I ever bag something like that?

The author with her trophy mule deer buck. A tough hunt and a little luck brought this deer down. This is proof that anyone can do it.

We were met in our host's yard with enthusiasm and advice on where to go, and an alternate plan if the first one failed. Off we set, walking breaks, buttes, and looking for miles at some of the most beautiful country I've ever seen. The air was cool and crisp, no breeze and wonderfully quiet. We trudged for several miles with no results. We didn't see a sign of a deer. Pondering the next action, I spied movement over on the right and there they were! Muleys! What a spectacular sight! Along with two does, a nice muley buck was standing at attention holding court on a butte about a half a mile away. They had seen us, ran off the butte and down to the breaks. We followed and caught up with a doe. I knew that buck was in the brush somewhere near. We were still and nervous, eyes scoping out everything we could see. Suddenly he bounded up another butte, within rifle range. I hurriedly dropped to my knees, aimed and fired. The shots were low and he took off in hasty pursuit of his does. I was disappointed but thought, well, I had my chance and blew it; at least I got to see him posing on the butte and I'll never forget that scene. Dejectedly we walked back to the truck and decided on "Plan B" as described by the rancher.

There was a trail beside his landing strip, and he told us that it was a favorite hang-out for muleys. We were only a short way down the trail when we heard some movement.

All at once the trees exploded and a herd of muleys crashed out of the woods, led by a huge beautiful buck. When they reached the safety of the middle of the field, they stopped, looked us over, then continued on over the fence and were gone. Needless to say, no words passed between Brian and I, and we just knew what our next step would be.

Meandering through the trees, carefully sliding through the field and crossing over the fence, we very slowly and quietly sneaked up the ridge. This was a wonderful chance and we knew we better not blow it by being seen. As we reached the ridge top, we dropped to our knees and froze! Down in the breaks were the does, staring up at us! Scanning for the buck, it felt like three days passed as we sat in the position, not moving a muscle, trying not to frighten the does. I shut my eyes for only a second to rest them from the strain; when I opened them I was looking straight at the buck's right antler, slowly bobbing up and down from behind a small knoll. My heart caught in my throat as I tried to whisper to Brian that the buck was there! We watched as all the muleys slowly walked behind that knoll and disappeared from sight. Our strategy was planned simultaneously! We had to get to the area they were headed without them seeing us! That meant crawling, climbing, and sliding up and down over three ridges.

I thought my lungs would burst, my legs would collapse and my beating heart would give away our position. Brian motioned to me to stay put as he sneaked to the very top and edge of the hill to see if we were in the right place. Absolutely. The does were just below him. Carefully he came part way down, and whispered that he was moving to the right to get a different angle and see if the buck was with them. After what seemed an eternity, he motioned with his hands to join him. The buck was there! Brian took a step down from the top of the hill and motioned for me to belly-crawl to the top. The buck was right out in the front standing broadside at only 60 yards. It was a perfect shot! I followed his orders and pulled up the rifle. I knew I needed a rifle rest and got situated fast, but, I could not find the buck in the scope! I looked up through the brush, saw the buck, and tried the scope again. He wasn't there! I couldn't believe it! Where was he? What was wrong? He wouldn't be standing there much longer as he had seen Brian by this time! And poor Brian was whispering/shouting "shoot"! I took just a second to settle down, thinking "I'm going to have to lift my head up a little higher so I can see, and that HAS to work!" The buck saw me all right, and this time he was in the scope! As the shot echoed off the surrounding ridges, the buck leaped up, jumped off the butte, tore down a gully and ran over to our left. Brian screamed, "Hurry up, get over there!" On knees that felt like water I stumbled over and watched as the antlers scraped the sides of the gully in one last head throw that dignified his life on earth.

It was then that my legs collapsed, I grabbed Brian as I fought back tears of disbelief. I had done it! I actually bagged a muley buck! And he was beautiful with his 5 x 6 antlers and a 27-inch spread! The beaming look of pride on Brian's face was also something to behold. When he left to go get the pickup I had time for one-on-one with MY muley. Countless times I ran my hands over each point on his antlers, petted his head, and smoothed his body hair, with reverence only found at times like this. He truly was a magnificent animal, and he was mine. He was so lucky to have lived four and one-half years in such beautiful country. Now he would live forever, worshipped by persons who can appreciate him and his life, and reminding us of moments when we really have to face ourselves and gain confidence to meet the challenges set before us.

I had a lot of fun with the "show and tell" part of all this as I was on the way back home. The most humorous episode happened when I stopped at the meat market. I asked the boys to come out and take in the deer meat for me.

This is what you're looking for. Mule deer inhabit rugged land in the American West. They grow larger than white-tailed deer and have the characteristic double-forked antler. (Photo by Kathy Butt)

One young man helped take a cooler from the back of the vehicle and immediately spied the trophy. The boy's eyes opened wide, he yelled a few unintelligible phrases including "they must have gotten this West River." I answered "yes." Then he asked, "Where West River did they get it?" I could hold back no longer so I said, "To tell you the truth, THEY is really ME!" He then turned and ran into the store calling for his buddy. "Come out here and see what this lady did! You won't believe it!"

"This lady did this?" "Wow!" As they finished loading up the meat, I followed them into the store as they yelled to everyone, "this lady did this"!

Before I left on the hunting trip, I had called my taxidermist to get the instructions on how to cape the deer out correctly if I was lucky enough to get one. He told me we probably shouldn't talk much about this as it might be bad luck. He wished me well and said he hoped to hear from me. He was coming out the door as I drove up to his house. He asked if I got one. My answer was "yeah, but I really don't know if it is worth mounting. I just want your opinion." As he looked into the vehicle, another case of shock, disbelief and pleasant surprise presented itself!

"Melvin the Muley" is beautiful and lives at our lake cabin where he holds court over a swan, turkey, ducks, fish, etc. I am thrilled that I get to enjoy him forever, and relive that dream and that hunt every time I look at him.

I still get a lump in my throat and get all choked up whenever I look at "Melvin," my wonderful mule deer mount. I had enjoyed many confidence-building experiences as I had learned to hunt, but the mule deer hunt out-shined them all! I'm sure beginners luck had a lot to do with it, I'll admit that, but for such a tremendous thing to happen to me on the very first hunt was unbelievable. I went from being terrified when I received my tags (after being "forced into applying" by my friends) to astounding disbelief, gratitude and pride when the good Lord saw fit to let me harvest Melvin.

I hunted the extreme northwest corner of South Dakota where the terrain could not be more different from the where I live, which is all flat agricultural land. I had heard about the muley's habitat and his country and was intrigued. However, it was still a surprise when I arrived in muley country — it looked like a lunar landscape! How could any deer live in this? Well, I watched, I listened and I learned. I was lucky enough to take a buck and a doe home with me. My muley allowed me to grow from being terrified and lacking confidence to a becoming a lucky, very humble but proud mule deer hunter. I will always be grateful to Brian Meiers, the local conservation officer and my friend for the understanding and patience (it took a lot, just ask him!) he had with me. His version of my hunting technique goes like this: "We will find a couple of bucks in the beginning of the hunt, she will take a couple of shots and miss, then she will settle down and the third critter she will take in one shot!" That happened with both mule deer and antelope while I was hunting with Brian, so I guess that's right! That hunt was a really big deal for me, as scared as I was that I would mess up, but Brian was a perfect teacher for a female novice. If I had had a guide with no patience, the story certainly would have had a different ending.

Brian's advice to a novice female mule deer hunter is "Have an experienced person with you. Besides teaching you, another person means extra eyes and ears and it is safer. Two women can hunt just as well as two men; having an experienced person with you is important. You have to just 'go do it.' You cannot learn it all from a book. Don't be afraid to make mistakes. If at first you don't succeed, try again and again. Be aware of all conditions. The weather determines a lot and the deer are smart. Be safe. You will be climbing and crawling and you have a loaded gun in your hands."

This is typical mule deer country. Steep hills and wide-open spaces make the hunting tough, but not impossible.

GETTING TO KNOW YOU

I found hunting the "great gray ghosts" to be fascinating and awesome. A big part of that is being in the rough country mule deer love. It's big, wide, open country, very different from the basic whitetail country that is either forest or agricultural lands. You catch the flavor of the old west; sometimes the land resembles a country that time passed by. In this big country, you get a feeling of vastness that makes a person feel very insignificant. It can be intimidating, downright scary, but very precious and beautiful all at the same time.

Today an estimated 2 million mule deer inhabit the western United States. Everything west of a line drawn down the center of the Dakotas to the west edge of Texas defines mule deer country. They are most numerous in the mountains and foothills, but can be found in other areas such as the prairie and badlands, too. They live in the deserts of the southwest where they are usually found in the brush areas along rivers and coulees. Mule deer like rough country including buttes, breaks, drainages, canyons and anywhere it is tough for us hunters to find them.

Mule deer are usually a brownish-gray, appearing mostly gray in winter. Where do they get their name? From their ears which are large and prominent like those of a mule. The large ears are beneficial as they enable the mule deer to have a fantastic sense of hearing. It is one of their main defenses. The mule deer's forehead is dark and its chin and throat are white. The tail is narrow and mostly white except for a solid black tip —completely different from the whitetail's. The antlers are also very different. The mule deer has antlers that fork, then fork again and are Y-shaped (bifurcated). Like the country they live in, their antlers are big. Mule deer are a large animal; bucks average between 200 and 300 pounds. Rare specimens weighing more than 300 pounds can be found. Does rarely exceed 160 pounds. Average height is 3-1/2 feet at the shoulder and average length is 6 to 6-1/2 feet.

How can you tell the difference between a whitetail and a mule deer? The mule deer are larger, have a different configuration of antlers, have bigger ears and narrow black-tipped tails.

Mule deer are browsers, utilizing a wide variety of brush and trees (more than 700 different plants). They depend heavily on the early stages of forest growth found at the forest edge. Mule deer are also picky eaters and look for the most tender and nutritious browse. Their seasonal eating habits vary greatly in different areas of the country. The West's large aspen stands are extremely important in their diet. There is great concern today that disappearing aspen stands are having a detrimental effect on mule deer survival; herds are declining. This is a result of human development of various types right in the core of wildlife habitat, and the fact that "recycling forest fires" very seldom sweep through aspen stands today to provide a regeneration of aspen sprouts. High in protein, sagebrush can be the mule deer's most important staple in winter. In fact, some people do not like to eat mule deer as the sage flavor is different and can be strong. (Jim Zumbo's venison cookbook will take care of this.)

Mule deer range farther and travel more extensively than do whitetails. They are also more gregarious and will form larger winter herds.

Mule deer are more curious than the whitetail and are often seen in open areas. When they are running from you, they often will run about 100 yards, then stop, turn and stare at you, giving you a good opportunity for a standing shot. That action can give the mistaken impression that they are "more tame" than whitetails.

Watching mule deer can be hilarious. When they are particularly frightened, they actually bounce and have acquired the nickname "kangaroo deer." The first time I witnessed this I just couldn't believe it. It really is funny to watch. This bouncing, called "stotting" is their most unusual characteristic. When stotting, all four feet come down together, their rear feet landing behind the front feet. Stotting is their adaptation to their terrain — they can quickly gain elevation on steep inclines and the action permits instantaneous, unpredictable changes in direction. This action results in a very difficult target for predators and hunters.

Mule deer and whitetails have basically the same rut habits. Since whitetails and mule deer can occupy the same habitat, there can be cross-breeding. The most notable characteristic of the hybrids is that they do not have the ability to stott. It's also true that hybrids don't often survive as long as the pure species.

GETTING READY

You definitely need a good pair of binoculars as you will be glassing great expanses of land. When purchasing your binoculars, stay between seven and eight power. Seven by thirty-five (7 X 35), seven by fifty (7 X 50), eight by thirty (8 X 30), eight by forty (8 X 40), eight by forty-two (8 X 42), and eight by fifty-six (8 X 56) are all good choices. Eight by forty (8 X 40) is the most common choice. Seven by fifty (7 X 50) allows the most light at dusk and dawn (your most important hunting hours) and is the best for those situations.

Do not get high-power binoculars, like those 10-power (10X) monsters. They are large and heavy and will be uncomfortable for you to carry, use and hold for any length of time. If they are not too heavy, they are so light you have to hold your breath to steady them. You will pay more for them in dollars

Good binoculars are mandatory in mule deer country. You need to see the deer before they see you.

and also in eye fatigue, which can ruin your hunt. Quality, not the power, is most important. Stay with the known brands, do not purchase something just because it is cheaper. Conversely, you do not have to purchase an extremely expensive pair, either. Start out with a "middle of the road" pair; you can always work your way up to the top of the line later after you have more experience. I have a small pair of camo Simmons binoculars that have served me well. I would like to have a large pair, but I've hesitated as I think they would be just too heavy to carry all day. When purchasing your binoculars, keep that thought in mind. You will be carrying your firearm, a fanny pack or backpack probably filled to capacity. A heavy set of binoculars will just add to the weight and be a strain on your neck and shoulders, and may interfere if you have to take a fast shot. Try different brands and sizes until you feel comfortable with a certain one. Be sure and get "waterproof" and not just "water-resistant" binoculars. Top-of-the-line binoculars include Bausch & Lomb, Swarovski, Ziess and Nikon models. Bushnell also has a good selection of binoculars and a wide price range. Tasco, is at the low end of the price and quality range.

Buy binoculars with individual eye focus — the kind you can set to your own eyes and leave there. Mark the settings with a fine-point felt marker or some liquid paper then look at the settings each time before putting them up to your eyes, making certain the glass is focused on your settings and ready to go. You'll avoid eyestrain and save precious time without having to adjust them constantly.

Rolling a single, center focus ring back and forth to get a clear picture each time you glass can be hard on your eyes. Most of these types of binoculars allow you to set the focus on one eye. But invariably while hunting, the focus ring shifts. To reduce eyestrain on one of these types, mark the center focus ring where the glass is in focus at about 100 yards. Set it there before you put them up to your eyes, allowing you then to make only small focus adjustments. When I found the right focus on my small binoculars, I used black electrician tape and taped them at that particular focus point. The tape is easy to use, is waterproof, yet will come off easily. This way, they are always "at the ready" and I don't waste time having to focus each time I use them. They look funny, but it works!

You will spend a lot of time behind your binoculars in mule deer country and you should know how to effectively use them and hold them. If you have been climbing and you are breathing hard and maybe shaking, take a minute to calm down. You do this before shooting your rifle; do the same thing when using your binoculars. This will help you keep the binoculars steady and find your game faster.

You need a "rest" for binoculars just as you do for your rifle. Sit down and place your elbows on your knees, as this will steady the binoculars. You can rest on a rock, downed tree or even use a tree trunk to steady yourself. A "last resort" method is resting your binoculars on your thumbs, then use your index fingers as braces against your temples.

If you see some game or what could be game with your naked eyes, don't look down to your binoculars. Stare at the spot and slowly bring the binoculars up to your eyes and scan. Don't move your head or shift your eyes.

Another piece of equipment that can help you find game is a spotting scope. This is not absolutely necessary but an option. A spotting scope on a tripod will help you see long distances when hunting the open country for big game. A twenty power (20X) scope is all the power you need for any big game. It will also let you look at a far-off deer and decide if you want to go after the animal. Trophy hunters live by their spotting scopes. Don't purchase a variable power — you will suffer eye fatigue. Look for optics that are clear and bright. You want as much light as possible during the pre-dawn and sunset hours. When you are trying out either binoculars or a spotting scope in the store, focus on a ceiling light and compare the difference in the brightness. As with binoculars, the spotting scope should be tough, durable and rubber-armored as it will receive some pretty tough treatment no matter how careful you are.

Because of the big country in which muleys are found, you may be shooting at a long distance, maybe 300 yards. That's why flat-shooting cartridges are best, like the 25-06 Remington (130-grain bullet) 270 Winchester (140- or 150-grain bullets), 280 Remington (150-grain), 7mm Remington Magnum (165-or 175-grain), and 30-06 Springfield (165-grain or even larger). You will be dealing with wind in mule deer country and therefore heavier bullets help keep you on target. It is a good idea to go to your local rifle range and review your yardage markings and practice shooting longer shots. Be prepared!

As for clothing, many of the same rules apply here as for white-tailed deer hunting. Use common sense and remember your blaze orange. Many of the Western states have less strict requirements on orange than do the eastern states. Get the regulation book and follow it, but remember, the regulations are only a minimum. Wear wool or fleece outer garments. You do not want to make any noise while you are stalking a mule deer. I was not aware of how quiet I needed

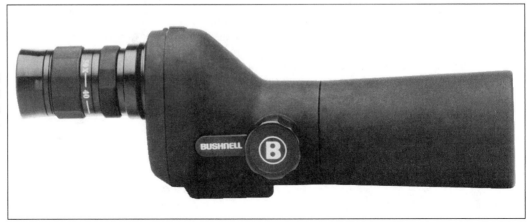

A spotting scope can help you locate deer a long way away and can tell you the trophy quality of closer deer.

to be when I hunted mule deer. I wore my waterfowl coveralls that really made loud "swish" noises when I walked. Brian had a fit and rolled his eyes whenever I forgot to walk with my feet spread apart!

You will definitely want sturdy, tough hunting boots with good traction. Also take along some very worn or soft-soled boots or shoes for noiseless stalking. Some hunters even take their shoes off and add another pair of socks so they can be as quiet as humanly possible while sneaking up on a mule deer. If you are in your socks, watch out for cactus!

One fact you must be cognizant of while in mule deer country is that rattlesnakes live there, too. Although encounters are extremely rare, it is good to know that they can be in your territory. If you hear a rattle, you will probably be within 4 to 5 feet of the reptile. If there is no wind and your hearing is good, you can hear them a lot farther away than that. If you do hear one relatively close to you, immediately freeze. Stay still and wait him out (snakes are always referred to as he or him). He will more than likely disappear. Do not run; if he is coiled and ready to strike, you will not be able to move fast enough, just stay still and then slowly retreat from the area. Rattlesnakes will strike half the length of their body.Take that into account as you appraise your position. Remember they would rather be left alone and would rather not bite you.

Rattlesnake bites are serious; they can be deadly serious. If you are bitten, forget about the old stories of "cutting and bleeding" the bite. It is safer to use an ace bandage or a cloth and place it between the bite and your heart. Do not tie it as tight as a tourniquet (you do not want to constrict the blood flow). In the first thirty minutes, the area surrounding the bite will swell up and get black and blue. After tying the bandage on, get to a medical facility immediately!

Thirty percent of the people who receive rattlesnake bites do not receive any venom. In many cases the fangs will not penetrate clothing, especially leather boots, etc. Ninety-eight percent of the bites occur on the hands and feet, so be aware of that fact. Do not be overly concerned or overreact because there may be some rattlesnakes in your hunting area. Sightings are rare and bites are even more rare. Simply be aware of these facts.

THE HUNT

Spot and stalk is the main method of hunting mule deer, but other methods discussed in the whitetail deer section may also be used. Terrain determines how to hunt them. First spotting a mule deer, then stalking him until you can get a good clean shot is an exciting part of mule deer hunting. You may be within good shooting distance when you first see the deer. In that case, you wouldn't have to stalk very far or at all. That would be more like stand hunting. If you spot a muley far away and decide that is the one you want, you must plan a stalk to get within rifle range. Hunting muleys means a lot of crawling, rolling over cacti, sliding on shale, climbing, dropping over ridges, etc. It also involves a lot of just plain waiting. Waiting for the deer to turn into the right position or to rise from his bed. Be ready for everything; this all makes the mule deer hunt challenging!

One thing to look out for... mule deer country is also rattlesnake country. If you see or hear a snake, stop, stay still and move away from the snake slowly. (Photo by South Dakota Department of Tourism)

Get out in the field before dawn and "glass" (look through binoculars) for mule deer. Watch where they go and where they bed down. The best times for a stalk are between 10 a.m. and 2 p.m. The deer are settled down and in their beds and that is when to start your stalk. If you have a chance to stalk some does and fawns, or even some whitetails, before the trip, do it to practice your stalking skills. It is fun and you will learn how to be quiet, crawl close to the ground and to stay still for a long time. Stalking will be done in all types of terrain, so be ready for thick brushy areas, timber, canyons, buttes, or draws.

In *Mule Deer: Hunting Today's Trophies* by Jim Van Norman and Tom Carpenter, they discuss three main considerations in beginning a successful stalk. "First, evaluate the overall opportunity. Given the deer's position, your position and the cover (vegetative or topographical) available to help you, what are your chances of getting where you need to be? Second, consider wind direction. Can you get there without the wind carrying your scent to the deer? Third, mentally map your stalking route. Is it a plan you can remember and follow?"

Make sure your planned stalk is realistic and that you are able to attempt it. Always be aware of wind conditions; make a different plan to accommodate the wind if necessary. Make a mental map of where you are going and where you need to be. Use trees, brush, rocks, etc. as marking devices. The terrain can be used to hide your movements. Take advantage of boulders, etc. that are in your path. Use your binoculars a lot while stalking. You may see other deer that you did not see before.

Mule deer are great at hiding in what looks to us as barren land. They can bed down in heavy cover but position themselves so they can see, smell and hear danger approaching from great distances. Don't expect to see the entire deer. Look for antler tips, legs, rumps, ears and faces. Remember the antlers are forked — look for the "Y". The rumps are white/gray and can appear to be a boulder; look for the tail to be sure what you're looking at is a deer. Pay particular attention to shady areas. They provide cover, security and heat relief. This is where the bucks will be hiding.

While hunting you must be careful not to "skyline" yourself. Do not go barging up over a ridge in full view of any mule deer in the county. You'll end up watching your chance at a good shot fade away fast. Very slowly, step by step, and under cover, crawl on your belly over the ridge. Stop before you are at the top and look and glass the country. Crawl a little farther up the ridge and repeat the procedure until you are sure you are at the top and have covered all the territory. If you do see a mule deer "waiting for you," plan accordingly and get a good shot.

The closer you get to the deer, the more important noiseless movements become. Remember those big ears and their fantastic hearing ability. Walk slowly and be aware of where you place your feet. Hunting with a rifle gives you more room for errors than hunting with a bow, but mule deer don't often hang around to see what's making all that noise. So be quiet. Move and wait. Move and wait. When you finally get

> **Mule deer are great at hiding in what looks to us as barren land. They can bed down in heavy cover but position themselves so they can see, smell and hear danger approaching from great distances.**

to the "right" spot where you can take a shot but find the deer is not in the correct position, you will have to quietly wait him out. This may take a long time; it would be good to "settle in" in a good comfortable position so your arms or legs are not numb when you have to move to make the shot. Have a doe bleat call with you in case you accidentally spook the deer; blowing that call can make him stop and give you time for a good shot.

You may be asking, "How can I handle sitting/lying there for a long time waiting for the deer to turn just right with my heart beating so loud I'm sure he can hear it? How do I control the flow of adrenaline for all that time?" Well, that is the exciting and thrilling part of hunting. And, that is why it is called "hunting" and not "shooting." A few deep breaths and forcing yourself to relax will help. Telling yourself to calm down will help. Just concentrate on what you are doing.

This is the basic way to spot and stalk hunt the West's great mule deer. For more detailed information, refer to *Mule Deer: Hunting Today's Trophies*, by Van Norman and Carpenter. It is packed full of information and gives you plenty of hunting tips.

Hunting mule deer may mean a trip out west for you and your hunting buddies. It is wonderful country. Refer to the "Finding A Place to Hunt" chapter for western lands information.

In his book, *To Heck with Deer Hunting*, Jim Zumbo describes the western badlands as off-beat, but terrific places to hunt deer. "The badlands are really lowland areas with lots of gullies, draws, sparse brush, and few trees. Much of the land in these regions is administered by the U.S. Bureau of Land Management, a federal agency that allows free public hunting. Some of them are a nasty maze of eroded hills and weird formations. Because of the topography and hiding places, plenty of deer live in them —both whitetails and muleys. Hunting badlands is a unique opportunity, being essentially a glassing and stalking exercise. Though deer usually aren't as numerous in badland areas as they are in more traditional spots, they often grow old and large because of the limited hunting pressure. One of the most proven strategies is to get into the hunting area before first light, looking for deer from a high vantage point as soon as it's light enough to see. It's often possible to watch deer bed down, and then make a careful stalk."

Mule deer hunting should definitely be on your list of new opportunities. They are truly a magnificent animal, majestic with their big racks. And they live in some of the most beautiful country on this planet. When you have hunted mule deer, you definitely will have had an experience of a lifetime.

Laura Merkwan of Sioux Falls, South Dakota loves to hunt mule deer in the mountains. "I really enjoy the excitement of being out there early in the morning and watching the sunrise over the mountains, watching the animals 'wake up' and hearing the sounds they make, and just generally enjoy their environment. The anticipation and preparation for the hunt is truly exciting, and knowing I hunted ethically and had a clean shot means a lot. Bringing meat home is a bonus! It's important for a woman beginner to be familiar with her rifle and to practice shooting and aiming from a variety of different positions. She needs to feel confident when conditions change. I also recommend researching the mule deer, how he lives and what his habits are. Scout the territory before you actually hunt so you will know how the mule deer react to you and you will be more prepared. Becoming familiar with the area is important. Also be prepared for changing weather conditions."

The Mule Deer Foundation raises funds through a local chapter and banquet system to promote management of the mule deer and protect and restore their habitat. You can have fun at the banquets and enjoy auctions featuring top-of-the-line sporting equipment, wildlife art and special hunts, while doing your part to preserve this magnificent animal. For membership details write: The Mule Deer Foundation, 1005 Terminal Way, Suite. 170, Reno, Nevada 89502, or call 1-888-375-DEER.

Expand your horizons, experience one of the most challenging hunts of your life and enjoy your newly-found confidence. Deer hunting can be one of the most amazing hunting outings you will experience.

CHAPTER NINE
ANTELOPE

The rain was smashing against the motel window between loud bursts of thunder as my alarm signaled that my day of destiny with antelope should begin. I remember moaning, "oh no" as I fumbled in the dark for the snooze button. It is not supposed to be raining when you hunt antelope. It is supposed to be nice, warm and maybe a little breezy — in other words — it is supposed to be perfect. That's what everyone told me. This was my first hunt in Butte County, South Dakota and I learned that the weather can be vicious. (I have since hunted there in rain, snow, sleet and hail (all at once) and have gotten so darned wet, there was even mud on the INSIDE of my underpants!)

Scott Mikkelson, the local conservation officer, was my guide and "antelope finder." I was hoping to hear "well, Berdette, it's raining so just go back to sleep and we'll wait for a nicer day," but I didn't hear that. Oh no, not Scott. He said, "What's the matter? You turning into a wimp? It might be a little wet out there, but the antelope are still there. Get ready!" The next thing I knew we were on the road out to the ranch where we would hunt. That road was gravel and didn't seem too bad, but the worst was yet to come. The rancher warmly welcomed us and graciously offered coffee and snacks. His wife had to leave, but made us promise that we would stay there at the ranch long enough for her to return and make homemade tacos for us. We had a delightful visit but I was getting antsy about getting out and finding some "goats," as pronghorn are called out West.

After explaining to us the areas in which we should hunt, the rancher told us how to get there. Each rancher owns thousands of acres and you really need to know exactly where you are going. Since it was so muddy, he offered to take us as close as he could to where we wanted to start since he had chains on his pickup. As I crawled into the vehicle, I realized I had changed gun cases and forgotten to attach my rifle sling. Both Scott and I realized neither one of us brought a camera! I bet the rancher was thinking, "Heaven help them. They are a couple of rookies." We finally got settled in the pickup and left for the hunting area. Even with chains, that was quite a ride — we could hardly drive in the wet gumbo mess. Gumbo is a mixture of clay, soil and dead vegetation that's common in the West. It turns slick as ice when it rains. I was wondering what walking would be like.

Walking proved easier than it looked once we got onto the grass. The excitement of finding a pronghorn took over and we began to concentrate on the hunt. After a long walk, we finally spied an antelope about 500 yards ahead of us, streaking across the prairie. We stopped and waited, he kept running and was not about to slow down. After walking for a long time and glassing the areas surrounding us, we found several antelope resting on the side of a knob about a half a mile away. We played the "spot and stalk" game, tried to come in around behind them so I could get a shot, but to no avail. (That's why they call it hunting!)

Finally, after we re-grouped with snacks, we planned a different strategy. We split up and covered some more ground. Before long, I could see Scott waving his arms and motioning me to come over. I immediately got excited and thought, "This is it!" After belly-crawling through the wet grass for about 100 yards, I could see two antelope standing down a small slope ahead of us. Just as I was about to raise the rifle and unfold the bipod, they took off — another foiled attempt! This antelope hunting wasn't as easy as everyone told me it would be. I was getting concerned! Scott was

THE BOTTOM LINE !

YOU'LL NEED THIS————————

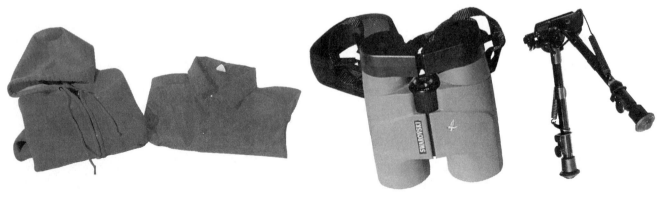

turned around, watching the pronghorns speed away from us when I saw him! Yes! There was a nice buck lying in the grass, right where the other two had been. They had run right by him and he never moved. I only could see his horns, then his head. Just as I whispered his presence to Scott, he ducked his head back down. Scott could not find him and I know he thought I was making it up!

"Well, forget him. I don't see him and besides, the buck that ran was a good trophy so let's go track them down," said Scott. Finally the buck lifted his head and Scott saw him. Then it was, "Well, it is your decision. The other buck was bigger, what do you want to do?"

I told Scott I had found him myself and because of that fact I already felt bonded to him and he was the one.

I flattened myself against the ground as much as possible as I unfolded the bipod and got the rifle in position. "Oh, please stay there," I prayed. I thought he was the most beautiful thing I had ever seen and I wanted him. Scott was nervously telling me to hurry and get into position because we were bound to be seen any second. Sure enough, the buck spied us and stood up and stared at us. I knew what to do and did it. The shot was perfect, in spite of my shaking! He was down and he was mine! As we ventured close to him, my emotions took over and a few tears fell. He was so gorgeous, his horns were so nice, the meat would be so good and, the best part about it, was that I found him by myself, it all worked and now he was mine. I gave thanks for the wonderful hunt, the great people I was with, and especially for God letting me have this creature.

After we field dressed the buck, Scott and I stood and looked at each other, knowing how far we would have to drag the antelope in the mud. If it had been dry, we would've walked back to the ranch and brought out the pickup. But no. Now it would be difficult. About half way back we heard a roar, looked up and here came the rancher, tearing through the mud. He had been watching us with binoculars and knew we needed help in the mud. After an unprofessional start, I

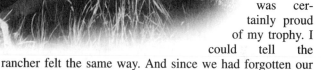

Arthur the Antelope fell to the author's bullet in Butte County, South Dakota. Antelope hunting is similar to deer hunting, but the shots are longer, the country is more open and you spend a lot of time crawling, trying to get close to the animals.

was certainly proud of my trophy. I could tell the rancher felt the same way. And since we had forgotten our cameras, the rancher came to the rescue with his so we got our pictures!

After we cleaned up, scraped mud off and had a cup of coffee we were ready to get back to town and start the skinning and cutting process. The rancher, more specifically, the rancher's wife, would not hear of it! As we rested with our coffee, she called the ranch on her way back home and demanded in no uncertain terms that we stay until she returned. We thought, "OK, but we are not going to put her to work making our supper." Well, wrong! Never underestimate ranching families. I have met some of the most wonderful people in this manner, and these people were at the top of the list. We certainly would have offended her if we had NOT stayed for those wonderful homemade tacos, bread and all the fixings. We could tell these people loved hunters, were proud of their land, loved the antelope that lived there and bent over backwards to help anyone who stopped there. The world is full of wonderful people!

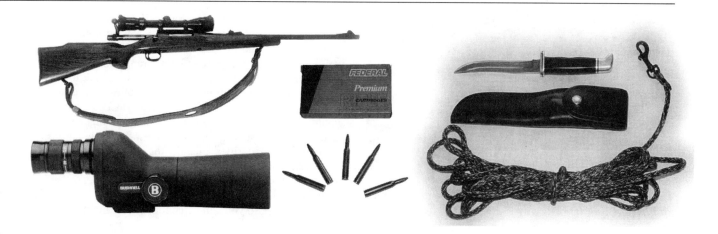

My buck antelope was a beauty then and he is a beauty now. That pronghorn became "Arthur, the Antelope" and now graces my wildlife wall. When I look up at him, I swear he winks those huge eyes at me and tells me he is glad to be mine!

GETTING TO KNOW YOU

Antelope are beautiful, graceful and intriguing critters. Their distinct coloring is unforgettable. They are a tan, with a dark muzzle and white cheeks and have two large outstanding white stripes on the front of their neck. Their eyes are large, almost appearing "buggy eyed." This sharp eyesight allows them to see hunters extremely well. They can recognize moving objects more than 2 miles away. Be sure you stay hidden from view when hunting them.

The male has a black patch back behind his jaw. Their brilliant white rump gives them away in the grasslands. The antelope can literally "make their hair stand on end," especially the rump, and signal danger to the rest of the herd.

A sheath, or skin covers the permanent horns on both bucks and does. This sheath is shed each year by the buck. The does' horns are shorter than the ears, while the bucks are tall, erect and sport a prong, facing forward. The black horns are curved at the tip and an average set will measure around 12 inches. The average pronghorn weights about 110 pounds. The "pronghorn" shares the same history as bison; eons ago the population is estimated to have been 30 million to 40 million.

Antelope range in about the western half of the U.S., primarily on grasslands. They are very dependent upon good winter weather for survival and that season can determine the population very quickly. Sometimes the entire herd will move more than 100 miles to escape bad winter weather.

Antelope are the fastest land animal in North America. Being capable of running at great speeds like 60 miles per hour on flat land is their best-known attribute. Their "cruising speed" is believed to be 30 miles per hour. At only about five days old, the fawns can outrun a man! The rut takes place late summer; does usually have single births the first year and twins will then follow.

Antelope usually inhabit prairie grassland areas — places where you can see forever. You will also find them in open range land moving carefully through herds of cattle. They live in areas of short and mixed prairie grasslands and areas of sagebrush-grasslands. Being browsers, sagebrush and forbs supplies them with needed nutrition. If they are in the vicinity of alfalfa and croplands, they will feed there from time to time. Their diet mainly consists of rough browse and sagebrush; therefore there is little competition with ranchers' cattle who graze the same range. They usually feed during the morning and evening hours, but are generally moving around all day. They will lay down to rest, then get up again and wander.

An amusing characteristic of pronghorns is their intense curiosity. When they see strange objects, they usually will not be frightened off until they catch a scent. Their top priority at first will be to find out what the strange object is. This is an important fact for you to remember as you can sometimes use this to your advantage. Even a fluttering piece of cloth may bring an antelope close to you as he investigates. My son-in-law, Mark, always reminds me of the story of his first antelope hunt. While he and the other hunters were concentrating on watching an antelope herd that was out in front of their vehicle, trying to decide the best plan of action, etc., one of the hunters happened to turn around and he was shocked to see two antelope, one a nice buck, standing behind the pickup, looking at the hunters!

It is here that I can give a promotional plug for South Dakota's beautiful Custer State Park. There is no finer place you can go to view herds of pronghorn! They will be grazing on open grasslands, along with the resident bison herd, just as they were centuries ago. Spending a summer vacation observing antelope or other big game is a great way to prepare for the coming hunting seasons.

GETTING READY

Contact your wildlife agency for the appropriate application blank for antelope hunting, noting the deadline. Deciding upon which unit to hunt will depend on where you want to go, antelope populations in the area, landowner permission, public lands, etc. Do your homework. Please refer to the "Finding a Place to Hunt" chapter. Antelope inhabit the grasslands, so you will be hunting in the wide open spaces. Most of the Western states issue antelope permits through a lottery. The season usually starts in early October.

If you will be staying in a motel during the hunt, make your reservations early. Antelope hunting is done in rural areas and small towns. The few local motels can fill up fast.

The weather can change drastically, so be prepared to dress for warm, cool or wet weather. I have hunted in 85-degree weather and in snow within three days! You may be walking a lot, so good hunting boots are needed. You may be doing some crawling on the ground as you sneak up on the antelope, so heavy hunting pants and a shirt with reinforced elbows are good. You don't really need brush pants, but they would help in the same situation. Blaze orange items are required in most states. Read and follow your regulations.

Good antelope rifles include the 243 Winchester, 270 Winchester and the 25-06 Remington with medium to heavy bullets. You will be shooting at fairly long ranges, so be sure to practice shooting before you hunt. Spend some time at your rifle range so you can be confident of a good shot up to

What's important about this photo is the bipod on the rifle. You need a steady platform from which to shoot, especially what you are thinking about taking a shot at an animal that is 300 yards away.

250 yards. A rifle bipod (two legs attached to the forearm or barrel of the rifle) is great, if you can get it set up easily. Practice with it. Some hunters will carry a small backpack and put the backpack down as a rifle rest. No matter what you choose, plan on using a rest. The shots are long and you want to make a good one to put the antelope down quickly.

Binoculars are a must. Please refer to the "Deer Hunting" chapter.

Take a large cooler and some ice with you. If you are hauling the antelope directly to a meat locker, you can put whole bags of ice into the body cavity to cool the meat as you head to the locker. Or, you can quarter or butcher the antelope and store the meat in the cooler. Ask your mentor about which option would be the best.

Remember to pack your camera. Antelope are very photogenic!

DECOYS

Decoys can be used for antelope hunting. An antelope decoy set up in the grassland area will bring the animals in simply because of their curiosity. I know some hunters who have had antelope walk up to within 10 feet of the decoy. Since the hunters were sitting behind the decoy, they got a great shot. A hilarious decoy to use is a cow--that's right--a wood cutout of a cow. Antelope are used to seeing them and will not spook. Just be sure your cow is the same breed as those grazing with the antelope! Hiding behind the cow will allow you another great shot. A mirror blind can also be used successfully. A 4-foot square piece of Plexiglas with a mirror-finish window film on one side and braces to place into the ground is all you need. While you are hiding behind it, all the antelope sees is a section of prairie reflected back at him. No matter what you choose for a decoy, the point is to remember to stay well hidden at all times.

THE HUNT

Antelope can be hunted throughout the day, so you don't have to worry about getting up way before dawn. Conversely,

don't party late the night before the hunt either — you need a steady hand for your rifle. If you are driving out to your hunting area and there are antelope there and they see the vehicle, they will probably only stand and look. Vehicles don't bother them as they are used to seeing farm trucks all the time. Humans are a different story. The human form seems to send antelope off like a shot. If you see antelope while you are in the truck, keep on driving until you get to a place where you can park and the antelope will not be able to see you. Probably behind a hill or knob in the area.

Then the hunt begins. The basic way to hunt antelope is to spot them, stalk them and then get in range for a good shot. You'll need to know exactly where they are when you start out walking. SNEAK up the hill or around the bottom of a knob. Do not walk up the hill and then pop over the top. You will spook them for sure. When you reach the top of the hill, take your cap off and keep your head down so there is very little chance of them seeing you. If this works and they are there and they are within range, slide back down the hill a bit, get your bipod legs or rifle rest set up and your rifle ready. Think about the yardage, how they are standing, and shot placement. Then when you move back into position for the shot, they will have moved. Deal with it. Aim for the area where the brown meets the white near the front shoulder. Be sure it is a safe shot. Take a few deep breaths. Position your rifle rest firmly, quickly and quietly. If the antelope have seen you by this time, they will probably be standing there looking at you, or about to start running. Take that shot as soon as possible, methodically, precisely, but in a hurry.

If this strategy does not work and the antelope take off, watch and see where they are going. For instance, if they ran behind some hills or knobs to your left, walk back around the hills and "head them off at the pass." Another option is for your hunting buddy to walk around those hills and move the antelope back towards you. Just remember, this is just an example — antelope will go where they want to go! It is to the hunter's advantage that antelope are curious. Many times they will just stand and look at you if they see you. That gives you time to make a good shot.

I have bagged antelope that were just standing out on the prairie, surprised them around the side of a hill, or sneaked over a depression to get near enough for a good shot.

Doing the dirty work. Antelope hunting is usually done in warmer weather. That makes it doubly important to get after the field dressing right away. You want to get the body heat out of the antelope as soon as you can.

The farthest I have ever shot was about 250 yards. The bipod works well in keeping the rifle steady. Be sure you have it placed on firm ground; do not let it be "tippy" on rocks, cactus or cowpies or your shot will not be accurate. That may be frustrating when you are in a hurry to shoot, but you must have that rifle firmly planted.

If you use a decoy, place it in the appropriate area and just sit behind it. Some hunters use a white flag placed on a stick, wave it and the antelope come in — their curiosity gets the better of them.

Do not "run" the antelope before you harvest it — the adrenaline will make the meat taste much stronger. Sneak up and take your shot. The sneaking is the hard part, but the shooting can be pretty tough, too.

Antelope hunting can really be exciting. I'll never forget how "exciting" it was the day it was raining, sleeting, snowing and the wind was blowing about 45 miles per hour. Poor Scott, my hunting buddy, very graciously volunteered to move the herd past my position on the top of this particular hill. The antelope however, did not want to cooperate. The "move" escalated into about five moves. Each of which took place in this terrible weather. I had never been so wet, so cold, so muddy in my life! My rain pants split on the rocks and I even ended up with mud on the inside of my underpants! Now THAT is being muddy! I was so wrapped up in my misery and the wind was so loud that I couldn't hear Scott's directions as he stood on the next hill screaming and waving his arms. He later told me there was a nice buck just over the crest of the hill to my left, within 50 yards of me and that is what he was jumping around about! The moral of the story is: don't bother antelope hunting in adverse weather like that. Wait until it clears up and you will have a much better hunt. Two days later the sun was shining and it was warm. All things worked together and I found a nice buck, made a good stalk and squeezed off a nice shot.

AFTER THE HUNT

When I started antelope hunting, several people told me I wouldn't like the meat, that the animals smelled bad and that it was not a good game animal. I heartily disagree! My husband and I have found that we like antelope meat very much. The first time I fixed antelope steak, my husband said, "If this is antelope, you can go hunt that whenever you want to"!

The problem with bad smelling or tasting meat is the way the hunters handled it following the shot. Antelope season is usually during warm weather so the meat has to be taken care of quickly. First of all, immediately field dress the animal and skin it as soon as possible. Do not place the carcass immediately on ice; there must be a natural "cool down" time to insure the quality of the meat.

Following the cool down period, the meat is then ready to cut. It is easiest to cut it into quarters. Put ice in your cooler and place the meat on top of the ice. If there is room, cover with ice.

It is at this point where some hunters run into trouble. They think all they have to do is clean the carcass, then they whip it into or on top of a vehicle, maybe drive around for another day or two, then drive home which could take another day. By the time they have the carcass home, because of the warm days, it has already started to spoil. This is when they say antelope meat is bad. Not! You simply have to take care of it and do it quickly. Get the meat cut up quickly and into the freezer.

Because sage is a large part of an antelope's diet, there may be a slight sage aroma to the meat, but it is not offensive. Antelope meat is sweeter than venison and wonderful any way it is prepared. The secret to having good antelope meat is to protect the meat quality by properly taking care of your animal after the shot.

Antelope hunting is not only for the guys. It is a fun and relatively easy big game hunt for women and youth. If you do not have antelope in your state, check with your wildlife agency and they can give you an information number for another state's agency. From them you can get information on antelope season.

Antelope hunting is another opportunity to learn, to enjoy, to meet new friends and visit old friends, meet another outdoor challenge and savor some wonderful wild game meat for your table.

CHAPTER TEN
WILD TURKEY

The hairs stood up on the back of my neck when I heard the gobble! "Dive for cover! Now!" I said. "You, here by this tree. You, over there. This is it! Set up fast and quiet!"

Lori and Lila did exactly as I said, and within seconds were ready to draw a bead on the beautiful Merriam's turkey we heard gobble not more than 100 yards in front of us. I waited for a few seconds, having set up behind them, before I started calling. I barely got the yelps out when he sounded off again. He was closer! I gave a couple more yelps and a cluck or two, then waited. He answered me every time I called. I just knew he had fallen in love with me and would come running into our laps giving the gals their first "raw, in the wild, wild turkey show" and chance to shoot. Suddenly, a new sound came from my left. It was a hen! She started yelping, cutting and coming in to me. I was hardly breathing as I prayed the gobbler was with her. But no, he stayed out in front of us, still gobbling but not moving. The hen poked around, trying to find the "other woman" and bring her back to the gobbler. Since she found nothing (just me), she wandered away, back to the tom. He was still gobbling as I resumed calling, but, "Oh no! Can't be! Please no!" Yes, he was headed away from us! I called my heart out, using three different calls and all the tricks in my arsenal, but to no avail. The live hen had won! The gobbler was leaving with her, thumbing his nose at us. How dare he? He was so close! He was hot to trot! He was coming in! What happened? As I sat there in a state of shock, not believing that he didn't show up and listening to the echo of his gobbles as they carried down the ridge away from us, I really had some angry thoughts about "Rim Rock Romeo." This had been my chance to prove to my friends that I really knew what I was doing and could get a turkey in for them. Now he made a fool of me! "Wait until tomorrow, guy, it's gonna happen," I vowed.

As I sat there, stunned at our bad luck, just waiting to see if the forest would produce any other birds, I reflected on my "turkey hunting life" and remembered my very first hunt. I could identify very easily with the gals, this being their first hunt. I remembered the apprehension, the nervousness, the "what am I doing?" expression on my face. Heck, I was just plain scared! From that experience to this one, now guiding and calling for my good friends, I have learned a lot. If I can do this, YOU can, too!

When I was on the game commission, one of the staff members, a real turkey enthusiast, started telling me about turkey hunting. He then encouraged me to attend the national convention of the National Wild Turkey Federation, representing the South Dakota game commission. After the things he told me, like how you must be all dressed in camouflage, get up in the middle of the night and sit under a roost tree, call to the tom, pretending you are the hen that "wants him" as his hormone level is skyrocketing, I was hooked. Watching the videos at the convention, hearing all these crazy people with their turkey calls, especially seeing no visible call but knowing the sounds were actually coming from a person, and then watching the national calling championships, where guys actually ACTED and DRESSED like turkeys, well, I thought they were all crazy! But fun! Somehow the entire situation took hold of me. I was caught up in this craziness and wanted to learn more. We had no turkeys in our area of South Dakota, and I never knew anyone who ever hunted any. But the entire atmosphere of fun, great people and turkey hunting stories did the trick! When I left the convention I knew that I would have to try it!

THE BOTTOM LINE !

YOU'LL NEED THIS————————————————

Here is a beautiful Merriam's tom strutting for some hens in South Dakota. Wild turkeys are among the most beautiful birds on the continent. (Photo by South Dakota Department of Tourism)

The next spring season I received an invitation to the Governor's Wild Turkey Hunt in the Black Hills. I was ecstatic and so grateful, but scared to death. I had been told at the convention what type of camouflage to get for general purposes, but beyond that, I knew nothing. I did have my Remington 11-87 12-gauge shotgun, my trusty waterfowl gun, and boots and that was it. When I learned the hunter list included the VIPs from the turkey hunting world, the officers of the NWTF, outdoor writers, etc., I just took a deep breath and prayed for survival without looking like a fool. The guys were great to me, lending me a face mask, shotgun shells, explaining the method of hunting and why arising well before dawn was important. They explained everything.

My first embarrassment was the fact that I could not keep pace with my guide, who was my son's age and ran up the ridges like a mountain goat. Already the first time out I felt like a failure, felt too old to do this, that he wouldn't want to be tied down with me. But I lived through it. However, the first three times out, the birds did not cooperate. The pressure was on for me though; being a commissioner I felt I had to learn as fast as I possibly could. I felt I was under the microscope the entire time, and prayed I did nothing foolish. I wanted to bag a bird so very badly, but as the hunting times passed and no opportunity presented itself, that looked rather remote. Saturday evening came and again we roosted no birds. Sunday morning would be my last chance; the pressure was on. After dinner that evening I saw a "meeting of the minds" and they were gesturing towards me. "Now what?" I thought. Well, they had a turkey roosted, within easy access and it was to be my bird! Now talk about pressure! There was not even an hour's sleep before the alarm rang!

I was ready! I had psyched myself up and tried not to shake as I whistled "Bridge on the River Kwai" on the way out the door. I now had not one, but two guides. One of the hunters who had roosted the bird gave me a shotgun shell loaded with #6 shot saying, "Take this. This will get your bird for sure!" I had just put it in my pocket with the rest of the shells and forgot about it. We were silent as they lead me up the ridge and pointed out my seat beside a tree. Then, we

waited. I just hoped and prayed all would go well and that I would at least hear and see a turkey. I was daydreaming of growing up fishing with my father when a loud gobble rocked the trees. Wow! What a sound! My heart started beating fast and the adrenaline was flowing just at the first gobbles! Then I heard Bo, my guide, behind me softly yelping. "So this is how it works," I thought. All kinds of questions went through my head. How long do they gobble? How long do they stay in the tree? When do they fly out? Which way do they fly? It was a few gobbles later and then only 30 seconds after he hit the ground that I saw him running up the

The author proudly shows off the gobbler she bagged during the South Dakota Governor's hunt in the Black Hills. It took a lot of work to bag this bird, but it was worth it.

ridge towards me. I was hardly breathing by this time and I know I was shaking. He wandered behind a tree about 15 yards in front of me and I was ready. But he surprised me when he appeared in full strut, walking straight towards me! That was one of the most beautiful sights I had ever seen and will never forget it! I just stared at him! He was incredible!

I almost forgot I was supposed to shoot. I tried to remember everything I had been told. But they never told me what to do in case the turkey charged me! He was coming closer, his feathers were coming down, and we were looking eye-to-eye! I couldn't shoot him in the face! He was too close! I just had to wait and see what he did and hope he didn't jump in my lap! I'm sure Bo was going through contortions there behind me as he couldn't figure out why I didn't shoot! Suddenly the bird turned and started running up the ridge to my left; that's when I pulled the trigger and Bo yelled "Shoot!" at the same time! A beautiful Merriam's was mine! Shaking, screaming, almost throwing up, I ran to the bird! I couldn't believe it! I suddenly heard someone saying, "Congratulations! I told you the shell I gave you would be the one!" It was the hunter who had roosted the bird and who had ridden up to the canyon with us. When I loaded my gun that morning, I had just reached into my pocket and grabbed three shells. I had no idea THAT shell I had placed into my gun first. He had marked the shell before he had given it to me, and sure enough, it was the same one! After a neat photography session there in the forest, we headed back to camp.

Well, I had done it! I was so proud! From the time of walking into camp knowing nothing, to leaving with a beautiful wild turkey, some changes had taken place within me. I learned all kinds of things. I went from being terrified of making a mistake to becoming so proud of myself for overcoming all the challenges that were presented to me in those three days. And, I found out I loved to hunt wild turkeys! This is why turkey hunting should be presented with a warning label: "Once you do it, you will become a wild turkey fanatic!"

I did become a wild turkey fanatic and now, having just completed the Great Wild Turkey Hunt of 1999 in the southern part of the Black Hills of South Dakota and Wyoming with master hunter, writer and speaker Jim Zumbo, my excitement for spring turkeys was still at fever pitch. There was a huge difference though this time. I was the sole guide and turkey caller for my two best women friends on their first-ever wild turkey hunt! I had everything set almost two months previous and all systems were "go." Then, of course, Murphy's Law set in!

As a result of my time on the Game, Fish and Parks commission, the conservation officers are still my very good friends and hunting guides. When I hunt antelope in the Black Hills, Scott has always been there for me. When he heard I wanted to bring my friends out turkey hunting, he jumped at the chance to guide and call for us, and even volunteered a fellow officer's talent at calling. I had hunted in the Black Hills before but always had a guide. Living the "flat-lander" life on the eastern South Dakota prairie where everything is straight north and south or east and west, I've always found the Black Hills to be intimidat-

ing and I get turned around very easily. Since I always had someone else with me, I could depend on him and really didn't have to worry about directions or anything else.

Scott told me to call him when I arrived in town and we would make the final plans. Well, THAT was a heck of a phone call! He then told me that he had to fly an antelope count and had a walleye tournament that weekend! The other officer was also tied to the job.

"Oh, I'll come over and show you on the Forest Service map where to go. You can do this on your own," he said.

Yeah, right. Panic? YES! But what else could I do? Another friend had offered to help us find turkeys but he ended up being too busy, also. So, it was up to me! I knew what I had to do and I better do it right as the gals were arriving the next evening!

Luckily, Zumbo had given me the map we used the five days before, so I grabbed a bottle of water, the map, crossed myself and left for the forest on my own! It worked! I only made two wrong turns, found the logging trails I

Karen Mehall, editor of the NRA's American Guardian magazine, bagged this Eastern wild turkey in Missouri.

was directed to and found my way back to town in time for dinner! Now, if my calling would be good enough; if the weather and the birds cooperated, all would be fine and we would be successful. Lori and Lila are good hunters. I knew they would understand my predicament and concerns but still be excited about hunting the wily bird. When I explained the situation, they both looked at each other and said, "We do not want a man to guide us! We want you! We want this to truly be a WOMEN'S turkey hunt! You will be just fine!"

Well, as I shuffled my feet and said "oh, shucks" I was really thrilled to death. We all know that meat on the table is a bonus. There is so very much more to hunting than bagging game. So we set off with the attitude of enjoying a new adventure — women only, thank you. Friends can surely inspire a person! The self-confidence they gave me as we embarked on our four-day excursion into the wild was fantastic!

GETTING TO KNOW YOU

The wild turkey almost became our country's symbol, losing out to the bald eagle. They greeted the colonists to this country and played an important role in their survival. In South Dakota, the wild turkey is considered a big game animal, not a game bird. This designation may vary from state to state, but the wild turkey is considered a most fantastic, beautiful and wily bird to pursue and behold as a true trophy.

Guide Les Rice, the author and Margaret McDonald display a fine Merriam's tom taken in South Dakota's Black Hills. (Mitch Kezar, www.kezarphoto.com)

Their iridescent and multicolored feathers can bring a tear to your eye with their beauty. The intricate patterns of light and dark feathers add a very dramatic touch. Their heads, which are not the most attractive wild game head we'll ever see, demonstrate emotions, especially in the toms during the springtime breeding season. When he is excited, his head turns brilliant red, white and blue and he courts his "ladies." That's why it is dangerous for hunters to wear those colors — you could be mistaken for a gobbler. Never, never wear red, white or blue in the turkey woods.

The male wild turkey sports a "beard" of hard feathers, jutting out from the chest. The turkey beard is one of the measurements used to determine a trophy. A shorter beard is found on a young tom, called a "jake," and a longer beard is found on the older toms. The birds also have "spurs" that grow on the backs of their legs, another measurement in determining age.

Wild turkeys have unequaled eyesight during the daytime. I've been told they can see a tick on a log at 300 feet. That's why it is so important to be perfectly still at all times when setting up to hunt a gobbler. Their sense of smell is not good, so that is one worry you can forget about while turkey hunting.

There are four subspecies of wild turkeys in the United States. The Eastern is the largest, some weighing in excess of 20 pounds. They are found in the hardwood forests of the eastern U.S. and west to Texas, Missouri, Iowa and Minnesota. They have been successfully transplanted in several other states, including South Dakota. Rust-colored feathers and brown tail feather tips identify the Eastern bird.

The Osceola is known as the Florida turkey. This one is smaller than the Eastern, with more iridescent green and red feathers.

The Rio Grande wild turkey inhabits warmer, dryer climates of the southern U.S. They are not as brilliantly colored as the other types of turkeys and have extremely long legs.

The white tail coverts and tail tips identify the Merriam's turkey. They appear to be black with the white "trim" setting them off from the background. How beautiful they are when you can see them flying with the white "accompaniment." Merriam's live in the pine and hardwood forests of the western U.S.

Turkey hunters call it a "Grand Slam" if they can bag one turkey from each subspecies. Of course, that means moving around the continent to find them in their habitat. The first people I met who had accomplished a Grand Slam were women, a mother and daughter. That is a neat "notch" to have on your hunting belt. So, the Grand Slam would include the Merriam's, Eastern, Osceola and the Rio Grande. This can become your goal, if you want! You could do this, you just have to get started!

In the spring, during the breeding season, the gobblers (the male turkeys) gather a harem of hens. A peak gobbling period at the beginning of the season is a good time for hunters. The toms are announcing their presence, telling the world they are ready for love. Attracting hens is their only goal. They can be so excited they may gobble at car doors slamming, crow calls, a jet overhead and thunder. He gobbles the most during the "wake up" part of the morning. The gobbling lessens during the day and picks up again as he flies up to roost in the evening.

The gobbler's ritual of "selling himself to the female" is called strutting. The males will fan out their beautiful tail feathers, drag their wing tips, dance in circles, "drum and spit." Through all this their head is brilliant red, white and blue and he gobbles up a storm. The first time I saw this I nearly cried. It was the most majestic, wonderful action I had ever witnessed in nature. To this day, if I am lucky enough to have a bird strut in front of me during hunting season, I feel the hunt was a success. It is so cool!

And again, we are faced with a paradox. When the gobbler is strutting in front of you, the killing shot is taken when he raises his head straight up or up and out, away from his body. But, you may ask, "If I am watching him strutting and dancing and being so cool for a hen (me), how can I possibly shoot him?" You have to settle this question with yourself before you ever embark on your hunting trip. Do not shoot the bird when his head is not stretched out away from his chest. While strutting and gobbling, the head and neck can stretch out a long ways; that is your moment to claim your trophy. If you shoot while he has his head tucked in close to his body, you will ruin both his feathers and the meat. A good, clean shot aimed at the head is what you want to do.

If he is looking at you straight on with head tucked in and will not put it up, then shoot straight at him.

During your hunting preparation time, rent turkey hunting videos. Learn to notice the turkey sign: scat, dusting places, tracks, and look for turkey habitat. Watch all the details very closely, and try to really learn as much as you can about the birds and where they live.

A good way to learn about turkeys and turkey hunting is to join the National Wild Turkey Federation and receive its magazine, *Turkey Call*. It's fun to read and educational and will give you good background on turkey hunting. The NWTF sponsors a turkey hunting program on TNN (The Nashville Network) found on Saturday mornings January through July. This is a great television program, showing turkey hunts, hints, tips, calls and a personal touch of one turkey hunter reaching out to another.

Meanwhile, back in the woods contemplating why the gobbler left us, what emotional feelings came upon me as I relived that very first hunt with all of its unknowns. I know how important that was to me and how that experience set the pace and paved the way for many, many wonderful wild turkey experiences. It's great to let nature be the teacher. I went out on my own, with some direction, sometimes the video camera was my companion as I played with the wild turkeys. I learned a lot about turkeys; the methods of hunting; what to do and not to do. I learned about myself, taught myself patience and enjoyed immensely the wonderment of the very first bird I ever called in all by myself! I did it! And you can do it, too!

Just as with everything else, it had been men who had told me about turkey hunting. When I started there were very few women involved. Today, there are many women who enjoy it and turkey hunting is becoming the fastest growing hunting experience in the country, enjoyed by thousands of women and youngsters. So let's get ready to hunt turkeys.

GETTING READY

The first thing you must do is decide where you want to hunt and then apply for your tag. Your state wildlife agency can supply you with applications for tags. If hunting unit information is not included with the applications, ask for them separately. All you have to do is contact your state wildlife agency and they can answer your questions. Be sure to have your application filled out correctly and returned ahead of the deadline. Know the regulations. The most important thing is that spring is usually "tom only" hunting and the fall season, if your state holds it, is usually "any turkey," meaning either hen or tom can be harvested.

If you desire guide service, call your wildlife agency and they can direct you. You can also call your local sportsmen's club or your local National Wild Turkey Federation chapter members. If you have chosen to hunt on private land and received your tag, your next step is to obtain hunting permission. Please refer to the chapter on "Finding a Place to Hunt." A quick call to the local conservation officer (their names are listed in the hunting handbook printed by the state agency) can get you started. You can also inquire at sporting goods stores and visit with personnel. When you have found a place, then scout it out thoroughly and get to know the land and the environment. Sometimes, in heavily hunted areas, it's better to get permission before you apply for a tag. That way you won't end up with a license, but no place to hunt.

If you will be hunting on public land, obtain all the necessary maps. They usually are available at convenience stores, game department offices and other areas where you can buy

 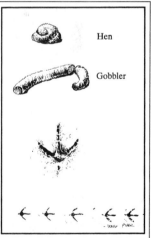

You can locate turkey flocks in spring or fall by finding dusting areas, droppings, scratchings, or tracks. Dusting areas are depressions in dry, sandy soil-sometimes on anthills. Scratchings are areas where turkeys scrape to the bare ground looking for food. J-shaped gobbler droppings are usually easy to distinguish from roundish hen droppings. Look for turkey tracks in mud and soft, bare earth such as cultivated fields. Authorized by permission of the National Rifle Association.

the licenses. Again, please refer to the chapter, "Find A Place to Hunt." After you have your maps, take some scouting time and drive up into the forest and become familiar with the logging trails, forest edges, streams, rocks and vegetation. Then you will know where things are. Dawn or dusk is the best time to hear gobblers because that is when they are the most vocal. Take some "locator" calls, usually a crow, owl or predator call. (They are called "locator" calls for a reason: they can locate gobblers for you--they are a loud, shocking noise and the gobbler just "has" to answer!) Walk, then stop and call; if a gobbler answers, try to pinpoint his location. Depending on the time of day, you can either set up and call him in or know the exact location of the roost he is in for the night.

When you are scouting you will be looking for specific signs that show turkeys are in the area. Turkey tracks, scratchings, droppings and dusting areas are clues that you are in the "turkey woods." You may even find a feather or two, telling you that turkeys have been in the area. If you see a small depression in the ground on dry soil, that is a dusting area. Scratching is just what it sounds like — you can see where the birds have scratched the ground looking for food. Turkey droppings distinguish gobblers and hens by the shape: The hens' droppings will be in a round, mound-type formation and the gobbler's will be in a J shape. The tracks are just that — turkey tracks on the ground, with the largest being the gobbler's. Check out water holes for tracks.

To mark locations for yourself, so you know exactly where to go the next morning when you want to find the same place, take along blaze orange marking ribbon and mark specific trees at certain points and tie the ribbon around the tree. My friend Lori always makes neat little bows! Guys are not going to do that, so you will always find YOUR tree! Be sure to find as many likely hunting places as you can on the scouting trip. You don't want to waste any time trying to find a specific area when you could be hunting.

A good compass is a necessity. You can purchase small ones that do the job but yet do not take up room in your pocket. To be thoroughly educated on the use of maps and compasses, it's a good idea to take the Becoming an Outdoors Woman workshop's Map and Compass class. Just remember, if nothing else, the red needle always points north and you can get your bearing from that. Be sure to stand away from your vehicle so you obtain a true reading.

It's important to have a set of binoculars, too. You might end up spotting turkeys on distant ridges and without binoculars you would miss them. Don't take a big, heavy pair with you. That's too much to carry. There are small sizes available on the market that are good and work just fine. Please refer to the Deer Hunting chapter.

Just because April and May are "springtime" and not in the middle of summer, don't think there would never be any mosquitoes! Bring your insect repellent and have it near at all times. I'll never forget one of my first encounters with mosquitoes while turkey hunting. I was out in the Black Hills of South Dakota where it is usually warmer than up in the northeast corner where I live. I never gave bug spray a thought. Well, as my guide/friend and I were sitting almost directly under the tree where our gobbler was waiting (we misjudged the distance the night before) the mosquitoes started buzzing around just as our gobbler started talking to us. Being so close under the roost, there was no way to swat them away. One mosquito landed on my cheek, just in front of my ear. I could not move! What would I do? It was driving me crazy, but I dared not move! So, I thought of the most painful experience in my life — giving birth! Now, this mosquito bite couldn't be as bad as that! If I survived childbirth twice, I could certainly survive this dumb mosquito bite. So I sat there, gritting my teeth as he bit me! Well, I lived through it, I didn't move, the gobbler flew down and walked in front of my gun barrel. When I told my friend later about the mosquito, he said, "Oh yeah, I had a bunch on me, but good thing I was sitting behind you and the tree so I could swat a few!" See what we women are capable of doing. The moral of the story: Bring your bug spray because you never know when you will need it. That was not a fun experience, believe me!

WHERE DO I STAY ON THE HUNTING TRIP?

If you cannot drive to your turkey hunting destination from your home or wherever you are, be sure to make motel reservations early. Motels can fill up in prime hunting areas very quickly, with some people making reservations from year to year. Call early so you don't have to worry about reservations. Make sure you choose a motel/hotel that is the most convenient and the closest to where you will be hunting. You don't want to have an hour's drive to get to your parking place, then another half hour to walk in--all after getting up at 3:30 AM. It's important to take the distances in consideration. Ask if they have game cleaning facilities and a freezer. Those are very convenient.

Since turkey hunting involves weird and early morning hours, make all food/eating arrangements beforehand. If you have the motel kitchen make your sandwiches, be aware that restaurant kitchens are not usually active before you would leave in the morning. Twenty-four hour convenience stores are great for gas, pop, coffee and breakfast snacks. Pinpoint a close one to the motel and know how to get there quickly.

If you are staying with friends that live near your hunting area, be considerate of them, especially if they are non-hunters. If they do not hunt with you, they will have trouble understanding your passion to obtain a turkey. They will not understand how you can leave at 4 a.m., not return until maybe 9:30 p.m., (after roosting a gobbler before dark). By that time all you want to do is grab a bite to eat and go to bed again. They will feel left out, maybe even "put upon" and taken advantage of in this situation. Make time for them such as getting back early one evening and taking them to dinner. Do not leave them completely out of the picture or you may not be invited to stay again. Treat them with consideration, even if they don't understand your schedule and demand some of your time. That might be your "fee" for staying.

If you will be staying in a campground be sure to take everything you need. If you are a veteran camper you will know the list; if you are not a veteran camper the first thing to do is to make a list of the equipment you must have. Cook-

> **Turkey tracks, scratchings, droppings and dusting areas are clues that you are in the "turkey woods."**

ing gear includes: food and drink, can and bottle opener, pans and kettle, serving and eating utensils, hot dog and marshmallow skewers, pitcher, plastic containers and bags. Camping gear includes: tents, poles, stakes, stake driver, sleeping bags, pillows, inflatable air mattress and air pump, blankets, lantern, cooler, charcoal grill or camp stove, fire starting materials, folding chairs, rope, ax, water jug, flashlight, first aid kit, wash cloths and towels, toilet paper, extra batteries and fuel, prescription medications, extra footwear and clothing, waterproof tarp, heater, and a dependable alarm clock.

TURKEY GUNS

One of the most important items on your preparation check-off list is the shotgun. You also have to patterning that gun. I have only used my Remington 11-87, 3-inch 12-gauge shotgun with a modified choke for turkey hunting. That has served me well in every situation. Some people recommend a full choke and you can do that, but I have been totally satisfied with my modified. Whatever gun you choose, be sure and have a sling installed on it. You may do a lot of walking and that sling will "save your life" during the day. I would not have my shotgun without a sling — it's great for all kinds of hunting as it frees up your hands to carry gear or for stopping and calling for turkeys, etc.

A 20-gauge shotgun may also be used for turkey hunting, but the 12-gauge throws a little more lead. That can mean the difference between a clean kill and a wounded bird. I started with the 12-gauge and feel most comfortable with it. I feel more confident if I have to take a rather long shot. I want the most power I can get to instantly kill the bird and not just wound him. That is another ethical discussion--feeling "right" inside and being completely confident about what you are doing.

Another point you should be aware of is the use of fiberoptic dots and scopes for turkey guns. I do not have either on my turkey gun, and I don't believe I really need extra help since I have been successful with the gun as is. I would not confuse the issue by adding either one of these to your gun as you are starting. When you are experienced and feel you'd like to try these products, then by all means do so. There are advantages and disadvantages to both products.

Lori Goldade patterns her shotgun with a turkey target and a hay bale as a backstop. To effectively hunt turkeys, you must know which loads work best with your gun and where they strike in relation to your point of aim.

As for ammunition, there are many "turkey loads" on the market. These are shells designed exclusively for turkey hunting. Don't be confused by all the kinds when you go into your sporting goods store or gun shop. I use #5 or #6 shot. I have used both Federal and Winchester. Both work fine. These sizes are simple to remember, pack the power I need, pattern in my gun well and are easy to find in the store. I have used other kinds and sizes but always come back to these. I have found the 3-inch #5 is my favorite.

Perhaps I forgot to mention it in the shotgun chapter, but the shot numbers discussed (i.e. #5 and #6) refer to the size of the pellets contained in the shotgun shell. The smaller the number, the larger the pellet. That is, #1 is bigger than #2 and so on. But the shotgun shells are always the same size, meaning you end up with fewer of the bigger pellets and lots more of the smaller pellets in any shell. What you are after in any shotgunning situation is to have enough pellets hitting the bird to kill it quickly. A turkey is a big bird, so you need bigger pellets, but the target you are shooting at (the head) is small, so you need plenty of pellets to increase the chances that you will put six pellets into the kill zone. So it becomes a compromise. Small pellets, even a lot of them, won't deliver enough energy down range to kill a turkey and too few big pellets won't be as likely to hit the target. So, you need to practice, read and learn to know what will work best for you.

While you are at the store, pick up some "turkey targets." These are outlines of a turkey head, showing where your pellets hit when you pattern your shotgun. I personally like the

Margaret McDonald and the author discuss turkey loads while hunting in South Dakota. (Mitch Kezar, www.kezarphoto.com)

Winchester shotgun pattern targets as they are large enough to see where ALL of your pellets hit. The circles are 30 inches wide; also there are pellet count charts on the bottom. If you cannot find any like these in a store, contact Hunter-John at P.O. Box 771457, St. Louis, MO 63177, or call 314-531-7250, or visit www.hunterjohn.com. They are sold only in cartons of 72 targets per carton, which cost around $50. You will use a lot of these throughout the year, so go ahead and get a carton and share with your friends. You must pattern your gun before you hunt turkeys so you know exactly where the pellets are hitting on the bird. Four to six pellets are sufficient in the head/neck area to kill a bird. If you cannot find a large 30-inch target sheet and only see small ones, they can be used. Tape them in the center of a wide open newspaper sheet. Tape it all together and you will have a target large enough for the patterning purpose. Before you leave the store be sure you have some shooting glasses and hearing protectors.

So, you have your shotgun, your shells, patterns, shooting glasses and hearing protectors. You are now ready for the final check in this area. The best yardage for killing a turkey is 45 yards or less, but shots closer than 10 yards are tough, too. Never take a shot beyond 45 yards; remember, you do not want to wound the turkey. You'll feel terrible about it. Forty yards is a good safe number to remember. To correctly pattern your shotgun, we will use a distance of 30 yards. When you are actually turkey hunting, you will be sitting on the ground, shotgun on your knee, aiming at the turkey's head and neck for a quick clean kill. Use this position when patterning your shotgun so conditions are identical. I use a big round bale of hay for a backdrop for my target. I set the paper up 30 inches off the ground, fasten it with big nails or spikes and I'm ready. If you have a farm friend you can use the same method. If you have to make other arrangements, speak to someone in your local sportsmen's club and ask where you can pattern your gun. There may be a gun range

or a location on public land nearby where you can do this. DO NOT TURKEY HUNT WITHOUT PATTERNING YOUR GUN FIRST!

Now is the time you must measure out distances and remember them. You will need to remember what 20, 30, and 40 yards look like when you are in the forest. The distance will look farther in the open. "Mark" the distance in your head and remember it.

When you are in position, on the ground, shotgun propped on your knee, aiming at the turkey's head/neck on the paper, slowly SQUEEZE the trigger. After the shot, make sure the gun is unloaded and place the safety on the gun, lay it down and go check and see the results. There should be enough pellets in the red neck area to quickly kill the bird. If there are less than 6 pellets, try the process all over again. Note if the pellets veer off to the right or the left, are high or mostly fall on the bottom. If you have shot several times and are not satisfied, then change to a different size shot. Maybe the #6's will work better in your gun, or the 4 x 6's (that's a combination of 4's and 6's together in one shell). You will know what is best in your gun only by trying different shells and choosing the correct one. Most guns these days have interchangeable choke tubes. Try a full choke in your gun and shoot once, then try a modified choke and compare the difference. Choose whatever makes the best pattern in your gun. Remember, confidence is important and this is another step.

The last step in gun preparation is cleverly camouflaging your gun so the turkey won't see it. You have to be still, quiet and completely covered in camouflage, including your gun. I tried using a gun "sock" but I didn't like it at all. It moved, it bunched up and I was afraid I would not be able to shoot properly. Do not buy a gun sock! I use an adhesive camouflage tape found in your sports store or discount store. Choose a tape with a dark pattern; do not choose one that has a lot of white in it. Start at the top of the gun barrel and continue on down, taping, turning and cutting as needed. This taping will do the trick. I asked a firearm manufacturer if the tape would in any way hurt or disfigure the gun and was told it would not. I therefore leave the tape on for waterfowl hunting, too. The tape never comes off of my gun — it serves my every hunting purpose. If you want to take the tape off after the season is over, to look at your pretty gun, that's fine, but you don't have to. Be sure and replace the tape at least every other season as the color can wear off and a lot of white will show. You do not want that.

The thrill of turkey hunting, for me, is calling the bird into close range; the closer he comes, the more exciting, thrilling and rewarding. That is why I use a shotgun. Rifles may be used in some states depending upon the regulations in your hunting area. The problem with using a rifle is that being able to ethically kill the bird without damaging or destroying any meat is very difficult. The base of the neck or a high body shot would be the best if using a rifle. A 22 Magnum, 223 Remington or a 22-250 would be the best choice calibers. Handguns, muzzleloading rifles and bow and arrow methods can also be used for turkey hunting. For a starting turkey hunter, I recommend using a shotgun and the rest of this discussion will be based on shotguns as the weapon to use.

CAMOUFLAGE YOUR BODY

You must have camouflage from head to toe while hunting turkeys. Their eyesight is phenomenal. Your face, your hands,

Lila Antonides and Lori Goldade all decked out in camouflage gear and ready for the hunt. Because turkeys have such great eyesight you need to blend in and sit still.

even your ears must be covered! Wild turkey hunting is probably the most demanding in terms of camouflage that matches your environment. You must be still and you must be quiet, but complete camouflage is also important. When you decide on a place to hunt, take note of the environment. Find out if the trees have sprouted leaves yet, if there is green grass or brown weeds, brown pine needles, black dirt, green bushes or bare branches. Then, choose the appropriate camouflage pattern. You do not have to go buy a whole new complete set of camo; you can mix and match. How green the area is will depend on how far along spring has progressed in your hunting area. You will probably want some brown and some green. For instance, I wear gray/brown camo hunting pants and wear a camo jacket that is mainly green (original Realtree). That way my legs are camouflaged and match the ground I'm sitting on and my upper body color will fit in with new leaves on the bushes at ground level. Depending on where you are, you may want all green, brown, gray or a combination.

You will be sitting with your back against a tree in most situations and will want to blend in with the surroundings. "Breaking up your outline" is most important. As previously mentioned, during the spring mating season, the gobbler's head will turn red, white and blue. DO NOT WEAR ANY OF THESE COLORS! Another turkey hunter could spot these colors and think you are a turkey. If this hunter fails to act responsibly you could be one of the few people hurt in hunting accidents each year. Again, for safety reasons, do not wear red, white or blue, ever.

Springtime can be cold, wet, windy or very hot. Choose your camo accordingly. You want to be as comfortable as possible. Dressing in layers is good; you can always remove sweaters, etc. You will be getting up very early, and

arriving at your hunting spot before dawn. It can get very cold while you are waiting for that gobbler to wake up, so it's better to be a little overdressed and remove some items than to be so uncomfortably cold that you are ultimately miserable. Be aware of the weather, the temperature forecasts and approaching rain. If you dress accordingly you will be fine.

I wear the same wool long underwear for turkey hunting that I wear for waterfowl and big game hunting. They feel good in the cold morning. Pantyhose or silk long johns are good to keep ticks from getting to you. I wear my polypropylene black turtleneck and wear a couple more light wool sweaters if necessary. If it is really cold, I even wear my camouflaged, insulated hooded sweatshirt under my jacket. That hooded sweatshirt has been my best investment by far! I wear it for everything and all situations. It is great to have the protection of that hood against the wind or some rain. If it gets warm you can take it off and its not heavy or bulky to carry in your hunting vest's back compartment. Be sure to have some good camo rain gear. Do not buy the cheap vinyl suits. They tear and are noisy. If the rain jacket is lined, then all you might need is a long-sleeved shirt. It is best to leave the diamond or crystal earrings at home or else in your backpack to be worn for the pictures. The flash of shiny jewelry could tip off your gobbler that he's walking into a trap.

I wear my regular hunting boots, with good grips on the bottom. Wear your regular hunting socks — no red, white or blue here either. Make sure that your boots have a brown sole. I have been in the woods with hunters who have had light-colored boots, including soles, and they really are prominent. I figure if I can see them that easily, a turkey can, too. If you wear a pair of dyed tennis shoes for hunting shoes make sure, absolutely sure, the soles show NO white. Sometimes your pant legs can ride up and you don't want any bright colors peeking out. Dark green or brown is great. If you are hunting in wet swampy areas (southern U.S.), waterproof camo boots are available.

A face mask is probably your most important item! Do not forget to include one or two in your hunting gear! Your face is easily seen by turkeys and absolutely must be covered. There are several styles of face masks; most are either mesh or a very thin material. That allows for visibility while still disguising your facial features. You can get a "half" mask, my particular favorite, which you wear

Here's a proper turkey set-up. Get your back against a tree and have your gun up in the ready position. Notice how well the camouflage breaks up the hunter's outline. (Mitch Kezar, www.kezarphoto.com)

A turkey hunting vest is a great asset in the woods. The pockets give you room to stow all your gear and the flip-down seat helps to keep you comfortable.

Gloves play an important role. You will be sitting against the tree, holding your shotgun on your knee so your hands will be visible. My favorite all-purpose hunting gloves are the brown Isotoner-type, with the vinyl on the inside of the palm. That makes for a good grip on the shotgun or calls. You can get them either lined or unlined. I've always used that type of glove and cannot get used to any other. There are lighter camo gloves on the market, some with vinyl "grippers" that work well. Just make sure that whatever gloves you purchase fit properly. You do not want to get them too large and then have them interfere with the operation of your gun. Make sure whatever you get fits well, is comfortable, and is preferably dark brown. You can use them for all of your hunting.

Another important item you need is a turkey hunting vest that includes a snap-down padded seat. The vest is designed as follows: there are adjustable straps for over the shoulders, big pockets on the sides, a game carrier space right behind your shoulders, and a seat that falls down when you unsnap it and is instantly ready for your behind when you need it. You need the pockets, but the most important function of the turkey vest is the seat. Sometimes you may be sitting for a long time and that ground can become awfully cold or hard, especially if you are sitting with a tree root at an inappropriate place on your anatomy! The seats are usually waterproof, but if you will be hunting in rain or snow, I suggest adding some more protection. I have a completely waterproof inch-thick seat that I carry with me for most types of hunting. I placed that inside the "envelope" that holds the seat pad and then had double waterproof protection. It makes the vest a little heavier, but I appreciated the extra cushioning.

There are different types of vests available. I recommend getting the most simple one, as long as it has all the features mentioned. There are some vests that have double and triple pockets, both on the inside and outside and if you would fill them all, that vest would become mighty heavy and uncomfortable.

With a common turkey vest, you can easily take all your gear with you. The easy and nice thing is that you can leave all your gear (calls, compass, etc.) right in the pockets and don't have to take it all out after every hunt. You know what is in each pocket, you get used to that while you are hunting and you will always know exactly where everything is, and it can stay there. Leave it in the vehicle in the evening so it's all ready to go in the morning!

Choose which camo pattern you think will be the most serviceable for you. I have a green/brown Realtree vest and it has fit every turkey hunting situation I have encountered. The pockets are large enough to bring a water bottle and a snack

around your neck then just pull it up over your nose, under your eyes and place the elastic around the back of your head. With glasses, I have found that to be the most comfortable. There are some face masks that have "ready made" glasses holes, but the ones I have tried have never worked. They are never the same size as your glasses, slip all over and then you cannot see anything. I have tried the kind that is attached to your cap and all you do is lift up the cap and the mask falls over your face. With that kind, I don't have the visibility I feel I need. This is personal preference; just make sure you have your face camouflaged by some type of mask.

If you do not want a mask there is an alternative. You can purchase camouflage makeup. With that, you must smear it all over your face, covering all exposed areas. But I don't want to run around all day looking like that. Then later remove it, apply regular makeup, then maybe run into another turkey later in the day and be caught without camo on my face. I probably look scary enough after being out hunting all day without showing off a brown and green face. The camo makeup does offer unlimited visibility because there is no mask to cover your eyes, but it's just not for me. I suggest saving it for the Halloween party.

Let's talk about caps. Of course it must be camouflage and with a bill to help hide your face and block the sun. There are other turkey hunting hats available, but I prefer the regular cap. The brims on the other types are not wide enough to shade my face and will blow off in the wind. Try several caps to see which ones work for you.

A good selection of turkey calls will help you to bring gobblers in close. You can learn calling by getting any of a number of good audio tapes and trying to mimic the sounds. Master one call first then move on to the next. (Photo courtesy of Hunter's Specialties) or two, also. If you are hunting hard, up and down hills or other difficult terrain, you will be thirsty, so be sure to bring water. A little snack is a neat treat, too.

TURKEY CALLS

As you will find out for yourself, the thrill of turkey hunting is calling the gobbler in close to you. Watching him strut for his "hen" (you) is beautiful and very much fun to watch. This particular situation, of hunter calling in the game, depends on the hunter's knowledge and ability to imitate an adult hen, a lovesick hen who will draw in her gobbler. The turkey hunter must be a decent caller, be quiet and still because this situation is turning nature backwards. We are making the tom come to the hen this time.

There are hundreds of turkey calls on the market today, all are supposedly "the best." The first woman turkey hunter I ever spoke with told me she takes 15 different calls with her into the forest. That scared me to death! How could I master one well enough to hunt turkeys, much less learn 15 different ones? The secret is not to be intimidated. I learned one type at a time and now I have taken seven different calls with me; however, I still use only three regularly. They are easy to master and you can do it, too.

Don't be confused by all the kinds, types, names, materials from which they are made, and all the "hype" that goes with them. I suggest you learn to use three basic types at first: the box call, the friction call (formerly known as peg and slate call) and the push-button call. I also suggest you master two specific turkey calls at first, the yelp and cluck. The three types of calls I mentioned will very adequately allow you to do that. Don't think you have to be perfect — turkeys sure aren't! On one of my early turkey hunts we heard a most horrible turkey call. We thought for sure it was someone using a call that they did not know how to operate. We started laughing because it was so awful. Well, a couple of minutes later a hen walked by on our left. The crazy calling was her!! Our eyes were wide as saucers as we tried to stifle our laughter. I've never heard anything like that since. It was almost scary! The yelp and the cluck are the two basic turkey calls that you will need to learn first. They are easy to master and you can accomplish your goals with the box call, friction call, and the push-button call.

The yelp is probably the most common turkey call, used both in spring and fall. It is used to let other turkeys know you want to associate with them, to locate other turkeys, and hens use it in the spring to let gobblers know where they are. The hen yelp consists of five or six "notes," sometimes preceded by a definite "whine." The cluck is shorter and is the sign of "happy and contented" turkeys. When you are learning these calls, be sure NOT to have your cluck sound like a putt, which is the alarm sound turkeys make. If you do you'd scare off the birds. (The putt is a loud, short type of cluck.) Turkey hunting videos and audio cassette tapes that come with the calls are good ways to learn these calls.

The box call is just that, a box with an attached cover (paddle) that you "chalk up" underneath, then slide back and forth on the edges of the box. Holding only the bottom of the box with your left hand, hold the paddle between the first and second fingers of your right hand. (If left-handed, do the opposite) Start moving the paddle on the box edges from the back of the box obtaining a whine and then a yelp. You will probably make a horrible, screeching, spine-chilling noise when you first try it. Just keep practicing and you will master it. The box call can be used for locating birds as well as calling them in to you and is a favorite of many turkey hunters. Here's a good tip: to keep your turkey box call quiet when it's in your pocket, wrap a wide rubber band between the box and the paddle, then make a second wrap with the rubber band around both the paddle and the box. This will ensure against unintentional squawks.

The friction calls consist of a round piece of glass, slate, copper, aluminum or some other material and a "striker" or stick to rub against on the material. Hold the striker like a pen and make small J-shaped strokes or circles on the plate. Again, at first you will probably make a horrible noise but you will gradually get it and calling will be easy for you. I called in my first turkey with a slate call like this. You should've heard me

The author, left, and Margaret McDonald look on as Les Rice demonstrates the use of a box call while hunting in South Dakota's Black Hills. (Mitch Kezar, www.kezarphoto.com)

the first I tried it! It was awful. With practice you can easily learn and be proud of yourself in no time!

The push-button call is operated by pushing a little peg inside a small box. My "Chatterbox" is my favorite call and makes wonderful soft yelps and clucks and is very easy to use. I have called in several turkeys so easily with this call I can hardly believe it. The beauty of it is that you only need one hand to operate it. As I'm sitting with the shotgun at the ready on my knee, being right-handed, I'm holding the Chatterbox call with my right hand right beside the trigger area. You can make yelps and clucks very easily by only moving your index finger. When the bird is in position and you are ready to fire, simply just drop the call (just let go of it), move your finger to the trigger and it's all over. Easy, simple, no movement and you have your bird.

My friend purchased a Chatterbox that attaches to the gun barrel. Your index finger fits through a ring that is attached to a cord that is attached to the call. You hold your finger close to the trigger, same as above, pull the cord and make your yelps. Again, there is minute movement; it's simple and easy. My friend Wayne Sande from North Dakota called in his first turkey using this call; he said it worked fine and he just loved it. You can purchase both kinds of push button calls and see which one will work for you. You will be very surprised how easy they are to operate and how good they sound.

There are gobbler calls available, usually for the reason of making a tom "shock gobble" (to scare or irritate him into gobbling). Gobble calls can be very dangerous, especially on public land, because another hunter may mistake you for a gobbler. Gobble calls really don't work that well anyway as they usually drive toms away rather than entice him in for a fight. I say leave the gobbler calls on the shelf.

A good tip to remember is to bring a plastic bag in which to carry your calls. If they become wet the sound can be altered greatly, or in some cases, they just won't work. Keep them dry.

There are a lot of "how-to" videos on the market. Along with one dealing with "how to hunt wild turkeys" be sure and get one that explains and teaches the art of turkey call-ing. Practice with the tape. You probably better do that when no one else is around — you will feel more free to "expand your turkey vocabulary" any way you want to, and no one will be there to laugh at you. If you are planning on hunting with your women friends, you can all get together and prac-tice, helping each other. I'm glad no one else could hear the three of us women, all yelping and clucking at the same time. We all learned from each other and had fun doing it.

As you browse through the sporting goods stores, cata-logs and magazines you will see various other types of calls. They are interesting and good but try those after you have experience with the ones I told you to learn first. The dia-phragm mouth calls (pieces of latex stretched in a frame that you insert in your mouth) are great, but can be difficult to master. I like them because they completely free up your hands so there is no chance of a gobbler seeing you move. Some of them take a lot of air to properly use and then the yelp becomes louder than you want. There are many hunters that cannot use them at all because of the "gagging" sensa-tion. I credit my saxophone playing with being able to quickly learn to use a diaphragm call! And speaking of hilar-ious situations, I have fun freaking people out by telling them "I took my diaphragm to the turkey convention and just had a ball!"

I cannot stress this point enough: do not take yourself too seriously. Yes, you are learning new things and facing new challenges; yes, you have the right to be a little nervous and worried about doing things right. But do not let these feelings overshadow the fact that you will have fun learning and expe-riencing new opportunities. We all make mistakes in the beginning (I sure did), but we learn from them and that makes us better persons and hunters. Just remember to enjoy yourself and HAVE FUN! In all the hunting I've done I think I've had more plain fun turkey hunting than anything else. Starting with learning the calls, there can be so many funny situations. Just think of explaining the biology of the gobbler's "hot hor-mones" and his running to breed the hen. It's hilarious when

Almost as good as the real thing. Outlaw Decoys makes a line of turkey decoys that uses photo reproduction to make the light-weight silhouettes look alive. (Photo courtesy of Outlaw Decoys)

you start telling your uninformed friends about all this! So, enjoy yourself and have fun learning, planning, hunting and making wonderful memories with your buddies.

DECOYS

A great way to insure that the gobbler comes all the way in to you is by using decoys. If he is just out of range but still interested, a decoy can be the "clincher" that will make for a successful hunt. A hen decoy can be used alone or a "set" including a hen and a jake (young gobbler) can be utilized. The gobbler is coming in to you because he thinks you are a hen he wants, in the worst way, to mate, so it's OK if just the hen decoy is there. If he sees the jake, he knows he can run him off and claim the hen for his prize so he will also come to you in that situation.

I have used two different kinds of turkey decoys. I have used the rubber/plastic type that resembles a full body and I have used the silhouettes. The rubber/plastic are bulky and very difficult to carry. They have to be folded to fit in anything, and sometimes "pop out" to assume their natural position and you end up fighting to keep them concealed. However, I have hunted with them and they work; they are just more complicated to carry and use.

My favorite decoys are the state-of-the-art silhouettes from the Outlaw Company (same company as the goose decoys). I think they are terrific because they present such life-like features. They are a photograph screen printed on heavy-duty vinyl and come with stakes to push into the ground. Since they are a photograph of a turkey, they are the most natural-looking decoys on the market today. They are not too expensive; it's great to buy turkey silhouettes as you only have to buy two, not a dozen as with geese! They are light to carry and since they are flat they fit well into a camouflage bag. Have three metal rods for each decoy—one for the stake and two for either side of the rear of the decoy to stabilize when its windy.

It is important that when you are transporting turkey decoys to always have them concealed well in a camo bag. If they are not, you take the chance of having another turkey hunter mistake them for the real thing and there could be tragic results. Always, always, be conscious of other turkey hunters in the forest. The decoys should be placed about 20 yards in front of you or your partner, in the open and in the path the gobbler will take to come in to you. Place the hen and jake facing each other. Set the jake facing your shooting position. An approaching gobbler will usually confront the decoy head-to-head, so its tail will be toward you. When he fans his tail he will be unable to see you raise your gun or move slightly if you must. Just using the lone hen decoy, place it broadside ahead of you so the decoy will intercept the gobbler's path to you. If all works correctly, the gobbler will need to "investigate" his hen and "show off" for her. The strutting can begin before he reaches the decoys, but he will really put on a show when he is dancing around the decoys.

On my most recent turkey hunt in northeast South Dakota I set up with my pair of decoys. The gobbler spied them from a long way off — remember their spectacular eyesight! He came in strutting from 100 yards away. It was fun to watch him look at the decoys, then dance around them, strutting his

> **A point to remember here is that every sound appears farther away than it actually is in when you are in the forest**

stuff like you couldn't believe. It was so much fun I didn't want it to end, but I knew this wouldn't go on forever and that he would soon catch on to the fact that he was fooled. If those decoys had not been there, I doubt he would have given the prolonged show that he did. The attraction of the decoys added to the splendor of the entire production. It was wonderful.

I have seen some video tape where gobblers were so enamored with the hen decoys that they tried to mount them! No kidding! It was hilarious! The gobblers received no satisfaction of course, so they tried it over and over again! I'm sure that turkey hunter had to make a trip to the sporting goods store for another hen decoy because that one was destroyed.

If you have located a gobbler and you instantly decide to set up where you are, set the decoys up as fast as you possibly can. A point to remember here is that every sound appears farther away than it actually is in when you are in the forest. That gobbler can hear you and see you from a long way off and if you are fooling around trying to get the decoys set up when you should be completely set up and ready yourself, your hunt might be ruined. I speak from experience. It happened to me. It was during the Black Hills hunt with Lori and Lila. We heard the gobbles; I had the women set up and then I was messing around trying to poke the metal stakes that hold the decoys up into the ground, It turned out to be solid rock. I finally just quit and gave up, quickly getting behind the gals to start calling. The gobbler never answered after that and I'm positive that I ruined it because I took so much time pounding into the rocks. That was a not-so-happy learning experience. Don't let it happen to you.

Using decoys is a personal preference. I have had good hunts without them. I just feel a turkey hunter needs all the advantages available and I believe decoys can add a final dimension. Try them and decide for yourselves. I can assure you, you'll have a story to tell.

Here are some tips from the National Wild Turkey Federation: whenever possible, set-up by a tree that is wider than your shoulders and taller than your head. From your seated position, identify the clearest line of vision to your front. Establish a "sight line" that allows you 100 yards visibility. Then set your decoys approximately 20 yards from your position on the line. Should you see another hunter (especially if he/she is close to your "line of sight") call out to the hunter in a loud, clear voice. Their presence has already compromised your location and a "soft" call may only confuse them, rather than alerting them to your presence. If you are calling over decoys and then elect to move to a new location, check carefully to ensure that no one is stalking your decoys. Check carefully before leaving your stand location.

THE HUNT

OK! You are ready to bag a beautiful wild turkey. You have completed all of your homework and are in turkey camp on a nice sunny, warm afternoon. You are ready to head out to the forest and find a gobbler. Remember the discussion on locator calls and be sure to have one with you. When you arrive at the forest, quietly — ALWAYS

Set up against a huge pine, Lila Antonides and Lori Goldade check their shooting lanes to make sure they have a clear field of fire in a safe direction.

BE QUIET — try a couple yelps on your turkey call and then pause and listen. If you hear nothing, move on, repeat the scenario, alternately using your turkey call and the locator call. How far should you walk between calling and repeating the procedure? Depending on the terrain, maybe every 150 yards or so. On a recent turkey hunt we called, stopped, and called but too far in between at one point. We rounded a curve in a logging road, called, and the gobbler was right there in front of us. If we had called sooner, BEFORE we rounded the bend, we might have had a turkey in our bag.

Picture yourself walking, stopping, calling, walking, stopping, calling and lo and behold, you hear a gobble in front of you. I wish I could be with each one of you when you hear your first turkey gobble in the woods. It will scare you, shake you, start your adrenaline to flow and you may even panic! Depending on how far you think he is from you, SET UP QUICKLY. I usually say 150 yards is a good number to remember no matter which scenario you use in setting up. Try to set up about that distance from the bird when you hear the gobble. Quickly and quietly find a suitable tree to sit beside, drop your gear there and place your decoys out about 20 yards in front of you. Get back to your tree, unsnap your vest's "sitting pad," sit down, pull your face mask up, position the gun on your knee in the ready position and have your call in hand (this is why I prefer the push button call — I can call and the gobbler can't see me move my finger and the gun is at the ready).

Do not take any more time than necessary to set up. Do not make the mistake of trying to "get in close" to him. I have made that mistake more than once and it's a disappointing, maddening feeling to be so close and then have it all go wrong. One of my first hunts I was calling to this gobbler whom I thought was a long way off. I thought it would be eas-ier and better to get closer before setting up — WRONG! I had just plopped down by my tree, didn't even have my face mask up yet and here he was! He knew EXACTLY where I was and as our eyes met I think I noticed a gleam in his that said "tee hee, I beat you here!" Of course I did not have a proper shot and the last I saw of him was his back end flying over the fence 50 yards away. THAT was a big lesson learned.

So you are all set up and ready. One mistake many hunters make is calling too much as the gobbler comes in to you. Just a couple soft yelps usually does the trick. Another method: instead of, or in addition to the soft yelps, loudly yelp, sounding extremely excited and raspy, and continue a long drawn out series of yelps. I have seen toms come in with both methods. For just starting wild turkey hunting, I recommend using the soft yelps first. The gobbler knows where you are — make him "want you so badly he can't resist" and use whatever it takes. If you hear him getting closer to you as he gobbles, BE READY! When he breaks out of the brush, or steps out from behind a tree, in a full strut, gobbling his head off and dancing around on his way to the decoys or to you (his hen) STAY STILL! HARDLY BREATHE! DO NOT MOVE! DO NOT CALL! When he is within range, up to a maximum of 40-45 yards and he positions his head straight up, SHOOT! (Even in all the excitement, please remember to put the safety back on your gun after you shoot.)

That is how it is supposed to work. There is Murphy's Law, you know. If you were all set up and waiting for the bird to show up and he does not show, what does that mean? It really means you must have patience and really become aware of absolutely everything around you. Watch to your right and left, moving only your eyes, as he could be coming in silently — they do that just to make your day more interesting! Be patient and sit still and wait. Maybe he caught a movement you made and left. If there was a hen with him, maybe he left with her thinking that would be easier than walking all the way to you. If he did leave with the hen, he may breed her and then come back to you! I have had that happen to me. I thought he was gone for good, but for some reason I just stayed put, and sure enough, here he came sauntering over the ridge top. His hormones wrote his future! You may try to call once or twice, maybe he will answer. If he has been silent and has not come in, wait about 20 or 30 minutes before moving. If the gobbler won't come to your calls, stop calling. Often the sudden silence will make him curious as to whether the "hen" that was calling has left him, and he'll usually sneak in for a look. It's quite disgusting to have been working a bird, have him go silent, wait and wait until you finally give up and get up to leave and have him explode out of the brush and fly out over the tree tops, especially when he was probably only 15 to 20 yards away in the thick brush.

Gobblers don't like to walk over things--like logs. They will walk around them. They do not like crossing fences or streams. When you set up, keep that in mind and be constantly watching your surroundings.

If your afternoon in the forest is unproductive, then take note of where the turkeys are roosting for the night. Roosting a bird, or "putting a bird to bed," and getting out to the roost well before dawn the next morning will give you the best opportunity in bagging a gobbler. Looking for sign, staying in the forest until dark and using your locator call will help you find where the roost tree is and you will hear the gobblers sounding off because they know they are safe from predators for the night. Look for trees that are largest in a particular area; that's where the birds will be roosting. When you have them located, mark your trail with the blaze orange ribbon as explained earlier so you will be able to find it in the dark in the morning.

Get back to camp, have your dinner, and get to bed. Do not have any "night before" parties, especially with alcoholic beverages; you will be getting up early, maybe even 3 a.m., depending upon how far you have to go to get to your roost tree, and you need all your faculties intact and you need to be sharp and rested.

Make sure your alarm clock is dependable; I always bring two in case one would fail. Limit your intake of coffee and other liquids before you arrive at the forest; you might be sitting for a long time waiting for a bird and there will be NO opportunity to go to the bathroom.

When you arrive at the forest, see the trail you have marked and park the vehicle. Don't slam the doors shut and be as quiet as possible. Load your shotgun quietly, making sure the safety is on. Carry your shotgun carefully and walk carefully. It will be dark. Safety in situations like this is another reason to have a sling on your shotgun--the barrel is always pointed safely up in the air. Quietly walk up the trail on the way to the roost, choosing to set up about 100 to 150 yards away from the roost tree. Set up the same way as described previously, quickly and quietly. Even if the bird hears you, you will be sitting there long enough that he will have forgotten about you by shooting time. Be cognizant of which way you will be facing when the sun rises.

There can be some hens who do have beards! And there are some hens who really do gobble!

Check your shooting hours in your hunting handbook. It is usually legal to shoot one-half hour before sunrise to sunset, but be sure to check for yourself. In order to know just when to arrive at your roost tree and set up, start working backwards from shooting time: If shooting is "X" time, you must be set up and waiting and ready by maybe one-half hour before that, then it may take you 20 minutes to walk in, maybe 30 minutes to drive from your "turkey camp," etc. Then figure accordingly on what time to get up. DO NOT BE LATE! Mother Nature's critters will not wait for you!

Do not make any turkey calls until it is legal shooting time when there is enough light, or until you hear the first hen yelp. Imitate the sounds you are hearing, then use soft yelps. You do not want to get him excited too early and have him fly down before legal shooting time. You never know how long a gobbler will stay in the roost gobbling before he decides to fly down. The first one I hunted gobbled 103 times before fly down! (No, I did not count them, an accompanying friend did. I was way too nervous!) Some other times, they have gobbled only a couple of times, then flew down. When a bird gobbles back to you, don't call anymore. He knows where you are. Sit tight, don't move and wait and watch for him to fly down. When you see him fly down, this is it! He should walk right into your gun range. If you have to move your gun to get a better shot, wait until he is behind a tree; quickly adjust your gun ONLY at that time. If the tom doesn't come in, it can mean he has spied some other hens and took off the other way with them or is coming in silently to you. Be patient until you are certain he has left the area.

If this strategy of trying for a roosted bird, still your best opportunity, has not worked, then try the method discussed earlier. At least you will know where the roost tree is and you can try a different idea. Turkeys may or may not roost in the same tree consecutive nights, but it's worth a try to set up and hopefully intercept them as they return that evening.

Even though roosting a bird or "putting a bird to bed" is the best opportunity to bag a bird, that does not mean you cannot hunt at other times during the day. In the middle of the season when the hens are still laying eggs, the hens leave the gobblers around midday to get to the nest to lay their daily egg (they only lay one a day). At this time when the gobblers are alone, they can become more vocal and more likely to come to a turkey call. Along this same line of thought, gobblers are probably most vocal at the very opening of turkey season as their hormones are really starting to bother them. They are "hot to trot" and will gobble to the world about it. They are easier to call in at this time. However, some places in the country, like the upper Midwest, the weather usually does not cooperate. There can be late spring snow storms and cold rains and wind. Another good time to hunt is the very end of the season when the hens are on the nest incubating eggs and the gobblers are completely alone. You can find some with hormones still running at fever pitch and they will be glad to share some time with you! When to hunt is an individual decision depending on your work schedule, family life and ability to go at a particular time.

We discussed the physical attributes of a gobbler — he possesses a beard, has big spurs, has a red, white and blue head, etc. The hen's head is pale in comparison and she looks rather "blah." However, THERE CAN BE SOME HENS WHO DO HAVE BEARDS! AND THERE ARE SOME HENS WHO REALLY DO GOBBLE! In all the turkey hunting I've done I have only heard one weird one, but I know they're out there.

I was hunting northeast South Dakota a few years ago and had set up a fishing date with some friends. I told them I was turkey hunting that morning and that I would be at the meeting place by noon. I was ready to call a non-productive hunting morning a day, in fact, I was on the way to the Jeep when I heard another gobble in the opposite direction. I moved over somewhat and set up and called. The gobbler was "hot" but yet he just wouldn't move. Time was drawing to a close for me, but no way would I leave this hot tom — my friends would just have to wait for me.

That was the most stubborn gobbler I'd ever worked. So, I moved closer to him and proceeded to call again with the same results. It was getting late and I knew my friends would start worrying about me, so I just thought "one more move." I had him pinpointed — he was just on the other side of a tiny knoll, gobbling his head off, but not moving. Now that he knew I had moved in to him, he figured I would come in the rest of the way to him (which is why you always stay where you are unless it's unusual circumstances like this).

He kept on gobbling and strutting, etc. I was extremely frustrated and thought "the heck with it, I'm gonna do it" and slowly and quietly crawled up to the top of the knoll. My shotgun was at my side and I thought I would be ready to surprise him when I looked over the top. I knew he was only about 30 feet away from me. As I peeked over the top of the knoll I don't know who was the most shocked, he or me! I was dumbfounded at what I saw! There was no red, white and blue head! It was just as plain and pale as a regular hen! I thought, "no, this can't be! He?? She?? gobbled its head off for a long time. It cannot be a hen!" The turkey's eyes locked with mine for a split second; I was too shocked to shoot and just laid there in limbo and then he (or she?) was gone! I did not shoot because I just had the feeling it had been a "gobbling" hen, which would've been illegal. It certainly was a hunt to remember! You can bet I really search for the red, white and blue head every time I'm in the turkey woods. You should've heard my fishing buddies. It was a good lesson to learn; Mother Nature is good at that!

Jakes are the young, inexperienced toms. The are fun to watch as they try to imitate a mature gobbler and maybe even "steal" a hen before the big guy arrives on the scene and runs him off. On a turkey hunt in South Dakota's Custer State Park, I was working on a bird who absolutely would not walk up the hill and over a big log to get to me. All at once there were three gobbling jakes (you can distinguish their immature gobbles) behind me and to my left. I thought for sure the big gobbler would come up the hill just to give the jakes a bad time. I lost track of him in the thick brush and waited. Hearing more gobbles from the jakes, I waited a little longer, then gave up on him. I was sitting in front of two trees which made a V-shape at the base. It was comical listening to the jakes, but I hadn't heard anything from them for awhile so I decided to turn around and see if I could spot anything. Just as I turned and peered through the "V" in the tree, the three jakes were right there and all three gobbled right in my face! I tried not to scream. They ran away and my friend, Conservation Officer John Wrede, who was calling for me, was laughing so hard he rolled down the hill. I did not bag a turkey on that trip, but so many funny things happened that it was a great time with lots of wild turkey memories.

There are fall turkey seasons in most states; check to see if you can hunt hens and gobblers at that time. I don't think it is as much fun or nearly as exciting as spring turkey season, but it is still a reason to get out and hunt and many hunters enjoy it. Use the same techniques in the fall as you do in the spring to find turkeys (sign, scratchings, tracks, etc.). Wild turkeys travel and live in good-sized flocks in the fall. The most popular way to hunt in the fall is to break up a turkey flock and try to intercept or call in a turkey as it tries to find its way back to the flock. Sit against a tree, just as hunting in spring.

You can use the "putting a turkey to bed" approach during fall hunting by splitting up a flock in the evening. Splitting up a flock involves finding a flock, sneaking close to the birds, then charging at them as you yell and scream.

This photo of the author shows the white bands on the tail of a Merriam's turkey

You need to startle the birds so they go in all directions. You can then return to call in the morning and hopefully bag a bird. The kee-kee run call is the most popular used in the fall.

That is the call of the young birds trying to find the mother hens. Any call that sounds like a young turkey will probably work. Watch your videos and listen to your cassettes to learn the kee-kee call.

For more information on fall turkey hunting, refer to the NRA Hunter Skills Series, *Wild Turkey Hunting*. Call 703-267-1531.

AFTER THE SHOT

"Tobias" is my full-body mount of a beautiful Merriam's gobbler and holds court, strutting, in my den. I love having him there. Every time I look at him I relive the hunt. He is so very beautiful in full regalia with all of his gorgeous colors! When I have non-hunting guests and they see a real wild turkey for the first time, they are astounded at the bird's beauty. They had no idea how iridescent the feathers

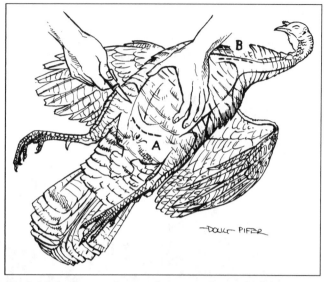

To field dress a turkey, make a cut shown by line A and pull out the innards. Remove the crop (undigested food) with an incision at line B. Wipe the exposed areas clean and protect them from flies. Authorized by permission of the National Rifle Association.

were and how large the tail fan can be. When you have a special souvenir of a hunt, it means the world to you.

If you hadn't thought about any taxidermy work on your bird before the hunt, then you must make the decision immediately upon harvesting him. By hitting the neck and head area, the rest of the bird is then intact and good for a full mount.

Do not ruffle his feathers, wring his neck or touch him in any way that would ruin any of his feathers. Carefully hold his wings down if he still has not "given up," so they are not damaged. Cut off the oxygen supply, if you have to, by applying pressure to the head. If you are having a full-body mount, do not clean your bird.

After the pictures have been taken, place him in a cool place, if possible, until you can get him to the closest freezer. When carrying the bird out of the woods be careful not to hit branches, etc. that would ruin any feathers. Wrap the head in paper towels and tuck it under a wing. Wrap him in plastic trash bags so there is no possibility of freezer burn and tie them tightly shut. Be sure and lay him flat in the freezer. Keep him in the freezer until you arrive with him at your taxidermist's shop. If you do not know any taxidermists, ask your conservation officer or local sportsmen's club members about who they would recommend. There are a number of ways you can have your bird preserved and your taxidermist will gladly show you pictures so you will have an idea of what you want.

If you want a full-body mount, choose a taxidermist who will use your bird's own real head. I have seen some work that was done using a plastic head and it was awful. It was a disgrace to the wild bird and I felt it showed a lack of

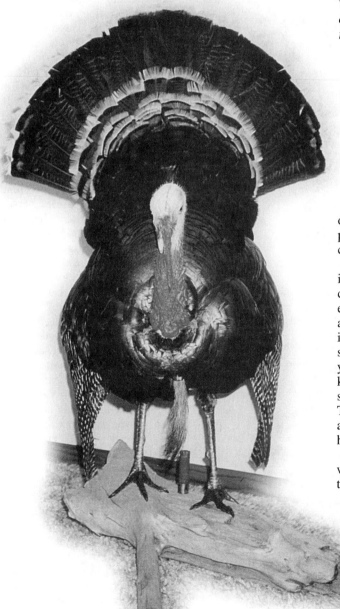

The final prize. After you've bagged a gobbler, like this one the author took in northeast South Dakota, you have several options for preserving the memories of your hunt. The author chose a full-body mount.

respect. Ask your taxidermist to "freeze dry" the head — that is the way it should be preserved

To clean and restore the luster to the feathers of your mount whether it is a tail fan or full mount, dust with a feather duster first then spray the duster with a little WD-40. That will bring back the brilliant colors and the sheen.

If you are not taking your bird directly to your taxidermist or placing it in your freezer, then it must be cleaned. See page 148 in the NRA book, and the illustration.

If not being used in a trophy situation, the turkey's beard, spurs and feet can be removed

Turkey guide Les Rice performs the ritual of dabbing of blood from a hunter's first bird on the cheeks of Margaret McDonald. (Mitch Kezar, www.kezarphoto.com)

and saved, especially the beard and spurs which can be made into jewelry. Necklaces, hatbands and bracelets are a few examples of what can be done with "turkey souvenirs." Ask some of your seasoned turkey hunting friends what they have done with theirs or create new ideas of your own. The most awesome necklace I've seen was worn by a turkey hunter at a National Wild Turkey Federation convention. It contained about 20 turkey beards!

Of course you must have a camera along with you during your hunt. Never fear, you WILL find room for it in your vest pockets. How neat it is to look at those pictures later and relive the hunt! A 35mm camera is best to have; the new disposable outdoor cameras are OK for some things, but not one of your hunting trophies. You want a good quality picture. Be sure to use the flash if necessary; be cognizant of the quality of light. You have just bagged a beautiful bird and you want him to look his best in your picture. The best position for this is to lay him out on the ground, tuck his wings under his body or spread them way out, stretch his head and neck out and while sitting or kneeling behind him hold his tail feathers in the fan position. You may position your shotgun across his neck or beside you for further effect. Another pose of holding your wonderful bird over your shoulder is nice, too. Just take the pictures and enjoy it! Be sure to have some of the surroundings included in the pictures. That adds a nice touch plus in later years you will be able to remember where it was taken.

If you or your friends have a video camera, consider taking it with you. Just remember the operator must be dressed all in camo, must be quick and quiet and must sit behind you or to the side. Give the camera person some quick lessons in turkey hunting so he or she will know exactly what to expect and how to act.

I must tell this story: When I bagged "Tobias," my nice Merriams's, a graduate student studying wild turkeys was with me and called for me. It was the first season in this special unit and since he worked with the birds he "had to be there." Well, his calling was almost supernatural! He sounded more like turkeys than the turkeys did! I had no idea that turkeys made all the special vocal effects that he imitated. That was quite an experience for me and I learned a lot. He insisted on taking his video camera because this would be the first hunt he would record. I was thrilled and agreed. I was even more thrilled when Tobias was in dancing and strutting around the decoys and putting on his show. I sat there, watching in wonderment, and was dreaming about having all this on video, how lucky I was, and how I could actually relive this hunt forever! After I pulled the trigger we ran to the bird, with the video tape still running as we "ohhhed and aaawwwed" over him. All at once Chad's face fell and he turned white as a sheet. A whispered "oh no" is all he muttered as he looked at me with a "hang dog" look. Asking what the problem was, he shook his head and told me. "I was so excited I pushed the wrong button and it was NOT recording, so I don't have anything of the hunt!" I felt like I had been slugged in the stomach. Things like "you're kidding" and "I don't believe it" just didn't seem appropriate. Talk about being disappointed! I still feel so badly about it — to have lost such a classic situation in the turkey world almost made me cry! Moral of the story: Whoever is videotaping for you must know exactly what they are doing and you just have to hope they don't get so excited they push the wrong button!

There are all kinds of new experiences out there for you, and wild turkey hunting stories are the most fun to share with family and friends. Along with that fun comes the responsibility of being a safe hunter. Use common sense when in the forest and while hunting and always remember that you are probably not alone and to act accordingly. I want you to have a great time, learn a new passion but be safe doing it.

One of the best things you can do as a wild turkey hunter is to join the National Wild Turkey Federation. Show your support of the bird we all love so much and meet new friends and have fun at the same time. The NWTF has accomplished great goals in the years since its inception. At the turn of the century there were only 30,000 wild turkeys left in the U.S. Thanks to NWTF's restoration and promotion efforts, today there are more than 4.8 million wild turkeys in the country. There are more than 200,000 members in 50 states, Canada and 11 foreign countries. There are 1,300 chapters spread throughout the U.S. and Canada. There are 55,000 JAKES members (Juniors Acquiring Knowledge, Ethics and Sportsmanship. These are members 17 years and younger). The new Women in the Outdoors program boasts 10,000 members. Contact your local chapter for more information or call national headquarters at 1-800-843-6983. You can also visit the Web site at www.nwtf.org and learn more about the NWTF.

Here is a Turkey Hunter's CODE OF CONDUCT (as published by NWTF): As a Responsible Turkey Hunter, I will:

1. Not let peer pressure or the excitement of the hunt cloud my judgment;

2. Learn and practice safe hunting techniques;

3. Hunt the wild turkey fairly;

4. Know the capabilities and limitations of my gun or bow and use it safely;

5. Obey and support all wildlife laws and report all violations;

6. Respect the land and the landowner and always obtain permission;

7. Avoid knowingly interfering with another hunter and respect the right of others to lawfully share the out-of-doors;

8. Value the hunting experience and appreciate the beauty of the wild turkey;

9. Positively identify my target as a legal bird and insist on a good shot;

10. Share responsible turkey hunting with others and work for wild turkey conservation.

The National Wild Turkey Federation has published a wonderful and very helpful book, *Guide to the American Wild Turkey*. It is a state-by-state guide of wild turkey populations and includes helpful information on every aspect of the wild turkey.

It is available by contacting the national headquarters.

Well, back to the saga of "Rim Rock Romeo".....all the while I had been lost in thought about turkey hunting, Lori and Lila had sat there, waiting, waiting and waiting for lover boy to show up. He never did; his gobbles had disappeared down the far ridge. Calling for any other gobblers in the area was to no avail; nobody answered. Patience having run thin, it was time to head back to the Jeep. Disappointed? You bet! Ready to give up? NEVER! We decided to come back and try for him again the next day.

Since we had no bird roosted, we actually slept in that last morning, but worked hard when we got to our hunting area. We were all calling, and came up with nothing. Rim Rock Romeo had completely disappeared. His friends weren't even around. It was windy, which makes for horrible turkey hunting. There were intermittent showers making life even more miserable, and finally when it really started to rain hard we knew we had to be headed back because we were parked on a mud road.

As we walked back to the Jeep I kept thinking of that disgusting hen that made Rim Rock Romeo run off. She had really made me mad. She had ruined everything!

Were Lori and Lila disappointed? Yes. But did they have fun? Yes. Do they want to go back next year? Yes. It was the camaraderie, the experiencing all this together for the first time, the laughter, the memories, THE HUNT. A bird or two would have been a bonus! We proved we women can do it!!

CHAPTER ELEVEN

BOWHUNTING

"Yea!! I did it again! I'm great!" I was probably only 10 years old but I remember patting myself on the back a lot when I was out by the old granary on hot summer afternoons. One of my fondest childhood memories was shooting with my bow. I had my father set up a square bale of hay for me and somehow I fastened my colored target paper to it. I still remember the colors and that red was the bull's-eye.

I had wanted a bow and arrow outfit for a long time before I finally got it. I daydreamed about it and thought how neat it would be just to shoot targets. I'll never forget the day my mother bought it for me and how excited I was when I first took it outside. My bow was a light-colored wood and it had a red and white bowstring. I even remember the colors of the feathers on the arrows. I never had any instruction, I just set everything up myself and started shooting. I would pretend the bull's-eye was anything and everything and would be out there for hours. My mother couldn't understand how I could be out there in the hot sun for so long. I loved it! My wrist and arm would have scratches and cuts but that didn't stop me.

Regrettably, that lasted only a few years. When I arrived at junior high and high school there were other interests and my archery set fell by the wayside. Our family then moved into town and by that time I had lost track of my bow and arrows.

Another love of mine while growing up was climbing trees back behind the house on our farm. I dragged all sorts of things up into the trees so I could have a house, a room or whatever to myself. Then I would watch for wildlife and be thrilled when something on the ground didn't even know I was up there. The only time I regretted being up there was when the cows decided to come over by my tree and park there for hours. Then I would hear my mom yelling for me, I would yell back, then I would scare the cows, they would run, then my dad would be mad at me. It certainly wasn't always as rosy as it sounded!

I love to stand hunt for deer and I've always said that I archery hunt with a rifle. When I put all of these experiences together, the childhood love of archery, the enjoyment of sitting up in trees and now my favorite method of deer hunting, I would have been a perfect candidate for an archery hunter. It's just too bad I got started hunting so darn late in life. I know the saying is "it's never too late," but that is not always true. I have physical problems with my shoulder and absolutely cannot pull on a bow. I have tried repeatedly after being told, "aww, come on, you can do it," or, "it's not as hard as you think." I've even had an expert recommend medication to enable my shoulder to cooperate. When I was on the game commission, I worked a lot with the bow hunting associations and they were always "working on me." How I hated to admit I just could not physically do it. I WANTED to, but I couldn't.

I have some women friends who are archery hunters and they just love it. How I envy them. I love to listen to their stories and I admire their prowess in obtaining their game. I have learned a lot from them and I know you can, too. This chapter is dedicated to those women who hunt with a bow. They know I am there in spirit.

One of the most fascinating women I've met is a great lady by the name of Brenda Valentine. This woman has hunted since she was 5 years old and has many "notches on her belt" when it comes to bagging game. You may see an

THE BOTTOM LINE !

YOU'LL NEED THIS———

article featuring Brenda in any hunting magazine. She is an outstanding bow hunter, a Becoming an Outdoors Woman workshop instructor, RedHead Pro Hunting Team member (the only woman), outdoor promoter and feisty Tennesseean. Brenda has this advice for archery beginners: "The first thing you would NOT want to do is take your husband's bow, or any man's equipment, for that matter. You will be turned off because it will be too hard to pull. The draw length will also be too long, which will automatically give you interference and make you hit your arm and hurt your breast. This would be all from improper stance and equipment that does not fit. A bow is more dependent on proper fit than anything there is. You can kind of get by with a shotgun or rifle that doesn't fit; a bow that does not fit is just like wearing someone else's shoes that do not fit. You just cannot handle it. Draw length and draw weight are the two major factors of fit, one being dependent on the length of your arms and the width of your shoulders, and the other is the weight that you actually pull.

"Most people think that you have to pull exorbitant amounts of weight to be an effective hunter. That is totally wrong. The equipment and the technology that we have now, the arrows and the broadheads allow any average to small-sized person, be it a woman or teenager, to easily pull 40, 45 or 50 pounds. That's not much. The lowest let-off most of the bows have today is 65 percent, and you are getting on up into the 80 percent range with some bows. So, in effect, if you are pulling 40 pounds, you may not be holding but 7 pounds at full draw. The creation of the compound bow and then the high let-off has made us more than equal with our male counterparts," said Valentine.

"On my bow," she continues, "I only have to pull 6 inches and it breaks over and lets off. It only weighs 2-1/4 pounds, that's less than my purse by about 400 percent! Fully rigged-out with six hunting arrows, broadheads, sights and stabilizer it is less than 3-1/2 pounds. (I shoot carbon arrows.) The bows for women these days are so light. The grips are formed down to fit your hands well; they are just totally

designed for women. You can sit on a stand and shoot. I shoot a Browning and it's 35 inches tall. Most men's bows are 39 to 42 inches tall and if you were sitting on a seat or chair, you'd have to stand up because the bottom limb would hit the bottom of the stand or the ground. These new little bows are so short, you can sit there and relax for hours and then make your shot without having to stand."

Brenda describes how to buy your bow: "Go to a pro shop, preferably one that has a woman working there. I don't want to take anything away from men, but a woman will better know how to fit you because she will realize the problems that you face. I don't know why, but women's arms are attached to their bodies differently. Men will invariably say, 'I don't know why you are hitting your arm, I never hit mine.' Of course they don't, because we are made differently. When women hold out their arms, their elbows stick right out, waiting to get hit. Men's arms are not like that. It's these little differences that men don't understand. If a woman has a man tell her to shoot and the string hits her elbow and hurts, then she says, 'This is not fun. I don't want to do this anymore.' If you can find a knowledgeable woman who has worked her way through these problems, it can be a go for you from the very beginning. It can be fun and you don't have to suffer to get into shooting a bow.

"One of the great things about bow hunting is it usually takes place early in the year while it's still warm. It's such a quiet, peaceful time, most women get caught up in it and it's not as much the actual kill for them as it is the quiet time, the actual stalking thing. I think most women enjoy the hunt probably more than they do the actual kill. It's such a close, personal thing with a bow, you usually have time to study the animal and decide if you really want that animal. A lot of times with a gun it's such a fleeting thing and you have to make snap decisions because of the time of the year the game is spookier and not as relaxed. Early in bow season, they haven't been hassled, they haven't been hunted and the game is relaxed and you can pick and choose and decide which one you want.

"For bow hunting I prefer a climbing stand because it's more mobile. I can sit in a different tree every day. Bow hunting is such a close sport and all animals are so bright

Brenda Valentine shows off a sizable buck she dropped with a bow. Anyone can become an accomplished bowhunter, but some people say it is easier for women because they are more patient.

when you are hunting that you need to change positions. You need to work the wind and not just leave your scent in the same place all the time. A climbing stand is one that you carry in with you and it attaches around a tree. You kind of use an inch-worm type motion and get yourself up the tree. When you are done hunting, you can take it down and sit in a different tree every time you go to the woods.

"The fixed-position or the hang-on type tree stand straps to the tree but you have to have some type of ladder or steps to get up the tree to get into it. These are usually set up before the hunt because it would make too much noise going in at hunting time. The day before or the month before is typically when they are set. They are somewhat mobile; you don't move them every time but they are not permanently attached to the tree. Most ladders are made for men whose legs are generally longer than women's, so add a few steps for your own safety. A pull-up rope for your gear and a safety belt should always be used. You want to be comfortable in your stand, so be sure to correctly adjust the seat height."

When I asked Brenda how long she stays in her tree stand, she said, "It depends on what is going on. Sometimes I have an animal in 15 minutes and sometimes I go and I'll stay eight hours. It was years, YEARS, before I could discipline myself to stay from before daylight until after dark. If I'm in a place and it is rut and I think that I have enough deer sign to make me believe that it's worth investing that time, I can stay in place for 12 hours and not go to the bathroom and eat very little. You have to train yourself and discipline yourself to do this."

Whenever discussing bow hunting I have always wondered how any woman could sit in a tree stand for long hours at a time and not have to go the bathroom. When I stand hunt with a rifle, or when I'm turkey hunting, both of which mean sitting for a period of time, I'm always ready to go to the bathroom when I'm finished hunting. I cannot imagine sitting in a tree stand for eight to 12 hours and not leaving to go to the bathroom or just to move. When in a tree stand, you can't leave or you don't dare go to the bathroom because of the scent, etc. So I wondered, do bow hunting women really dehydrate themselves before they go? Brenda says, "I really don't. Shoot! A Ziploc bag is perfect; I can tinkle in a Ziploc bag on the stand if I want to! I keep a safety harness on and in super, super cold weather, that makes one of the best hot water bottles there is! Most of us have these (warm up) pouches in our coat or vest; when it is miserable cold, that warm Ziploc bag is welcome! I think people took jars and bottles for years. I have a girlfriend who camouflaged a 2-pound coffee can and she keeps that around her stand. She

fixed some kind of rope for it where it will just hang off her stand. I've tried jars and things, but they all make noise. I've hunted a lot of men's stands that have had milk jugs sitting in them. The Ziploc bag is the best thing for me." (Author's note: place a plastic-coated pop cup into the baggie first for stability.)

"I try to limit myself to just one or two cups of coffee in the morning before I go to the tree stand, but I think your kidneys just learn. In fact, your whole body kind of shuts down. Your senses and your instincts are running overtime and it seems your bodily functions just shut down. When you come in you are just totally worn out. People ask, 'How can you get so tired just sitting in a tree?' I think it is because all of your senses are on edge the whole time; there's no let down. Even if you close your eyes for a second, your ears take over to totally pick up any sounds. When your eyes are open, they are just constantly scanning for any break in the scenery that you might think may be an animal. Many women catch on real fast because they have good eye-hand coordination and they like the quietness, the peacefulness of bow hunting opposed to the boom of the gun."

Kathy Butt is a freelance writer/photographer from Tennessee who hunts with a bow. Her "getting started" advice is this: The best thing I can tell women who want to start bow hunting is to go to an archery pro shop and be properly fitted for a bow. That's the basis for everything — using the right equipment. That will make you more confident with that bow and you will enjoy shooting. Finding someone who will work with you, someone who really knows what they are doing, someone who is easy to work with and is very patient is also very important. There is a lot of good equipment out there right now, especially for women. When I started bow hunting 15 years ago, I had to use equipment made for men. We had to make a lot of adjustments. I didn't let it keep me from bow hunting with my husband; but as time went on manufacturers started creating better bow equipment for women, it made it much easier, much more enjoyable. Getting fitted with the right bow is all-important.

When teaching the waterfowl class at my first Becoming an Outdoors Woman workshop, I met a most delightful lady bow hunter, Skip Meisenheimer. I regretted I did not have time to attend her archery classes. The women who were in her classes were continually expounding upon how exciting it was, how much they liked the instructor and how much they learned. They were instilled with new confidence for a new activity. After spending time with Meisenheimer in her archery shop, I felt the same way. She still teaches at BOW, has been her city's children's archery instructor for more than

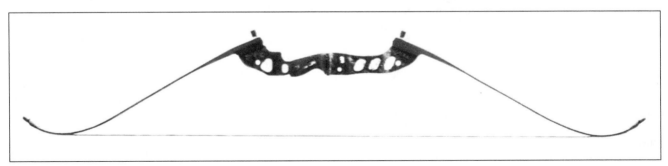

This PSE Coyote is an example of a modern recurve bow. The recurve is relatively simple when compared to modern compound bows.

30 years, and is a private instructor. She seems to glow when talking about bow hunting and sharing her experiences.

Skip told me, "my husband and I started shooting archery in 1965. I had over a year of target shooting which consisted of a recurve bow and shooting with wooden arrows because that was the thing at that time. I practiced a lot outdoors. I started bow hunting in 1966; I hunted with eight or nine guys so I had some very good instructors. In 1967 my husband and I both went to instructor school and we both received our patches."

When I told Skip about hurting my arm when I was a youngster shooting my bow, she said, " The reason your arm gets black and blue is because women try to make themselves stronger. We may not hit ourselves to begin with because we have extended our arm. We are not tired. We pull back and everything is correct. The more we use our upper body muscles, the more tired we get because we are not strong enough to begin with. Then we start turning our arm and hitting our elbow. My husband and I named this elbow turning procedure 'milkmaid's elbow'. Men hardly ever hit themselves because they are a lot stronger in the upper body. Even though my husband had great upper body strength, he had a terrible tear in his shoulder that had to be repaired surgically. To be able to keep on bow hunting, he switched from right-hand shooting, to left-hand shooting and got along fine. Once you learn the basics, it doesn't matter if you shoot right or left-handed; you must do everything correctly and practice."

When discussing pounds of pull, Skip says consistent correct shot placement is more important. She says, "I don't care if you are pulling 30, 50, 60 or 80 pounds, shot placement is critical. I remember this one guy told me he pulled a great amount of pounds and was proud of it, but because he

had been sitting in the cold so long waiting for an elk, when the time came, he could not pull back at all."

When asked how she starts bow hunting instruction, Skip answered, "Basically I like to introduce the people to the recurve, not a compound bow to begin with. My theory is a bow should be an extension of your arm. When I put that bow out there, it should be just like I was using my hand to try to get something. If I extend my hand out there, that bow should be right where that target is, where it is comfortable to you. I think when women look at compound bows and see all the wheels and gadgets and things, it is overwhelming for them. I like to start by introducing new students to what a bow is and the correct way to use it. I like to start everybody out then let them develop their own style."

Skip decided she needed a compound bow during antelope hunting after the antelope watched the arrow from her recurve bow approach him and then he stepped aside. The compound is twice as fast. "If you could see the arrow from a recurve bow in slow motion, the arrows will come out and gain height and then drop. They almost make an arch. With a compound they are a lot flatter and go straight in. They are much faster and that is why everyone goes eventually to a compound. I feel that speed and poundage is the frosting on the cake; accuracy is the cake. If you can put the arrow where you want to, in the same spot all the time, that's what counts. If you put that arrow in the same spot every time, it really doesn't matter how much speed you have or how much poundage you have. That's what's going to get you your deer," Skip explains.

Skip's advice includes telling women "they must have their own bow for which they have been measured. She believes all aspiring bow hunters should have professional instruction and lessons and purchase their equipment at a pro shop so they know exactly what they are getting. At the pro shop, they can shoot and find out if this is what they really want to do, if it is their "thing." The women can try different bows and see what they really like. If women have tried their husband's bows and were discouraged, they should run, not walk, to the nearest pro shop for assistance with a woman's bow."

"The first thing to do is get measured for a bow and the length of the arrow; then work with the weight of the pull. Start with low poundage and then work up from there. Then decide if you want to just target shoot or hunt. If a person can handle 28 to 30 pounds to just target shoot, that's fine. If you decide to hunt then you would get set up with a bow that would adjust to a higher poundage pull. You would also need a larger arrow as the heavier the pull, the heavier the arrow you need. You can start out with low poundage and go higher; they are adjustable. The equipment must be the correct fit; you do not want to get discouraged. Skip likes to work with a 35- to 50-pound pull for women and young adults. You should check with your state's wildlife agency to know what poundage is legal where you are going to hunt as some states have a minimum pull weight requirement. Women should learn to pull with their shoulders, not just their arm. Isometric exercises will help you strengthen your neck/shoulder/back area. Another important point is to learn right away to anchor your pulling hand beside your face and always hold that position."

After being correctly measured for a bow, you will want to find the correct arrows. Your instructor will have a chart to show you. Arrows must be compatible with the bow weight

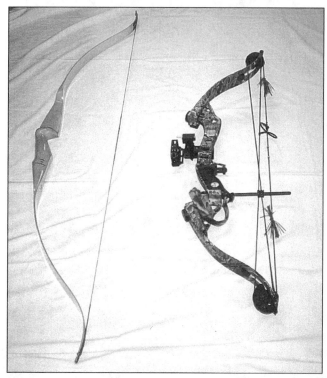

Side-by-side the differences between a recurve bow and a compound bow are very apparent. Both have their benefits. Both have their drawbacks. You should try shooting several types of bows before you purchase one.

and draw length. The most popular arrows used today are aluminum (Skip uses aluminum for hunting). They are light, can be straightened and re-fletched (reattach feathers). There are also fiberglass, carbon and wooden arrows available. There are even special arrows made just for bird hunting: flu-flu arrows! They have large feathers on them so they don't fly as far and you can find the arrow when it hits the ground (if you miss!). If you want to hunt small game, use specially designed blunt-tipped arrows. Skip hasn't hunted geese with a bow but she has successfully hunted pheasants and gophers! Did she hit them? You bet! She says, "gopher hunting is very good for you. You have to have the patience to stand there and wait until they come back up out of their hole. It gives you a little education for hunting deer because you have to learn to deal with your shadow. If that gopher sees your shadow, he is gone and so is the deer. When the gopher comes up out of his hole, you will have time to draw."

Besides the bows and arrows, there are other items you will need for the best bowhunting experience and success. Your instructor will explain the use of pins and sights, a "stay put" to hold your arrow, a bow rest or "hook and sling" to free up your hands if necessary while on stand. There are other items like the "kisser button," finger tab and arm guard that all go into improving your performance with the bow. When I walked into the archery shop, I was intimidated when I first saw all the equipment. DON'T BE AFRAID OF THE EQUIPMENT! It just takes a little time to absorb all the information. Once you see that each item has a purpose, it is very simple. Skip took me step-by-step and very care-fully, patiently and cheerfully explained each piece and why it was needed. I'm sure she was very tired of me asking "why?" and "what for?" constantly. Your instructor will teach you the same way. If he or she doesn't answer all your questions, insist upon it. If he or she still doesn't, then find another instructor. There are good ones out there and many bowhunters will also volunteer to help you.

I shot a recurve bow at Skip's shop and loved it! She was very good with me, showing me how to stand, how to pull, how to drop my shoulder and not hold it so tight and stiff. I learned how to hold my elbow down (not pointed out so it would get hit) and learned not to push too hard. This is why it is so important to have a FEMALE instructor — she will KNOW what to tell another woman!

Because of a woman's anatomy, a female bow hunter must ask herself "where does the bow string hit?" Well, you can guess where it may hit, but Skip has a solution for that. She has a chest protector. It is a piece of heavy vinyl that covers one breast and is attached by fitting your arm through the strings and fastening it. She says it works "like a charm." It pulls the shirt in and you don't catch the bow string on anything. She tells women students that if they don't pull into the side of the arm and come around in front, they will hurt themselves. Practice with layers of clothing on; when you will be out hunting, the temperature will not be the same as when you practiced. You do not want to think you are all ready and confident, then have a shot ruined because you forgot to allow for the extra sweatshirt or jacket that you may be wearing. If you do not have an arm guard to keep your sleeve

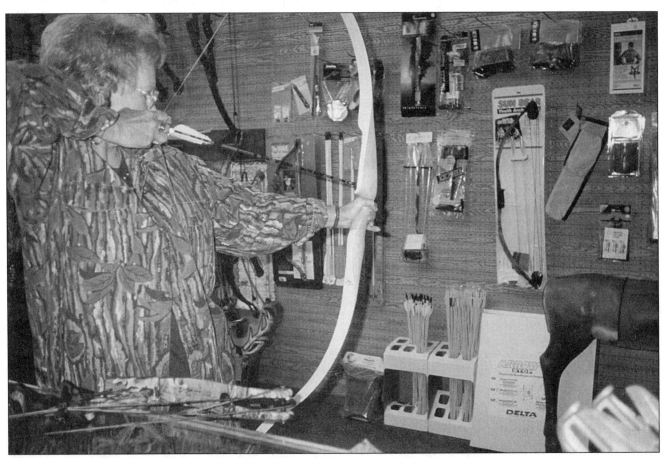

To really get a feel for a bow, you've got to pick it up and look it over. Here the author tries her hand at drawing a recurve in a local archery shop.

tight to your arm so it does not interfere with your shot, you can use duct tape or electrician's tape and wrap it around your arm several times.

Practice is important; practice every day. If you have no outdoor area in which to practice, you can use a hallway in your home as Skip did. "It doesn't matter the length that you practice, it's IF you practice. It's like brushing your teeth or tying your shoes; if you practice doing it the right way all the time pretty soon it gets to the point where you can do it and you don't even think about it. There are some good instructional tapes available today. Check out your video rental store. If you can't find them, then ask your instructor. A beginning bow hunter must take a Bow Hunter Education Course." (Contact your wildlife agency for places and times.) If there is not a "women's only" Bow Hunter Education Course available to you, urge them to start one. Learning in a non-competitive and non-intimidating atmosphere is important.

Because bowhunting requires you to be very quiet and still to allow the animals to get in close to you, it is important to try to cover up your human scent. Using commercial potions like "Doe in Heat" scent will help draw bucks in close to you. Skip keeps the scent on cottonballs inside a 35mm film canister. They should be placed away from you on the ground in a good shooting area. Never take them up into the stand with you as that would immediately give you away. "You can also place the scent on a rag, attach a string and drag it behind you to cover up your human scent you left as you walked into the woods. Just do not use skunk scent! I was told to use skunk scent and then the deer would really come in to me. I was skeptical, but I tried it. I watched deer a ways off, but they would never come in. I had a lot of time to sit and think about it. It finally dawned on me that if I were an animal, why would I come in to a skunk smell, because the skunk only sprays when there is danger. A lot of guys disagree with me and I just don't understand that. The best smells are those that the animals are used to. For instance, if there are no apple trees or acorns around where you are going to hunt, do not take any in with you. That smell would be foreign to the deer and they might not come in to you. Even if we cannot smell it, the deer certainly can."

Skip answers the question, "How many yards is a good shot?" this way: "Not any more than 10 yards. I like to have them very close. The longest shot you should take would be between 20 and 40 yards for deer, 30 yards for antelope. But 10 yards is even better. You should use your cover-up scent and be hidden well enough so you can get them to come to you. If you have them closer to you, you will have a much better chance to make a killing shot. If the deer are in close, you will have less chance to have your arrow deflected by a branch which could make a bad hit. Make sure you clear the area and know the yardage of that cleared area. I have passed up shots which I thought would injure the animal, so I let them go. You can't get them back once you've shot at them, you know! It's like being in a bowling alley — you throw the ball and it goes in the gutter; you'll never get it back. You might as well take your time and throw the bowling ball correctly the first time. It's the same way in archery. You get one chance. If you can't make a good hit, don't shoot at all because there is always tomorrow. If you stand very quietly and don't let that animal know you are there and don't disturb anything he will be back because that is his territory and you will see him again."

Skip has a practice hallway in her shop and has set up a video shooting system. With bow at the ready, you watch the video of the animal and when it is time for the best shot, a green line moves across the top of the picture. You then shoot. At the end of the series of videos, you compare your score with what is on the picture. It is fun and it's a great training tool. Ask your instructor to inform you about this video system — you'll love it!

Because bowhunters want the animals so close, they have to do everything possible to completely hide (cover up scents, staying perfectly still and quiet, full camouflage). Since normally deer do not look up as they are walking or running through the woods, bowhunters usually elect to hunt from a tree stand so they are above the deer. As for tree stands, Skip used to use a portable one. Now she thinks it's easier to build a permanent stand and put a wooden ladder on it. "I have quite a few tree stands in different places in the shelterbelt (A grove of trees protecting farm buildings or animals from wind.). You have to take the wind direction into consideration.

Skip Meisenheimer, an archery professional shows the proper stance for shooting a bow. It's important to get training before you try archery hunting. It will help you get rid of any bad habits before they work their way too deeply into your shooting style.

You sit where you are DOWNWIND from the animals (the wind is blowing TOWARD you so they cannot smell you). That means you have to move around so you always stay downwind. To test the wind direction, tie a small feather on a string or just use a small piece of string and attach it to your bow. Watch it and you can see the wind currents and directions. The currents change in the morning one-half hour before sunrise and again at night one-half hour before sunset. The wind will stop and that is when it will change. This really makes you aware of how strange nature can be. If it does change, you might have to get down off the stand and go to a different spot. One time I saw this deer coming toward me and then she just stopped. She had me. I finally figured out what it was — the wind had changed.

"The major bowhunting clothing tip I can give you is this: you must be quiet and that means wearing quiet clothing," said Skip. "Fleece is great, but it is notorious for picking up cockleburs. You do not want to sit in your tree stand for hours twitching from the cockleburs that are stuck on the backs of your legs or your bottom. Put your fleece clothing in a plastic bag and carry it in to your stand. You may even need that plastic to help drag your deer out later. You can then stuff the plastic bag into your fanny pack that you hang on the branches behind you.

"I use a safety harness (a big belt that connects your body to the tree behind you so you do not fall off the stand) every time I go up the tree. You should not go up in any tree stand without your harness. Make sure it is attached in a high enough position on your body so if you would happen to step off the stand platform your legs will not be dangling way below the stand. That would make it very difficult to climb back up on the stand. Remember, higher is better and safer," says Skip.

Skip also uses ground blinds utilizing tumbleweeds, grass, broken branches and anything that is natural to the animal. She adds, "Make sure you have an opening to plainly see the deer trail and are able to shoot. Also take into account where you will be sitting when the sun rises so you will not cast a shadow. You want to be able to move around in your blind because you have to sit there for a long time and you want to be comfortable. If you are not comfortable, you will be fidgeting and you will never see that deer."

Deer, as a rule, will not look up into a tree. But Skip thinks they are more educated. When she first started hunting she said she always got deer in very close. Now there are many more hunters in the field and people have a lot more recreation time than they used to. This makes a lot of difference. Deer get educated very fast.

"I have used a doe decoy that folds up," said Skip. " I've had does come in and look at it, but I'm still waiting for the big buck to come in and take a look. It's a portable decoy and folds up quite flat, but I have to haul it in quite a ways and it gets heavy. As for using decoys, I think it depends on what time of the year it is. I would not use a buck decoy at the beginning of the season, but I might use one during the rut, especially if I had a buck decoy and a doe decoy. (Bucks tend

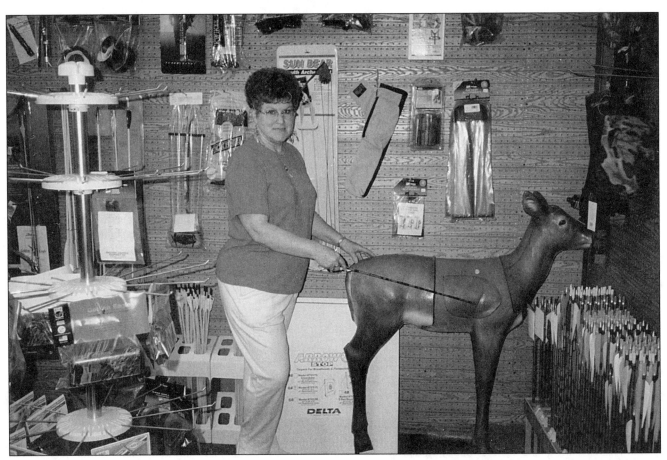

The vital area on a deer is relatively small and it takes a good hit with an arrow to bring down a deer quickly. Here Skip Meisenheimer shows one of the best places for an arrow to enter. This shot, just behind the shoulder, will hit the heart and lungs.

to stay by themselves during the beginning of the season. During the rut they become territorial and will chase off other smaller bucks.) I would use a smaller size buck. If you have seen a 10-point buck in the area and you bring out a 12-point decoy, the 10-pointer will not mess with it. If you have a smaller decoy, he'll probably come in and try to take the doe away from the smaller decoy."

Skip hunts with a bow "because it's just me out there. I am the one who is doing it. It's just me and the animal. I like close shots. I am invited into their territory. This is their home. I'm their guest. It's a challenge to see how close you can get to something. If you can get deer to come to you without them smelling you or being aware of your movement, you know you've done your job. Then the shooting becomes easier. The day my heart stops racing 50 miles per hour when I see an animal come upon me, then that's the day I'm going to hang it up. It's the excitement of it! It's the fun of the trip — it's the seeing the ones that got away. One of the other advantages and exciting things about bow hunting is that when you are making the shot at an animal, you can see the vision line of the arrow going to the "X" (the vital area or target area). You can't do that with a rifle. You do not always have to get the game. There's always tomorrow; you can hunt and also enjoy seeing the animals. It's interesting and it's fun. If you score and bring meat home for the table, it's just the frosting on the cake; but you have to learn how to really enjoy the cake before you can enjoy the frosting."

Like all hunters, bowhunters have to pick the spot on the deer where they want the arrow to hit. Says Skip, "You cannot

shoot at the whole animal. If you just shoot at the animal, you will hit the horns. Believe me, you will! For some reason, your eye goes towards the horns. I've seen guys do it! I've experienced it myself. If you stand there and you practice at your target enough so that you can say 'OK, I'm shooting this or that,' then you pull, release, keep your whole arm out and follow that arrow. Look at that spot and you can actually see that arrow going into it. So when you are hunting, and you practice that and you have picked a spot on that animal, then you let go, you follow that arrow, then you can see the arrow hit the animal. I have a lot of tapes that actually shows this happening."

If you are asking, "Where do I shoot when the deer comes in? What is the vital area?" Skip recommends a lung shot. Always remember to go straight up from the front leg, then back behind that front leg a bit. When shooting from a tree

stand, Skip says to remember the angle at which your arrow will fly. Shoot lower than normal if you are shooting from a tree stand.

Skip has a great training tool for correctly placing your shot. It is a 10-inch tall buck deer on a platform. Skip handed me a large pin and told me to put it in the "right spot" — the vital area if I were hunting. When the long pin was placed, she then turned the deer around and we saw exactly where that deer would have been hit. The back side of the deer model is cut out and all the vital organs are showing. You will be able to see if you are aiming in the correct place or need to move "your spot" somewhat. If your instructor does not have one of these deer, try to find one.

With deer as close as 10 yards, it can take some time for the animal to get into a perfect position for a shot. You may draw the bow and have to hold it there for a while. Skip had this to say when asked how long the average time is that you hold the bow drawn: "When your heart is beating 50 miles per hour, it seems like forever. If a deer is coming through and you have your hand on the bow and you are standing and waiting, remember to 'pick a spot' and to keep breathing because if you hold your breath you may fall off the stand. Bide your time a little bit, and you will have the deer come right in. I really can't tell you how long I hold the bow drawn because I've never counted or even thought about it. It's just something you do instinctively. I would guess that I hold the bow drawn no longer than one or two

Archery pro Skip Meisenheimer brought down this deer while hunting the edge of a corn field. Good shot placement is very important while archery hunting. It can mean the difference between a clean, quick kill and a long tracking job.

minutes. If you draw too early you will lose your form and that means the arrow will shoot lower. It's better to wait until the animal gets close, quietly raise your bow, then proceed in your form and shoot."

Does Skip use a grunt call to attract deer? "No, I don't want to. If you are grunting and you are trying to get that animal in to you and get it close enough, they have ears and they are going to hear it come from a tree! So, I think it's best not to grunt. My theory is, if you have a buddy, and you want the best way to hunt, have your buddy grunt away from you. Work on the buddy system. Really, you should not go hunting by yourself anyway. My husband has a fit because I like to go by myself so he makes me take the cell phone. I keep it turned off and he yells "it will be no good if you fall out of the tree.' Maybe the cell phone should be left at the bottom of the tree — if you fall it's already there!"

It is wonderful to become acquainted with women who have hunted for a long time and are so proficient at what they do. Skip has an electric personality — she almost shoots off sparks when talking about her passion for bow hunting and her love of the outdoors and the resources. When watching Skip pull back on her bow so fluidly and easily, and with a million dollar smile, I silently gave thanks for the opportunity to have met her. How great it is to have a teacher like her! She instills confidence and ethics and makes people feel good about themselves and what they want to do. I would hope that every woman meets an instructor like Skip. Because she has hunted for so long and experienced so much, she is full of neat and funny stories. I have to share this one with you in Skip's words: "I had some guys come up from Georgia and we bowhunted up in the northeast South Dakota hills. There are real nice ravines there and the farmers had electric fencing on their land. I knew the wires were 'hot', and I knew how to cross them. Well, these guys were southern gentlemen, right down to the core. We had to go across the fence. I got ahold of the top wire of the barbed wire fence and I knew which wire was hot. I was careful to not touch the two wires together. Two of the southern guys came up to me, took ahold of the wires and pushed them down!! My legs aren't very long so you know what happened! When it was all over, the insides of both my legs were burned--you could see the little burn marks right through the coveralls! Whew! Was that hot! Here these guys were just being kind to me! After that happened, it's just LEAVE ME ALONE! I CAN DO IT!"

Brenda Mitzel, an accomplished bowhunter, was a rifle hunter who turned to bowhunting because of the safety factor and to be able to have deer come in close to her. She spent two years observing deer and their habits before actually hunting them with a bow. She liked the solitude and quiet of the woods and the excitement of watching animals and their behavior. She likes the challenge of having deer come as close as possible to her. Brenda gives these tips to beginning bowhunters: "Go out to the woods, spend time observing your game, know what they do and when and where they do it. Read bowhunting magazines and educate yourself. When using a compound bow, start at a low poundage pull, like 20 to 25 pounds. Turn it up every week and practice until you can pull the required 40 pounds. Practice, practice, practice! You can go to your local archery range or take a target out to public land. Never use broadheads to practice — you want them to stay sharp for your hunt. Use field tips that are the same weight as your broadheads. Practice shooting from your tree stand before hunting season so you know exactly what to do and how to hold your equipment and shoot. Take a target out with you and practice shooting down. You always want to mark off where 10 yards is and where 20 yards is. Walk it off and know where those marks are at so when a deer comes by you will know if that deer is 10 yards or 20 yards away. I have never shot anything beyond 10 yards. Knowing distance is important; if you think a deer is 20 yards away and you shoot and it's 30 yards away, chances are you will not hit it. When you shoot from a tree stand, you must take into account exactly where you are standing. It's not like a rifle and you can just pull up and shoot; you have to pull back so you have to allow for your arm to have freedom and not hit the trunk of the tree. That happened to me my very first time out. I watched this nice buck come down the cornfield for half an hour, he came right by me and I couldn't pull back because the trunk of the tree was there and away he went!

"I only take four arrows with me; you can only use one, you know! I use aluminum arrows, and being a female, I use smaller arrows. Men have teased me about my 'puny arrows' until I successfully bagged a deer and they didn't!

Brenda Mitzel bagged this nice little whitetail buck with a well-placed shot. It takes practice, but if you really want to learn to hunt with a bow, you will love the experience.

"Always use a safety belt to attach yourself to the tree. Include a bow rest in your equipment, especially if you rattle antlers where you will need to use both hands. (Please refer to the Deer Hunting chapter.) The bow rest wraps around your leg and has a cup you put the end of your bow into so your bow can rest in the cup and always be ready. I also recommend a 'stay put' on the riser of your bow; it will hold your arrow on your rest. You will need this because if you sometimes pinch the string, your arrow will fling right off the rest and that's not a good thing! The 'stay put' will keep the arrow right on there and it doesn't interfere when the arrow lets go."

Brenda says her average length of time in a tree is four hours. "I always get impatient. Actually, noon is the best time to go hunting. Deer move at noon, especially during the rut. I've watched them at noon season after season. I suppose they've eaten, they went back and bedded for awhile and their instinct tells them to 'go back and check the rubs and scrapes again to see if anything has come by.' Rubs are the areas on small trees where bucks have rubbed the bark off with their antlers. Scrapes are areas where bucks have pawed the ground, cleaned off the area and then urinated on it. Scrapes are usually underneath a tree with nibbled-off twigs hanging down. I have watched deer do this. Scrapes are very important, especially if looking for a buck. A doe may just walk by and relieve herself in it. Don't set your tree stand right on top of a scrape. Place yourself 10 or 20 yards away from it. If you find a scrape when you are out scouting, cover it back up and check it the next day to see if a deer has been there. That's a good way to see if that is a route they are traveling a lot. If they are traveling it a lot, most likely it will be opened up again. If after two days it's not open again, then move on to a different area."

Brenda uses permanent, built-in tree stands. "If you hunt on private land, you can build your tree stand and just leave it there forever. If you are going to hunt on public land, know your state's regulations for the allowable time that the stands can be in the tree, if your name and address needs to be on it and any other regulations. I would not take a portable stand with me because I would have to take it with me every time I went or else take a chain and padlock it to the tree if you are going to leave it there for a period of time."

Getting a good shot is very important. Brenda says she likes to visualize: "When I am sitting in my deer stand and I see a deer coming, I have a point in mind where I know the deer would come to, so before it got to where it could see me, I would pull back and hold on it. As soon as the deer walked in, then I could let the arrow go. If you wait to pull back until the deer is at the spot, you will scare it and it will be gone. One time this doe mingled around for 10 minutes while I was in position; I didn't think I was able to hold it anymore. I just had a point and I waited until she walked into that and then I let the arrow go. Ten yards is not very far away; in a blink of an eye they can be gone."

Brenda has a good tip for noise elimination on the tree stand. Cover your floor with carpet. Her husband made a rubber cover for the carpeted floor. It is attached to the tree stand and can be pulled over the carpet and latched. When you leave the tree stand at night your carpet will be covered to protect it from freezing rain or snow which could be dangerous and noisy the next morning. Your floor will be clean, dry and ready.

To eliminate human scent on clothing, Brenda suggests storing your hunting clothes in a plastic bag with a piece of a pine tree branch and placing it out in the garage or in the basement. She also advises that rubber boots are best as they leave no scent in the woods. Brenda uses the commercially available Scent Shield and sprays her clothes and bottom of her boots before walking in to the hunting area.

"A successful season doesn't always mean that I got a deer," she says. "The things that I saw were sometimes better than getting a deer. One time I heard this terrible crashing coming down the trees and I thought 'this is it!' Here came this deer running as fast as it could by me, all of a sudden here came another one running like crazy. They went around underneath my tree, round and round like for half an hour. As they were doing this I thought 'gee, this stinks!' Well, the one had been sprayed by a skunk and it apparently just wanted to be friends with the other one but it smelled so bad the other deer wanted nothing to do with it!"

Brenda knows confidence plays a large part of women's hunting activities. She says, "You have to be confident when you go out there. If you have any doubts about your shooting ability, you shouldn't be out there. You need to know that when you shoot, it's going to be right. If you don't have the confidence that you KNOW exactly where your arrow is going to hit, and that you will hit the vital area, then you need to practice some more."

Brenda says, "When you are in your tree stand with all your equipment ready and your confidence level is high, and that big deer comes, watch out! Honest to God, your heart beats so loud in your ears you think your head will explode, and you think your heart will explode! You shake and you tremble! They say the best thing you can do is keep taking deep breaths because that helps to relax you and calm down a little bit. This will all happen when you get to shoot your deer, too. It's a tremendous experience! If you lose all this, then you shouldn't be hunting any more. When this excitement leaves, then that's the time to quit."

Gail Swanston is a four-year veteran of Becoming an Outdoors Woman workshop archery instruction, a life member of the Whitetail Bowmen archery club, teaches bowhunting at various other locations and events, owned an archery shop for 14 years and has hunted for 20 years. Gail recommends that beginners start at a professional archery shop and get fitted for a bow. "It's important," she says, "to be fitted exactly for a bow because if she pulls it too far, she will not be accurate. A beginning woman bowhunter should have a light enough weight so that she is comfortable with pulling. She

Gail Swanston's buck sports a broken antler, likely from a fight with a bigger deer. Bowhunting will allow you to get closer than you may have ever thought possible to game animals.

can always work into the hunting weight of the draw. She should speak with someone who owns an archery shop, try out a bow, then go on for instructions. She should start with an easy weight that she is comfortable holding. Start at a close-range target and when you can group your arrows into a pie plate, you can start moving back and increase your yardage. Starting at 8 to 10 yards would be a comfortable range with which to start. When I hunt, I won't shoot anything over 30 yards away because I'm real confident that I'm accurate at that distance. The challenge of hunting is getting close to your game anyway."

Gail said there are two kinds of compound bows, they just have different wheel attachments on the top or bottom. "There is the wheel bow and the cam bow. A wheel bow has a round wheel on the axles. A cam bow has a half-wheel or an oval, so that when it comes over you actually pull it over the top which is your let-off point, and what you are holding may be 50 or 60 percent less than what it is when it breaks over the top. A wheel bow just continually rolls back. The wheel bow is a smoother bow but it won't shoot as flat as the cam bow which launches the arrow faster. The beginner should try both to see which one she would be comfortable with. The cam bow is a little harder to pull back over the center, but when you do hold it back it has a greater drop-off than a wheel bow, which means you are actually holding less weight than a wheel bow when the cam bow is drawn back. Wheel bows are usually used for target shooting. A beginner would be more comfortable with the smoother action of a wheel bow. I shoot a PSE (Precision Shooting Equipment, Inc.) FIREFLITE wheel bow. It is a light-weight and I shoot it at 42 pounds draw which is the minimum weight you can legally hunt with; it's what I'm most comfortable with if I have to hold waiting for the deer to come in. I can hold it there for a long time. I shoot aluminum arrows; never shoot a wooden arrow out of a compound bow as they will shatter."

Gail is not your typical bowhunter in that she usually hunts from the ground. "I don't like heights! Instead of clutching the tree, I stay on the ground and hide behind a tree or bushes. I have never hunted from a 'set-up' blind. You do not HAVE to hunt from a tree stand. I have stood in the crotch of a tree that was only 3 feet off the ground and leaned against a very wide tree that was behind it. A deer walked right underneath the fallen tree that I was in. So you don't have to be up very high to be able to shoot deer. There are portable tree stands just big enough to put your feet on. If you can get those up about chest or head height and then just stand on those, that's high enough. The higher you get off the ground the more difference in the trajectory of your arrows, so you will want to practice from a tree stand if you are going to shoot from a tree stand."

Her clothing and scent control isn't always conventional, either. "I have worn a red flannel checkered shirt and stood behind a tree and shot at a deer 8 yards from me! When my husband and I were hunting one Sunday after church, I even had cologne on and a deer came in toward me. It was vanilla scent — I swear that's what it liked! It was a doe and I could've just stuck my hand out and rubbed its back, it was that close! I didn't move and it just walked right on by me. She had a fawn with her so I didn't shoot."

Gail says she wouldn't recommend wearing cologne, but she also wouldn't recommend overdosing with all the scent eliminators or cover scents currently on the market. "The name brand "Cover Up" is good because it neutralizes the human scents," said Gail. "All the lures and other cover scents I don't think are necessary. I have gotten very close to deer, within 3 feet of them, without any scent at all. You want to get downwind from the game so they don't smell you. I don't believe in washing your clothes in a special soap or this ultra-violet stuff that supposed to neutralize things. I have used buck lure twice during the rut and it does work. They do come in to it. They have actually come right up to it and smelled it. I sprinkled it as I walked in. If you know the trail or path that they are taking, they will come down it anyway. But they will stop and smell that. Buck lure and doe-in-heat lure is the same thing. The thing is to get in early before the deer move. Be in your place before the deer start coming through so you are not going in at the same time they do. It takes a lot of patience to hunt with a bow."

Gail said the longest she usually stays in her hunting place is two hours. "The deer start moving at dusk so you go in an hour before, get in and get situated, then just stay alert! Watch for them because they are quiet. Since I'm not in a tree stand and I'm on the ground, I have to be very conscious that I do not move a lot or move rapidly. I scan with my eyes and turn my head very slowly. I just don't jerk it around back and forth to look and see if something is coming. If you have watched while you are hunting, you generally know which way the deer move in the evening versus the morning so you have an idea of where to sit on the trail."

Be in your place before the deer start coming through.

As far as bowhunting clothing is concerned, Gail says, "wear any camo that breaks up your pattern and is warm and comfortable. If you can afford to purchase the different camo that blends with different backgrounds (different seasons, the darker and the lighter, etc.) it would be good to have that. Anything that breaks up the pattern is good. I wear a face mask. I have worn face paint but I don't like to take the time to clean it off. The only hindrance with a mask is if the eye holes are not big enough and when you turn it may cover your vision somewhat. I always wear gloves because it covers the shine from my rings and my hand. I like light-weight camouflage gloves. I shoot with a finger tab (a device that protects your fingers while pulling back on the bow) so I need the light-weight gloves."

Gail advises first time hunters to get "...warm boots and a chest protector. The chest protector is very, very important. When you first draw the bow back to shoot for the very first time, be sure that you either draw the string in to the side of your chest or else you are 'small enough' so that the string will miss you because it hurts like heck if it hits you! You will be bruised for three days at least! Not fun! The chest protector is great; I wear it over my coveralls. While wearing the chest protector I don't have to worry about catching things on pockets or buttons."

Gail and her husband don't do a lot of scouting because they usually hunt in the same place and they know there are deer there. They find the trails and sit off to the side. They go out before dawn and an hour or two before dusk. Gail says, "I do most of my hunting in the evening. I don't have much luck in the morning. I have sat there and watched the frost build up on my arrow and the sun melt it off and never saw a deer! The bucks cheat and move after dark, you know!"

I asked Gail what she does when she is all settled in her hunting place and a deer comes along. "I like to get the deer in about 20 yards before I ever draw back," she said. If the deer walks behind a tree that is between me and the deer, then I will draw back and wait for it to get closer. It's important to just draw your bow back many times beforehand and hold it to build up those muscles so when this time comes, you can draw back and hold for as long as you need to. If you draw back too soon and you have to let down, the deer may detect that motion and run away. When you have an open 'alley' with no branches or any interference between you and the deer, and it's within a range that you know you can have a killing shot in the heart/lung area, then you release the arrow. You don't usually get a chance to shoot a second arrow so you want that first one to be very accurate. You do not want to wound a deer, so you make that first shot count. Besides, if you let them in close enough and get a real accurate shot, there is no tracking to it!"

Lori Goldade is a good friend of mine and besides being a proficient bowhunter of deer and bear, serves on the Board of Directors of Outdoor Women of South Dakota. Lori says, "My first lessons in bowhunting were at the Becoming an Outdoors Woman workshops. You can learn from those workshops, there is reading material available, and there are television shows and tapes. There is a lot of information out there. It took a lot of time before I felt I was ready. The first year I went out I had no intention of shooting a deer. I just wanted to experience pulling the bow back. The most important thing I learned when I first started to hunt with a bow was to be prepared. You have to shoot a lot and be confident in your shot placement. You have to know mentally that you can make a good, clean shot, and to know when to make that shot."

It has been my experience that ladies are excellent students. They learn the sport much faster than men because they LISTEN.

Lori has taken two Canadian bears and talks about the equipment: "You use the same equipment hunting bear as you use deer hunting. The poundage has to be set higher. I started pulling about 20 pounds and worked my way up to the required 40 pounds. You must be able to pull 50 pounds to hunt bear in Canada. I really enjoyed my bear hunts. Yes, they were scary! Before I went, I read books on bear biology and recommend that everyone do that, but I was on edge. It's hard to believe that you do not hear the bear in the woods. They're just there. When my first bear finally came in, I was just shaking—really shaking—muscles were shaking that I didn't even know I had! Shaking that hard, you think you are never going to be able to pull the bow back. I did get it pulled back but it was too dark and I couldn't see through the peep sight. He wasn't there very long; he grabbed meat out of the bait and went behind me and was chewing on it. I could hear his jaws crunching bones! He would come out, grab some more meat, go back behind me and crunch some more. It was dark and here was this bear crunching bones behind me! While I was waiting for the guide to come pick me up with his four-wheeler, I was nervous. I was staying right up there in the tree. I would have stayed there all night if I had to!

When the four-wheeler finally came, I had to climb down out of the tree and walk to it! I had hoped the four-wheeler had frightened him away! Obviously, I returned safely, but it was quite exciting to say the least!"

Lori says, using a bow for black bear hunting is a great option because you can get them to come in close to you. "This year I had two of them climbing up the tree at the same time!" she said. "If you move even a bit, they run away. The challenge of bear hunting is not there while hunting with a rifle — you are not that close. The game is right there when you are hunting with a bow. That's the thrill of it!" (Lori points out that you should have a buddy with you and make sure you can run faster than the bear!)

I discovered a most delightful, enthusiastic and extremely knowledgeable man who is working very hard to bring women into the archery and bowhunting field! Mr. George Chapman is affiliated with the archery manufacturer PSE, Inc. (Precision Shooting Equipment, Inc.) in Tucson, Arizona. Mr. Chapman began the PSE Shooting School in 1989, and since that time has given archery instruction to more than 2000 archers. His career in archery spans more than 50 years and includes tournament competition, with numerous national tournament victories, a lifetime of bowhunting, equipment design and manufacturing. He has also been involved in both shooter and dealer education.

Chapman has this to say: "In archery, we are fascinated with crowns and jewels. The International Bowhunting Organization has the National Triple Crown. There are also dozens of smaller or less well-known aggregate tournaments known as "crowns," and the individual tournaments are sometimes known as "jewels." But, there is a missing jewel in the archery industry crown. That jewel is women. Look around at most tournaments and you will see about 85 percent of the people are men. There is an even smaller percentage of women taking to the fields as bowhunters. Archery remains a male-dominated sport.

"Yet archery is one sport where a mother can take her children, and they can all participate. It is good exercise for almost anyone, even the physically challenged. It teaches discipline and concentration. It gives its participants a sense of self-worth and accomplishment. It is an almost spiritual link to an ancient heritage. Best of all, it's fun!

"It has been my experience that ladies are excellent students. They learn the sport much faster than men because they LISTEN. They don't try to apply what they think they already know to what I'm trying to teach them. Most women are motivated to learn as quickly as possible. They are very stingy with their time and will work hard on a project — like archery lessons — to get it accomplished. Women are generally less competitive with less ego. Most women are not bothered nearly as much by peer pressure as male students.

"I've always enjoyed working with women as students in my schools. Many of them have gone on to make the sport a part of their lives. They buy equipment and teach archery to their children. Attracting women into archery is a job for each of us, and to show my commitment I

The Lil' Ol'Man is a tree stand designed for women. It is light-weight and easy to carry. Hunting from a tree stand puts you up above the deer's line of sight.

You'll need a basic understanding of archery equipment before you walk into a store and start asking questions. First, there is the bow. There are basically two types of bows available now: recurves and compound bows. As discussed before, compound bows use either pulleys or cams to reduce the amount of weight you have to hold when the bow is pulled all the way back. With a recurve, the bow is basically a stick and a string. You hold the whole weight. It is simple, but it can be tough to hold the weight for any length of time. As a result, compound bows have come to dominate the market and there are several variations on the design. Ask several people and you'll get several answers as to which is best.

Arrows are made of aluminum, carbon fiber or wood. You'll need arrows that work well with your bow, are the right length for you and fit your budget. The stiffness of the arrow is call its spine. An arrow with the correct spine for your bow will fly straight and true, one that is too flexible or too stiff will wobble all over the place.

When you hold back the string you can use a mechanical release device (basically a simple trigger), a finger tab, a glove or have pads attached to the string. Try them all to see what you like.

There are also any number of accessories on the market. If you like to shop you'll like archery. It is a sport you really can explore.

Archery equipment companies have recognized that the future lies with drawing women and youth into target shooting and bowhunting. The top three companies all have light-

coach Ladies Only Schools. Men are not allowed at these schools because whether husband or boyfriend, they intimidate the women. SHE is shooting, SHE is listening. SHE is learning."

Like all the other hunters I've met, Chapman suggests that women interested in archery get proper instruction. "The first thing a female beginning archery student should do is find a coach," he says. "Don't wait until you run into trouble and then go see the coach. Getting started right is necessary, so find that coach first. Don't accept your husband's or boyfriend's archery equipment; you are built differently and hand-me-downs will not work properly for you. See the coach before you buy any equipment. You should be fitted for a bow and shown what to do with it. The coach will tailor the bow to you. The woman should have poundage that she can handle; she should start low and work up."

Chapman coaches shooting schools around the country each year. Besides the women-only shoots, he hosts schools open to everyone. For information, see the PSE, Inc. Web site www.pse-archery.com and click on schools.

"Women can be a major positive force for our sport and industry," says Chapman. "The ladies participating in archery today are adding a great deal of class to the sport. Increased numbers of women can also give our industry more political clout, something we need to save our bowhunting rights."

EQUIPMENT

Never go up in a tree stand without a safety harness. Most falls occur when you are getting into or out of your tree stand. Buckle-up for safety. Falls from tree stands can be fatal.

weight bows made for women and youngsters. PSE, Inc. has a "bow system that grows with the archer." It is designed to meet the needs of archers between the ages of 6 to adult. There are three bows in the system; different equipment is added as the person grows. PSE, Inc. also has "Kidz Bowz," specially made for children ages 4 through 10 years. The easiest way to stay current with PSE technology is through the Web site: www.pse-archery.com.

Golden Eagle/Satellite Archery has a special bow made for young children as they are starting archery. They also have three models of a compact size bow that women archers will appreciate. There are some accessories available. Call for information at 813-920-5407. Web site is: http://www.webpagers.com/golden.

Browning has bows for youth and women in their Micro Class line. They are "high-tech, compact, and lightweight." They also have some accessories available. The U.S. consumer hotline is toll-free at 1-800-333-3288.

Tree stands are a matter of personal preference. Some bowhunters don't even use them, others go high-tech. It is completely up to the hunter and what she decides is the most comfortable and allows her adequate movement, concealment and safety. Some people build their own and leave them as permanent stands. They are made out of wood or steel and anchored to the tree. You can either use a metal ladder or construct a permanent wood ladder. The design is completely up to you, but keep safety in mind. Of course, the time to construct and place these is well before the season; you do not want to be working in your hunting spot and making all kinds of commotion during hunting season. Be prepared. (You can learn how to construct a tree stand when you attend the Becoming an Outdoors Woman workshop.)

Portable tree stands are popular and there are various designs on the market. Portable means you can move the stand from tree to tree as you desire. Ol' Man Treestands believes in the family and has designed a tree stand that is just the right size for the young hunter and the woman hunter. "It is safe, comfortable and easy to use. The Lil' Ol' Man will climb trees from 8 inches to 18 inches in diameter. It is easy to carry, light, compact, and attaches and adjusts on one side only which makes it easy to use. The Ol'man net seat insures that it is comfortable. It weighs 18 pounds, the seating platform is 18 inches wide by 34 inches long, standing platform is 14-1/2 inches wide by 29 inches long and it has a weight capacity of 175 pounds.

Ol' Man Treestands has a new large-platform fixed position tree stand that is light to carry, easy on the pocketbook and will accommodate larger people. It is the new Tara AirElite that is light weight, big and roomy, economical for its size, loaded with features and super comfortable with the net seat. Weight, with the chain needed to attach the stand to the tree, is only 13 pounds and the platform has more than 4 square feet of room.

This is only a smattering of items that are available. The bowhunting market is huge, much bigger than can be covered in one chapter. Hunting with a bow is a learning experience and it takes a bit of experience to get proficient at it. When you walk into an archery shop, don't be overwhelmed by everything you see. Ask questions. If you don't get answers you understand, ask again. If the clerk or store owner gets impatient, find another store. Don't give up.

Hunting with a bow is certainly a challenge; you will become a very skillful hunter as you learn how to bow hunt. Enjoying the thrill of having the game in close to you is what bowhunting is all about, as the women hunters have told us. For another opportunity, for more time in the woods and to meet another goal, consider bowhunting.

A ladder stand offers some people a bit more of a feeling of security, but it is also more difficult to carry and erect in the woods. You make the choice.

CHAPTER TWELVE
OFF-SEASON ACTIVITIES

When the hunting seasons are over, you may have the same "let-down" that comes at the end of a wonderful vacation. After all the preparation, all that you have learned, all the fun you had and all the challenges you have met, you will probably think "What do I do now?" This is, believe me, a normal reaction. Don't despair! There are many outdoor and hunting-related activities that you can become involved in all year round.

The seasons will most likely be over at the end of December or early January. Some rabbit hunting seasons go well into February in some areas. If you live in the northern regions of the U.S., January through the end of March means ice fishing. It's not for everyone, but it can be great fun, especially if you get a group of women on the ice. Contact your sportsmen's club for suggestions. Snowshoeing and cross country skiing will also keep you in the outdoors. Winter has a lot to offer photographers; if that is your interest, take advantage of the season.

Check with your wildlife agency to see what, if any, other seasons such as crow, squirrel, rabbit, etc. are open in your area. Predator hunting (usually fox and coyote) can also take place in the winter months. That is a good time to field test your warmest clothing and boots! Call your sportsmen's club to obtain information on predator hunters. They may take you with them! It is a great way to test your rifle skills.

If you are into archery, you can shoot with a local league to sharpen your skills. If there is an indoor shooting range, spend some time there. Don't hang up the rifle just because the hunting seasons are over. I shoot my .22 rifle a lot in the winter. If I can't get to the rifle range, I set up pop cans in interesting configurations out on the river bottom. There are many ways you and your friends can enjoy a "shooting afternoon." Set up little competition events — use your imagination. Just always remember to shoot safely.

Springtime brings the rounds of conservation organization banquets and auctions. Sportsmen and women contribute their time and resources to help raise money for habitat and work toward the preservation of our hunting traditions. Choose your favorite interest and join the ranks of people

Getting involved in outdoor groups during the off-season is a great way to meet people and learn more about the outdoors. Here, the author, right, Lori Goldade and Gayla Baker take a break during an outdoor show where they are representing a local sportsman's club.

The author is also very active in the Rocky Mountain Elk Foundation. Here, she's getting ready to give a speech at a fund raising event.

working together for wildlife. Each specific organization has a local committee that organizes the event in your city or area. Find out who is on that committee from your sportsmen's club, call them and offer to volunteer. Those committee volunteers work hard, but they enjoy it and have a great time. You can meet new friends, new hunting buddies and enjoy the feeling of working for something really worthwhile. A sense of fulfillment overcomes you when the event is over — you know you have done your part for the wildlife.

Conservation organizations have been described in detail in each appropriate chapter in this book. I want to inform you here about the Rocky Mountain Elk Foundation, a terrific way to work for wildlife. The RMEF is an international habitat conservation organization with nearly 110,000 members. It was founded in 1984 and its corporate offices are in Missoula, Montana. The RMEF has generated $90 million to conserve and enhance nearly 2.7 million acres of wildlife habitat throughout North America. Their mission is to ensure the future of elk, other wildlife and their habitat. The RMEF is committed to conserving, restoring and enhancing natural habitats; promoting the sound management of wild, free-ranging elk which may be hunted or otherwise enjoyed; fostering cooperation among federal, state and private organizations and individuals in wildlife management and habitat conservation; and educating members and the public about habitat conservation, the value of hunting, hunting ethics and wildlife management. The RMEF recognizes the great potential of female hunters and was one of the first national sponsors of the Becoming an Outdoors Woman workshops. I am very proud

of the fact that I was the first female invited to present the keynote speech at the national convention's opening ceremony — that was quite a show of support for females involved in the outdoors! Whether you hunt elk or enjoy watching the magnificent animals, working with the RMEF gives you the chance to become involved, not only for the preservation of elk, but other wildlife as well. The RMEF raises funds through a local chapter system and female committee members are increasing all across the country. I belong to two dif-

Prairie dog shooting can be great fun and a good way to hone your rifle skills. Use a small-caliber varmint gun because you will be shooting all day. The author likes this mini-shooting bench because it is light and portable and it provides a great shooting support.

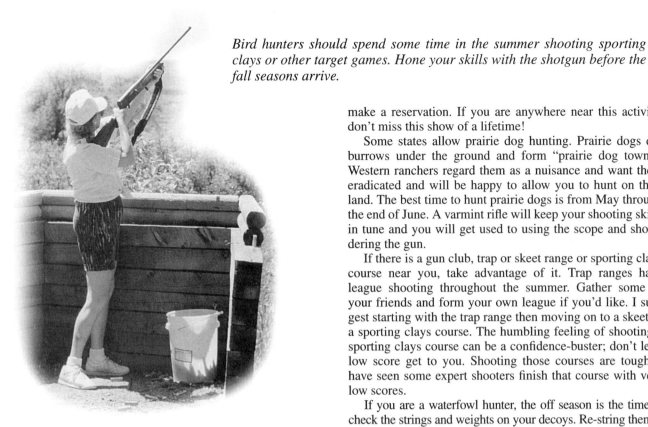

Bird hunters should spend some time in the summer shooting sporting clays or other target games. Hone your skills with the shotgun before the fall seasons arrive.

make a reservation. If you are anywhere near this activity, don't miss this show of a lifetime!

Some states allow prairie dog hunting. Prairie dogs dig burrows under the ground and form "prairie dog towns." Western ranchers regard them as a nuisance and want them eradicated and will be happy to allow you to hunt on their land. The best time to hunt prairie dogs is from May through the end of June. A varmint rifle will keep your shooting skills in tune and you will get used to using the scope and shouldering the gun.

If there is a gun club, trap or skeet range or sporting clays course near you, take advantage of it. Trap ranges have league shooting throughout the summer. Gather some of your friends and form your own league if you'd like. I suggest starting with the trap range then moving on to a skeet or a sporting clays course. The humbling feeling of shooting a sporting clays course can be a confidence-buster; don't let a low score get to you. Shooting those courses are tough. I have seen some expert shooters finish that course with very low scores.

If you are a waterfowl hunter, the off season is the time to check the strings and weights on your decoys. Re-string them if necessary and get them all ready for the waterfowl season. When that time rolls around, you will be glad you took the time earlier so you are not working on decoys until midnight the night before season opens.

Birdwatching can be a fascinating hobby and millions of people are avid birdwatchers. Whether it is watching birds on a feeder in your yard or walking through the woods, bird-

ferent committees and I believe the women in both committees have more fun than the guys!

For more information on how you can become a member, call 1-800-CALL ELK, visit the Web site at www.rmef.org, or write Rocky Mountain Elk Foundation, PO Box 8249, Missoula, Montana 59807-8249.

Whether it is the Rocky Mountain Elk Foundation, National Wild Turkey Federation, Pheasants Forever, Ducks Unlimited, or whatever organization you choose, just GET INVOLVED! We all must do our part for preservation of our traditions and working for the welfare of wildlife.

February and March are also the sports show season in most major cities. These shows highlight destinations, gear and all sorts of sporting activities. Take one in to see what you are missing.

Learning and practicing your wildlife calls is a good activity in the off-season. You may be an expert when the next season rolls around if you spend some time practicing during the off-season. If there are crows in your region, take a crow call outside and "play" with them. It can teach you a lot about calling all kinds of birds.

Early spring you can find prairie chickens and sharp-tailed grouse performing their mating rituals on their leks (dancing grounds). Please refer to the sharp-tailed grouse section of the Upland Game chapter for a complete description of this activity. Call your wildlife agency or the U.S. Fish and Wildlife Service office for locations near you. In some areas the USF&WS rents blinds to the public for viewing or photography purposes. You will have to call ahead and

Small water can mean big fish. This bluegill came out of tiny farm pond. You don't need expensive equipment to enjoy fishing. A few simple items will put you on the road to fun.

watching can be amazing. Use your good hunting binoculars and purchase a good bird guide book. This is an activity you can do alone or with a group of people. Contact your state wildlife agency and order a book that shows you how to plant your yard to attract wildlife; that can mean entertainment for you year round.

If you have a national wildlife refuge near you, stop at their office and ask about the different activities they sponsor throughout the year. Some of them have special volunteer days that would allow you to help with some of those activities. Ask them what birds and animals inhabit the refuge, then go out and try to find them. A favorite activity at the refuge near my home is watching bald and golden eagles during the spring migration.

Observing certain animals, such as deer, at a wildlife park or a side trip to a game farm will allow you to observe the animals and their habits. Take your rattling antlers or deer calls with you and see what happens!

A visit to a taxidermist's shop can also be rewarding. Besides viewing all the mounts, you may be allowed to observe how the mounting process is done. You will learn more about the particular animal, how it lived, what its hair or fur is like "close up", what feathers are crucial to flying and tons of other information. The taxidermist is a wealth of knowledge, so don't be afraid to ask any question.

Summer fishing, boating and canoeing are wonderful activities and if in the right place at the right time can afford you a look at wildlife on shore.

Taking care of hunting equipment is an important part of the off season. Gun cleaning, rearranging "hunting" drawers, organizing your equipment and clothing are only a few items on the list. If you had trouble with a gun or rifle malfunctioning or jamming during hunting season, summer is the time to take care of it. If you still aren't sure what size shells shoot the best in your gun, summer is the time to find out and this is the time to pattern your shotgun.

Perhaps the most important thing to do in the off season is to not ignore your shooting. Practice, practice, practice! Whether with your shotgun shooting trap, shooting cans with a 22-caliber rifle or target practicing with your big game rifle, just practice and have fun doing it! "All through the year check out the wildlife/shooting/hunting and related web sites. There is a ton of information there and always something to learn."

"The off season is a time to reflect on past hunts, to remember, to appreciate, to give thanks for the experience and the wildlife, and to look inside ourselves and know why we are out there. It is the time to think about our mistakes and how to correct them, to be a better conservationalist, hunter, wife, mother, friend and person."

Practice makes perfect. Don't put your guns away just because the hunting season is over. Get out to the range and sharpen your skills.

Summertime means fishing time. These walleyes fell to the author, left, and her partner, Gloria Erickson of Nebraska, on the Missouri River near Pierre, South Dakota. Fishing is a great way to get outdoors and learn a new skill.

When the hunting seasons close for the winter, it's time to try ice fishing. Again, it's not about the kind of gear you own. It's all about having fun.

EPILOGUE

I am concerned about the future of hunting and preserving this wonderful American tradition. This book was written to help women "find themselves" in the hunting arena, become proficient at hunting skills and love it so much they will feel the need to pass their enthusiasm and knowledge to their children, their grandchildren, the neighbor's children. What a wonderful way to perpetuate our tradition. It is extremely important in this day and age to remember that "family values" are not just political buzzwords. We must embrace the "real world" of the outdoors and the dimension that involvement in outdoor activities can bring to a family.

In the past decade there has been much discussion of "bonding." I have found no stronger bond anywhere than that bond forged by families and friends who hunt together. Even though I discovered hunting relatively late in life, it quickly became my obsession — my passion. I learned as much as I could as fast as I could. I have experienced this bonding and found it strongest the day I was waterfowl hunting with my son and son-in-law.

Our son, Rod, is a career officer in the U.S. Air Force and had not been "home" during a hunting season for many years. Although he had hunted with his buddies during high school and college, I was not into hunting then. It wasn't until 1998 that he and I had ever had the opportunity to hunt waterfowl together. My son-in-law, Mark, lives only 200 miles away and we hunt together a lot. When Rod finally had leave that coincided with waterfowl season and Mark was also at my home, I happily got to play the part of "ramrod" for the hunt. This was a really big deal for me. "Mom" would be goose hunting with her Lt. Col. son for the first time ever and her son-in-law would fill out the trio. No one could ever be more proud than I was when all three of us were in the rushes and I was waiting to call in some geese for my boys.

Since my daughter had married Mark and brought him into our family, he and Rod had never been able to spend any real meaningful time together, even though they had known each other for 10 years! What a thrill when we all found ourselves together at goose hunting time! We started the day with duck hunting on the river bottom. After three hours of standing in 6 inches of water and breaking ice to get there, I had had enough and left for home. The two boys stayed out there until noon and came back with their limit of ducks. I immediately noticed a closeness between the two that I had never seen. Later in the day, we decided to try a different side of the river bottom because there were giant Canada geese over there. We took off, goose decoys in tow, to try our luck at the "big guys." We scared up hundreds of birds, both Canada geese and ducks, which immediately disappeared. "Oh, well," I thought, "they will return. And if they don't, the boys had a great day of hunting already anyway." After we were settled in the rushes on the riverbank we sat and waited.

About 15 minutes later, my son-on-law Mark said, "Be quiet! I hear the geese! They're coming back!" Sure enough, they were! I started calling with all that I had in me and Mark was calling, too. They were not only just coming, they were headed straight for us! The only thought I had at that moment was "Please, let them come over us. This is so special. Help me do everything right so the boys have a shot!" As the geese flew in, they did fly right overhead. Unbelievably, I didn't even think to take a shot. The only thing I wanted was to get those geese in the correct position for both Mark and Rod to connect. I heard one shot, then two, and watched as two giant Canadas sailed down toward us. I had done it! I had successfully called the geese and both boys had

The author's son, Rod, left, and son-in-law, Mark, pose with a pair of geese the author called in during the first hunt her two "boys" ever shared together.

made good shots. I had tears in my eyes as they waded out into the water to retrieve their game. Both of them were bringing back 14-pound birds that Mom had called in. What an experience! What a day! Words cannot explain the feelings that I had as I watched them proudly bring these beautiful giant Canadas back to the rushes.

That evening we had a surprise birthday party for my husband. They didn't know it, but I was watching the two boys. There was a certain feeling, a closeness, a connection that had not been there before. Hunting is truly a terrific experience. When shared, it can create feelings beyond description. I was so happy to have been the catalyst. Calling in the geese for these boys and seeing the happiness, fulfillment and the bonding that took place between the two was unforgettable.

I wrote this book with the purpose of helping to perpetuate the future of hunting. When I saw it happening in my family it was a very emotional experience. We are now a true hunting family. Our daughter, Andrea, her husband, Mark, our son, Rod, and his wife, Carol, both have two boys. I am thrilled, excited and thankful that I have four grandsons to introduce to the outdoors. I have had a lot of fun already. Andrea and Carol still prefer to do their hunting in the malls, which is OK, but I'm working on them! Since I missed out on introducing my own children to hunting, I feel I have my second chance with our grandsons and I'm going to give it all I've got! I thank God I get to play a part in the preservation of one of the most meaningful activities we humans can participate in — hunting His wonderful creatures. I hope when you get started hunting, you will have the same feelings and will want to share it with the world around you.

The picture of a hunting family: Back row, from left, Andrea, Mark, Rod and Carol. Front row, Drake, Dylan, Bruce, Berdette, Chandler and Colton. The tradition of hunting can only be preserved by keeping family ties strong.

Index

R

S

T

LEARN FROM THE OUTDOOR EXPERTS

DEER & DEER HUNTING
MAGAZINE

Contains practical and comprehensive information for ALL whitetailed deer hunters. You won't need to buy separate magazines about deer, bow and gun hunting, **DEER & DEER HUNTING** covers it all.

1 year (9 issues) only $19.95

www.deeranddeerhunting.com

WISCONSIN
OUTDOOR JOURNAL
WISCONSIN'S HUNTING & FISHING AUTHORITY

Gives you 100% Wisconsin quality hunting and fishing articles, photos and news. You'll get twice as much essential Wisconsin outdoor information than any other full-color state magazine.

1 year (8 issues) only $17.97

www.wisoutdoorjournal.com

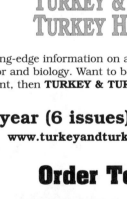

TURKEY & TURKEY HUNTING
MAGAZINE

Leading-edge information on all aspects of wild turkey behavior and biology. Want to be more successful on your next hunt, then **TURKEY & TURKEY HUNTING** is for you!

1 year (6 issues) anly $13.95

www.turkeyandturkeyhunting.com

Order Today!

Credit Card Customers Call Toll-Free

800-258-0929

Offer ABAZPN

M-F, 7 am - 8 pm • Sat, 8 am - 2 pm, CST
Or send order on a 3 x 5 card with payment to:

krause publications, Offer ABAZPN, 700 E. State St. Iola, WI 54990-0001

write for foreign rates

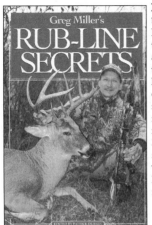

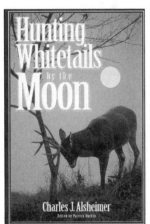

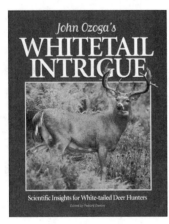
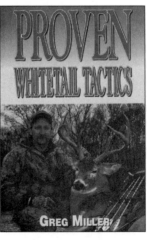

Oh Deer! The Venison Cookbook for Beginners

by Cheri Helregel

Wondering what to cook now that there's venison in the freezer? With chapters on everything from incorporating venison into your current recipes to choosing the right spices for a venison roast, this book has the solutions to serve up fabulous meals from your hunter's harvest. Nearly 100 easy-to-fix recipes give you plenty of options.

Softcover • 6 x 9 • 150 pages
20 illustrations
Item# DRCB • $13.95

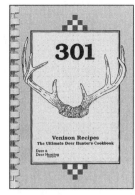

301 Venison Recipes

The Ultimate Deer Hunter's Cookbook
by Deer & Deer Hunting Staff

Mouth-watering recipes have made this cookbook a hunter's classic. If you need to feed a hungry bunch at deer camp, or serve special guests in your home, look no further.

Comb-bound • 6 x 9
128 pages
Item# VR01 • $10.95

The Complete Guide to Game Care & Cookery

3rd Edition
by Sam & Nancy Fadala

Everything from harvesting and preparation to cooking and serving is quickly referenced in this cookbook. Nearly 500 recipes for delectable entrees, side dishes and more from a hunter trained by a master chef.

Softcover • 8-1/4 x 10-11/16
320 pages • 500 b&w photos
Item# GCC3 • $18.95

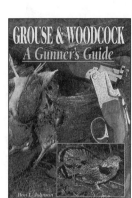

Grouse and Woodcock

A Gunner's Guide
by Don Johnson

Join Don Johnson to find out what you need in guns, ammo, equipment, dogs and terrain. Acquaint yourself with the history of grouse and woodcock and the tactics for a successful, exciting hunt with his expert advice.

Softcover • 6 x 9 • 256 pages
50+ b&w photos
Item# GWH01 • $14.95

Whitetail Behavior Through the Seasons

by Charles J. Alsheimer

More than 160 striking action shots reveal a rarely seen side of North America's most impressive game animal. In-the-field observations will help you better understand all aspects of the whitetail deer, from breeding to bedding. Nature lovers and hunters will love this stunning book.

Hardcover • 9 x 11-1/2
208 pages • 166 color photos
Item# WHIT • $34.95

Spring Gobbler Fever

Your Complete Guide to Spring Turkey Hunting
by Michael Hanback

This anecdotal book illustrates specialized tactics and entertains readers with great ideas, diagrams and strategies for calling and taking all four subspecies of wild turkey.

Softcover • 6 x 9 • 256 pages
153 b&w photos/diagrams
Item# SGF • $15.95

The Complete Book Of Outdoor Survival

by J. Wayne Fears

Prepare for the unexpected, and survive. Technical tips, useful skills, and real life examples, the information covered in this comprehensive guide benefits all outdoor enthusiasts from scouts & hikers to hunters & adventurers. Topics include edible plants, edible animals, smoking meat, making solar stills and more.

Softcover • 8-1/2 x 11
368 pages • 550 b&w photos
Item# OTSUR • $24.95